Gender and Crime

NEW PERSPECTIVES IN CRIME, DEVIANCE, AND LAW SERIES
Edited by John Hagan

*Clean Streets: Controlling Crime, Maintaining Order, and
Building Community Activism*
Patrick J. Carr

Gender and Crime: Patterns of Victimization and Offending
Edited by Karen Heimer and Candace Kruttschnitt

Gender and Crime

Patterns of Victimization and Offending

EDITED BY

Karen Heimer and Candace Kruttschnitt

New York University Press

NEW YORK AND LONDON

NEW YORK UNIVERSITY PRESS
New York and London
www.nyupress.org

Library of Congress Cataloging-in-Publication Data
Gender and crime : patterns of victimization and offending /
[edited by] Karen Heimer and Candace Kruttschnitt.
    p.   cm.
ISBN-13:978-0-8147-3674-6 (cloth : alk. paper)
ISBN-10: 0-8147-3674-2 (cloth : alk. paper)
ISBN-13 978-0-8147-3675-3 (pbk. : alk. paper)
ISBN-10: 0-8147-3675-0 (pbk. : alk. paper)
1. Crime—Sex differences. 2. Female offenders. 3. Women—
Crimes against.   I. Heimer, Karen. II. Kruttschnitt, Candace.
        HV6158.G457 2005
    364.3'74—dc22   2005017343

New York University Press books are printed on acid-free paper,
and their binding materials are chosen for strength and durability.

Manufactured in the United States of America
c 10 9 8 7 6 5 4 3 2 1
p 10 9 8 7 6 5 4 3

Contents

Introduction

New Insights into the Gendered Nature of Crime and Victimization

Karen Heimer and Candace Kruttschnitt

It has been almost thirty years since the publication of Carol Smart's classic book, *Women, Crime and Criminology,* which highlighted that the study of crime had been "gender blind."[1] Smart showed that by ignoring gender differences in crime, criminology had been particularly remiss; indeed she called the discipline to task. Research has made important strides since then. Criminology now recognizes that women do commit serious crime and that the pathways to crime clearly are gendered. Unique aspects of violence against women have also come to light, launching new lines of scholarly research as well as attempts at social action to reduce women's victimization.[2]

Much of the recent research on gender and crime has been shaped by feminist perspectives that show that gender is a social construction, produced and reproduced in social interactions.[3] Feminist criminology is often premised on the assumption that gender is a "social institution" that organizes daily life and "is built into the major social organizations of society, such as the economy, ideology, the family, and politics, and also is an entity in and of itself."[4] The bottom line is that gender shapes human behavior in all arenas, and crime and victimization are no exceptions.

Our understanding of the ways in which crime is gendered has been advanced by numerous empirical findings and, more recently, theoretical insights.[5] Yet many gaps in our knowledge remain. This book presents a series of studies that advance our understanding of the gendering of crime and victimization in several ways. The chapters report patterns of women's offending and victimization that have not yet been reported in the research literature. Some of these patterns emerge from new data sets, and others are drawn from novel analyses of existing data. All these essays speak to key theoretical and substantive issues in research on gender, crime, and victimization.

One such issue is the debate over the usefulness and compatibility of feminist versus traditional theoretical constructs and arguments. Studies of gender and crime have long been criticized for simply assuming that theories designed to explain male behavior are equally applicable to females. Such studies are constructed on the basis of male criminality and historically have "added gender and stirred." The end result is that "gender" often has been treated as a variable to be controlled rather than as a theoretical construct. One approach to this problem is to eschew existing criminological theories and constructs in favor of novel theoretical approaches. Another approach is to synthesize constructs from traditional criminological or sociological theories with feminist theory and research. Indeed, in a recent review of feminist criminology, Jody Miller and Christopher Mullins argue that the "best feminist research in criminology is explicitly attentive both to gender and to useful insights from broader criminological thought."[6] One outcome of this approach is the uncovering of some similarities in the factors associated with female and male offending, as well as gender differences.[7]

A variation on this debate also appears in the victimization research. Here, concern is focused on the relative isolation of research on violence against women, especially intimate-partner violence, from the larger bodies of research on violence in general. As a recent national workshop on violence against women concluded, there is considerable evidence that research on violence against women could benefit from its integration with the broader study of determinants of "the causes, consequences, prevention, treatment and deterrence of violence more broadly."[8] By looking at multiple forms of victimization across the life course and across different social settings, and by examining the relevance of nontraditional responses to female victims of violence, the research on women's victimization presented in this book broadens our understanding of victimization generally as well as the gendered nature of some aspects of violent victimization.

Another issue in research on the gendering of crime and victimization concerns the use of qualitative and quantitative methods.[9] On the one hand, qualitative studies allow for deep-level contextualized analyses that are often not possible in quantitative studies of survey data or crime statistics. On the other hand, quantitative studies can allow for comparisons across groups and subgroups, over time, and across place that are difficult to achieve using qualitative methods. This book includes a fairly even balance of essays based on qualitative and quantitative analyses. Our premise is that these different methodologies are compatible and coalesce to help produce a richer portrait of the gendering of offending and victimization than is possible from either qualitative or quantitative studies alone.

A third important issue that has recently emerged in some studies of gender, offending, and victimization is the movement to cast women as active agents in their social worlds, responding to constraints but also engaging in decision-making. This stems in large part from the recognition that in criminology, as in other areas of social science,[10] we often strip women of their agency and capacity for free will. But as Belinda Morrissey points out in her book *When Women Kill: Question of Agency and Subjectivity,* this movement also has been fueled by popular narratives and legal discourses on women offenders, especially violent female offenders.[11] Several chapters in this book show that agency is a key to understanding women's and girls' offending and their responses to victimization, even when situations and social structures constrain individual motivations and decisions.

A fourth important issue in recent feminist criminology is the intersectionality of crime and victimization—the ways in which gender, race, ethnicity, and social class converge to shape perceptions and experiences in daily life. This issue has been central in recent years to feminist theory and feminist criminology.[12] Even so, research on intersectionalities and crime is in the relatively early stages, and our understanding of its complexities is still emerging. The chapters in part 3 of this book assess gender-race-class patterns of offending and victimization, in an attempt to further illuminate these intersectionalities. Other chapters are based on data from predominantly minority samples and thus contribute to the discussion of the gender-race intersection. Because these chapters speak more explicitly to other issues, we have not located them in the section devoted to intersectionalities.

Finally, as a set, the essays in this book speak to the connection between women's victimization and their offending. This linkage was initially forged with the important works that focused on women's "pathways" to offending.[13] Several essays build on earlier work that connects childhood abuse, relationships with antisocial men, drugs, and offending. They do so by highlighting the equally important contributions of other well-known predictors of offending and by illustrating the neighborhood and criminal justice experiences that further contextualize victimization experiences.

Part 1 of this book includes studies of women's and girls' offending. Part 2 presents studies of victimization. Part 3 addresses gender, race, and class intersections in offending and victimization.

Gendered Offending: Pathways, Situations, and Social Contexts

The essays in part 1 address several of the theoretical and substantive issues just discussed, namely, the cross-fertilization of feminist and traditional criminological research, the contributions of qualitative and quantitative research, the agency of women offenders, and the interplay between victimization and criminal offending. Each essay focuses on different aspects of pathways, situations, or structural contexts of gender and offending.

The chapter by Peggy C. Giordano, Jill A. Deines, and Stephen A. Cernkovich is based on the first life course study of female offenders to date. The authors present a qualitative analysis of interviews with and detailed narratives from female offenders who were first interviewed as adolescents and then were interviewed again thirteen years later, when they were in their late twenties. The chapter focuses explicitly on the question of whether traditional criminological theories can be combined fruitfully with feminist arguments to generate a more complete understanding of female delinquency and crime. Giordano and her colleagues answer this question with an unqualified yes. They report that concepts from traditional criminological theories, such as poverty, peer influence, and parental inattention and neglect, are central to our understanding of women's offending over the life course. But Giordano and her colleagues show that constructs from feminist explanations also are essential for understanding female crime. For example, physical and sexual victimization, as well as associations with older antisocial men (who foster women's involvement with drugs, prostitution, and other crimes) presage women's offending and contribute to their inability to desist from crime. The authors also suggest that desistance from crime is due in part to individuals' "motivational stances," specifically their openness to conventional influences. In sum, the study acknowledges that poverty, peer influence, and other environmental factors increase the chances of offending throughout the life course, but at the same time, individuals' motivations and actions shape their own trajectories of crime.

Jody Miller and Christopher W. Mullins's study also is based on unique data, in-depth interviews with at-risk and delinquent girls that focused on situational contexts and the meanings that girls give to their violent and aggressive interactions. The findings in this chapter emphasize the complex negotiations of status that occur within girls' interactions. Miller and Mullins note that although the causes of girls' conflicts look stereotypically female at first glance, there are important ways in which these interactions parallel those reported by research on male conflicts. Specifically, the researchers show how girls' interpersonal conflicts often reflect attempts to gain respect in interactions, especially respect based on toughness. At the same time, they emphasize that the negotiations and conflict arise from "highly gendered social structures," such that fights over status play out in the form of fights over boys or challenges to appearance and style. Overall, this chapter illuminates a neglected issue in research on gender and offending—how females create meaning in situations of violence and how they *use* violence as a means to achieve goals. Like the study by Giordano and her colleagues, Miller and Mullins's essay shows that there are important points of overlap between explanations of female and male violence, though the specific elements of violent interactions manifest themselves in highly gendered ways. Moreover, Miller and Mullins's study clearly shows the importance of girls' agency in violent interactions—the girls in their study were not propelled into violence by forces they could not control but, rather, used the display of toughness to achieve valued statuses and reputations among their peers.

The chapter by Hilary Smith, Nancy Rodriguez, and Marjorie S. Zatz turns attention to the pathways of girls and boys to juvenile court. This study takes as its starting point previous research on delinquency that has emphasized the role of victimization and drug use for girls while emphasizing the impact of delinquent peers for boys. The qualitative analyses in this chapter show how juvenile-court personnel view the interconnections between gender, victimization, delinquent peers, and drug use. The data in this study are case-file narratives written by probation officers and semi-structured interviews with juvenile probation officers. The findings reveal histories of abuse among both boys and girls, but they also show that sexual abuse is more commonly reported in girls' files. Smith and her colleagues find no gender differences in reports of the extent of negative peer influences, but the reports showed that boys were more influenced by peers in their own age group, while girls were more influenced by older males. This point parallels the finding of Giordano and colleagues that older antisocial males often exert negative influence on marginalized girls and women. Smith, Rodriguez, and Zatz also uncover important gender differences in disposition and treatment, largely due to limited resources and constrained treatment options. Overall, the chapter reports some similarities across girls' and boys' cases and also emphasizes important gender distinctions. It draws attention to the gendered pathways that lead boys and girls into the juvenile court and shows that court officials have few avenues for addressing these gender differences.

The chapter by Rosemary Gartner and Bill McCarthy shifts the focus to women's offending, specifically to one of the most highly publicized forms of crime—mothers killing their own children. Although this phenomenon is sensationalized in the popular media, it has received surprisingly little attention in scholarly research. Gartner and McCarthy's chapter addresses this phenomenon using new data and a sociohistorical approach. They develop a historical map of neonaticides and infanticides in two U.S. cities, Seattle and Buffalo, over a ninety-year period. Their analysis uncovers some findings that are unexpected, given typical portrayals of mothers who kill children as mad, bad, or victims. By including types of cases that have not been examined by previous research, Gartner and McCarthy discover that the common images of mothers who kill may be accurate for a smaller proportion of cases than has been suggested by either academic research or the popular media. They argue that in some cases women acted more as rational actors, making what seem to have been conscious decisions in response to the perceived constraints of poverty or social consequences of their children's births. Clearly, this essay emphasizes the agency of women offenders, yet it also acknowledges that murder is the outcome of decision-making within situations of perceived constraints, both economic and social.

Many of the studies in this part acknowledge the overarching effects of structural constraints—often poverty. The chapter by Karen Heimer, Stacy Wittrock, and Halime Ünal focuses explicitly on how women's poverty and economic marginalization affects their material lives as well as their violent offending. Specifically, this study examines variations in women's arrest rates as compared to men's arrest rates (i.e., gender ratios of crime) for one hundred large U.S. cities from 1970 through 2000. This is the first study to examine these patterns across cities, as well as over time, thereby revealing findings that have been obscured by studies that use national-level data. The authors report that in cities and decades where women's economic oppression is greatest, the gender ratio of crime increases, with women accounting for a larger proportion of all arrests. Given the significant role of poverty in explaining male crime, it seems only reasonable to assume that it similarly plays a role in female crime. But Heimer, Wittrock, and Ünal's chapter moves beyond the focus on the poverty of the community as a whole to address the poverty and marginalization of women specifically.

Gendered Victimization: Trajectories, Social Contexts, and Justice

As is true for female offending, we have made significant progress in understanding the ways in which criminal victimization is a gendered experience. Although women are much less likely than men to be the victims of crime, they are much more likely than men to be the victims of intimate-partner violence, especially lethal violence.[14] Efforts to discern such gendered patterns of victimization arose from the vast amount of research, public attention, and especially congressional funding devoted to the topic of violence against women.[15] Nevertheless, as is true of research on offending, important gaps in our understanding of this phenomenon still remain.[16] We believe that the research included in part 2 will, in some very important ways, address some of these gaps.

Because women are much more likely than men to be violently victimized by someone known to them, scholarly research on women's victimization has been compartmentalized into specific forms (spouse abuse/partner abuse) and types of victimization (sexual assault). Although this research has been instrumental in identifying the prevalence of these phenomena and some of their social and individual correlates, it has left us with virtually no understanding of how victimization experiences might be linked over time within individuals' lives. This omission can be attributed in large part to the limitations of the data that has been the primary resource for assessing national trends in victimization: National Crime Victimization Surveys (NCVS).

Candace Kruttschnitt and Ross Macmillan utilize the National Violence against Women Survey (NVAWS) to provide the first life course analysis of women's experiences of violent victimization. The NVAWS is unique among national surveys in its focus on respondents' lifetime experiences of violence and its attention to gathering detailed information on perpetrators that can be linked across violent incidents. Capitalizing on these design attributes, Kruttschnitt and Macmillan develop and test a life course approach to women's victimization that focuses on three central questions: First, to what degree do relationships shape the types of violence that occur within them? Second, how do victimization experiences in one relationship and at one point in time influence subsequent victimizations? And, third, does the historical context surrounding relationships shape women's violent victimization experiences? The answers to these questions suggest far more diversity in the types of victimization women experience within one type of relationship and across relationships than previously thought. However, the findings also suggest that there is much more that we need to know about the sources of this diversity. Although Kruttschnitt and Macmillan consider some of the major risk factors associated with certain patterns of victimization, they are unable to speak to the social and ecological factors that contribute to these patterns of victimization.

One important attempt to contextualize women's victimization experiences can be found in the chapter by Laura Dugan and Jennifer L. Castro. Their research substantially expands our understanding of women's victimization by examining the victimization experiences of a jailed population in comparison to the conventional population contained in the NCVS. By so doing, they uncover not only extensive histories of victimization among jailed offenders but also direct links between their victimization and retaliatory offending. Further, because Dugan and Castro frame their analysis of women's victimization experiences within routine-activities theory, they can explicitly address the relevance of this theory for a marginalized segment of the population. For example, from their analysis we learn that although partnering with a male may provide substantial protection from victimization for conventional women, it offers little protection for marginalized women. Similarly, what are often considered high-risk contexts for violent victimization—living in public housing, having a low income, and having high mobility—have relatively little effect on marginalized women. As the authors conclude, this research clearly demonstrates that context matters and that contexts differ depending on the women being studied.

The third chapter in this part focuses on the cross-national context of women's violent victimization. Gary LaFree and Gwen Hunnicutt examine World Health Organization data on men's and women's homicide victimization rates in thirty-five nations covering the years 1950 to 2001. The last large-scale analysis of World Health Organization data that addressed the gender gap in homicide victimization covered the period 1950–1980. Notably, that analysis revealed that changes in women's social status conditioned the relationship between gender stratification and the gender gap in homicide victimization.[17] The changes in women's labor-force participation, even since 1980,[18] have had consequences for men's and women's social roles and relationships. Recent analyses of homicide victimizations in the United States, for example, have drawn attention to a "backlash" thesis, arguing that changes in women's working lives, and in attendant cultural norms about family responsibilities and even sexuality, have made women more vulnerable to physical violence.[19] As such, a temporal and cultural analysis of changes in female homicide victimization rates is long overdue.

LaFree and Hunnicutt dissect gender differences in trends over time, assessing both whether these trends show signs of convergence or divergence and how shifts in male or female rates may be influencing these patterns. Although these aggregate-level data cannot reveal which men and women are most vulnerable to violent victimization, they do help us to understand the importance of cultural context to our understanding of homicide trends. Not only are there substantial differences among nations in their homicide victimization rates, but nations with less gender stratification also have less gender disparity in these rates. Further, since trends in homicide victimization co-vary for males and females within nations, there is evidence that social context may be more important than gender per se in influencing vulnerability to lethal violence. Such enduring and culturally specific gendered patterns of victimization offer a promising lead for theory development and, in particular, understanding what types of social contexts are most and least conducive to lethal violence.

The final chapter in part 2 examines how victimized women are treated in the criminal justice system. Going beyond the more conventional approaches that focus on domestic violence courts and rape processing, Kathleen Daly and Sarah Curtis-Fawley instead examine one of the most important criminal court interventions of the twentieth century—the development of restorative justice. Despite its growing popularity in the United States and its more extensive development in other nations, there have been serious questions about whether this alternative to traditional criminal court sanctions can be used in cases that involve serious interpersonal violence. Daly and Curtis-Fawley provide the first assessment of the use of restorative justice in sexual assault cases. As they indicate, worldwide there are only two jurisdictions that routinely use restorative justice in sexual assault cases involving youthful offenders: South Australia and New Zealand. This path-breaking research takes us deep into the discourse and negotiations that occurred in two sexual assault cases that involved very young female victims in South Australia. Additionally, by drawing on a larger pool of archived sexual offenses, the study also addresses the relative merits of this process and the courtroom process for victims of sexual violence, and it acknowledges factors (e.g., seriousness, victim-offender relationship) that influence whether a case ends up in a restorative conference. We believe that both advocates and critics of the restorative justice process will find this research compelling.

Intersectionalities: Gender, Race, Poverty, and Crime

The final two chapters in this book focus explicitly on a central issue in contemporary research on gender and crime, namely, the ways that race/ethnicity and social class condition the offending and victimization of females and males. Although there have been numerous calls for research on intersectionalities, there have been relatively few empirical studies. Most of the existing research has been qualitative and has added to our understanding of this phenomenon, especially by showing how race and class influence perceptions of and structure opportunities for crime.[20] Quantitative studies of intersectionalities, by contrast, have been few and far between. The chapters in this part target this omission by using a variety of quantitative methods and data sources to study race, class, and gender intersections in offending and victimization.

Sally S. Simpson and Carole Gibbs begin their chapter with an insightful review of feminist scholarship on intersectionalities that devotes special attention to the question of why qualitative methods are more often preferred in studies of this phenomenon. They note that some authors, such as Kathleen Daly, have argued that qualitative methods are better suited because it is often difficult to make categorical distinctions necessary for quantitative analyses.[21] But Simpson and Gibbs add that qualitative methods may be preferred simply because they are more consistent with feminist epistemology. To address the lack of quantitative research examining gender-race-class patterns of offending, Simpson and Gibbs analyze the National Longitudinal Survey of Youth. These data are particularly well suited to analyses of intersectional groups because minority youth were oversampled and the survey contains multiple indicators of social class. Using these data, the authors examine whether constructs developed from traditional male-centered criminological theories (e.g., general strain theory, control theory, social learning theory) are neutral with respect to different intersectional groups. Their analysis reveals that taking account of subgroup variations is essential for explaining self-reported delinquency by youths. Indeed, they find that there are important gender-race-class patterns of juvenile offending that are not accounted for fully by constructs from traditional "general" theories of crime. They conclude, consistent with the spirit of the studies in part 1, that constructs from traditional theories may play a role in helping to explain gender-race-class differences in offending but that traditional theories clearly need to be extended or modified to offer reasonably complete explanations of delinquent patterns across different intersectional groups.

The chapter by Janet L. Lauritsen and Callie Marie Rennison focuses on the well-known disproportionately high rates of violent victimization among minority women. The authors note that although recent studies of violent victimization suggest that race and ethnic differences in levels of victimization may be due to community poverty, family structure, and other aspects of disadvantaged structural locations,[22] research has not yet assessed whether there are in fact racial and ethnic differences in these predictors of violent victimization. Lauritsen and Rennison address this omission by using the National Crime Victimization Survey to assess similarities and differences across African American, Latina, and white women in levels, trends, and factors associated with violence against women. Their results show, first, that the trends in victimization are similar for African American, Latina, and white women and, second, that almost all the individual, family, and community characteristics they examine have similar effects on violent victimization in these racial and ethnic subgroups. Lauritsen and Rennison therefore conclude that race and ethnic differences in *levels* of violent victimization can be explained by the same individual and structural factors, such as poverty, family structure, community context, and so on. As such, their research highlights the importance of acknowledging economic and other structural constraints in explanations of racial disparities in victimization, consistent with the findings of many of the studies on criminal offending in this volume and elsewhere.[23]

Toward New Understandings of Gender, Crime, and Victimization

The chapters in this book further illuminate the gendering of crime and victimization, as well as provide direction for future research. As a set, they make important statements about the cross-fertilization of feminist theory, gender theory, and traditional criminological perspectives. Indeed, the theme that emerges from many of the essays echoes Miller and Mullin's point in their recent review that the synthesis of feminist theory with ideas from traditional criminology constitutes an important avenue for the advancement of research on gender and crime.[24] Further, the essays demonstrate that the findings of qualitative and quantitative methodologies are quite complementary and together offer a deeper understanding of gender, crime, and victimization than would be possible from either approach alone.

The chapters in this volume also suggest that a more complete understanding of the gendered nature of crime requires viewing women as active agents, albeit subject to different constraints than their male counterparts. Several of the chapters demonstrate how crime and victimization reflect choices made within social parameters, especially poverty and gendered normative structures. And, finally, these chapters highlight the importance of further theoretical and empirical work on the offending of marginalized women, especially poor women and women of color.

Of course, no single volume is ever all-encompassing or the final word, and ours is no exception. For example, the present volume does not include treatments of hegemonic masculinities and crime, sexualities and crime, women in the criminal justice system, or the role of critical race theory. These topics, as well as others not mentioned here, certainly are significant and must be addressed before we can have a complete understanding of the gendering of crime. But, in setting the scope for this volume, we focused on the issues outlined in this introduction, issues which we maintain are fundamental to contemporary research and debates about gender, crime, and victimization.

This book is the result of the creative energy and hard work of a group of researchers who are dedicated to advancing knowledge about gender and crime. We cannot thank them enough for their contributions. We hope that you will enjoy reading these chapters as much as we have enjoyed working with this outstanding group of scholars.

NOTES

1. Carol Smart, *Women, Crime, and Criminology: A Feminist Critique* (London: Routledge and Kegan Paul, 1976).

2. See Candace Kruttschnitt, Brenda L. McLaughlin, and Carol V. Petrie, eds., *Advancing the Federal Research Agenda on Violence against Women* (Washington, DC: National Academy Press, 2004).

3. See, for example, Candace West and Don H. Zimmerman, "Doing Gender," *Gender and Society* 1 (1987): 125–151.

4. Judith Lorber, *Paradoxes of Gender* (New Haven: Yale University Press, 1994).

5. One of many excellent reviews of research can be found in Nadine Lanctot and Marc Le Blanc, "Explaining Deviance by Adolescent Females," in *Crime and Justice: A Review of Research,* vol. 29, ed. Michael Tonry (Chicago: University of Chicago Press, 2002), pp. 113–202.

6. Jody Miller and Christopher W. Mullins, "Taking Stock: The Status of Feminist Theories in Criminology," in *Advances in Criminological Theory,* vol. 15, ed. Francis Cullen, John Paul Wright, and Kristie Blovins (New Brunswick, NJ: Transaction, forthcoming).

7. See Peggy C. Giordano, Stephen A. Cernkovich, Jennifer L. Rudolph, "Gender, Crime, and Desistance: Toward a Theory of Cognitive Transformation," *American Journal of Sociology* 107 (2002): 990–1064; Karen Heimer and Stacy De Coster, "The Gendering of Violent Delinquency," *Criminology* 37 (1999): 277–317.

8. See Kruttschnitt, McLaughlin, and Petrie, *Advancing the Federal Research Agenda,* 2.

9. See Kathleen Daly, "Different Ways of Conceptualizing Sex/Gender in Feminist Theory and Their Implications for Criminology," *Theoretical Criminology* 1 (1997): 25–51; Candace Kruttschnitt, "Quantitative Contributions to the Study of Gender and Crime or Bootstrapping our Way into the Theoretical Thicket," *Journal of Quantitative Criminology* 12 (1996): 136–161.

10. Denise Wrong, "The Oversocialized Conception of Man in Modern Sociology," *American Sociological Review* 26 (1961): 183–193. We note the irony of this title, given the focus of the present volume.

11. See Belinda Morrissey, *When Women Kill: Questions of Agency and Subjectivity* (London: Routledge, 2003).

12. Daly, "Different Ways of Conceptualizing Sex/Gender," 25–51.

13. Kathleen Daly, *Gender, Crime and Punishment* (New Haven: Yale University Press, 1994); Beth Richie, *Compelled to Crime* (New York: Routledge, 1996).

14. Candace Kruttschnitt (with assistance of Rosemary Gartner and Kathleen Ferraro), "Women's Involvement in Serious Interpersonal Violence," *Aggression and Violent Behavior* 7 (2002): 529–565.

15. See Kruttschnitt, McLaughlin, and Petrie, *Advancing the Federal Research Agenda.*

16. Ibid., vii.

17. Rosemary Gartner, Kathryn Baker, and Fred C. Pampel, "Gender Stratification and the Gender Gap in Homicide Victimization," *Social Problems* 37 (1990): 593–612; see also Rosemary Gartner, "The Victims of Homicide: A Temporal and Cross-National Comparison," *American Sociological Review* 55 (1990): 92–106.

18. See Howard N. Fullerton Jr., "Labor Force Participation: Seventy-Five Years of Change, 1950–1998 and 1998–2025," *Monthly Labor Review* (Dec. 1999): 3–12.

19. Rachel Bridges-Whaley and Steven F. Messner, "Gender Equality and Gendered Homicide," *Homicide Studies* 6 (2002): 188–210; Lynne M. Vieraitis and Marian R. Williams, "Assessing the Impact of Gender Inequality on Female Homicide Victimization across U.S. Cities: A Racially Disaggregated Analysis," *Violence against Women* 8 (2002): 35–63.

20. See, for example, Lisa Maher, *Sexed Work* (Oxford: Oxford University Press, 1997); Richie, *Compelled to Crime.*

21. Daly, "Different Ways of Conceptualizing Sex/Gender."

22. See Janet L. Lauritsen and Robin J. Schaum, "The Social Ecology of Violence against Women," *Criminology* 42(2) (2004): 323–357.

23. See, for example, Lauren J. Krivo and Ruth D. Peterson, "The Structural Context of Homicide: Accounting for Racial Differences in Process," *American Sociological Review* 65 (2000): 547–559.

24. Miller and Mullins, "Taking Stock."

Gendered Offending
Pathways, Situations, and Social Contexts

Chapter 1

In and Out of Crime
A Life Course Perspective on Girls' Delinquency

Peggy C. Giordano, Jill A. Deines, and Stephen A. Cernkovich

This chapter draws together two areas of considerable interest within contemporary criminology: (a) issues of gender and (b) the life course perspective on crime.[1] Researchers who rely on longitudinal studies (those that follow the same youths over time, particularly as they make the transition to adulthood) have learned a great deal about the factors associated with the initial movement into delinquency and recently have given increased attention to processes linked to "exiting," or giving up, a criminal lifestyle. Most of these studies, such as the influential work of Sampson and Laub, have relied on samples of male offenders.[2] We recently completed the first contemporary long-term follow-up of a sample of girls who had been involved in serious acts of delinquency during their adolescent years (the Ohio Serious Offender Study), and these data allow us to examine the phenomenon of female delinquency from this longer "life course" vantage point. These data provide a window on the girls' lives as children and adolescents, as well as on the adult life experiences of highly marginal respondents who are often not included in large numbers in typical youth surveys.

The study, which includes a male comparison group, addresses several basic but important questions. How do young girls become involved in serious levels of crime and violent behavior in the first place? Are theories developed to understand male antisocial and violent behavior useful in explaining female delinquency, or is it necessary to develop distinctly gendered theories? How do these disadvantaged young women with significant delinquent histories fare over the long haul, when compared to males with similar backgrounds? Does gender influence the process of exiting from a criminal lifestyle; that is, are "desistance" processes also distinct for women and men? This chapter presents an overview of results from the Ohio Serious Offender Study, focusing on the key issue of whether girls' involvement in crime (initial causes, life course consequences, and processes associated with desistance) reflect gendered—that is, unique to girls —or more "generic" processes.

Background

Steffensmeier and Allan highlight a continuing controversy, one that many of the chapters in this book directly or indirectly address: "Criminologists disagree as to whether gender-neutral (i.e., traditional theories derived from male samples) or gender-specific theories (i.e., recent approaches derived from female samples and positing unique causal paths for female as compared to male criminality) are better suited" to explain female criminality.[3] Our own view is that the either/or dichotomy suggested by the contrast between traditional and feminist frameworks is neither necessary nor helpful to the theory-building process. Results of the Ohio Serious Offender Study indicate that basic tenets of these seemingly opposing viewpoints are not in themselves fundamentally incompatible, and the results show that a comprehensive understanding of girls' delinquency requires a more integrated approach. Particularly when the focus is on the relatively small but important subgroup of girls with serious delinquent histories, we believe that it is necessary to draw from and work toward integration of these different perspectives. A brief review of traditional and feminist theoretical positions will provide a conceptual backdrop for our discussion of the study's major findings, and set the stage for this type of theoretical integration.

Traditional "Male-Based" Theories

Strain theories. Researchers have long stressed the intimate links between poverty and movement into delinquent and criminal activity. *Strain* theories, such as the original formulation developed by Robert K. Merton, focus on the notion that commonly accepted cultural goals in a class-based society such as the United States often center on financial and occupational success. Yet there are notable disparities, linked to one's class position, in the legitimate means to reach these desired ends. Thus, strain theorists emphasize that crime can be an attempt to achieve these goals by "innovating," that is, by attempting to achieve them through illegitimate rather than legitimate means.[4] Other researchers do not focus as narrowly on monetary success but instead have documented numerous ways in which disadvantaged neighborhoods provide a social environment in which crime and violence are more likely as a response, survival strategy, or lifestyle.[5]

Learning theories. Learning theories are another important general framework for understanding delinquent and criminal behavior. Edwin Sutherland's theory of differential association stresses that criminal behavior is learned, as are other behaviors, through communication in social interactions. Particularly important are those interactions that occur within intimate personal groups such as family or peer networks. Through these interactions, individuals learn norms and values that either support or oppose criminal behavior. The central proposition of the theory is that an individual becomes delinquent or criminal "because of an excess of definitions favorable to violation of law over definitions unfavorable to violation of law."[6] The individual learns not only criminal techniques from others but also the rationalizations and defenses (attitudes) that are associated with taking delinquent action. To explain the varying degrees of impact that associations have on individuals, Sutherland further emphasizes that "differential associations may vary in frequency, duration, priority, and intensity."[7] Associations that occur more often, start earlier, last longer, and are more intense or intimate will likely have a greater impact. Researchers in this tradition have thus focused on family effects—for example, the role of parental criminality—and have also found that the attitudes and behaviors of one's peer group are significantly related to the likelihood of becoming involved in and sustaining a pattern of delinquent behavior.[8]

Control theories. Travis Hirschi's theory of social control attempts to explain conformity rather than deviance.[9] Hirschi stresses that most youths will not engage in delinquent actions because of their links to conventional institutions such as the family and school. Individuals with strong attachments to parents, teachers, and school activities will not want to jeopardize these bonds and relationships. In contrast, "delinquent acts result when an individual's bond to society is weak or broken."[10] Hirschi argued that attachment to parents is the most important element of this bonding process, and research has consistently documented that strong ties to family, including parental warmth and caring and consistent supervision are indeed reliably associated with lower levels of delinquency.[11] Commitment to conventional lines of activity, especially academic achievement, has also been shown to be significantly related to the likelihood of involvement in delinquency.[12]

Although these theories differ in approach and emphasis, it is nevertheless possible to sketch an overall portrait of the "typical" delinquent that emerges from research based on these traditional theoretical frameworks. Such a youth likely

- lives in a poverty area;
- has a family background characterized by lack of parental warmth and caring and inconsistent and harsh discipline, including physical abuse;
- does poorly in school and is alienated from it—may drop out or attend erratically;
- learns about crime from parents, siblings, or others in the immediate environment;
- makes a connection with members of a delinquent peer group, who provide further delinquent definitions and a social context for carrying out delinquent acts.

Feminist Perspectives

Researchers who have adopted a feminist theoretical perspective have sought to draw more attention to the unique concerns of girls and women and to highlight the ways in which gender inequalities structure criminal and noncriminal options, definitions of self, and processes of social control.[13] This body of work focuses on the reality that most women do not become involved in criminal activity, but it also has included more attention to delinquent girls and women offenders. Moving beyond early critiques that lamented a lack of attention to girls' lives, more-recent analyses have specifically critiqued the "male-based" theories and research deriving from them and in the process suggested the need for distinct theoretical frameworks. Leonard, for example, systematically reviewed the classic theories of delinquency and concludes that they are "biased to the core, riddled with assumptions that relate to a male—not a female—reality."[14] For example, after discussing social learning theories, Leonard concludes,

Generally speaking, women are shielded from criminal learning experiences. Even within the same groups as males (like the family), their social position is unequal, and they are frequently taught dissimilar attitudes. More isolated from criminal norms and techniques, they are also more consistently taught law-abiding behavior and are expected to act in accordance with the law. . . . Boys and girls are taught quite different standards and, with this, subtly different attitudes toward law breaking.[15]

Although we agree that boys and girls are often socialized quite differently, this kind of assessment helps to explain the continuing differences in male and female rates of involvement but not the actions of young women who fail to adopt a law-abiding lifestyle. Yet the overall conclusion here is that explanations other than those deriving from basic social learning principles (or other "male-based" approaches, such as those reviewed above) need to be marshaled in order to adequately explain the conduct of girls who do become involved in delinquent activity.

Scholars such as Chesney-Lind and Shelden have offered more in the way of specifics, focusing attention on the role of victimization experiences, in particular the role of sexual abuse, often within the family, as a particularly critical and uniquely gendered background factor that helps to explain girls' involvement in delinquency.[16] This focus on victimization has been an important development within the field and illustrates that a comprehensive approach will sometimes require asking different kinds of questions (in this case about prior victimization) from those that have typically been included in studies and surveys focused on male offenders. Chesney-Lind and Shelden describe a sequence that often flows from victimization, suggesting that the status offenses (e.g., running away) that bring girls to the attention of the juvenile justice system often relate directly to these abuse experiences. These authors indicate that interviews with young women reveal that once "on the streets, they were forced into crime in order to survive. The interviews show very clearly that they did not have much attachment to their delinquent activities."[17] The specific nature of girls' and women's crimes (especially prostitution) also provides evidence of the pervasive influence of gender inequalities of power—that is, the effects of patriarchal arrangements.

Another theme highlighted within feminist theoretical frameworks is the idea that negative and/or coercive relationships with males provide an important social context within which girls' delinquency often unfolds. For example, Bottcher suggests that "studies of adolescent gender show that patterns of male domination and female subordination are increasingly apparent during the teenage years," noting also that "the portrayal of female subjugation and sexual exploitation is unremitting in qualitative and journalistic accounts of delinquent youths and gangs."[18] This theme is also quite prevalent in research focused on the criminal behavior of adult women, usually based on studies of incarcerated women. Researchers such as Richie have found that the crimes of many women offenders can be traced to the coercive actions of male partners, and some offenses are actually better viewed as attempts at self-defense or self-preservation rather than criminal actions.[19] This focus on relationships characterized by constraint, control, and coercion contrasts with the relatively more egalitarian world of peer relations stressed in traditional delinquency theories. In summary, the "typical" delinquent that emerges from feminist analyses includes one who

- is sexually abused by a stepfather or other male relative;
- runs away from home to escape from the abuse;
- engages in illegal activities as a survival strategy;
- comes into contact with other males who either foster or demand further involvement in illegal activities, including prostitution;
- may self-medicate with drugs and/or alcohol to cope with the abuse and other demoralizing experiences she has encountered on the street, including violence from a male partner.[20]

Desistance from Crime—Is It Also a Gendered Phenomenon?

Researchers who have conducted follow-up studies of boys with significant delinquent histories have found evidence of both continuity and change in their lives and criminal careers. On average, boys with more serious levels of involvement in delinquency during childhood and the adolescent years tend to offend longer and at more serious levels in adulthood.[21] In addition, researchers such as Moffitt have pointed out the myriad ways in which early delinquency involvement, including arrests and periods of incarceration, tends to negatively impact other areas of adult functioning—such as marriage and marital stability, school achievement, and occupational success.[22] Although delinquent youth may tend to incur more problems in these areas than their more conforming counterparts, researchers such as Sampson and Laub have also documented that offenders may experience adult transitions and turning points that come to be associated with making beneficial life changes.[23] Thus, important goals of the Ohio Serious Offender Study were to determine how these young women with significant delinquent histories have fared as they have matured into adulthood and to assess whether factors associated with men's desistance are similar for understanding girls' movement away from crime.

Sampson and Laub developed an *age-graded theory of informal social control* that focuses particular attention on the positive benefits of a strong marriage and job stability on the process of desisting from criminal activity; unfortunately, the sample used in Sampson and Laub's study was composed entirely of (white) boys who had grown up in Massachusetts during the 1950s, thus leaving open the question of whether the theory is a good fit with the life course experiences of contemporary female delinquents.[24] In one study of desistance among women, Baskin and Sommers interviewed thirty women who had desisted from crime and found the reasons women gave for desisting were generally similar to those found in studies of male offenders.[25] In a study of British offenders, however, Graham and Bowling found that desistance tended to occur more abruptly for women than men and was often linked to the birth of a child.[26] Studies of gang involvement also show that "female members typically leave the gang if they have a child, but male members do not."[27] Other factors that may influence desistance processes relate to the greater societal stigma attached to female compared to male antisocial behavior, violence, or drug abuse. This could result in greater motivation for women to move away from crime, but it could also make it more difficult to connect with "conventionalizing" influences (employers, prosocial marriage partners).[28]

On balance, since women have historically maintained closer relationships to the family and have been more likely to derive status from marital partners, while enjoying less power and success in occupational arenas, we began the Ohio Serious Offender Study expecting that (a) women would be more likely to desist from crime than their male counterparts and that (b) marital attachment and childbearing would be critical as influences on women's behavior, while employment experiences would be less important as predictors. The Ohio Serious Offender Study thus adds to prior work, not only because it provides new details about initial causes of female delinquency but also because it allows us to understand more about later processes of adjustment, as these young women have matured into adulthood.

The Ohio Serious Offender Study

In 1982, we conducted a study of male and female adolescents' involvement in delinquency, relying on in-home interviews with a random sample of youths who resided in Toledo, Ohio (the "neighborhood" sample). Yet because we wished to focus special attention on girls' delinquency, we were concerned that this sample might not contain a sufficiently large pool of girls who had backgrounds with serious levels of delinquency. Thus, we also conducted interviews ($n = 127$) with the entire population of the only state-level institution for delinquent girls in Ohio; the sample of males was drawn from the populations of three institutions for males ($n = 127$).[29] In 1995 we were able to locate and interview approximately 85 percent of the serious offenders who had participated in the adolescent interviews. The final sample was 48 percent white and 37 percent African American. The average age was approximately twenty-nine years. These respondents completed a structured interview, and after this was completed, we also elicited detailed life history narratives from a total of 180 respondents (97 women and 83 men). Many of these narratives exceeded one hundred pages in length, and most contain information relating to the childhood, adolescent, and adult experiences of these respondents. Some of the narratives are less complete than others, particularly concerning the "early years"; thus, for some of our analysis we tabulated results based on sixty-six of the most complete narrative accounts provided by women in the sample. We also analyzed male narratives extensively, and in a few instances draw on these for comparison purposes. These narrative materials were supplemented with arrest information obtained from searches of all the jurisdictions in which respondents were known to have resided. In addition, we collected incarceration histories from the Ohio State Department of Rehabilitation and Correction. These sources provided external checks on the information provided in the life history narratives and supplemented the respondents' own reports of their current levels of criminal involvement.

Getting into Crime: The Childhood and Adolescent Years

The girls who participated in the Ohio Serious Offender Study, like their male counterparts, most often grew up in neighborhoods characterized by extreme poverty, and their marginal social and economic positions form a basic but important backdrop for understanding the character of their lives, as well as their delinquent conduct. Our initial interviews took place in the rather neutral location of the state institution for girls, but many of the life history narratives elicited at the follow-up contain frequent references to a lack of economic resources during childhood and adolescence and make more concrete the realities of their disadvantaged backgrounds. For example, Jessie, a thirty-year-old respondent, reflected on why she was always reluctant to invite other young people over to her house:

> Because our house was . . . ruins, a place that I didn't like. It was, it was always a mess, you know. It wasn't presentable for other people to come . . . 'cause a lot of times we didn't have electricity. . . . A lot of time we didn't have running water. . . . You know, a lot of times we didn't . . . you know, have lights like I got now. We used to have kerosene lamps, you know, just things that were inconvenient. . . . I just kind of felt bad about that.

Other girls undoubtedly lived in better housing circumstances, but many made references to the character of neighborhoods in which they were brought up:

> It was all the neighborhood. They always called the north end the bad end . . . 'cause, you know, everybody does it (drugs, crime) on that end.

These young women did not always forge a direct connection between their early circumstances and delinquency involvement, but some, like Angie, did develop themes that appear consistent with the basic elements of a Mertonian strain theory argument:

> It was the people I hung out with at the time. . . . It was what they did . . . and they walked around . . . furs . . . leather . . . gold . . . you know . . . had this and had that. . . . So, you know . . . things like that attract your attention when you've just been trying to work a little regular . . . little old Burger King job.

This developing world view seems to generally parallel that of a male respondent, Matt, in his discussion of his own early forays into delinquency:

We both [he and best friend] wanted more. . . . You know . . . we were wearing our old worn-out tennis shoes . . . and we were wanting Nikes and . . .
you know . . . thinking about what we could get.

As we analyzed the lengthy narrative accounts, we began to recognize
the difficulty of isolating a single conceptual theme. In a majority of instances several influences combine to increase the likelihood that delinquency, drug use, and/or violence will occur. For example, the quotations
above contain references not only to economic disadvantage but to themes
stressed by differential association theories ("everybody does it on that
end [of town]"; "it was the people I hung out with at the time"). Another
example that illustrates this idea of a constellation of mechanisms is provided by Jana's story of her adolescent years:

The biggest motivation was the money. . . . It was a lot. . . . I was selling like
100 to 300 hits of acid. I would get 100 to 300 hits at 75 cents a piece. Then I
would turn around and sell it for $1.75 a piece. . . . [I] helped pay the rent,
bought groceries. . . . My sisters and my brother knew, but mom . . . she . . .
she like drank and smoked dope and she had no idea I was selling drugs. . . .
My mother was not a real enforcer or anything, and my father was older . . .
so I was basically raised myself alone. My mom was just too lenient. . . . I
had no discipline. . . . I basically, basically did as I pleased.

Jana clearly stresses an economic motivation, but a lack of supervision and
parental neglect (consistent with control theory emphases) and parental
deviance (consistent with themes stressed by differential association theorists) are also an important part of her story. Since most contemporary
feminist theories highlight the ways in which social class (as well as race
and ethnicity) act as influences on the character of women's lives, the
more controversial assertion is that principles of differential association
and mechanisms associated with control theory are also useful theoretical
frameworks for understanding female as well as male delinquency.

In our view, the emphases within these latter theories are particularly
important to consider, given the reality that even in extremely disadvantaged areas, only a small subset of girls ever become involved in delinquent activities. Thus, the narratives we analyzed support the notion that
these more localized social influences within the family, wider social contacts that often connect to family affiliations, and later on, association

with delinquent peers significantly increase the likelihood of delinquent involvement (consistent with the logic of differential association). Some treatments of negative social influences on girls have tended to stress the role of association with males, particularly romantic partners. We agree that romantic involvement sometimes plays an important role in the etiology of girls' delinquency, but the "bad boyfriend" may be only one of many actors that make up a girl's total network of affiliations. The sections of the narratives focused on the early years very frequently contain references to family members who play a pivotal role in the initial development of delinquent definitions:

On their drug abuse:

My mom, she was an addict herself. I started noticing things about her when I was about nine. She seemed to have got . . . real withdrawn from us. One day, this particular day, she was in the bathroom and I crawled on my hands and knees and I peeked through the little door. I wanted to know what was making my mom change . . . why was she treating us like this, as far as neglect and not giving us attention or a hug or something. . . . I cracked it and I seen her, she was shooting dope.

There was always drug abuse in my family. . . . My father was a junkie. . . . He had been to prison several times. . . . Ever since I was a kid I knew about drugs. . . . It was there.

Interviewer: Who turned you on to crack? *Answer*: My mom, ... [but] I got my own stems and stuff [drug paraphernalia] now.

Influences on violent behavior:

They [mother and aunt] would show me how to fight and how to get better.

My grandmother said she wasn't going to let me in the house until I learned how to fight my way out of it.

I got a whoopin' when I was a kid for not fightin'. I got beat up, and every time I ran home my mama beat my ass. . . . So I learned how to fight and I start beatin' everybody's ass that said something to me and I got suspended from school. [Eventually] I got my ass whooped [for fighting].

I got in a fight with this girl, and then the teacher, Miss Johnson, she said I was getting suspended, and I ended up getting into that fight with her and arguing with her and she kicked me. . . . She still had her foot print on my pants where she kicked me. And I went home and I told my mom. And my mom came back to the school and said, "You want to see what it's like to get kicked?" And my mom kicked her butt . . . period. . . . She hit, my mom fought the teacher . . . and said "no one touches my daughter." . . . They took us to court, and they kicked me out of school.

Concerning property crimes:

[I started out] stealing bicycles with my brothers. . . . We'd take them across the bridge [into Kentucky to steal them].

Like when I got the Reeboks, the Reeboks I got caught with, they wasn't even for me. They was for my Aunt Linda, and I would, would take them, and then she would pay me for them so I would have some money.

These sections of the narratives also frequently referenced a lack of success along conventional lines (particularly at school) and, consistent with control theory emphases, often centered on low levels of parental supervision and sometimes severe neglect. The women often spoke with much emotion about the impact of this pattern of neglect:

I spent years trying to make her be a mother to me. . . . But you cannot make someone be what they had no intention of being . . . and she had no intention of being a mother.

I had nobody [to] tell me what to do. . . . I did what I wanted to do. [Yvette said her mother was "strung out" or drunk most of the time; at age twelve Yvette witnessed her mother being killed by her own sister: "She stabbed her in the jugular vein."]

My parents didn't give me much attention in the proper areas, or I would have felt more like staying home.

As noted, the various influences (poverty, parental deviance, low supervision) unfold in a seamless, interconnected way within the women's life history accounts; similarly, it is useful to consider these as an intimately linked package of risks from a conceptual standpoint—parental neglect and criminal involvement/drug use set against a background of poverty decrease girls' abilities to succeed through traditional avenues; at the same time, such processes increase their exposure to and potential influence from a variety of criminal elements. As the girls entered their teen years, they were undoubtedly more likely than those with close family ties and high levels of supervision to come into contact with extrafamilial influences who provided further delinquent definitions and opportunities:

> This was an older woman. . . . She took me under her wing. First I started out to be the babysitter. . . . She let her nine-year-old son smoke black African hash. She left it there with us . . . said "smoke this." . . . I didn't know what the heck it was. . . . She was a bad influence . . . because she shouldn't have been giving me all that stuff . . . and then she had me selling it.

The women described the adolescent years as a period of heightened receptivity to peer influence, a social dynamic that has been a centerpiece of prior work on male delinquency:

> "Come on, Nancy, you know you want to do this. . . . Come on, you want to go out and eat some soapers. . . . Come on, let's go smoke some dope." Well, being a teenager, . . . off I went, you know. I thought right then my friends were more important than my family.

> I was kind of misled. . . . I was trying to hang with them to have friends, and in order to have them as my friends I had to do what they do. . . . I was just interested in them. . . . I would follow them to go steal. I would follow them into smoking marijuana.

The last quotation, from Marie, sounds remarkably similar to the following comments from Tony about the role of peer influence in relation to his own involvement:

> I was just kind of misled real bad. . . . [I wanted] to fit in with them.

Taken together, the life history narratives reviewed here suggest that we should not bracket off social processes stressed in traditional delinquency theories if we are to understand girls' own patterns of involvement. Indeed, it is unfortunate and something of a misnomer to consider these "male-based" theories. Although most of the classic theories were developed using samples of males, in our view there is nothing particularly male about poverty, school failure, parental deviance, or neglect. Based on our analyses of these life history materials, we offer the following proposition: The more serious young women's levels of involvement in delinquency, drug use, or violent behavior, the more likely it is that social processes described within traditional theoretical perspectives such as control, strain, and differential association will be implicated as causes of their problem behaviors.

These narrative data also reveal, however, that we cannot afford to bracket off mechanisms and dynamics that have been stressed by feminist theorists. An analysis based on traditional variables alone provides a useful but far from comprehensive understanding of the "early years." As Chesney-Lind and other researchers have emphasized, victimization experiences and other gendered processes are as integral to an understanding of these narratives as are the more "generic" causal influences mentioned earlier:

> I've just had men tampering with me since I was seven years old.

> Uncle Jamie, he's dead right now. He died of AIDS, and I tell you I'm so happy to hear he was dead. I never had to hate more than he. You know, him and Danny [brother] raped me. I had no hate in my body till him. . . . There's so much trauma in my life. It was when I was real young, like when I was about nine or ten years old.

Marie not only describes her abuse experience but also a sequence of behavior and reaction that directly parallels that outlined by Chesney-Lind and Shelden earlier:

> When he [brother] dared you to tell, you wasn't going to tell . . . because you knew what was going to happen . . . and plus, from the way we seen [what] he used to do to his girlfriends and stuff like that . . . 'cause he used to beat them up and stuff. . . . What happened to [us] made us go to the streets or, you know, to drugs . . . first the drugs, then the streets. . . . Getting high was the only thing that we could do that we didn't have to think about nothing.

Danielle is even more blunt and unsparing as she tells her story, but she makes a similar connection between repeated sexual abuse and her later involvement in prostitution:

I was raped by just about every man my mother ever had. . . . I told the judge, he say, "Why you keep runnin' away from home, Danielle?" I said, "Well, hell, if I gotta stay home and get fucked by all her men, I might as well be out on the street and get fucked and get paid for it."

Feminist perspectives have also illuminated multiple deleterious effects of relationship violence on girls' and women's lives. April describes her mother's struggles with an abusive partner, a recurrent fact of life that likely had a deep impact on April's own development and subsequent life choices:

My mom used to run to the battered women's shelters, and she used to take us with her. . . . I tried to break them up and they just kept fighting, so I called the cops on them. . . . He was, you know, beating her pretty bad.

Later on, young women may themselves forge relationships with antisocial, violent men, who not only are more likely to use violence against them but may directly foster or amplify girls' levels of involvement with drugs, alcohol, or other illegal activities, including prostitution. Tina's narrative includes frequent references to the negative impact of Donny, a boyfriend she had as a teen:

That was the only thing I didn't like about him was he wanted women to make money for him. [Interviewer notes: this boyfriend would actually drop her off at the truck stop, so that she could solicit there. Sometimes truckers would take pity on her, and pay her to simply talk with them ("I used to cry and cry at the things done to me"). . . . One time a man threatened her with a knife, and she was forced to run away from his truck, dressed only in a shirt. Another trucker drove her home].

Our data, then, underscore the importance of the themes in feminist treatments of female delinquency as well as the processes described by traditional delinquency theories. But how can we reconcile these distinctive portraits? Our view is that when these more highly gendered processes take place within a social context characterized by poverty, many criminal associations, and little parental care and control, delinquency becomes more likely as a possible adaptation. In contrast, where sexual victimization (as an example) occurs within a more affluent neighborhood and family setting, and a young woman's life is characterized by a generally high level of family support and supervision, delinquent behavior is not likely to be a common coping mechanism. In those situations, psychological distress or anorexia may be more likely as negative (and more traditionally "gendered") long-term consequences.

To assess these issues more systematically, we analyzed the most complete life history accounts and coded their content with respect to the different thematic elements contained within them. More than 70 percent of these narratives contain references to both gendered and more generic themes. No narrative produced by these young women contained only references to gendered processes, and just 29 percent consisted of references only to mechanisms stressed by traditional delinquency theorists. This offers strong support for the idea of an integrated approach.

We also examined these relationships using data from the structured interview. Sexual abuse has a modest statistical relationship to the level of self-reported delinquency involvement within the neighborhood sample, but it does not remain a significant predictor once other family dynamics, the respondent's orientation toward school, and the level of peer support for delinquency are taken into account. Similarly, a history of sexual abuse was not significantly related to variations in the level of delinquency involvement reported within the Serious Offender sample.[30] These analyses suggest that such victimization experiences are most often catalysts for delinquency involvement when they occur in tandem with other traditional predictors of delinquency. Such findings are also in accord with previous studies that focused on the long-term effects of various types of child abuse. For example, Widom found that while abuse was important as a risk factor, a majority of the abused children in her study did not go on to become involved in adolescent delinquency or adult criminal behavior.[31]

Getting Out of Crime: The Lives of the Serious Offenders at the Time of the Adult Follow-Up

We began the long-term follow-up expecting to find that the women in our sample were more likely than their male counterparts to have desisted from their earlier pattern of serious delinquent conduct. We did find a somewhat "protective" effect of gender in quantitative analyses that examined respondents' self-reported criminal involvement (at the time of the follow-up) as well as their patterns of adult arrests.[32] Yet focusing on the comparison with men does not adequately capture the marginal social and economic positions of these women and the difficulties many had encountered as they matured into adulthood. When we consider the women's own self-reports about their levels of involvement in crime or drug abuse, recent arrest histories, and information from the narratives, we find that a majority (74 percent of African Americans and 57 percent of white women) could not be clearly categorized as having desisted from criminal activity. It is important to recognize that some of this involvement relates to low-level offending or drug use and also to reiterate that men did in fact report higher levels of involvement. In addition, men were more likely to have experienced recent arrests or periods of incarceration (using all sources of information about their criminal involvement levels, 96 percent of African American and 90 percent of white male respondents could not be classified as clear desisters).

Differences between this study and results based on other long-term follow-ups became even more apparent as we examined other areas of the respondents' lives. In some respects this basic contrast overshadows the gender differences in overall rates of criminal involvement. For example, while Sampson and Laub found that a majority of the men who had participated in the Gluecks' study were married and had stable employment by the time of the follow-up study of the men at age thirty, we found that only a small percentage of respondents in our study—whether male or female—had achieved the "respectability package" emphasized by these researchers.[33] Only about eight percent of the women (a) were married, (b) reported an average or better level of marital attachment, and (c) had secured a job working above the 1995 poverty line. Males were significantly more likely to be employed, but a similar small percentage (8.6 percent) had been able to put together this total "package." Societal-level transformations, such as the decline of solid manufacturing jobs, and changes in the likelihood and permanence of marriage are undoubtedly important elements that help to explain this pattern of results.

In addition, this cohort of young people came of age during a time when drug use, especially crack cocaine, had a particularly debilitating and marginalizing impact on the character of their lifestyles and subsequent opportunities to move in a more prosocial direction. (As one male respondent put it succinctly, in describing the impact of crack cocaine, "You smoke it, you own it.") The majority of both women and men (83.2 percent of the women and 82.7 percent of the men) failed to graduate from high school, a statistic that stands in stark contrast to societal trends—

further marginalizing this group of respondents. Jenny's narrative, for example, telegraphed her own awareness of this lack of access to what have come to be considered achievement "basics" in U.S. society. Jenny described how she always cried when she watched the movie *Grease*. At first the interviewer thought that Jenny was referring to the love story between the lead characters. Later, however, this respondent made clear that she was most moved by the scene at the end of the film, showing all the young people walking across the stage to receive their high school diplomas.

The narrative accounts and interviewer notes also provide evidence that most of the women and men, consistent with their low annual earnings, tended to reside in extremely marginal housing circumstances. Almost no respondents owned their own homes, and there are frequent references to dangerous neighborhoods, cramped apartments, and even time spent in shelters or other temporary housing:

> I know these roaches are bad. . . . I'm sorry—please excuse this!
> *Interviewer*: don't worry about this. . . . I'm telling you don't worry about the little critters they don't bother me in the slightest—I just flipped them off the paper.

> The conditions that surround the house were just chaotic and just unimaginable. . . . The homeless shelter and the Catholic Mission on the end of her street, those were the only buildings that seemed to have any hope for any residents in them. [Interviewer comments]

Even though early family circumstances and later involvement in delinquency typically connected respondents to highly disadvantaged adult lives, the follow-up nevertheless documented a significant range of criminal involvement—some respondents had clearly desisted, others were much less involved in crime, drug use, or violence than when they were first interviewed as adolescents, and still others were actively seeking to make or sustain a lifestyle change. Marital attachment and job stability were not strong, reliable predictors of desistance for either the women or men, but these factors were important for a smaller subset of respondents, particularly those who had established a strong bond to a highly prosocial spouse.

We found that it was important not only that the respondent had formed a strong bond with another person but also that the partner presented a significant contrast in orientation and lifestyle ("he's the calm one," "she's a real goody-goody"). The presence of this contrast element was related to variations in desistance of both women and men; yet because women in general are much less likely to be involved in criminal activity, it was more likely that marriage, on average, would serve as a positive social force or dynamic for male respondents. The pool of romantic partners available to many of the women did not as often present this element of positive contrast ("he's a known alcoholic," "he's got a temper on him; that's mostly what gets him in trouble," "he was stealing from drugstores at the time").

Our analyses of the life history narratives of more and less successful "desisters" also led us to see the important role of cognitive (perceptual) and motivational changes in understanding mechanisms linked to desistance. Some of the respondents managed to effect significant life changes even though they were not married or while they were still actively involved with antisocial partners. These respondents often crafted new lives using what appeared to be very little in the way of raw materials—that is, having few available sources of positive influence or financial or other resources. We observed significant variations in and saw a significant role for the individual's motivational stance—that is, openness to change and receptivity to elements in the immediate environment likely to have a "conventionalizing" influence. For example, some women resonated with religion at a particular point in their lives; spiritual transformations then became a catalyst for making a variety of other beneficial life changes. Others focused heavily on the effects of their children and on their own desire to be more effective, loving parents than their own had been. Although men also frequently mentioned that they wanted to be a good influence on their children, this theme was more often a centerpiece of the women's narratives. The role of children in the desistance process is complex, however; we found that childbearing experiences did not inevitably lead to desistance within this sample of serious offenders. This again suggests the important role of cognitive changes—for some of the women with extensive criminal backgrounds, the birth of children did not result in the type of motivational change that was associated with a sustained move away from criminal activity.

This lack of an automatic or abrupt effect is suggested by the finding that more than 50 percent of the women did not have physical custody of at least one of their minor children at the time of the adult follow-up. In addition, child-endangerment charges were frequently mentioned in the adult arrest histories. In other instances, women (and some men) described how the experience of having children indeed had a transformative effect ("Having a baby, that changed a whole lot of me. . . . It wasn't about me no more"). These narratives also focused on how respondents had taken concrete steps to distance themselves from environments likely to have a negative influence ("I just stay away from people that is going to get me in trouble. . . . I don't need it"). Future research using larger samples of offenders should examine in more detail the conditions under which children successfully operate as a catalyst for making life changes. This research would ideally involve samples of men as well as women, recognizing that childrearing is typically still very highly gendered—women remain the close-in caregivers for a majority of children, and these issues are generally lifelong, core concerns in women's lives. In addition, women who have difficulties related to their role as parents face greater social stigma than comparably situated men, thus adding to their sense of burden and marginality. It will also be important to explore differential effects of men and women's desistance/persistence processes on their children's own well-being and risk for future involvement in delinquent behavior.

Conclusion

Feminist theories have illuminated multiple ways in which societal, familial, and individual-level social forces combine to make it much less likely that girls will ever become involved in criminal behavior. Patriarchal arrangements and institutions have produced effective systems of control over girls' actions that are direct (e.g., higher levels of supervision of girls) or subtle and indirect (socialization messages that discourage assertive or aggressive behavior, or various types of risk-taking). Yet in every jurisdiction and era, a small subset of girls do "act out" in ways that result in social sanctions, including official intervention—that is, arrest and periods of incarceration.

Results of this long-term follow-up study of young women who had evidenced serious levels of delinquency as adolescents suggest the following conclusion: a comprehensive explanation of their actions (as compared with explanations for the relative lack of involvement on the part of most girls) requires that we draw from both the classic explanations of delinquency and the contemporary perspectives that tend to emphasize uniquely gendered processes. Within the life histories of these young women, we find ample evidence of both types of social dynamics. Economic marginality, disadvantaged neighborhoods, and an "excess of definitions favorable to the violation of law" are frequent themes within the narratives, but these themes are often intertwined with stories of sexual abuse and a recurring pattern of negative male influence. Boyfriends and other older males are important actors within the social networks of these respondents, but they are not the only sources of antisocial influence—we found that parents' criminal involvement and/or severe drug and alcohol problems frequently emerged early on and continued throughout the women's childhood and adolescent years. These family processes not only proved to be a source of criminal learning (consistent with differential association theory) but also decreased the type of family bonding and supervision that generally serve to inhibit girls' opportunities for and exposure to delinquent actions (consistent with social control theory). Feminist perspectives have provided a nuanced portrait of the distinct dynamics that may be involved when male partners influence girls in a delinquent direction (e.g., focusing attention on asymmetries of power); yet the narratives also underscore the importance of more-general processes of social influence, such as the adolescent girl's developmentally appropriate desire to be well-liked and respected by her same-gender peers.

The adult follow-up study also supports the idea that some processes associated with continued crime or desistance appear "generic" (that is, they have a good fit with the life experiences of women as well as men), while others appear to be more heavily gendered. For example, some women in the sample were able to benefit from a strong bond to a prosocial romantic partner, a "good marriage effect" that has been described in prior research on male offenders. Yet this process can appropriately be conceptualized as "practically speaking" gendered, in that many of the women seem to have had greater difficulty finding and thus benefiting from this type of respectable partner. We also focused on the role of motivational changes, and again, future research may support the idea that these attitudinal and perceptual changes are more central to an understanding of mechanisms involved in women's as compared with men's desistance efforts. Future research can usefully explore in much greater detail processes that may be more and less salient for girls (and under what conditions), an approach that seems preferable to the either/or theoretical stance that has sometimes dominated discussions of these issues.

Another important consideration is that some areas of inquiry emphasized by feminist scholars are important in their own right, without necessarily requiring a direct causal association with either the onset of criminal behavior or desistance processes. For example, research on violence against women has resulted in heightened social awareness and has often been directly responsible for legal and social interventions aimed at interrupting patterns of relationship violence and other types of abuse. These social change efforts improve the lives of all women, including those with greater criminal justice system contacts. Similarly, research and programs focused on women offenders' role as mothers are important to pursue, whether or not such programs link immediately and directly to the desistance process. A multifaceted approach, including attention to generic (e.g., poverty status, housing difficulties) and gendered processes will likely be required to interrupt the array of disadvantages that for these women have taken a "life course" to accumulate.[34]

NOTES

1. This project was supported by grants from the National Institute of Mental Health (MH2905/MH46410).

2. See Robert J. Sampson and John H. Laub, *Crime in the Making: Pathways and Turning Points through Life* (Cambridge, MA: Harvard University Press, 1993). See also John H. Laub and Robert J. Sampson, *Shared Beginnings, Divergent Lives: Delinquent Boys to Age 70* (Cambridge, MA: Harvard University Press, 2003).

3. Darrell Steffensmeier and Emilie Allan, "Gender and Crime: Toward a Gendered Theory of Offending," *Annual Review of Sociology* 22 (1996): 459–487.

4. See Robert K. Merton, "Social Structure and Anomie," *American Sociological Review* 3 (1938): 672–682. See also Robert K. Merton, *Social Theory and Social Structure* (New York: Free Press, 1968).

5. See, e.g., William Julius Wilson, *The Truly Disadvantaged: The Inner City, the Underclass, and Public Policy* (Chicago: University of Chicago Press, 1987); Elijah Anderson, *Code of the Street: Decency, Violence, and the Moral Life of the Inner City* (New York: W. W. Norton, 1999); Albert J. Reiss and Michael Tonry, eds., *Communities and Crime* (Chicago: University of Chicago Press, 1986).

6. Edwin H. Sutherland and Donald R. Cressey, *Criminology*, 8th ed. (Philadelphia: J. B. Lippincott, 1970), 75.

7. Edwin H. Sutherland, *Principles of Criminology* (Philadelphia: J. B. Lippincott, 1947), 7.

8. For discussions of familial effects on criminality, see, e.g., David P. Farrington, Darrick Jolliffe, Rolf Loeber, Magda Stouthamer-Loeber, and Larry M. Kalb, "The Concentration of Offenders in Families, and Family Criminality in the Prediction of Boys' Delinquency," *Journal of Adolescence* 24 (2001): 579–596; Joan McCord, "Family Relationships, Juvenile Delinquency, and Adult Criminality,"

Criminology 29 (1991): 397–417. For discussions of peer-group effects on delinquency, see, e.g., Dana L. Haynie, "Friendship Networks and Adolescent Delinquency: The Relative Nature of Peer Delinquency," *Journal of Quantitative Criminology* 18 (2002): 99–134; Terrence P. Thornberry, Alan J. Lizotte, Marvin D. Krohn, Margaret Farnworth, and Sung Joon Jang, "Delinquent Peers, Beliefs, and Delinquent Behavior: A Longitudinal Test of Interactional Theory," *Criminology* 32 (1994): 47–83.

9. Travis Hirschi, *Causes of Delinquency* (Berkeley: University of California Press, 1969).

10. Hirschi, *Causes of Delinquency*, 16.

11. See, e.g., Sung Joon Jang and Carolyn Smith, "A Test of Reciprocal Causal Relationships among Parental Supervision, Affective Ties, and Delinquency," *Journal of Research in Crime and Delinquency* 34 (1997): 307–336.

12. See, e.g., Terrence P. Thornberry Alan J. Lizotte, Marvin D. Krohn, Margaret Farnworth, and Sung Joon Jang, "Testing Interactional Theory: An Examination of Reciprocal Causal Relationships among Family, School, and Delinquency," *Journal of Criminal Law and Criminology* 82 (1991): 3–35.

13. Karen Heimer, "Gender, Interaction, and Delinquency: Testing a Theory of Differential Social Control," *Social Psychology Quarterly* 59 (1996): 39–61.

14. Eileen B. Leonard, *Women, Crime, and Society: A Critique of Theoretical Criminology* (New York: Langman, 1982), 181.

15. Ibid., 108.

16. Meda Chesney-Lind and Randall G. Shelden, *Girls, Delinquency, and Juvenile Justice*, 3rd ed. (Belmont, CA: Thomson/Wadsworth, 2004).

17. Chesney-Lind and Shelden, *Girls, Delinquency, and Juvenile Justice*, 146.

18. Jean Bottcher, "Social Practices of Gender: How Gender Relates to Delinquency in the Everyday Lives of High-Risk Youth," *Criminology* 39 (2001): 893–932.

19. Beth E. Richie, *Compelled to Crime: The Gender Entrapment of Battered Black Women* (New York: Routledge, 1996).

20. It is important to note that this sketch of the feminist perspective tends to create an image of women offenders as rather passive victims of patriarchal arrangements, coercive experiences, and the like—a view that recent feminist scholarship within criminology has critiqued and attempted to complicate. For example, researchers such as Lisa Maher (*Sexed Work: Gender, Race, and Resistance in a Brooklyn Drug Market* [Oxford: Clarendon Press, 1997]) and Deborah R. Baskin and Ira B. Sommers (*Casualties of Community Disorder: Women's Careers in Violent Crime* [Boulder, CO: Westview, 1998]) have noted that women do exert "agency," that is, make their own choices within certain boundaries or constraints. They may also develop a more positive, active view of themselves and their behavioral choices than is implied by the "passive victim" portrait (see also Emily Gaarder and Joanne Belknap, "Tenuous Borders: Girls Transferred to Adult Court," *Criminology* 40 [2002]: 481–517).

21. David P. Farrington, "Key Results from the First Forty Years of the Cambridge Study in Delinquent Development," in *Taking Stock of Delinquency: An Overview of Findings from Contemporary Longitudinal Studies,* ed. Terrence P. Thornberry and Marvin D. Krohn, pp. 137–183 (New York: Kluwer Academic, 2003).

22. Terrie E. Moffitt, "Adolescent-Limited and Life-Course Persistent Antisocial Behavior: A Developmental Taxonomy," *Psychological Review* 100 (1993): 674–701.

23. Sampson and Laub, *Crime in the Making.*

24. Ibid.

25. Baskin and Sommers, *Casualties of Community Disorder.*

26. John Graham and Benjamin Bowling, *Young People and Crime* (London: Home Office Research Study, 1996), 145.

27. Bottcher, "Social Practices of Gender," 899.

28. See, e.g., Edwin M. Schur, *Labeling Women Deviant: Gender, Stigma, and Social Control* (New York: Random House, 1984); Richie, *Compelled to Crime*; Carol Gilligan, *In a Different Voice: Psychological Theory and Women's Development* (Cambridge, MA: Harvard University Press, 1982).

29. For a more detailed discussion of the early delinquent backgrounds of the respondents in the sample, see Stephen A. Cernkovich, Peggy C. Giordano, and M. D. Pugh, "Chronic Offenders: The Missing Cases in Self-Report Delinquency Research," *Journal of Criminal Law and Criminology* 76 (1985): 705–732.

30. Peggy C. Giordano, Jill A. Deines, and Stephen A. Cernkovich, "Gendered or Generic Theories of Delinquency Causation? Evidence from a Long-Term, Follow-Up of Serious Adolescent Offenders" (paper presented at the annual meeting of the American Society of Criminology, Denver, CO, November 22, 2003).

31. Cathy Spatz Widom, "The Cycle of Violence," *Science* 244 (1989): 160–166.

32. Peggy C. Giordano, Stephen A. Cernkovich, and Jennifer A. Rudolph, "Gender, Crime, and Desistance: Toward a Theory of Cognitive Transformation," *American Journal of Sociology* 107 (2002): 990–1064.

33. Giordano, Cernkovich, and Rudolph, "Gender, Crime and Desistance"; Sampson and Laub, *Crime in the Making.*

34. See, e.g., Kristy Holtfreter, Michael D. Reisig, and Merry Morash, "Poverty, State Capital, and Recidivism among Women Offenders," *Criminology and Public Policy* 3 (2004): 105–208.

Chapter 2

Stuck Up, Telling Lies, and Talking Too Much

The Gendered Context of Young Women's Violence

Jody Miller and Christopher W. Mullins

Although the largest gender gaps in offending are for violent crimes, recent studies of girls' violence suggest that their "involvement in physically aggressive behavior seems to be rather more common than previous research would suggest."[1] A few works emphasize similarities across gender, and many focus on gender differences in the causes and consequences of violence. Only a handful of studies have simultaneously addressed overlap and divergence within and across gender. This is the approach we believe is most fruitful for understanding the nature of girls' violence, particularly when such an approach attends to the important but complex role of gender inequality in creating gender differences.[2]

Here our goal is to provide a contextual examination of the nature, circumstances, and meanings of fights between girls. We draw from a broader qualitative study of violence in the lives of urban African American youths to examine thirty-four young women's accounts of the situational context of girl-on-girl fights. The examination of situational context has been popular in studies of male violence for decades; recent scholars have called for this approach in the study of female violence as well.[3] This contextual focus allows for examinations of gender as an integral facet of the everyday world that structures social life and provides a meaning system for interpreting social action. The strength of in-depth interviewing for situational analyses is that we can examine young women's subjective interpretive processes vis-à-vis violence and thus gain insight into the meanings and normative place of violence in their social lives.

Gender and Violence

Situational examinations of male violence have a long history. Despite different theoretical traditions and empirical emphases, the depiction of young men's violence has remained remarkably stable across the decades: it is characterized by focal concerns that strongly emphasize autonomy, respect, and the defense of reputation. Recent scholars have explicitly linked these concerns to gender: they are core features of hegemonic masculinity on the streets.[4]

Ironically, while the study of young women's violence has a much shorter history, there is considerably less consistency among researchers regarding its causes, nature, and meanings. These variations are rooted in the problem of gender inequality. For instance, though hegemonic masculinity encourages the use of aggression, dominant features of femininities have emphasized passivity and obedience. Violence runs counter to such hegemonic behavioral demands. Thus, the emphasis on "doing gender," popular in explaining masculinity as a key facet of male violence, proves more problematic for explaining female violence. Likewise, research has consistently shown that gender stratification is widespread and results in structural limitations on women's street participation and activities. Broader features of gender inequality, which include institutional inequalities as well as social norms and arrangements built on the notion of gender difference, strongly influence both the emphases and interpretations scholars bring to bear on female violence.[5]

Feminist scholars have been at the forefront in emphasizing the "blurred boundaries" of women's victimization and offending. Attention to gender inequality has led feminist scholars to examine "the gendered and sexed contexts that bring adolescents to the street [and] the gendered and sexed conditions of survival on the street."[6] This work is important for emphasizing how gendered structures differentially affect girls. Several scholars suggest that women's violence is qualitatively different from men's: women use violence as a protective measure, in response to their vulnerability to or to their actual victimization.[7] Though important for understanding facets of female offending, this approach may be less successful in explaining girls' aggression toward other girls.

A number of scholars argue that female violence is expressive and relational, whereas male violence is instrumental. For instance, Hagan and Foster make a distinction "between indirect, relational forms of aggression that are more common among girls, and direct, physical aggression that is more frequent among boys."[8] Steffensmeier and Allan suggest that "[s]ituational pressures such as threatened loss of valued relationships may play a greater role in female offending. . . . women take greater risks to sustain valued relationships, whereas males take greater risks for reasons of status or competitive advantage."[9] Likewise, although Adams critiques other scholars for assuming that issues of respect are only relevant for males, her analysis of young women's violence frames respect in the same explicitly gendered way: "respect transcends the masculine understanding of respect . . . as a personal and individual issue, to encompass a relational understanding of respect in which respect for others is paramount in maintaining solid, stable relationships." She claims that girls' fights can be interpreted as "an affirmation of normalized femininity" because they often occur in the context of conflicts over boyfriends, friends, and family.[10]

Our concern with this approach is whether such interpretations are themselves based on taken-for-granted assumptions about gender difference. "Women are relational, men are instrumental" resonates with popular notions of gender but ultimately is one-dimensional for understanding young women's violence. It is belied, as well, by evidence that men sometimes engage in violence to maintain relational obligations or defend loved ones.[11] Even gang violence is often for the defense of one's group or retaliation for a gang peer.[12] However, scholars have not framed such incidents as "relational." Likewise, social meanings of gender often undermine women's uses of aggression precisely by framing it as expressive and emotional. This characterization discounts women's instrumental goals and may result in an interpretation of women's violence as ineffectual.[13] Assumptions of gender difference are based on deeply entrenched cultural beliefs that persist, despite empirical evidence to the contrary.[14]

Rather than starting from a premise of gender difference, our analysis attempts to specify when and how gender matters in the enactment of violence. In analyzing girls' accounts of girl-on-girl violence, we ask these questions: What facets of girls' conflicts appear to be gendered, and what is the nature of such gendering? What similarities exist across gender, when we compare our findings with studies of male violence? In what ways are the gendered facets of girls' aggression the result of a desire to meet gender-specific goals that are rooted in gendered social structural constraints? We take a skeptical approach to the idea of dichotomous difference to provide a nuanced analysis of girls' violence.

Methods and Study Setting

Our data come from a broader study of gender and violence among urban African American adolescents. We draw from surveys and qualitative interviews with thirty-five girls in north St. Louis, Missouri, conducted between 1999 and 2000. Respondents were twelve to eighteen years old, with a mean age of sixteen. They were recruited for the project with the cooperation of several organizations working with at-risk and delinquent youths, including a local community agency and two alternative public high schools. The schools were designated to serve youths expelled from St. Louis public schools for chronic in-school disruptive behavior or violence. Counselors approached youths to participate in the study when they were known to reside in disadvantaged St. Louis neighborhoods.

Sampling was purposive. We interviewed girls at risk or involved in delinquent activities, all of whom had experience with girl-on-girl violence as perpetrators, victims, or witnesses.[15] Respondents came from neighborhoods characterized by intense racial segregation, social isolation, limited resources, concentrated poverty, and high rates of violent crime. Though Anderson and others have examined male violence in such milieus, such research has had little to say about young women's violence. There is evidence that African American girls in distressed urban communities have higher rates of violence than their counterparts in other racial groups and settings,[16] but qualitative analysis of the phenomenon has been limited.

Data collection began with the administration of a survey, and youths were then asked to participate in an audiotaped in-depth interview, typically on the same day. The primary data for this contextual examination come from the in-depth interviews. Girls' responses in the survey were used to help guide the conversation in the in-depth interviews. These were semistructured, with open-ended questions that allowed for considerable probing. Our goal was to gather data that could provide a relatively holistic assessment of the nature of girls' violence, situated in the context of girls' perceptions of female violence, general patterns of girl-on-girl conflicts, and the features and motives behind specific arguments and violent events. Young women were first asked about the nature of conflicts between girls and to describe recent examples, including those they had participated in or witnessed.[17] They were then probed for details about the incidents, including what happened and why, where it happened, and how third parties responded. Rigorous examination of such accounts offers a means of "arriving at meanings or culturally embedded normative explanations" for behavior, because they "represent ways in which people organize views of themselves, of others, and of their social worlds."[18]

In our analysis, we took care to ensure that the concepts developed and illustrations provided typified the most common patterns in girls' accounts. This was achieved using principles of grounded theory, including the search for and explication of deviant cases.[19] Reliability was strengthened through our triangulated data collection technique, by asking questions about violence during multiple points across both interviews, and by asking for detailed accounts during the in-depth interviews. Though not generalizable, the study raises significant issues that may guide further inquiries into the nature of girls' violence.

The Gendered Context of Young Women's Violence

Asked to characterize the nature of girls' conflicts, young women often framed them as petty events that were part and parcel of both the trouble-making nature of girls and their quick tempers. Alicia said girls' fights were "stupid. If a girl look at another girl, it's a fight. If a girl say something to a girl, it's a fight. Over boys. Stupid little stuff, girls'll fight over anything." Sharmi laughed as she explained that girls fight "all the time. *All* the time. . . . [It can be about] shoo, everything, he say/she say stuff, lookin' at you the wrong way, *anything*." Consequently, Tami explained that while she had two or three close female friends, "you mostly gotta hang out with the males 'cause females start too much stuff."

Compared to these general characterization of girls' fights as trivial, young women's accounts of actual conflicts revealed a complex negotiation of status, respect, and relationships. Here we discuss the most common proximate triggers for girls' conflicts: he say/she say; status challenges concerning style and reputation; and boys. These were often cited as the immediate causes of conflicts but were layered with accounts of the tenuous nature of girls' friendships, the role of third parties, jealousies, and the desire to create a reputation as "tough."

He Say/She Say

Young women used the phrase "he say/she say" to refer to several types of events (e.g., spreading rumors, "telling your business," and name calling); what these have in common is their occurrence behind an individual's back. Gail explained, "he say/she say [is when] somebody said something about this, or started a rumor about this person, and then they wanna know who said it and all that." Ramara's description of a such a fight was typical:

A girl that didn't like me . . . I guess [because] somebody told her something about me or something, and she wanted to fight me. And I started talkin' about her 'cause she started talkin' about me and stuff. Then people started tellin' her, "Well, she said this about you," and they'll tell [me] what she said about me. I don't really trip off like what people say about me 'cause I know whatever they saying about me ain't true and stuff. But I still went along with it and stuff, until it came down to where we was about to get suspended for disruption of classes and stuff 'cause we was just in the hallway, heated and stuff.

Sometimes rumors or comments were sexual in nature. Dawanna complained of sexual rumors people had spread about her that resulted in a fight with a girl at school. When Dawanna confronted the girl about spreading rumors, "she got attitude and junk, and talkin' 'bout she gonna kick my butt after school and stuff. So we got into it [fought] after school." Likewise, Felicia described a fight that emerged when a girl told others of her sexual activities:

A girl up here . . . know that I talk to this dude up here, and we don't let everybody know that we talking because it's not nobody's business, so we keep it on the hush. And she told everybody that we was sleeping together. . . . So I told her, her best bet for real was to keep my name up out of her mouth from now on. She [got] an attitude, so I had to smack her.

Just as often, however, he say/she say conflicts involved other forms of name-calling. For instance, Sharmi described an incident that escalated after a girl at school had called Sharmi's friend "ugly" in front of Sharmi's sister. Her sister "went and told my friend," and the friend "was like, 'I'm getting her' or whatever, 'cause the girl had kept talkin' stuff or whatever." Later they attended a seminar together, and the girl who called Sharmi's friend ugly was there. Sharmi went up to the girl and said, "'yeah, you know her, you tryin' to call her ugly' or whatever, and she called me a 'B' [bitch] or whatever." Sharmi's friend got involved in the altercation at that point as well: "They was lookin' at each other, talking stuff . . . like sending messages back and forth, whatever, like [after school] they was finna [getting ready to] fight."

As Sharmi's discussion highlights, third parties played an integral role in he say/she say conflicts: they routinely passed on information about who said what to the individuals involved. Gail pointed out that fluctuations in girls' friendship networks were often involved: "It'll be one girl who think this person her friend, and she'll tell her something. And that person who she thought was her friend'll go back and tell the other girl or just accidentally let it slip out or something, and then everything else get started." Likewise, Katie noted, "they be hangin' around each other but then they talk about somebody in they group. Then when that person leave, then someone outta the group, they tell 'em what someone said and they start arguing about that." She described a recent incident:

> One of the girls was hangin' with them and so they got into it 'cause they just talkin' about her clothes or whatever. . . . "She tacky, she don't know how to dress." . . . So somebody overheard, and they told her—'cause they talk real loud—and so they told her what had happened, and so she went back and asked them and they start arguin'.

Christal described a series of conflicts between herself and three friends —Shauntell, Ashley, and Jameesha—who "call ourselves cousins." Shauntell told Christal that Ashley said she wanted to fight her. Christal confronted Ashley in the cafeteria, the conflict escalated, and then Ashley said that the fourth friend, Jameesha, had also said she wanted to fight Christal. Christal complained, "Every time you get into it with one of them, they tellin' you what the other person suppose to be saying." Ashley's comments succeeded nonetheless, and Christal began arguing with Jameesha, with both threatening to "whoop" each other.

Girls' friendship circles sometimes included young women who did not like one another; their mutual friends either kept the peace or escalated the conflict. Gail noted, "It's enemies at our school who got the same friends though. So when they around they friends they just gotta get along, you know. People be like, 'don't fight, don't fight,' breakin' it up, pullin' them back and stuff." On the other hand, mutual friends sometimes heightened rather than reduced conflicts. Anishika provided a lengthy account of the disruption of a friendship that began with he say/she say:

> These two girls was best friends. I mean, both of 'em, they real short, real . . . little, you know, like, they suppose to be in elementary school or something. . . . So they was like best friends and the lil' short dark one,[20] she was real cool. . . . Every time one fight, the other short one will help, right. . . . [Then] they let this girl come up here and mess it up for 'em. [One of the best friends was suspended, and] when she came back [the third girl] was like, "you know, so-and-so [i.e., the lil' short dark girl] was talkin' about you. . . . [She said] you fake." Which is all a story, they just wanted them to fight.

The story succeeded: "So [the best friend] was like, 'You said I'm fake.' [The dark one] was like, 'Naw, I ain't say that.'" Her friend didn't believe her and continued to confront and accuse the girl:

> [The dark one] didn't want to fight her 'cause they was real cool. So the other girl, she frontin' [acting tough in front of others] and stuff, knowin' the other one [wouldn't fight her]. . . . She was just doin' all this [hitting gestures] behind her head . . . like we'd be in the lunchroom, [the dark one]'d sit by me and stuff, [the other one]'ll come over there and kick her chair and stuff, [the dark one]'ll start crying. . . . She really [was] doin' [it to] get all this attention, makin' everybody think she hard and stuff. She use to always act like she goin' smack her and stuff. . . . [But] she know if she would have hit her, [the dark girl] woulda just whooped her. And she know. They was best friends, they both could fight, and she know she would have got whooped. Everybody was like, "aw, you a punk" to the one that was cryin', "'cause you know so-and-so'll whoop you, whyn't you gon' fight her?" Dudes ampin' it up [attempting to escalate the conflict], "whyn't you gon' fight her?"

The girl was heartbroken that her best friend had turned on her. Anishika told her,

> "That's not your friend 'cause yo' friend wouldn't've been doin' all that. She wouldn't've let nobody come to her with no he say/she say, and she didn't hear you say it yo'self. . . . Friends don't do all that, they do not let nobody come to them tryin' to break they relationship up." . . . I mean, it

just hurt her, you know what I'm saying. She was upset, crying and stuff. I told her she have to know she didn't have friends. I told [her] I thought I had friends, I ain't wanna listen to my mamma, but I had to find out the hard way.

Anishika's story encapsulates the disruptive effect of he say/she say on girls' friendships and the distrustful attitude young women often developed about their relationships with other girls. Additional themes emerged in this narrative that will be followed up later, including Anishika's emphasis on the confrontational girl's desire for others to see her as "hard" and the role of third parties in "amping up" fights. First, we move to another proximate trigger for girls' fights: status challenges.

Status Challenges: Style and Reputation

We distinguish status challenges from he say/she say based on their face-to-face rather than "behind-the-back" nature. Young women consistently described two basic types of status challenges between girls: those that concerned personal style, including dress and hair; and those that were reputational in nature, particularly concerning girls' desire to project images of toughness and an ability to stand up for themselves. Girls linked the former status challenges to issues of jealousy and the latter to both disrespect and "showing off." Both concerned girls' place within social hierarchies.

Style challenges. Many girls emphasized the role of jealousy to explain conflicts about personal style. Janelle said, "I think [jealousy] occurs more between females than the guys. They just, you know, a girl can walk in and her outfit will be cuter than the other girl's, and she'll be like, 'ah well.'" Cherise noted, "most of the fights that I have had occurred because the girls may have been jealous of me, the way I look, the way I dress, how many boys like me. Jealous." Describing what girls "get into it" about, Shauntell summed up:

Hair, nails, clothes and shoes. And the way you walk. . . . You know, some people get into it and be like, "you think you smarter than everybody." Oh naw. Not up here. They ain't worried about smartness. You come to school [and] you got jewelry, yo' nails done, yo' hair done, shoes, clothes, pretty— they gon' hate. That's all it is, a matter of hatin'.

Conflicts emerging over personal style typically played out in a face-to-face manner, as Felicia noted, with girls "always [having] something to say." Ramara described a "playful" friend who would "just go up to a girl and [say] 'girl, yo' hair is just too nappy,' you know, even if they hair be the straightest hair in the world, she'll just do it." She continued:

> Then the other girl like, "well yo' hair nappy too, and look at yo' clothes and they wrinkled" and blah, blah, blah. And then they lead into a big argument and everybody around them soupin' they head up to fight and stuff. [My friend] don't really trip off of it until . . . it go to where they gotta fight. Then she be like, "well, I was just playing with you in the first place, so if yo' hair wasn't nappy you wouldn'ta even gotten mad."

As Ramara's story suggests, a powerful means of disrespecting a young woman was to imply that her clothing or hairstyle was inexpensive, in poor taste, or not well tended to. We were given several versions of a single set of incidents that involved face-to-face affronts about hair. Christal described the altercations her friend Shauntell had with an older girl at school:

> Some high school girl got into it with Shauntell because the girl came to Shauntell and Shauntell had her hair [in microbraids]. . . . And then the girl came to her and was like, "who did your hair?" And Shauntell was like, "my play momma." And then she was like, "well, when you got it done, was it *done* done?" And then Shauntell was like "what you trying to say?" . . . A couple of days later Shauntell saw the girl and [her] braids was getting raggedy and Shauntell asked the girl, "who did yo' hair?" and she was like, "some girl," and then Shauntell was like, "when you got yo' hair done was it *done* done?" And then she was like, "yeah." So it all started from there. . . . [They didn't fight,] they just argued. 'Cause [this girl] in the tenth or eleventh [grade], one of 'em. And Shauntell ain't in nothin' but the seventh. She say she ain't gon' even stoop down to Shauntell['s] level, she'll [get] somebody to fight Shauntell for her 'cause she ain't finna fight Shauntell herself."

The charge "was your hair *done* done?" was an insult that implied the girl's hair had not been braided professionally at a beauty shop but instead was done by an amateur at home. It called into question the girl's capacity to invest in her personal grooming. Christal also noted the age difference between Shauntell and the "high school girl"—Tisha—implicated in the conflict. Tisha provided her own version of these events:

> [The last time I got into it with a girl] it really wasn't about nothin'. It was a lil' middle school girl. She had thought I was somebody else, and she came and said something to me. And I ain't understand what she was sayin', you know, 'cause I wasn't the one that said something to her. So when she came back to me sayin' whatever she had said, all that lil' remark or whatever, I ain't know what she was talkin' about. So then all that day they was like, "you let that lil' girl say that to you?" blah, blah. I'm like, "what she say?" 'Cause I really didn't understand it. Somebody had said something to her about her hair, so she came to me, ask me something about my hair. . . . She was like, "who did your hair, and when they did it was [it] *done* done?" Something like that. I had some braids comin' into a ball or whatever. I had had 'em for like three months so my roots was kinda thick or whatever. So I was like, "yeah." So she just walked away then. So everybody was just talkin' about it all that day or whatever, and she just kept sayin' lil' stuff. But I wasn't payin' her no attention 'cause she a lil' girl, she only in seventh grade. . . . I know she was sayin' something, but I wasn't hearing it. I'd just see her laugh with her friends and all that kinda stuff. They was ampin' her up, all that. . . . She'll stand back and say stuff [rather than approach me again]. She'll try to send lil' messages from her friends . . . and I'll be like, "I don't wanna hear that" or whatever. . . . I guess she figured out I wasn't paying her no attention so she moved on and got into it with somebody else.

Tisha's account not only emphasized that it had been a case of mistaken identity but also that their age difference precluded her from engaging in the conflict. Refusing to fight back sent the message that Shauntell—particularly because of her youth—was not capable of engaging Tisha in a challenge worthy of her attention. Tisha would not have raised her status by fighting Shauntell, because her larger stature would have made the match unfair. On the other hand, older girls were in something of a bind, as Tisha's comments suggest. "Everybody" at school was talking about the incident "all that day," and they were challenging Tisha's willingness to allow a "lil'" girl" to disrespect her. The age problem was likely heightened because many of the young women we interviewed were at an alternative school that included both middle and high school students. Middle school girls in particular were attempting to build their reputations, which caused unique dilemmas for older girls that they would not have faced in a regular school setting. Age was also an undercurrent in girls' narratives regarding reputational status challenges, to which we now turn.

Reputational challenges. Conflicts regarding reputation frequently arose when young women read the actions of other girls as disrespectful, or they were provoked when their own actions were perceived as disrespectful by others. Like style challenges, these occurred face-to-face. They involved a variety of acts, including staring, eye rolling, making inappropriate comments, and generally "getting an attitude." At their extreme, these challenges focused on girls' sexual reputations. Anishika described a recent incident that involved inappropriate sexual comments:

> Serena gotta lotta mouth . . . but the other lil' girl [Justine], she could fight though. And Serena was runnin' her mouth, talkin' 'bout Justine a rat [sexually promiscuous] and stuff. . . . And Justine was like, "whatever, whatever." They was going back and forth, and the gym teacher broke them up so they wouldn't fight 'cause he know the one that's running her mouth [Serena] gon' [get] beat up, and he know that Justine can fight.

According to Anishika, the gym teacher took both girls to the office, and they were suspended. "So Justine was like, 'aw, she talked all this stuff and got me suspended for three days, and we didn't do nothin'. I'ma give them a reason to suspend me.'" Anishika continued:

> Soon as that bell rang, Justine was standing outside looking for Serena. . . . She [had] ran all the way up [the street] somewhere . . . tryin' to hide . . . and they seen her. Justine went over there, she was like, "what you say?" and she just stole her [punched her in the face], she just knocked her, right then and there. . . . Serena got beat up. She shouldn'a talked all that stuff, talkin' about Justine is a rat, tellin' everybody . . . 'bout she got caught sucking somebody stuff under the bleachers. So Justine, she just whooped her.

More often than sexual reputational challenges, however, young women described conflicts that evolved out of broader perceptions of disrespect. For instance, Tami said, "it's like if you bump into 'em or something they get a attitude. [Even] if you say sorry and stuff, they still be trippin' off of it, and then that'll go on for like three days or whatever." Janelle described the situation:

I was walking through the hall and there were two girls playing in the hall and I was trying to get through. And they was swinging on each other. I'm like, you know, trying not to get hit, trying . . . to get . . . to my locker. And I was like, "whoa, chill out." So she got an attitude about it, and she was like, "what'd she say?" and, you know, she got loud with me so I got loud back, and we had an exchange of words, but we didn't fight.

Looking at someone the wrong way also was read as a sign of disrespect. Sharmi noted, "I don't like it when females look at me [a lot]. . . . I get mad." Alicia described one such event:

They was in art class and the girl was talking real loud, just being ghetto, and the one girl kept staring at her. And the girl that was talking real loud was like, "she hate when people stare at her." So the girl who was staring at her said, "if you wouldn't be talking so loud, I wouldn't be staring at you." They got to passing words or whatever, they didn't fight, they was just arguing and from then, like this week they just been staring at each other, rolling they eyes. But they ain't fight. . . . They always getting into it, saying stuff to each other. . . . [And] more people getting involved in it . . . adding they little parts, saying stuff to them. They just adding they own two cents in it . . . wanting [them] to fight.

Likewise, Lisa complained, "Why-come every time you walk past you gotta roll your eyes, curse her out, say a lil' something so your friends can laugh? What's the point? Just walk away . . . just leave her alone. But these lil' girls don't."

As both girls' comments suggest, these face-to-face conflicts were exacerbated by the presence of third parties. In addition to third parties amping up conflicts, young women believed that girls often were disrespectful to other girls to show off to their friends and convince others that they were "hard." Anishika noted this earlier, in her account of the best friends who had a falling out. The one girl repeatedly confronted her ex-friend, threatening to "whoop" her. According to Anishika, "she really doin' [it to] get all this attention, makin' everybody think she hard and stuff." Janelle said girls sought out fights when they were "trying to make their name. . . . They'll go fight somebody so somebody can be like, 'so-and-so fought her,' just so their name will be known." Likewise, Cleshay said girls' conflicts were due to "people trying to be something that they ain't, that's all. Trying to make an image for theyself."

Girls' characterizations of other young women's actions typically focused on their showing off and trying to be tough. However, they often characterized their own behaviors as a reflection of their ability to stand up for themselves. Janelle, who earlier described an "exchange of words" she had with a girl in the hallway, explained why she "got loud" with the girl: "one of my friends was trying to tell me to calm down, don't worry about it, and just go on to lunch. But, me being the person I am, I don't let people talk to me any way without me saying anything back." Likewise Kristy got "kicked out of school" after fighting a girl who "disrespected" her. She was frustrated when the school counselor "kind of reversed it, made it seem like it was my fault. Like I should've just ignored that girl. But some things you just don't say to me." Justifying her own fights, Cherise surmised, "I'm not no punk. My mom told me not to be no punching bag."

On the other hand, many girls criticized the routine nature of girls' conflicts, often attributing it to other girls' lack of maturity. Yvonne complimented herself for "my attitude, how cool and calm I am about things that most people get all rowdy about." Once when a girl wanted to fight her, she told her, "you're not worth me getting suspended from school. You're not worth none of that, and I'm not gonna stoop to your level." Yvonne explained her rationale: "I don't gotta try to act like I'm hard. It's not about me trying to act like I'm hard. It's about me trying to accomplish something."

Lisa's comments were the most explicit in linking girls' fights to their lack of maturity. She was seventeen and complained that "these lil' girls, they stupid up here." Several girls had an ongoing conflict with Lisa's sister. Lisa insisted, "I'm not finna let them mess with my lil' sister while she pregnant. My lil' sister too old for that now. . . . She ain't got time for that no more. She ain't tryin' to fight." Likewise, of herself and her friends, Lisa explained, "we don't get pulled into a lot of arguments with girls and stuff. . . . The three of us is probably the oldest girls in this school or whatever. We just feel like we more mature than them." Despite her proclamations, Lisa herself was involved in an ongoing conflict, and much of it centered around her boyfriend.

Boys and Boyfriends

A common source of conflict for young women was their interactions with one another's boyfriends. Ostensibly, these were fights about maintaining the integrity of boyfriend-girlfriend relationships. These conflicts flourished because a prominent model for male behavior was the "playa," which encouraged boys to involve themselves with multiple girls simultaneously.[21] As Katie explained, "it's usually not the girl['s] fault. It the boy['s] fault 'cause" they talk to other girls. Kenisha provided a typical account:

> A girl up here didn't know that this other girl was goin' with this boy, and they got into it. And the boy was like [telling each girl it was her that he really liked]. And they thinking that the boy just wanted to be with one of 'em. He was really being with both of 'em at the same time, and they ended up fighting over him or whatever. In the end, they found out that both of 'em was getting played by him.

Because these gender dynamics were common in relationships, many young women found girls' fights over boys "stupid." April explained:

> Like this girl talking to that boy and another girl supposed to be talking to the same boy, so they want to fight after school. It is just stupid. They fight over the dumbest things to me. . . . It ain't no way in the world I'll argue over a dude. . . . You want him, he want you, 'bye. Have a nice life. . . . Don't sit and argue over no dude.

Rarely, however, were fights over boys exclusively about girls fighting *for* their boyfriends. In some cases, this did not appear even the primary concern. Instead, like those conflicts described earlier, fights over boys were very much about status hierarchies among girls. Despite girls' admonitions that such conflicts were "stupid," they often paralleled the types of status contests described earlier: talking to someone's boyfriend was a sure-fire means of disrespecting her. Such fights were often a facet of ongoing conflicts between girls, and third parties were frequently implicated for either transmitting information or amping up the conflict. Gail explained: "Like this girl'll go with this boy . . . and then somebody'll like say, 'she said she'll take him away from you.' And then they'll get mad and want to fight or something. . . . It's like, 'he playin' you anyway.' They'll just say something to make somebody feel bad or something." Such contests over boys were avenues through which girls established their social status, challenged other girls' standing, and attempted to put other girls in their place. Shauntell's account is illustrative:

We was at [a fast food restaurant near school] and this boy, my friend, he had on my headphones . . . and I was just standing against the wall while my friend was ordering the food. So [this girl] say, "I know he don't call hisself goin' with that lil' biddy girl." I looked at her, I say, "gimme my headphones so I can start blocking stuff out." I took my headphones and put 'em on my ear. So he looked at her, she talkin' 'bout, "you outta be ashamed of yo'self. Why go with something like that when you coulda had this?" And I turned my headphones off . . . [and] said, "you wanna fight me?" She said, "what made you think that?" . . . I say, "now you don't wanna fight me 'cause you ain't in school?" I say, "but when we at school, you wanna talk stuff. . . . Why you just don't fight me now?"[22] She was like, "I don't wanna talk to you, lil' girl. You'll get whooped too bad." I said, "well, if you gon' whoop me, fight me." "I ain't even worried about it," [she replied]. I said, "well don't." And then we came to school another day, and she was tryin' to act all hard, "why don't you fight me now?" . . . I said, "you a punk," and I walked away. But every time we get this close together through the halls, she'll bump into me. I look at her and laugh.

Alicia described an incident in which two groups of girls fought, ostensibly because of a conflict between two girls over a boy: "one of the girls [was] pregnant by a boy on the basketball team, and the other girl go with the boy or whatever. And they don't like each other because of him, and they got different groups [of friends] or whatever, and they got to arguing, fighting and stuff." She explained how the incident started:

The girl[friend] walked right past 'em right as the pregnant girl was talking about her, and she asked her if she was "talking about me." And she said, "if I ain't talking to you, don't worry about it." "Are you talking about me?" She said, "yeah, I'm talking about you." She said that as she was coming in the lunchroom and her friends was standing over there. . . . One word led to another, the B word came on out, and they wanted to fight anyway . . . so they start . . . fighting. . . . [Each girl's group of friends] didn't like the other group, so the groups fought.

Alicia said that the girlfriend and the pregnant girl—the two with the primary conflict—"fought different people" rather than each other. Thus, some fights, though seemingly over boyfriends, were more-layered events that involved ongoing clashes between both individuals and groups of girls.

Lisa, who earlier prided herself on her maturity in staying out of "lil' girls' stupid fights," provided a lengthy account of her ongoing conflict with a girl at school who also lived down the street from Lisa's boyfriend. Their feud had been going on for months, beginning in "the summertime" when Lisa was "jumped" by the girl's friends and then "jumped on her friend" in retaliation. Lisa recounted:

> You should see the lil' biddy, ugly girl. She so little and ugly. . . . [On Friday] she [told me that my boyfriend] like her and this and this and that. He came and picked me up from school, and me and my lil' sister in the car with him. . . . She at the bus stop [so] we goes up to her, [and my boyfriend] fronted her out [confronted her] or whatever. And she like [telling him] she didn't say all that. But she did say it. So he tellin' me to beat her. . . . I'm like, "I'm not finna beat her up 'cause we right . . . across the street from the school and they gon' lock us up."

Though the conflict began the previous summer, it was further exacerbated when Lisa was placed at the same alternative school as the other girl. Lisa explained:

> My boyfriend told her I was comin' up here, and she was like, she was gon' beat me up, wootie woo. But he was like, "if I was you I wouldn't do that 'cause all her people [friends] go here." And so when she seen me, I guess she thought that I was lying [about having friends at the school. When I started,] she didn't even see me [before] she heard everybody saying, "what's up, Lisa." . . . They was like, "what's up," givin' me hugs and whatever. . . . She hurried up and ran over there to me. . . . She came to me, and she was tryin' to talk to me. But she knew I wasn't even feelin' her like that. 'Cause I ain't feelin' nobody that try to come down there and fight me . . . and now you wanna be in my face [and be friendly]. I'm not feelin' you like this. [Since then,] she like, start tellin' me, tryin' to throw me off by talkin' [to] me about my boyfriend, talkin' 'bout my boyfriend all up in her face and stuff, which I know is a lie.[23]

Lisa provided numerous additional examples of her ongoing conflict with this young woman, many of which involved the girl trying to undermine Lisa's confidence in her relationship with her boyfriend. These included talking to Lisa about his past girlfriend and how "different" he had been with her and driving up to Lisa's house horning for her boyfriend. None of these incidents were apparently propelled by the girl's interest in Lisa's boyfriend; instead, the goal was to disrespect and challenge Lisa as part of their longstanding conflict.

Discussion

Research on the situational dynamics that shape interpersonal violence among young men highlights how violence emerges in response to "masculinity challenges"—direct affronts to young men's masculinity that require response in order to maintain respect and reputation.[24] These are often grounded in the perception of "disrespect," which can result from both minor (an accidental bump, a sideways glance) and more serious actions. Comparing this stable finding with our research here, young women's violence appears to be highly gendered. Most antecedents to girls' conflicts—he say/she say (i.e., gossip), evaluations of other girls' appearance (which girls linked explicitly to jealousy), and boys and boyfriends—seem to fit easy stereotypes of "feminine" concerns.

A careful read of girls' accounts, however, suggests that their aggression is more complex. There are notable differences when comparing the situational contexts of young men's and young women's fights, but there are equally important areas of overlap. Most significant, issues of respect are central to both male and female conflicts, including the altercations reported here. This is most obvious in our discussion of what we refer to as "reputational challenges." Though occasionally sexual in nature, most often these conflicts parallel reports of male conflicts with regard to how disrespect is both enacted and read into the actions of others (e.g., staring at or bumping into another, making disparaging remarks). Moreover, these conflicts allow young women to build and project reputations as "tough" and demonstrate that they are not to be "messed with."

Likewise, other proximate triggers for girls' violence are rooted in issues of respect, perceived disrespect, and status hierarchies between girls. Yet key elements of respect and status—and thus of what constitutes disrespect—arise from highly gendered social structures. For example, Eder and Enke's research on the functions of adolescent gossip—what girls here refer to as "he say/she say,"—emphasizes its importance for strengthening group bonds, "projecting a positive self-image by discrediting others, [and] solv[ing] interpersonal problems."[25] Although these authors did uncover male gossip, they nonetheless trace the ways in which female gossip

—and its particular focus on physical appearance and "conceited" behavior (what the girls here would refer to as "thinking she's all that")—is "a particularly powerful way to reinforce traditional gender concerns."[26] Likewise, Goodwin's groundbreaking study of the social organization of talk among African American children found that he say/she say is a uniquely gendered dispute activity. She describes he say/she say as "among the most significant of the girls' political activities; through it they are able to realign their social organization."[27]

Goodwin's findings are particularly relevant for our goal of elucidating both overlap and divergence across gender. While she found that he say/she say was a gendered social interaction, she also stresses the challenge her findings pose to notions of gender difference. As we highlight with regard to our own study findings, Goodwin did not find evidence that these disputes were distinctively expressive or relational—as evidence of girls' unique ethic of caring and responsibility—but rather that they were instrumental status contests through which girls addressed grievances with and sanctioned other girls and their actions.

Moreover, as with our research, Goodwin emphasizes the importance of third parties in managing and escalating disputes. Here again is an important area of gender overlap. It is widely known in the literature on violence that bystanders increase the probability that a disagreement will become violent. Girls' narratives here routinely highlight the role of third parties in "amping up" the dispute and disputants. Situationally, the presence of third parties intensifies the potential loss of face if a girl backs away from a disrespectful challenge. In addition, third parties may perceive fights as entertainment and thus goad combatants on to further levels of aggression for their own amusement. Girls appear to guard their reputations just as boys do and thus appear similarly subject to this process.[28]

The two themes in our data with the strongest gendered elements are fights over personal style (including dress and hair) and conflicts over boys and boyfriends. Our data suggest that both are strongly tied to status contests and hierarchies between girls. However, given their emphasis on physical appearance and attachment to males, both also speak clearly to the problematic nature of gendered reward structures. Conflicts over personal style appear both to sanction girls who are deemed too physically attractive (and who dress and behave as if they know it) and to ridicule girls who fail to live up to feminine standards of beauty. An interesting parallel exists in research on young men's street-based contests over what they term "flossing"—public displays of financial capital such as flashing money, dressing in expensive clothes, and driving expensive cars. Flossers are likewise simultaneously admired and derided for their conspicuous consumption.[29] These disputes also reflect gendered—in this case, masculine—reward structures: the focus of conflict is financial rather than "attractiveness" capital. However, both are rooted in inequalities. For young men, contests over flossing are tied to concentrated disadvantage and the lack of access to mainstream outlets for status and material success; for young women, this is coupled with gender inequalities that evaluate women according to their physical appearance.

Likewise, girls' fights over boys and boyfriends appear uniquely gendered, as attachments to males continue to be a central aspect of gendered reward systems for females. It is notable that girls were particularly derisive of girls' fights over boys, despite the fact that these were a frequent source of conflict. Recent work has shown that men similarly denigrate violence spurred by disputes over women. As with the girls here, men suggest that such fights are trivial and that women are not worth the effort or risk. Particularly in the context of nonfamilial relationships, men do not report frequent fights over women and insist that other men instigated the fight when they do. Fighting over women is perceived as unmanly precisely because it prioritizes emotional attachment to a particular female.[30] Yet despite their frequent disapproval, the young women in our sample routinely described their own and other girls' fights over young men.

Simon, Eder, and Evens argue that "relationships with boys are a means by which girls attain social status and popularity" among other girls.[31] Thus, it is not surprising that our findings suggest that girls do not simply fight other girls in order to maintain the integrity of their relationships but rather that these conflicts frequently arise as explicit status challenges among girls. This facet of girls' fights over boys may be tied specifically to the social location of girls in our sample. While Simon and colleagues suggest that the white middle-class girls they studied learned strong "feeling norms" about love and romance, the urban African American girls in our sample come from communities of concentrated disadvantage that limit opportunities for marriage, encourage what youths dubbed "playa" behavior among young men, and also emerge from historical conditions that have pushed women toward greater independence.[32] Thus, our lack of robust findings linking girls' conflicts over boys to the defense of strong emotional attachments (or at least girls' unwillingness to frame their fights in these ways) is likely buttressed by the intersections of inequality they faced.

Our findings suggest that the situational contexts and antecedents of girls' violence are complex. Likewise, teasing out differences and similarities across gender, without adopting easy notions of gender difference, is a complicated task. Respect—even when constructed in a gender-specific fashion—was central to young women's narratives of violence, just as it is to young men's. Girls' accounts here emphasized the construction of identities as individuals who were tough, unwilling to allow others to disrespect them, able to stand up for themselves and to use violence when necessary. Although previously seen as quintessentially masculine, these qualities emerged here as a powerful set of situational motivations for girls. The same structural conditions that make reputation essential for men on the street may be responsible for girls' attention to reputation and respect here. Thus, we can read these young women's aggression as a product not just of gender inequalities that lead to gender-specific meanings of "respect" but also of concentrated disadvantage and lack of access to mainstream outlets for status and prestige. Alternatively, it could simply be that, due to broader expectations of femininity held by society (and researchers), earlier studies simply overlooked the possibility that routine aggression is part of the structure of adolescent female social networks.[33]

Even given that status contests are a key organizing principle of both boys' and girls' social interactions, the conflicts that emerge may ultimately hold gender-specific meanings. For men and boys, it is possible that a violent encounter is the desired end result—the fight and its outcome "makes" reputation and solidifies social position. However, some work suggests that for girls, dispute encounters are more about the girl demonstrating her ability to stand up for herself.[34] Violence may only be necessary if the disputants lack a face-saving way out of the aggressive encounter. Girls and women may gain status less from the actual violence than from the appearance of solidity in the face of disrespect. If this is true, it would help explain the biggest difference we uncovered between girls' conflicts and those reported of young men: girls conflicts were slow to escalate to violence, they did not mention using weapons, and they did not describe "serious" violence episodes that resulted in severe injury or death. This also makes sense in terms of girls' navigation of the conflicting demands of respect maintenance and the negative evaluations ascribed to female violence and aggression in general.[35]

One final note: a strong theme running through girls' accounts was the devaluation of female fights as "silly" and "stupid." The nature and tone of girls' narratives speaks to the problem of girls "buying into" misogyny and the devaluation of women. Girls' internalization of these beliefs, and their enactment of them through violence toward other girls, clearly demonstrates how structures of gender inequality pit girls against one another. Schaffner suggests,

> Girls themselves absorb misogyny from the larger culture, particularly when they witness other women being devalued. This harms them in two ways— it leads to girl-on-girl violence, and it prevents them from forming the friendships that might help them thrive in adolescence or escape other violence in their lives.[36]

Thus, the harms of violence accompany the harms that arise from the very nature of gender inequalities and their interpersonal enactment. They disrupt the creation and maintenance of the very sort of social support structures that would most benefit these young women in traversing the hierarchical and exclusionary social terrains in which they live.

NOTES

1. Coretta Phillips, "Who's Who in the Pecking Order? Aggression and 'Normal Violence' in the Lives of Girls and Boys," *British Journal of Criminology* 43 (2003): 713. See also Sally Simpson, "Caste, Class, and Violent Crime: Explaining Differences in Female Offending," *Criminology* 29 (1991): 115–135.

2. For an example of research emphasizing gender similarities, see Ira B. Sommers and Deborah R. Baskin, "The Situational Context of Violent Female Offending," *Journal of Research in Crime and Delinquency* 30 (1993): 136–162. For an example of work that emphasizes gender difference, see Ann Campbell, *Men, Women and Aggression* (New York: Basic Books, 1993). Studies that have examined differences and similarities include Jean Bottcher, "Social Practices of Gender: How Gender Relates to Delinquency in the Everyday Lives of High-Risk Youths," *Criminology* 39 (2001): 893–932; Karen Heimer and Stacy De Coster, "The Gendering of Violent Delinquency," *Criminology* 37 (1999): 277–317; Jody Miller, "Up It Up: Gender and the Accomplishment of Street Robbery," *Criminology* 36 (1998): 37–66; and Jody Miller, *One of the Guys: Girls, Gangs and Gender* (New York: Oxford University Press, 2001).

3. For early works on male violence, see Albert Cohen, *Delinquent Boys* (Glen-

coe, IL: Free Press, 1955); Walter Miller, "Lower Class Culture as a Generating Milieu of Gang Delinquency," *Journal of Social Issues* 14 (1958): 5–19; and Marvin E. Wolfgang and Franco Ferracuti, *The Subculture of Violence* (London: Tavistock, 1967). For a discussion of the benefits of examining the situational contexts of female violence, see also Sommers and Baskin, "Situational Context of Violent Female Offending." For a general discussion of gender and situational context, see Candace West and Don H. Zimmerman, "Doing Gender," *Gender and Society* 1 (1987): 125–151.

4. For contemporary works that highlight the role of masculinities, see Elijah Anderson, *Code of the Street* (New York: Norton, 1999); James W. Messerschmidt, *Nine Lives: Adolescent Masculinities, the Body, and Violence* (Boulder, CO: Westview, 2000); and Christopher W. Mullins, "Masculinities, Streetlife, and Violence: A Qualitative Secondary Analysis," Ph.D. dissertation, Department of Criminology and Criminal Justice, University of Missouri–St. Louis. Mullins's work blends analysis of street-life subculture with masculinity and crime, and it highlights the continuity between contemporary and traditional research on male violence.

5. For a discussion of the strengths and limits of the "doing gender" approach, as well as an analysis of the problem of gender difference in scholarly work on female violence, see Jody Miller, "The Strengths and Limits of 'Doing Gender' for Understanding Street Crime," *Theoretical Criminology* 6 (2002): 433–460. Analysis of gender stratification in street networks can be found in Lisa Maher, *Sexed Work: Gender, Race, and Resistance in a Brooklyn Drug Market* (Oxford: Clarendon Press, 1997); and Darrell J. Steffensmeier, "Organizational Properties and Sex-Segregation in the Underworld: Building a Sociological Theory of Sex Differences in Crime," *Social Forces* 61 (1983): 1010–1032.

6. Kathleen Daly, "Women's Pathways to Felony Court: Feminist Theories of Lawbreaking and Problems of Representation," *Review of Law and Women's Studies* 2 (1992): 14. Feminist analysis of the blurred boundaries of victimization and offending can be found in Meda Chesney-Lind, *The Female Offender: Girls, Women, and Crime* (Thousand Oaks, CA: Sage, 1997); and Mary E. Gilfus, "From Victims to Survivors to Offenders: Women's Routes of Entry and Immersion in to Street Crime," *Women and Criminal Justice* 4 (1992): 63–89.

7. See Campbell, *Men, Women, and Aggression*; Karen A. Joe and Meda Chesney-Lind, "'Just Every Mother's Angel': An Analysis of Gender and Ethnic Variations in Youth Gang Membership," *Gender and Society* 9 (1995): 408–430; and Maher, *Sexed Work*.

8. John Hagan and Holly Foster, "S/He's a Rebel: Toward a Sequential Stress Theory of Delinquency and Gendered Pathways to Disadvantage in Emerging Adulthood," *Social Forces* 82 (2003): 75–76.

9. Darrell Steffensmeier and Emilie Allan, "Gender and Crime: Toward a Gendered Theory of Female Offending," *Annual Review of Sociology* 22 (1996): 467, 478.

10. Natalie G. Adams, "Fighting to Be Somebody: Resisting Erasure and the Discursive Practices of Female Adolescent Fighting," *Educational Studies* 30 (1999): 130.

11. See Mullins, "Masculinities, Streetlife, and Violence."

12. See Scott H. Decker and Barrik Van Winkle, *Life in the Gang* (Cambridge: Cambridge University Press, 1996).

13. See Jody Miller and Norman A. White, "Gender and Adolescent Relationship Violence: A Contextual Examination," *Criminology* 41 (2003): 1501–1541; and Jacquelyn W. White and Robin M. Kowalski, "Deconstructing the Myth of the Nonaggressive Woman: A Feminist Analysis," *Psychology of Women Quarterly* 18 (1994): 487–508.

14. See Michael E. Barber, Linda A. Foley, and Russell Jones, "Evaluations of Aggressive Women: The Effects of Gender, Socioeconomic Status, and Level of Aggression," *Violence and Victims* 14 (1999): 353–363; Celia L. Ridgeway, "Interaction and the Conservation of Gender Inequality: Considering Employment," *American Sociological Review* 62 (1997): 218–235; and Karen Walker, "Men, Women, and Friendship: What They Say, What They Do," *Gender and Society* 8 (1994): 246–265.

15. All the girls we interviewed had at least minimal involvement in minor delinquency. About half engaged in serious delinquency. All the girls had exposure to violence as witnesses (97 percent), victims (91 percent), or perpetrators (83 percent).

16. See Deborah Baskin, Ira B. Sommers, and Jeffrey Fagan, "The Political Economy of Violent Female Street Crime," *Fordham Urban Law Journal* 20 (1993): 401–417; Gary D. Hill and Elizabeth M. Crawford, "Women, Race, and Crime," *Criminology* 28 (1990): 601–623; Coramae Richey Mann, "Sister against Sister: Female Intrasexual Homicide," in *Female Criminality,* ed. C. C. Culliver, pp. 195–223 (New York: Garland, 1993); Simpson, "Caste, Class, and Violent Crime."

17. Our initial focus concerned problems in school, so most girls' accounts are about fights in school. Some girls also described incidents that occurred outside school, and many conflicts that began in school escalated on the outside and vice versa. The social location of schools is an important arena for examining girls' conflicts. Schools are embedded within broader communities, and these often "bleed over" into school interactions, particularly in communities of concentrated disadvantage. See Denise C. Gottfredson, *Schools and Delinquency* (Cambridge: Cambridge University Press, 2001); see also John H. Laub and Janet L. Lauritsen, "The Interdependence of School Violence with Neighborhood and Family Conditions," in *Violence in American Schools,* ed. Delbert S. Elliott, Beatrix A. Hamburg, and Kirk R. Williams, pp. 127–155 (Cambridge: Cambridge University Press, 1998).

18. Terri L. Orbuch, "People's Accounts Count: The Sociology of Accounts," *Annual Review of Sociology* 23 (1997): 455. See also Jody Miller and Barry Glassner, "The 'Inside' and the 'Outside': Finding Realities in Interviews," in *Qualitative Research,* ed. David Silverman, pp. 99–112 (London: Sage, 1997).

19. Anselm L. Strauss, *Qualitative Analysis for Social Scientists* (Cambridge: Cambridge University Press, 1987).

20. Girls were asked not to use real names during the interviews. Sometimes they described girls by their physical characteristics, as Anishika has done here. In order to make the narrative as clear as possible, we use Anishika's characterization of the "dark girl" throughout this passage to distinguish her from the girl who antagonized her.

21. The playa model for male behavior emphasized using girls for sex, having multiple sexual conquests without emotional attachment, and stringing along multiple girls simultaneously. It offered status and prestige within male peer groups. See Miller and White, "Gender and Adolescent Relationship Violence."

22. Shauntell's accusation that the girl wasn't willing to fight her out of school was a challenge to the girl's "toughness." Many girls believed that girls talked tough in school precisely because they knew adults would intervene before the conflict escalated to serious violence.

23. Lisa's confidence that the story was a lie was not as strong as she suggested here. She had a swollen black eye the day she was interviewed that was a result of a fight she started with her boyfriend after she accused him of cheating with the girl. See Miller and White, "Gender and Adolescent Relationship Violence," 1527.

24. Anderson, *Code of the Street*; Messerschmidt, *Nine Lives*; and Mullins, "Masculinities, Streetlife, and Violence."

25. Donna Eder and Janet Lynne Enke, "The Structure of Gossip: Opportunities and Constraint on Collective Expression among Adolescents," *American Sociological Review* 56 (1991): 494.

26. Ibid., 506.

27. Marjorie Harness Goodwin, *He-Said-She-Said: Talk as Social Organization among Black Children* (Bloomington: Indiana University Press, 1990), 142.

28. Nonetheless, it is likely that gender shapes and constrains the extent of girls' aggression toward other girls, as we will address. See Miller, *One of the Guys*, for a discussion of how girls use gender to limit their involvement in serious violence.

29. See Mullins, "Masculinities, Streetlife, and Violence."

30. Ibid.

31. Robin W. Simon, Donna Eder, and Cathy Evens, "The Development of Feeling Norms Underlying Romantic Love among Adolescent Females," *Social Psychology Quarterly* 55 (1992): 30.

32. See William Julius Wilson, *When Work Disappears* (New York: Knopf, 1996); Patricia Hill Collins, *Black Feminist Thought* (Boston: Unwin Hyman, 1990). In fact, in the survey portion of the interview, half the girls we interviewed reported that "being in love" was not too or not at all important, and more than a third reported the same for getting married. Only 15 percent reported that being in love and getting married were very important.

33. See Phillips, "Who's Who in the Pecking Order?"; Goodwin, *He-Said-She-Said.*

34. See Goodwin, *He-Said-She-Said.*

35. See Barber, Foley, and Jones, "Evaluations of Aggressive Women."

36. Laurie Schaffner, "Violence and Female Delinquency: Gender Transgressions and Gender Invisibility," *Berkeley Women's Law Journal* 14 (1999): 59.

Chapter 3

No Place for Girls to Go

How Juvenile Court Officials Respond to Substance Abuse among Girls and Boys

Hilary Smith, Nancy Rodriguez, and Marjorie S. Zatz

Studies of juvenile delinquency have identified the critical role prior victimization and delinquent peers play in juvenile offending, particularly in cases of substance abuse. Specifically, prior research suggests a strong relationship between victimization and substance abuse among delinquent girls, while for boys delinquent peers are especially salient.[1] We draw on this research on the gendered contexts of substance abuse to explore how juvenile court staff perceive the linkages between victimization, delinquent peers, and drug use. We are sensitive to prior studies that have shown that court officials respond to delinquency and make attributions based on perceptions of race, class, and gender.[2] We take this research a step further, identifying what juvenile court officials see as the antecedents associated with drug use and how these perceptions of gendered pathways may influence their decision-making processes.

Review of the Literature

Gender, Victimization, and Drug Use

Research depicting girls and women in the criminal and juvenile justice systems has illustrated the complex histories of female offenders' lives.[3] One of the most striking findings is the centrality of a history of abuse and neglect. Research conducted with female offenders since the 1980s has consistently identified their experiences of emotional, physical, and sexual abuse as a "first step" into juvenile and criminal justice involvement.[4] In 1999, the Bureau of Justice Statistics reported that 60 percent of women under correctional authority were physically or sexually assaulted at some time in their lives. Of these women, 69 percent reported that the victimization happened before they were eighteen.[5] The U.S. Department of Health and Human Services estimates that girls are three times more likely to have been sexually abused than boys.[6] Other research confirms this pattern, showing girls and women to be far more frequent victims of (sexual) abuse than boys and men.[7]

Substantial research links childhood victimization to the use of marijuana and other illegal substances.[8] For instance, Ireland, Smith, and Thornberry found that the risk of using drugs is one-third higher for youths with prior abuse histories than for nonvictimized youths.[9] Several retrospective studies of adult women offenders have also found that drug use could be traced back to prior victimization, with many women reporting drug use as a means of coping with past abuse.[10]

The Influence of Peers on Juvenile Substance Abuse

The role of peers in delinquency, including the use of drugs and alcohol, has been well established.[11] This research often suggests that associating with delinquent peers increases one's risk for delinquency and substance abuse. Some research has found that peers' substance abuse may be a more important predictor of drug use than of other forms of delinquency.[12]

Aspects of peer influences appear to be important throughout adolescence and across racial/ethnic and gender lines. As Heimer has noted, "the omission of peer influence from much of the work on gender and delinquency may have produced a somewhat biased picture."[13] Indeed, both quantitative and qualitative investigations of the relationship between peer influence and gender suggest that relationships with delinquent peers are consequential for predicting adolescent delinquency, including substance abuse, for both boys and girls.[14] For instance, Andrews et al. found that peers had similar effects on boys' and girls' initiation of substance abuse, with the use of drugs by male peers positively influencing subsequent use by both boys and girls.[15] However, the nature of the relationship with those male peers may differ for boys and girls. Giordano, for example, asks about the potential importance of boyfriends to the social context in which female delinquency occurs.[16] These types of relationships are often defined as safe (i.e., not abusive), yet the relationship may be far more risky than is typically assumed. As we will show, romantic involvement with older males is a significant contributor to girls' involvement with drugs and alcohol.

The Gendered Nature of Substance Abuse and the Juvenile Court's Response

Although literature on delinquency and peers suggests boys and girls are both strongly influenced by peers, important gender differences exist.[17] Inciardi et al. found that while boys and girls are both likely to *begin* using drugs out of curiosity and peer pressure, their motivations for *continued* drug use differ. For instance, girls are less likely to continue drug use because of peer pressure or pleasure. Rather, they are more likely than boys to continue drug use as a means of coping with psychological stresses.[18]

Although there appear to be different pathways of drug use for boys and girls, juvenile court responses to such abuse are strikingly similar for boys and girls. For instance, juvenile drug courts tend to focus explicitly on youths' use of drugs and alcohol and do not address coexisting problems such as victimization, school difficulties, or family trouble.[19] This, coupled with the perceptions of youth held by juvenile court actors, may hinder access to appropriate substance abuse treatment.

Attributions of Race and Gender

Finally, a number of studies have examined how race, ethnicity, and gender influence court actors' decision-making processes.[20] These studies have found direct and indirect influences of race and ethnicity in court outcomes.[21] Bridges and Steen applied attribution theory to explore the role stereotypes have on creating and maintaining racial disparities in the juvenile court and found a direct relationship between race and attributions of personal responsibility and wrongdoing as compared with external causes of delinquency.[22] Although research has found juvenile court actors often view girls as manipulative, deceitful, and even hard to work with,[23] little is known about how attributions of gender may facilitate or hinder particular court actions (e.g., the treatment of drug use).

The Present Study

Notwithstanding the contributions that have been made to the literature on victimization, offending, and substance abuse, and despite what the addiction literature has taught us about the similarities and differences among males' and females' involvement with drugs and alcohol, little, if any, research has explored how court officials perceive and respond to substance abuse by boys and girls. We argue that focus must be placed on the *gendered contexts* that bring boys and girls to use (and continue to use) drugs and alcohol. That is, antecedents of drug use, the social context in which drugs are used, and social and legal responses to drug use may differ for boys and girls in some fundamental ways—ways that are in part influenced by stereotypic images and expectations held by probation officers and other court officials. Consequently, in this study, we analyze case file narratives and interview data to illustrate how probation officers, psychologists, and other juvenile court officials describe drug use by boys and girls and to identify the gendered nature of court responses to substance abuse. Specifically, we explore the following research questions:

1. How do juvenile court officials report the association between delinquent peers and drug use among boys and girls?
2. How do juvenile court officials report the association between prior victimization (e.g., sexual abuse, physical abuse, and neglect) and drug use among boys and girls? and
3. What treatment recommendations are most prevalent for boys and girls with histories of drug use, and how do treatment recommendations vary by gender?

Methodology

We draw on two distinct data sources to assess how juvenile court officials perceive drug use and its antecedents among boys and girls. The first data set consists of official case file narratives from court records for a random sample of 174 girls and a matched sample of boys referred to juvenile probation in Maricopa County, Arizona, during 1999. Matching was based on age and zipcode, with zipcode serving as a proxy for neighborhood factors such as income and local educational system. These files include juvenile court petitions (including background information), disposition reports and decisions, progress reports, and psychological evaluations normally maintained by the juvenile court, both from the 1999 case and from any earlier referrals to juvenile probation.[24] Given our interest in drug use, we excluded cases in which the court file did not explicitly mention substance abuse problems, leaving us with seventy-five girls' files and ninety-nine boys' files. The girls and boys in this sample were racially and ethnically diverse. Of the seventy-five girls, 62 percent were White, 20 percent Latina, 12 percent African American, 5 percent American Indian, and 1 percent Asian American or Pacific Islander. Of the ninety-nine boys in this sample, 52 percent were White, 33 percent Latino, 10 percent African American, and 5 percent American Indian. The juveniles were between the ages of twelve and seventeen and were referred to juvenile court for person, property, drug, and status offenses, as well as for probation violations.

In selecting case file narratives, we retrieved statements about boys' and girls' substance abuse, histories of victimization, and peer relationships. The majority of the narrative statements were written by probation officers, but we also include psychological reports in our data. Although these are not written by probation officers, they are used by probation and other court officers to assess drug use, its antecedents, and appropriate court responses.

We supplement the case file narratives with semistructured interviews with fourteen juvenile probation officers. A diverse list of probation officers (with respect to gender, race/ethnicity, years of experience, and probation jurisdiction) was provided by the director of juvenile court services. The probation officers averaged just over eleven years of experience in juvenile probation, with a range from one to twenty-four years. They represented most of the units within the juvenile court (e.g., standard probation, intensive probation, detention, treatment services). These interviews shed light on probation officers' perceptions of the youths on their caseloads, the paths that led them to court, and appropriate treatment programs for them. Of the ten female probation officers we interviewed, five were White, two African American, one Asian American, one Latina, and one of Middle Eastern descent. Two African American men, one White man, and one Latino were also interviewed.[25] The interviews lasted between forty-five and ninety minutes. All interviews were taped and transcribed by the interviewer.

We focus in this chapter on how a history of victimization, delinquent peer relations, and substance abuse problems intersect as they are understood by probation officers and other court actors, and how the effects of

victimization and delinquent peers are seen as relevant, or not, to boys'
and girls' substance abuse problems. We conduct thematic content analyses of the case file and interview data, using a systematic coding scheme
we created to empirically analyze these data.[26]

Findings

Victimization, Gender, and Drug Use

Consistent with prior studies that highlight the relationship between
prior abuse and delinquency, case file data reveal that prior victimization
plays an important role in boys' and girls' drug use.[27] A total of 19 percent
of girls' files had a documented reference to physical and/or psychological
abuse, compared to 12 percent of boys' files. Three cases presented below
illustrate how physical abuse, including domestic violence, and psychological abuse play out in juveniles' lives:

- (Youth) has a history of both physical and psychological abuse in his
  natural family.
  (Youth) was drinking and using drugs while he was on runaway status from home.
  There have been issues with (youth's) choice of friends throughout
  the year.
  (Youth's) natural mother was killed in October of 1998 by the natural father. (Male, Hispanic, #91)
- (Youth) is 14 years, 8 months of age and before this court with her
  third referral. Her pending offense is for marijuana at school. When
  this officer first met with (youth), she was very cold and defiant.
  Behind (youth's) gang attire and hard-core attitude is a sensitive
  and very hurt young lady due to the emotional abuse she has en-
  dured throughout her childhood due to domestic violence. Much of
  (youth's) defiant behavior is out of lack of respect for her mother for
  enduring physical and verbal abuse inflicted by the stepfather over
  the past ten years. (Youth) feels rejected by her mother's choice to
  remain with this man. (Female, Native American, #63)
- The juvenile has reported that her stepfather, "Beats up mom, and
  has punched me in the stomach and slapped me in the face." (Youth)
  further stated that (youth's stepfather) does mean things and that

he is an alcoholic. "I prefer to be away from them" (youth) further added. (Female, White, #10)

The relationship between sexual abuse and girls' delinquency has been substantially documented in prior studies.[28] As reported in such studies, findings here show that 24 percent of girls' files had a documented account of sexual abuse, whereas less than 3 percent of boys' files held such accounts.[29] The following excerpts demonstrate the extent of their abuse:

- By her account, the sexual molestation discontinued because by her account, the mother was present in the home on a higher degree of frequency and the family at one point relocated to Mexico. By her account, the family was all sleeping in the same room at this time and this made it essentially impossible for the father to molest her. By her account, this did also occur to her older sister. She states that she, at one instance, witnessed this occurring to her older sister. She indicates that this would occur in the morning when the mother was not present in the home. She then states that her father would tell her that she should not run away and she indicates that her father did, in one instance, question her, "Do you like what I'm doing to you?" She also states that the father instructed her not to inform her mother. (Female, Hispanic, #29)
- (Youth) was victimized by a 40-year-old man who molested her; 19-year-old brother who emotionally and physically abused youth. (Female, White, #163)

Court officials may find it difficult to address the sense of powerlessness experienced by girls in such situations. Although removal from the home may be one option, treatment for substance abuse may be perceived as a more immediate need than responding to former abuse.

Drugs may be viewed as a means of coping with emotions such as anxiety, depression, avoidance, anger, and worthlessness caused by prior abuse.[30] For example, a probation officer writes,

- Father admits he was physically abusive with (youth). According to her family, she is associating with friends who use drugs. History of sexual abuse at the hands of her father from the ages of five to eight, which is said to have included sexual intercourse. I suspect substance abuse is as well a major issue, but also functions as again a means to attack self and revictimize self. (Female, White, #87)

The connection between drug use and victimization was also highlighted throughout our interviews. In fact, twelve of the fourteen probation officers discussed the impact substances have on youths' lives, specifically relating victimization histories to current substance abuse problems.

- When I worked in the unit back in detention, you would hardly ever get a girl that hadn't been raped, sexually abused, or physically abused. The whole time I was there, I can maybe think of two girls who came from so-called good families. Hundreds of hundreds of girls who came in; so I think it's a direct correlation.
- I would say 90 percent of them at least have been sexually abused or molested and at least that many, 90 percent, if not all of them, have substance abuse or alcohol problems.
- I'm dealing with a case like that right now. There is a girl who ran— there is a court order saying no contact with her father, and when she ran, she got in touch with him. And he molested her. So, after the molestation happened, she got caught on her warrant for being a runaway. When she got locked up again she kept saying she wants contact with her father. We didn't know at the time she was being molested. . . . But she's been saying this whole time she wants contact with her father, even though he molested her. . . . But yeah, a lot of it, there is drug-seeking to get away from it. They will tell me it makes them forget about their troubles, it makes them forget about a lot of stuff, bad things in the past. Yeah, they do run away to seek drugs, to escape their problems.

One probation officer clearly relates the connection between victimization, drug use, and other delinquent behavior:

Probation Officer: The biggest one I'm thinking of is a girl I ended up sending to Black Canyon (the state's facility for girls). She was out of control. Crack addict, prostitute. Her father was a convicted child molester. He didn't molest her, supposedly. He got out of prison, and mom let him back into the home with her. And mom wonders why she's out in the streets using crack. It's like—you have a child molester living in your home; he's probably abused your kid growing up.

She had been raped two or three times. . . . The mom is like, "Oh, I give her so much support, I'm always there for her, blah blah blah." Just no clue why this girl is out using crack and chose to live on the streets. When I say the streets, I'm talking like a sleeping bag out on the side of the road. . . . She'd be like out in crack houses; you'd see her walking down the streets prostituting, and I know when I worked in the unit back in detention you would hardly ever get a girl that hadn't been raped, sexually abused, or physically abused.

Interviewer: And is that something you approach with them, something you try to make a connection for them?

Probation Officer: A lot of the girls do believe that. They don't try to hide it, and they tell you, "You know, I was raped five times and I can't deal with it. That's why I use drugs."

However, a few court officials expressed doubts regarding the girls' abuse histories, indicating that they felt some stories may be untrue or exaggerated. For instance, a probation officer recalled:

- I don't know if I believe her or not—she said the car stopped, they picked her up, they made her take all these drugs, and they raped her. She's a drug addict and she does drugs. I don't know, it might have happened, it might not have. I don't really know.

In this case, the officer discounts a history of abuse and places the focus on the girl's use of drugs. Consequently, in such instances, the sexual assault appears to be nonexistent or unimportant in the eyes of the court officer.

In sum, data from both case files and interviews reveal how substance abuse by boys and, in particular, girls is also often characterized by experiences of physical and emotional abuse and by extensive violence in the home. Moreover, court actors' perceptions of the relationship between sexual abuse and girls' drug use highlights the complexities they face when they attempt to work with the girls.

The Role of Peer Influences in Drug Use

Prior studies have documented the important role peer relations play in juvenile drug use.[31] Consistent with such findings, case file narratives indicate that boys and girls are depicted as being heavily influenced by their peers. We found no statistically significant differences in the documented presence of peer influences in boys' and girls' cases. Specifically, 41 percent of boys' cases and 45 percent of girls' cases included some notation regarding peers. Juveniles' poor decision-making processes regarding peers and peer pressure were most commonly noted by juvenile court officials. The following excerpts illustrate this point:

- The juvenile also makes poor choices in his friends. The juvenile had in his house at the time of the shooting, (youth's friend), who ended up mortally wounded. The deceased had a long history with the juvenile court. (Male, White, #120)
- (Youth) is a 17 year, and 3 month old juvenile, who continues to abuse marijuana. In this officer's opinion, the juvenile gives in to peer pressure and accepts the responsibility of smoking marijuana socially with his friends and has taken probation and the terms and conditions of his probation very lightly. (Male, White, #174)
- (Youth's) peer associations are of concern. Her codefendant has a referral history with the juvenile court and has been a chronic runaway. Mom says kid has been using drugs in the past and hanging with gang members. (Female, White, #90)

Such perceptions present two options for the court: treatment programs to instill skills to make better choices or removal from the home to distance youth from peers, both of which are costly options.

Although there were no quantitative differences in the extent of negative peer influences in boys' and girls' case files, a closer analysis showed an important *qualitative* difference in peer relations. According to the social files, boys were described as interacting with delinquent peers in their age group; girls, in contrast, were depicted as heavily influenced by adult males. The influence of older peers was only noted in one boy's file. The following case narrative describes the influence of older men in girls' lives:

- (Mother) states that she found most of (youth's) friends to also be rebellious and feels that they are bad influences on (youth). She denies gang affiliation. (Youth) has recently taken up with a 27-year-old man who seems to be an extremely poor influence on her and is interfering with her relationship at home in addition to her following through with the terms and conditions of her release as related to the court. (Youth) is currently on runaway status. She is smoking marijuana and using what is believed to be amphetamines as tested through TASC. There are reports from school indicating that this man drops her off and picks her up, and the car that he drives reeks with marijuana. He is with her overnight where they have parties in the apartment which involve alcohol. (Youth) is a very young girl and certainly, this is a situation in which she is being endangered. (Female, White, #20)

In some cases, court officials report that these older individuals use or sell drugs. For example,

- (Youth) chooses to hang around with other people who use drugs. They are usually much older than (youth) and her mother does not approve of them. (Female, White, #132)
- Mother reports youth is "extremely promiscuous" and that even though (youth) is only 14 years old, she generally associates with male adults. Both youth and her mother state that in the past (youth's) choice of peers has been inappropriate. (Youth) reports that most of her friends in the past have been drug users. (Female, White, #87)
- This officer has learned the name of the adult male this juvenile has been leaving to spend time with. His name is (——). He is 22 years of age and on adult probation for drug offenses. (Female, Hispanic, #121)
- Of concern was the fact that (youth) tended to hang out with her older sister and a lot of her friends were older. She has been involved with known drug users that are known to the police department as selling drugs. (Female, White, #32)

In one girl's case, the options for friendships seem to be a gang or young adults:

- According to the juvenile, she has been affiliated with a gang known as (——). The juvenile indicated that she joined the gang so that she would have friends. The mother reports that when the juvenile did have friends, they were much older than she was. The mother stated that they were already young adults. Mother also stated that when the juvenile began to have these friends is when she began lying to her. (Female, Native American, #136)

Interviews with probation officers revealed similar findings. Several probation officers described the influence of older men in girls' lives and hypothesized as to why girls seek out and maintain these relationships. For example,

- The majority of girls back in detention when I worked there chose guys who were twenty to twenty-five years old. What are they looking for? The father figure and acceptance, feeling like they belong.
- Many of them have older boyfriends in their twenties, thirties, and some even in their forties. And that's that need to have somebody that loves them or that fathers them. For Father's Day recently, we did a lot of programing on qualities of fathers. Ah . . . what they had or did not have in their own fathers . . . what they're looking for in a male relationship . . . and we mentioned to them the father figure type of older male relationship. And for some of the girls that was the first time they heard of that. And they were really looking at that like, "Gosh, I wonder if that's why I'm dating older men."

Based on interview data, court officials appear to at least see a relationship between older males and dysfunction in girls' lives. However, their options for treatment are limited, making it unlikely such relationships will be addressed.

Juvenile Court Responses to Drug Use

At the time when youth in our sample were adjudicated, it was relatively early in the development of drug courts and other specialized drug programs. Perhaps for this reason, we found that standard probation and out-of-home placements were the most common court dispositions. Out-of-home placement in state facilities were especially likely dispositions for boys, with 32 percent of boys' cases resulting in recommendations for out-of-home placement as compared with 15 percent of girls' cases.[32] The following three cases illustrate the limited options available to court officials in responding to juveniles' drug use.

- Admitted to getting high and smoking marijuana with his friends for about the first month of his warrant status, he said he gave it up because his girlfriend did not like it. Has 3 felony petitions in his short life and has been unsuccessful on both standard probation and

JIPS [Juvenile Intensive Probation Supervision] during the last 37 months. Recommend that he be committed to the Arizona Department of Juvenile Corrections in a secure facility placement for a period of six months. (Male, Hispanic, #77)

- It is my opinion that the Court has invested many rehabilitative services into this young man, but he continues to refuse to be accountable for his behavior even though the juvenile's VOP [violation of probation] is for basically incorrigible behavior. He has a long history of exhibiting such behavior that will eventually result in him being involved in a serious crime. He continues to be a significant risk to himself and others. He has received the most restrictive services available, but continues to act out. Unfortunately, to this officer's knowledge, residential placements are not available as a treatment alternative due to the moratorium placed on such referral. Even though the juvenile only scored a 1 on the ADOJC [Arizona Department of Juvenile Corrections] risk assessment, and he does not fall within the Level IV category for secure care, I would ask the Court to go outside the guidelines and place the juvenile at Adobe Mountain. (Male, Hispanic, #159)
- No place to put a girl with substance issues (it would take her well beyond her 18th birthday-no place except Black Canyon unless CPS [Child Protective Services] in involved). CPS is the only agency that contracts with Parc Place. (Female, Hispanic, #16)

In one case, the juvenile court official did not perceive residential treatment for a boy as appropriate given his "manipulative" behavior. Instead, community supervision was recommended even though its ill fit was recognized. The anticipated and inevitable failure of probation by this juvenile would make state confinement easier to justify and process in the future.

- He is not the type that I usually recommend for residential treatment because he can easily manipulate others and could have a negative influence on those in treatment with serious mood or other psychiatric disorders. This juvenile is the type that I feel needs a boot camp type of program of strict discipline, work requirements, and no tolerance for excuses or manipulative behavior. I do not know if such programs are available. I doubt this juvenile would make any substantial change in his attitude if he were in a residential treatment program. I am more inclined to recommend the juvenile for intensive probation services. I suspect that he will violate, and then needed documentation can be obtained to support commitment to Department of Juvenile Corrections. (Male, White, #57)

The limited resources for treating youths with histories of abuse clearly weighed on probation officers, and how best to treat girls and young women who have been sexually victimized emerged repeatedly in our interviews with probation officers. For example, one officer recounted how she responds to youth who openly discuss prior victimization and drug use:

- Sometimes the girls will open up and say things like, "My stepfather molested me when I was eight" or . . . "something happened to me when I was twelve, and that's when I started doing drugs." We try to bring it back and say, "Do you think that might have been a catalyst? And if you deal with that, do you think possibly you could deal with your substance abuse issues also?"

Similarly, another officer highlighted the need for expanded resources, especially as they apply to medication:

- I would like to see more mental health assistance. Like I said, the girls who come in who are depressed, who come in who should be on medication but aren't, who come in on meds and feel that they shouldn't be, because this is a holding place, we don't have a lot of services set up.

Although this sentiment may be prevalent among court officials, case file data contained a significant number of youths already medicated in response to their drug use. One of our most interesting findings is that use of medication as a treatment for drug abuse ran along gender and racial/ethnic lines. That is, our data suggested that medication was largely limited to White females. Fewer than 3 percent of boys' files recommended medication for treatment, whereas 16 percent of girls' cases ($N = 12$) recommended medication alongside other treatments. Of the twelve girls for whom medication was prescribed, eleven were White and one was African American. The following cases illustrate this court-mandated process:

- The primary negative influence has been her sister. (Youth) explains that her sister got her started on drugs. (Youth) is a fairly serious drug user. She lacks goals and a direction. She has not gone to school in nearly a year. Her family cannot control her. On and on it goes. Because of her psychological complexity and clearly unstable emotions, this youngster would benefit from a psychiatric consultation to determine the efficacy of a mood-stabilizing medication. (Female, White, #90)
- This juvenile has a history of depression and prescribed medications. She also is a chronic and habitual user of drugs which negates any positive effects from her medication. She is believed to associate with peers who are also involved in the illegal use and sale of drugs. (Female, White, #103)
- (Youth's) boyfriend is over 20 years of age. In the past, (youth) was associating with a young girl on my caseload, who is 16 and currently pregnant. Her emotional condition should be monitored. She is prone to develop symptoms of depression, much like her mother. If she does, she would be a candidate for medication intervention. (Female, White, #146)
- The juvenile noted her father had taken her to see a psychiatrist for prescription of medication and monitoring. She stated the doctor had prescribed Paxil, however, according to the juvenile, "I didn't want any more drugs in my system." Therefore, she chooses to discontinue taking them. Uses marijuana to cope with various stressors. While the juvenile's dependence on marijuana is seen as the major problem at this time, she does have clinical symptoms of depression that do seem to have been present since childhood, before she began to abuse marijuana. Medication for clinical mood disorder will probably be needed, but it would be best to wait for the juvenile to begin a drug rehabilitation program. . . . Other symptoms of depression, such as hopelessness, low self-esteem, suicidal ideation and irritability, are not likely due to marijuana and probably will need medication and counseling to effectively treat. For now, I recommend starting the drug rehabilitation program and then working with that program to get the psychiatric evaluation done later. (Female, White, #163)
- She expressed strong affiliation with her new gang friends, revealing intention to nurture this relationship further. (Youth) is at a point of high risk in her life, a crossroads in which she can choose further

involvement in antisocial conduct, which will inevitably lead her toward promiscuity, substance abuse, and other delinquency, or placing herself under the caring authority of her parents, her father in particular. This is a highly distressed, angry, and depressed individual who is in urgent need of psychiatric and psychological interventions. In light of these findings, I would recommend the following: First and foremost, this individual must be immediately evaluated for medication interventions that may prove beneficial to ameliorate depression. A psychiatric evaluation is needed. (Female, White, #162)

These case file narratives serve to highlight several revealing aspects of the data, primarily the higher prevalence of "court-mandated" drug use by girls than boys. Boys were more likely to be detained or confined in response to their drug use, while girls, and specifically White girls, were more likely to receive medication as part of their treatment. Thus, for both boys and girls, but especially for girls, the most telling finding regarding juvenile court disposition recommendations is the extent to which limited resources confound the opportunity to provide appropriate treatment for drug use.

Discussion

Juvenile court decision-makers often respond to girls and boys as though the stories of their drug abuse are the same. We examined court social files of girls and boys with documented substance abuse problems and found that their stories are quite different. Although some similarities exist (e.g., the influence of delinquent peers on adolescent substance abuse), key distinctions emerged. Most important among these are histories of sexual and physical abuse among girls, the influence of older peers (especially men) in girls' lives, and recommendations for treating girls' drug use through medicalization.

Our findings support previous studies documenting the gendered relationship between physical and sexual abuse and delinquent activities, including substance abuse.[33] Women and girls who use drugs often have histories of extensive physical and sexual victimization, and drug use is often seen as a way to escape emotions associated with abuse.[34] In fact, the American Correctional Association found that almost half of the girls in training schools took drugs (34 percent) or drank alcohol (11 percent) as a form of self-medication.[35] Yet even though 24 percent of girls' files noted abuse histories, not all victimization stories were believed by juvenile court officials. As noted in Gaarder, Rodriguez, and Zatz's study of this same court,[36] some probation officers assume that girls are fabricating reports of abuse, perhaps not wanting to believe that so many girls share similar patterns and pathways to the court.[37] We argue that overlooking girls' abuse histories will result in a failure to address the impact victimization has on girls' lives and the role it plays in their offending histories, particularly regarding substance abuse.[38]

The data indicate a number of ways in which substance abuse and its antecedents vary by gender. Although boys and girls are both heavily influenced by their peers, girls' case files produced an important qualitative difference in the type of peer relations—the significance of older, male individuals in these young women's lives. Juvenile court officials note that these older males contribute to poor decision-making by the girls, including the decision to engage in drug use and sometimes to commit other delinquent and criminal acts. Often, the men in their lives are using and/or selling drugs, making access especially easy for the girls. According to many probation officers interviewed for this study, relationships with older males are sought out and even maintained for their ability to meet girls' needs for attention and/or acceptance. Despite the notations in the files regarding the negative influence of older men in girls' lives, our reading of the case files and interviews with probation officers suggests that there is not much attention paid to ways in which the men's influence might be mediated or reduced. This is particularly troubling because these older men appear to have an especially deleterious effect on the girls, far exceeding that of peers in general. We also found that the influence of older peers cuts across racial/ethnic lines; therefore, older peers seem to have a harmful effect regardless of race and ethnicity. There was also little variation by race or ethnicity in the influence of prior victimization on drug use; rather, the strong relationship between prior victimization and current substance abuse was consistent across racial/ethnic groups, at least as depicted in probation files.

Our findings suggest that girls have fewer options for treatment and services in juvenile court, further confounding treatment recommendations. As Chesney-Lind notes, 5 to 10 percent of federal, local, and private funds for juvenile justice are designated for girls.[39] Given the limited resources available, confinement appears to be one of the few courses of action available for responding to girls' drug use. One probation officer told us,

- As we have no funding for a Residential Treatment Facility at this time and because we do not have one that would be appropriate to address her substance abuse issues and be secured, we feel that there is little left to recommend at this time other than that this juvenile be committed to the Arizona Department of Juvenile Corrections, preferably in a drug rehabilitation program.

Yet a second, more perplexing, option for treating female substance abusers is medicalization. Due to the limited resources available for girls, and their complex social histories, juvenile court officials were most likely to recommend court-mandated drug use as a treatment response for drug-using White girls. For whatever reason, depression, anxiety, and similar disorders were not identified as critical problems for girls of color, although victimization histories (which might reasonably be seen as creating or exacerbating these mental health problems) were similar for White girls and girls of color.

Although we recognize that youths may have mental health problems that respond to medication and for which medication is an appropriate treatment, we argue that medicating as a means of control, without a mechanism to deal with other, co-occurring, issues (e.g., histories of victimization, influence of older peers) is problematic. A by-product of this medicalization is that girls maintain a continued dependence on a substance/drug, whether that substance is illegal or court mandated. As depicted in case file narratives, when a girl's doctor attempted to prescribe Paxil she countered that she "didn't want any more drugs in her system."

Despite the mounting research documenting that girls have rather complex risk histories that differ in significant ways from the experiences of boys, court responses to juveniles have largely ignored the specific needs of girls. Traditional treatment approaches have been shaped largely by what boys need, with the assumption that these same programs will work equally well for girls. Instead, we suggest that programing for girls must take into consideration their unique situations and special problems, including recognition of the gendered pathways to substance abuse and to the courts. A recent example is the use of juvenile drug courts. Drug courts have been designed to provide intensive judicial supervision and services to address substance use and related behaviors.[40] As a result, they are pragmatic and often neglect aspects that differentiate substance use among boys and girls. Indeed, the presence of girls in co-ed drug courts may help the boys, who may benefit from the positive attention they receive from girls when they are successful in their treatment. But if we want girls to address the root causes of their substance abuse, they need to feel comfortable talking about their histories of abuse and their involvement with older men. This, we suggest, is not likely to happen in a mixed-sex drug court, requiring us to reconsider available options to ensure that gender-specific treatments exist.

Conclusions

The findings reported in this chapter demonstrate the importance of considering the gendered contexts of substance abuse. Analysis of juvenile court social files and interviews with probation officers indicate that the pathways bringing girls and boys with substance abuse problems to court are quite distinct. We discover that probation officers and other court officials recognize that girls and boys have different histories, with prior sexual victimization a much larger issue for girls than for boys. Delinquent peers, we find, are referenced in both boys' and girls' files, but even here the relevance of peers is gendered, with the negative influences for girls coming from their involvement with older men, many of whom are using and/or selling drugs. Nevertheless, it is apparent that probation officers have few available treatment options in working with girls, forcing them perhaps into an overreliance on medication alone without treating the base problems that the substance abuse may be covering up.

Given that our data come from probation case files and interview data, several limitations arise. Although it is important to understand the antecedents and contexts in which drugs are used by boys and girls, reliance on probation reports may present a biased view of what actually occurs in girls' lives. That is, we do not know what the youths themselves perceive to be the causes or consequences of their drug problems. Our understanding of these relationships is limited to what probation officers perceived as sufficiently important and relevant to document in the files. We readily acknowledge that there may be significant differences between court officials' perceptions, as written in case file reports, and the reality of girls' lives. These reports are influenced by the gender, racial/ethnic, and cultural attributes probation officers assign to youth and are often based on what they think is real. Ultimately, these perceptions can have a troubling effect on youth, especially girls, in the juvenile justice system. Also, our data are limited to one jurisdiction. Further research in other locales will be needed to confirm the cross-jurisdictional validity of these findings, as will analysis of actions taken by this court in response to these and related findings.

Although our focus here has been on the gendered contexts of substance abuse, we also urge future researchers to examine more carefully the ways in which culture, language, and structural factors such as income inequality and racial discrimination constrain and shape the understandings of youths' problems held by court officials and the resources and treatment options available to them.

NOTES

1. See, for example, Dawn R. Jeglum Bartusch and Ross L. Matsueda, "Gender, Reflected Appraisals, and Labeling: A Cross-Group Test of an Interactionist Theory of Delinquency," *Social Forces* 75 (1996): 145–176; Robert Svensson, "Gender Differences in Adolescent Drug Use: The Impact of Parental Monitoring and Peer Deviance," *Youth and Society* 34 (2003): 300–329.

2. George S. Bridges and Sara Steen, "Racial Disparities in Official Assessments of Juvenile Offenders: Attributional Stereotypes as Mediating Mechanisms," *American Sociological Review* 63 (1998): 554–570; Emily Gaarder, Nancy Rodriguez, and Marjorie S. Zatz, "Criers, Liars, and Manipulators: Probation Officers' Views of Girls," *Justice Quarterly* 21 (2004): 547–578; Jody Miller, "An Examination of Disposition Decision Making for Delinquent Girls," in *Race, Gender, and Class in Criminology: The Intersection*, ed. M. D. Schwartz and D. Milovanovic, pp. 219–246 (New York: Garland, 1996).

3. Meda Chesney-Lind and Lisa Pasko, *The Female Offender: Girls, Women, and Crime*, 2nd ed. (Thousand Oaks, CA: Sage, 2004); Meda Chesney-Lind and Randall G. Shelden, *Girls, Delinquency, and Juvenile Justice* (Los Angeles: Wadsworth, 2004); Kathleen Daly and Lisa Maher, *Criminology at the Crossroads: Feminist Readings in Crime and Justice* (New York: Oxford University Press, 1998).

4. Leslie Acoca, "Outside/Inside: The Violation of American Girls at Home, on the Street, and in the Juvenile Justice System," *Crime and Delinquency* 44 (1998): 561–589; Joanne Belknap, *The Invisible Woman: Gender, Crime, and Justice*, 2nd ed. (Belmont, CA: Wadsworth, 2001); Chesney-Lind and Pasko, *Female Offender*; Chesney-Lind and Shelden, *Girls, Delinquency, and Juvenile Justice*; Daly and Maher, *Criminology at the Crossroads*; Barbara Owen, *In the Mix: Struggle and Sur-*

vival in a Women's Prison (Albany: State University of New York Press, 1998); Cathy Spatz Widom, "Childhood Victimization and the Derailment of Girls and Women in the Criminal Justice System," in *Research on Women and Girls in the Criminal Justice System,* ed. B. Richie, K. Tsenin, and C. S. Widom, pp. 27–36 (Washington, DC: National Institute of Justice, 2000).

5. Bureau of Justice Statistics, *Women Offenders* (Washington, DC: U.S. Department of Justice, 1999); Chesney-Lind and Pasko, *Female Offender.*

6. U.S. Department of Health and Human Services, *Third National Incidence Study of Child Abuse and Neglect, 1986–1993* (Washington, DC: U.S. Department of Health and Human Services, Administration for Children and Families, 1996).

7. Chesney-Lind and Pasko, *Female Offender*; Chesney-Lind and Shelden, *Girls, Delinquency, and Juvenile Justice*; David Finkelhor and Larry Baron, "Risk Factors for Child Sexual Abuse," *Journal of Interpersonal Violence* 1 (1986): 43–71.

8. Regina Arnold, "Women of Color: Processes of Victimization and Criminalization of Black Women," *Social Justice* 17 (1990): 153–166; Richard Dembo, Linda Williams, Werner Wothke, James Schmeidler, and C. Hendricks Brown, "Examining a Structural Model of the Role of Family Factors, Physical Abuse, and Sexual Victimization Experiences in a Sample of High Risk Youths' Alcohol and Other Drug Use and Delinquency/Crime over Time," *Violence and Victims* 7 (1992): 245–266; Timothy O. Ireland and Cathy Spatz Widom, *Childhood Victimization and Risk for Alcohol and Drug Arrests* (Washington, DC: National Institute of Justice, 1995).

9. Timothy O. Ireland, Carolyn A. Smith, and Terence P. Thornberry, "Developmental Issues in the Impact of Child Maltreatment on Later Delinquency and Drug Use," *Criminology* 40 (2002): 359–399.

10. Arnold, "Women of Color"; Chesney-Lind and Pasko, *Female Offender*; Barbara Owen, "Perspectives on Women in Prison," in *Women, Crime, and Criminal Justice: Original Feminist Readings,* ed. C. Renzetti and L. Goodstein, pp. 243–254 (Los Angeles: Roxbury, 2001).

11. Robert Agnew, "The Interactive Effects of Peer Variables on Delinquency," *Criminology* 29 (1991): 47–72; Bartusch and Matsueda, "Gender, Reflected Appraisals, and Labeling"; Peggy Giordano, Stephen A. Cernkovich, and M. D. Pugh, "Friendships and Delinquency," *American Journal of Sociology* 91 (2003): 1170–1202; Dana L. Haynie, "Delinquent Peers Revisited: Does Network Structure Matter?" *American Journal of Sociology* 106 (2001): 1013–1057; Ross L. Matsueda and Karen Heimer, "Race, Family Structure, and Delinquency: A Test of Differential Association and Social Control," *American Sociological Review* 52 (1987): 826–846; Daniel P. Mears, Matthew Ploeger, and Mark Warr, "Explaining the Gender Gap in Delinquency: Peer Influence and Moral Evaluations of Behavior," *Journal of Research in Crime and Delinquency* 35 (1998): 251–266; Ira B. Sommers and Deborah R. Baskin, "The Situational Context of Violent Female Offending," *Crime and*

Delinquency 30 (1993): 136–162; Svensson, "Gender Differences in Adolescent Drug Use"; Mark Warr and Mark Stafford, "The Influence of Delinquent Peers: What They Think or What They Do?" *Criminology* 29 (1991): 851–866.

12. Kristan G. Erickson, Robert Crosnoe, and Sanford M. Dornbusch, "Social Process Model of Adolescent Deviance: Combining Social Control and Differential Association Perspectives," *Journal of Youth and Adolescence* 29 (2000): 395–425.

13. Karen Heimer, "Gender, Interaction, and Delinquency: Testing a Theory of Differential Social Control," *Social Psychology Quarterly* 59 (1996): 39–61.

14. Peggy C. Giordano, "Relationships in Adolescence," *Annual Review of Sociology* 29 (2003): 251–281; Jody Miller, *One of the Guys: Girls, Gangs, and Gender* (New York: Oxford University Press, 2001); Terence P. Thornberry and Marvin D. Krohn, "Peers, Drug Use, and Delinquency," in *Handbook of Antisocial Behavior,* ed. D. M. Stoff, J. Breiling, and J. D. Maser, pp. 218–233 (New York: Wiley and Sons, 1997).

15. Judy A. Andrews, Elizabeth Tildesley, Hyman Hops, and Fuzhong Li, "The Influence of Peers on Young Adult Substance Use," *Health Psychology* 21 (2002): 349–357.

16. Giordano, "Relationships in Adolescence," 265, 274.

17. See James A. Inciardi, Dorothy Lockwood, and Anne E. Pottieger, *Women and Crack-Cocaine* (New York: Macmillan, 1993).

18. Ibid.; Chesney-Lind and Pasko, *Female Offender.*

19. Caroline S. Cooper, *Juvenile Drug Court Programs* (Washington, DC: Office of Juvenile Justice and Delinquency Prevention, 2001).

20. Chesney-Lind and Shelden, *Girls, Delinquency, and Juvenile Justice*; John M. MacDonald and Meda Chesney-Lind, "Gender Bias and Juvenile Justice Revisited: A Multiyear Analysis," *Crime and Delinquency* 47 (2001): 173–195; Donna M. Bishop and Charles E. Frazier, "The Influence of Race in Juvenile Justice Processing," *Journal of Research in Crime and Delinquency* 25 (1988): 242–263; Philip E. Secret and James B. Johnson, "The Effect of Race on Juvenile Justice Decision-Making in Nebraska: Detention, Adjudication, and Disposition, 1988–1993," *Justice Quarterly* 14 (1997): 445–478; Bohsiu Wu, Stephen A. Cernkovich, and Christopher S. Duncan, "Assessing the Effects of Race and Class on Juvenile Justice Processing in Ohio," *Journal of Criminal Justice* 25 (1997): 265–277; Marjorie S. Zatz, "The Convergence of Race, Ethnicity, and Class on Court Decision-Making: Looking Toward the 21st Century," in *Policies, Processes, and Decisions of the Criminal Justice System: Criminal Justice 2000,* ed. J. Horney, pp. 503–552 (Washington, DC: U.S. Department of Justice, 2000).

21. Donna M. Bishop and Charles E. Frazier, "Race Effects in Juvenile Justice Decision-Making: Findings of a Statewide Analysis," *Journal of Criminal Law and Criminology* 86 (1996): 392–413; M. A. Bortner and Wornie Reed, "The Preeminence of Process: An Examination of Refocused Justice Research," *Social Science Quarterly* 66 (1985): 413–425; Secret and Johnson, "Effect of Race on Juvenile Jus-

tice Decision-Making in Nebraska"; Wu, Cernkovich, and Duncan, "Assessing the Effects of Race and Class on Juvenile Justice Processing in Ohio"; Bishop and Frazier, "Influence of Race in Juvenile Justice Processing."

22. Bridges and Steen, "Racial Disparities in Official Assessments of Juvenile Offenders."

23. Kimberly Kempf-Leonard and Lisa Sample, "Disparity Based on Sex: Is Gender Specific Treatment Unwarranted?" *Justice Quarterly* 7 (2000): 89–128; Margaret Baines and Christine Adler, "Are Girls More Difficult to Work With? Youth Workers' Perspectives in Juvenile Justice Related Areas," *Crime and Delinquency* 42 (1996): 467–485; Joanne Belknap, Kristi Holsinger, and Melissa Dunn, "Understanding Incarcerated Girls: The Results of a Focus Group Study," *Prison Journal* 77 (1977): 381–404.

24. In Maricopa County, the county attorney files a petition (i.e., referral) against a juvenile who has allegedly committed a delinquent and/or incorrigible act. The adjudication process begins with a hearing to determine whether a juvenile is delinquent and whether a juvenile is a status offender. A disposition occurs when a juvenile offender is assigned treatment and/or placement.

25. Since the fourteen probation officers we interviewed could be readily identified, to protect the confidentiality of their interviews, identifiers based on sex, race/ethnicity, and caseload assignment are not provided.

26. John Lofland and Lyn H. Lofland, *Analyzing Social Settings: A Guide to Qualitative Observation and Analysis* (Belmont, CA: Wadsworth, 1995).

27. Chesney-Lind and Pasko, *Female Offender*; Chesney-Lind and Shelden, *Girls, Delinquency, and Juvenile Justice*; John Hagan and Bill McCarthy, *Mean Streets: Youth Crime and Homelessness* (Cambridge: Cambridge University Press, 1998); Les B. Whitbeck and Dan R. Hoyt, *Nowhere to Grow: Homeless and Runaway Adolescents and Their Families* (New York: Aldine de Gruyter, 1999).

28. Acoca, "Outside/Inside"; Arnold, "Women of Color."

29. It is important to note, however, that this is likely an underestimate of the extent of abuse in the juveniles' lives, and especially in the girls' lives, as these figures only represent instances where a court official was informed of such abuse and documented this abuse in the case file (see similarly Gaarder, Rodriguez, and Zatz, "Criers, Liars, and Manipulators").

30. Arnold, "Women of Color"; Eva Y. Deykin, Janice C. Levy, and Victoria Wells, "Adolescent Depression, Alcohol, and Drug Abuse," *American Journal of Public Health* 77 (1987): 178–182; Owen, "Perspectives on Women in Prison."

31. Judith S. Brook, David W. Brook, Mario de la Rosa, Luis F. Duque, Edgar Rodriguez, Ivan D. Montoya, and Martin Whiteman, "Pathways to Marijuana Use among Adolescents: Cultural/Ecological, Family, Peer, and Personality Influences," *Journal of the American Academy of Child and Adolescent Psychiatry* 37 (1998): 759–766; Thomas J. Dishion and Rolf Loeber, "Adolescent Marijuana and Alcohol Use: The Role of Parents and Peers Revisited," *American Journal of Drug and Alcohol*

Abuse 11 (1985): 11–25; Gerald R. Patterson and Thomas J. Dishion, "Contributions of Families and Peers to Delinquency," *Criminology* 23 (1985): 63–79; Laurence Steinberg, Anne C. Fletcher, and Nancy E. Darling, "Parental Monitoring and Peer Influences on Adolescent Substance Use," *Pediatrics* 93 (1994): 1060–1064.

32. Data on court recommendations are based on the most recent disposition found in the juvenile's records.

33. See, for example, Baines and Adler, "Are Girls More Difficult to Work With?"

34. Arnold, "Women of Color"; Chesney-Lind and Pasko, *Female Offender*; Daly and Maher, *Criminology at the Crossroads*; Owen, "Perspectives on Women in Prison."

35. American Correctional Association, *The Female Offender: What Does the Future Hold?* (Washington, DC: St. Mary's Press, 1990).

36. Gaarder, Rodriguez, and Zatz, "Criers, Liars, and Manipulators."

37. See similarly Kathleen Daly, *Gender, Crime, and Punishment* (New Haven: Yale University Press, 1994).

38. It is worth noting that the jurisdiction of our study concurs with this argument and is taking steps to address the perceptions of some probation officers in the study.

39. Meda Chesney-Lind, *The Female Offender: Girls, Women, and Crime* (Thousand Oaks, CA: Sage, 1997); Chesney-Lind and Shelden, *Girls, Delinquency, and Juvenile Justice*.

40. Caroline S. Cooper, *Juvenile Drug Court Programs* (Washington, DC: Office of Juvenile Justice and Delinquency Prevention, 2001).

Chapter 4

Killing One's Children
Maternal Infanticide and the Dark Figure of Homicide

Rosemary Gartner and Bill McCarthy

Women who kill their children have rarely been the focus of criminological attention. For the most part, criminologists have left the study of these killers to psychologists, psychiatrists, social historians, and family violence researchers. The absence of a conceptual framework within criminology for understanding this type of female killer has indirectly encouraged popular discourses and legal responses that construct them as either mad or bad.[1] Recently, feminist criminologists and legal scholars have challenged this binary characterization, offering a different view of women who kill their children. Highlighting a host of structural and cultural forces—gender inequality, women's relative powerlessness, unrealistic expectations and myths about motherhood, and the stresses and isolation of childcare—they portray these mothers as desperate and overwhelmed, as victims of circumstance and larger structural forces who could hardly have acted otherwise. The problem with each of these discourses, as Morrissey has observed with respect to female killers generally, is that they "restrict their portrayal to that of mythic evil or else to the impotence of victimhood or madness. Nowhere, it seems, is the presentation of a woman who is both violent and agentic, responsible and human, possible in these discourses."[2]

In this chapter, we discuss these stock narratives about mothers who kill newborns and infants. Drawing on historical and contemporary data, we do not so much challenge their accuracy as question their scope and implications. Our basic argument complements that of Morrissey, who used a series of case studies of notorious homicides by women to identify the limitations of dominant constructions of female killers. In contrast to her approach, however, we suggest that by considering a very different type of female homicide—that is, undetected cases or the "dark figure" of homicides by women—an alternative, more agentic characterization of mothers who kill may emerge. Dominant narratives, after all, are constructed from cases that come to the attention of legal authorities and that are classified as homicides. Yet there are well-documented problems with drawing conclusions about the larger population of offenders based on what is known about those who are apprehended. We provide data that speak to unsolved and undetected infant homicides. This evidence suggests an image of women who kill their children that is similar to one offered by some feminist social historians. Extending Morrissey's argument, we propose that some female child killers' actions "may be read as intentional and legitimate responses to personal and structural forces" without naturalizing these acts or denying women's responsibility for them.[3]

We focus on killings of newborns (neonaticide) and infants less than a year old (infanticide) because these are the children at greatest risk of being victims of maternal lethal violence.[4] Our analysis draws on two types of data. The first data set includes all neonaticides and infanticides known to the authorities in Seattle, Washington, and Buffalo, New York, from 1900 through 1989.[5] Homicides in which parents were identified as the culprits, as well as cases for which an offender was not identified, are included in this data set. We collected information on these cases from police files, coroners' records, and newspaper articles.[6] The second, smaller data set is based on death records for newborns and infants in King County, Washington (where Seattle is located) between March 1895 and September 1904.[7] Our purpose in collecting these data was to allow us to consider one source of the "dark figure" of newborn and infant homicide, that is, the potential misclassification of homicides as due to other causes.

Previous Research on Neonaticide and Infanticide

Research on the maternal killing of newborns and infants spans a number of disciplines. Early medical and psychiatric studies of clinical samples of killers[8] introduced typologies that have become "whipping boys" for social scientists, feminist and otherwise. Critics claim that by focusing on women's mental health problems—from severe postpartum depression to altruistic delusion—such typologies are tautological and decontextualized. Moreover, these accounts deny female agency and subjectivity, and they encourage characterizing women who use violence as either "mad" or "bad."[9]

By the 1980s, social and legal historians, evolutionary psychologists, and other social scientists took up questions about the killing of infants and the social and legal responses to these crimes.[10] Many historical studies are informed by feminist perspectives on gender inequality and emphasize the ways in which the constraints of social norms and laws provoked some women to commit infanticide. Though not uniformly inattentive to gender inequality, evolutionary psychology has typically framed neonaticide and infanticide as rational (and at times socially approved) acts of a genetically evolved human psyche oriented toward reproductive fitness. The interest of other social scientists in infant and child homicide increased in the 1980s in part because of growing attention to family violence.[11] Much of this literature treats the killing of one's children as an extreme instance of child abuse rather than as a phenomenon in its own right.

By contrast, criminologists have largely ignored the killing of infants by parents. This neglect implies that these acts are unsuitable for criminological theorizing. Two recent developments, however, have stimulated criminological interest in these crimes. First, macrolevel analyses of homicide have increasingly disaggregated homicide rates by victims' age and sex. These studies have found that homicides of children and adults are influenced by a combination of common, as well as unique, factors and that child killings follow patterns consistent with the predictions of criminological theories of violence.[12] Second, feminist criminologists have argued —with some success—for more research and theorizing on crimes against and by women, on family violence, and on the gendered nature of crime and its control.

In the past decade, several feminist-informed analyses have appeared that discuss the influence of gender, gender relations, and gender inequalities on lethal violence by parents toward their children. Many of these works focus on women and provide new classification schemes or typologies that attempt to address the shortcomings of earlier efforts. They typically critique and reject the "mad versus bad" dichotomy, drop categories for types of child killing that are rare among female offenders (e.g., as a form of spousal revenge), and add ones that are more specific to female experiences (e.g., denied pregnancy).[13] Although these approaches better reflect the complexities of neonaticide and infanticide, many of them also struggle with their own proclivity to construct women who kill their newborn or infant children in a unidimensional fashion. In particular, a number of these analyses construct mothers who kill their children as essentially victims.

Women Who Kill Their Children as Victims

For analysts who take this approach, women who kill their children are desperate and emotionally overwhelmed, victims of both circumstance and larger structural forces. This characterization is accomplished in a series of steps. Forming the backdrop for violence by women is the axiom that, as a group, they are fundamentally disadvantaged relative to men. In other words, patriarchy, which is reflected in a network of economic, social, and political inequalities, constrains the lives of all women. These disadvantages are reinforced for mothers by the oppressive nature of child rearing in societies that fail to provide adequate resources, by socially constructed myths about the rewards of motherhood, and by idealized expectations about the characteristics of good mothers.[14]

The stage set, the spotlight turns to the characteristics common to women who are charged with killing their newborns and infants. Here, the killers' social isolation, poverty, childhood and adult abuse, and tendency to be young and unmarried are highlighted to signal their disadvantaged status.[15] Rendered powerless by these forces, these women are either prevented from or incapable of exercising agency. In some analyses, the women's situation allows them no choice. Jensen, for example, describes infanticide as the "last desperate act of a woman who could see no other way out."[16] For Smithey, "the mother [is] powerless to select alternative action or escape the frustrating encounter"; the infant "dies as a result of the mother's inability to assuage her own pain."[17] In other analyses, a woman's mental condition negates her ability to make choices. According to Oberman, women who kill newborns "tend to be exceedingly passive, and they respond to pregnancy with a combination of denial, wishful fantasy and terror."[18] As evidence of these women's mental confusion and passivity, analysts point to their ineffectual efforts to disguise their crimes, such as wrapping their infants' bodies in newspapers and hiding them under their beds or placing them in shoe boxes in their closets.

The construction of women who kill their newborns or infants as lacking in violent intent is also accomplished by portraying them as loving and altruistic mothers concerned about their children's comfort even as they end their lives. Neonaticides, "as horrible as they are," do not have the "sadistic quality" of other kinds of homicides, according to Schwartz and Isser.[19] Smithey notes that "infants in this study *died* at the hands of their mothers due to an escalation of violence during which *the mother sought to comfort* the inconsolable victim" (our emphasis).[20] Others point to the care with which many women prepare for the killings and their tendency to smother, gas, or drown their infants (or to neglect to care for them) rather than to do direct violence to them. These methods lead some to conclude that many "murdering mothers . . . killed their children in relatively loving ways."[21]

The portrayal of these killers as victims who could hardly have acted otherwise, who were highly distressed and may have been unbalanced, and who killed their children gently and without malice introduces several problems. This construction reinterprets premeditation, an aggravating factor in law as well as in the feminist research on violence against women, as a mitigating factor for mothers who kill their children. Also, the language used to describe these female-perpetrated killings tends to characterize the women as either passive participants or benevolent actors and the deaths as uncaused—as in the frequent references to the victim "dying," rather than the mother "killing."[22] Hovering in the background is the specter of the mad mother and, along with it, the image of women's violence as pathological, a portrayal that feminists have long critiqued. More broadly, as Morrissey has pointed out, "recasting the criminal acts of women as tragic accidents is to deny the agency and responsibility of women in general and to delay recognition of a female ethical subject within contemporary Western legal discourse."[23]

Women Who Kill Their Children as Rational Actors

There is another sort of portrayal of women who kill their infants, however, which gives greater attention to the rational and self-interested motives behind these acts. Many social and legal histories of infanticide provide examples of this approach. This work often emphasizes the commonplace character of infanticide, especially in contexts where contraception and abortion were largely unavailable, and the tolerance of and, at times, popular sympathy for the killers.[24] Most historical treatments highlight the economic and social disadvantages of infanticidal mothers, thereby leaving some room for the possibility that these circumstances might produce, in Shapiro's words, an "acute mental derangement."[25] However, an overriding concern in much of this work is to construct these women not as simply or largely helpless and overwhelmed but as active subjects responding rationally to a situation structured by gender inequality and contradictory gender norms. As Laster observes with regard to the nineteenth century, simultaneous messages about purity and chastity, alongside those about the beauty of motherhood, created a context in which women's commission of infanticide can be seen as the response of normal, reasonable, and well-socialized (if distressed) women to a dire set of circumstances.[26]

Most recently, some of this historical work broadens the scope of the rational female killer's ability to act decisively and vigorously. Geyer-Kordesch, for example, argues for a characterization of women who kill their children that acknowledges their exercise of power, including the power to "reject the gendered trajectory."[27] The woman in this portrayal seeks to "annihilate her child . . . to bury this thing, this birth: to throw it in the river, to put it down a well . . . to invalidate her motherhood," in clear contrast to the women described earlier who kill their children passively or in ways that demonstrate their motherly love. By challenging "the anthropocentric sympathy" for "the innocent seduced girl," Geyer-Kordesch wants to give the woman who kills her infant "an authentic voice, not a sentimental one, since sentimentalizing has a powerful purpose" and precludes her telling "of her aspirations . . . her desire for life."[28]

This construction of the woman who kills her infant as a responsible, powerful agent faces its own pitfalls. The most obvious is the danger of resurrecting the stereotype of women who kill their infants as "bad," as malignant mothers, as evil personified. This danger should not be underestimated, particularly in the United States, where even women with extensive histories of mental illness are demonized when they kill their children.[29] Another problem with constructing mothers who kill their infants as primarily rational and self-interested is that, as Laster notes, doing so "converts the nature of their offending behavior from artlessness to callousness, distorts their 'true' subjective motives and oversimplifies the complex web of causes and motives for such crimes."[30]

A third problem with this characterization of women who kill their infants is the thinness of the evidence supporting it. Many historical and contemporary studies that challenge discourses that disable and pathologize these women nonetheless at times portray them in ways consistent with such discourses. Those who have killed newborns are described as denying their pregnancies, being unprepared for birth, and undergoing "an unusual psychological process" even though they typically lack histories of psychiatric illness.[31] Those who ended the lives of older infants faced "environmental circumstances . . . considered relevant to postnatal depression"[32] and were "emotionally overwhelmed,"[33] "incapable of rational thought," and deserving of sympathy "because of their mental confusion."[34]

Why do efforts to understand women who kill their children in more complex and diverse ways than allowed by the "mad," "bad," and "victim" categorizations end up with similarly narrow and standardized characterizations? What restricts empirical analyses of mothers who kill their children to a narrow range of accounts? One reason may simply be that existing characterizations are an accurate set of representations that capture the range of women who kill their infants as well as the range of circumstances in which they act. But there is a second possibility. These portrayals and the evidence on which they are based include only those women who have come to the attention of authorities. Women who killed their children but were able to avoid detection are missing. We contend that information on these unidentified killers might well challenge the portrayal of mothers who kill their infants as disproportionately distraught, unbalanced, powerless women unable to cope with their situations. To explore this possibility, we draw on two types of data: neonaticides and infanticides known to authorities in Seattle and Buffalo and the deaths of newborns and infants in Seattle.

Neonaticides and Infanticides in Seattle and Buffalo

Of the 4,857 homicides known to authorities in these two cities for the years 1900 to 1989, 53 were neonaticides and 54 were infanticides, of which about half occurred in each city. Because the number of killings is relatively small for a ninety-year period and because our focus is not on trends in either the incidence or the detection of neonaticides and infanticides, we have chosen to aggregate these data over time.[35] Table 4.1 indicates who the killers were in these cases. Of the fifteen neonaticides in which offenders were identified, thirteen (87 percent) were committed by mothers acting alone (eleven) or with the cooperation of fathers (two).[36] Of the forty-one infanticides in which offenders were identified, twenty-one (51 percent) were committed by mothers, all of whom acted alone. In other words, as other studies have consistently shown, mothers

TABLE 4.1
Neonaticides and Infanticides in Seattle and Buffalo, 1900–1989

	Neonaticides	Infanticides
Total number of cases	53	54
Number killed by mothers of the victims acting alone	11	21
Number killed by fathers of the victims acting alone	1	14
Number killed by mother and father acting together	2	0
Number killed by other known offenders	1	6
Number killed by unknown offenders	38	13

predominated among those known to have killed newborns and infants in Seattle and Buffalo over this ninety-year period.

Neonaticides and Infanticides Known to Have Been Committed by Mothers

Who were the women who came to the attention of officials for killing their newborns, and what were the circumstances of the killings? As other studies have found, these women were young. They ranged in age from sixteen to twenty-eight, with an average age of twenty; six were teenagers. All those for whom we have information on marital status were unmarried. In ten of the thirteen cases, mothers suffocated, strangled, or let their babies die from exposure or neglect; none of the mothers used excessive violence to kill. In all but one case, the women appear to have given birth alone; following the birth, most of them disposed of their newborns' bodies in ways that made it relatively easy to identify them as the killers. Six of the thirteen mothers left their victims in their bedrooms or other parts of their residence, two placed the bodies in the immediate vicinity, and one left her dead child outside her workplace. Most of the women made little attempt to hide their having just given birth, often because they were physically incapacitated at the time they were discovered. The following are three examples of these cases.

> A twenty-year-old, unmarried white woman appeared at a rooming house complaining of a severe headache and asked for a room in which to lie down. Several hours later residents of the house heard her moaning and sent for a doctor. The doctor determined the woman had just given birth. The body of a newborn male was found inside a suitcase in the room, strangled with a handkerchief. (Buffalo 1913)

The killer, a twenty-one-year-old white, unmarried beautician, lived with her sister and mother, neither of whom knew she was pregnant. She gave birth at home, wrapped the infant in clothing and newspaper, and dropped it down the coal chute of a nearby house. The infant subsequently died of exposure. The killer was identified because she went to the hospital for treatment of complications due to the unattended birth. She confessed, but said she thought the baby was born dead. (Seattle 1928)

The white, unmarried offender (age unknown) lived at home with her mother. She gave birth in her bedroom, wrapped the baby in pajamas, and placed him in her closet. Her mother found the body shortly thereafter. The offender said that she did not know she was pregnant and that the baby was stillborn. The postmortem indicated the baby was born alive and died from suffocation. (Seattle 1960)

These and the other cases of neonaticide in our sample fit comfortably into the characterization of mothers who kill newborns as hapless and desperate victims of circumstance and larger structural forces. In other words, these women can plausibly be described as passive, mentally confused, unprepared for births that they may have denied to others and to themselves, and/or so emotionally and physically overwhelmed as to be incapable of acting with much forethought or intent.

What do we know about the women who were accused of killing older infants and the circumstances of these killings? Consistent with the findings from other studies, these women differ in some important respects from those who killed newborns. The twenty-one women who killed their infants were older: their ages ranged from sixteen to thirty-eight, with an average age of twenty-four. Of the twenty women for whom we have information on marital status, sixteen were married. In half these cases, the infants were killed in ways similar to the neonaticides; but in ten cases the infants were beaten to death, a method generally considered in the literature to be more violent than exposure, suffocation, or strangulation. The circumstances of these killings follow the two distinct patterns that have been identified in other research on mothers who kill infants. The first pattern comprises thirteen cases in which the women had histories of mental health problems or recent experiences of severe depression; in three of these cases the women killed themselves along with their infants, and in two other cases the women attempted suicide. The second pattern is represented by eight cases in which women struck out violently because they were angered over their infants' crying and/or because they experienced extreme stress from the demands of being the sole care givers to their children. The following are three examples that represent these two patterns:

> A twenty-one-year-old mother of two took a dose of rat poison after administering some to her three-month-old son. Both died. She left a note to her husband expressing her fear that she was insane and asking him to take good care of their other child. She was reported to have been suffering from "nervous trouble" for about a year. (Seattle 1910)

> A twenty-year-old woman with a history of psychiatric illness called her sister-in-law to tell her she could no longer look after her three-week-old son. The child was found underwater in the bathtub with a fractured skull. The woman had been declared an unfit mother three years earlier, and her only child (at the time) had been taken from her. Her husband knew she was mentally unstable but thought her condition was improving. (Seattle 1973)

> A one-month-old baby girl died from internal injuries after her unmarried, eighteen-year-old mother hit and "yanked" her. The mother claimed the victim cried constantly and had been sick quite a bit. (Buffalo 1984)

The predominance of cases that fit the first pattern—that is, infanticides by psychologically distressed mothers—suggests an apparent commonality among women known to have killed their newborns and infants: evidence of psychiatric illness, mental disturbance, or—as Alder and Polk refer to it—an "unusual psychological process."[37] As noted earlier, in most neonaticides, the mothers claimed they did not know they were pregnant, were found incapacitated by the birth process with their dead newborns close by them, or made only feeble attempts to disguise the killings and dispose of the bodies. Similarly, in the majority of infanticides detected by authorities, there was evidence that the killer suffered from a psychiatric illness or mental disturbance. Moreover, like women who killed newborns, infanticidal mothers rarely attempted to disguise the deaths of their infants or dispose of their children's bodies without being detected, reinforcing the conclusion that these killers were not overly concerned about their fates or futures. These women, then, fit the categorization of mothers who kill their newborns and infants as victims—whether of their own mental disturbance, the burdens of motherhood in a context in which they had little support, or both. And they seem a distant relation to the more rational, self-interested, unsentimental woman put forward by Geyer-Kordesch.

Might our failure to find evidence for self-possessed, future-oriented women reflect, as we have suggested, a systematic bias in cases of neonaticide and infanticide that come to the attention of authorities and for which they identify a killer? To explore this possibility we examine two sets of cases: neonaticides and infanticides in which no offender was identified and deaths of newborns and infants in suspicious or ambiguous circumstances.

Neonaticides and Infanticides by Unknown Offenders

One of the striking findings reported in Table 4.1 is the large proportion of infanticides and, especially, neonaticides for which offenders were never identified. In more than 70 percent of the neonaticides (thirty-eight out of fifty-three) and 24 percent of the infanticides (thirteen out of fifty-four), the killer was unknown. The following are a sampling of these cases:

The body of a newborn male was found wrapped in newspapers in Love Alley. His head showed signs of bruising; cause of death listed as neglect and exposure. (Buffalo 1900)

The body of a newborn male, with surgical gauze tightly wound around his neck, was found wrapped in newspapers under a seat at the Princess Theater. A woman had been seen entering the theater earlier in the afternoon with a package. (Seattle 1923)

The body of a three-month-old boy was found at Alki Beach. He had been dead about two weeks. The police and coroner believe the infant had been beaten to death, thrown in the water from a boat, and then washed ashore. (Seattle 1924)

The body of a four-month-old female baby was found in a city park with obvious signs of trauma. Cause of death was listed as homicide. (Seattle 1948)

The body of a newborn female, dressed in an infant suit, wrapped in a blanket, and placed inside a gunny sack, was found in a garbage dump. Death was caused by asphyxia and exposure. (Seattle 1957)

A newborn male's body was found in a lumber pile near railroad tracks. He died of a blow to the head. The body may have been thrown from a car passing on a nearby expressway. (Buffalo 1974)

The bodies of the vast majority of these victims were found by accident, and almost all had been wrapped up and then disposed of in streets, fields, ash heaps, garbage dumps, and bodies of water. In only four of these fifty-one cases did it appear that the victims were left alive someplace where they might be found (e.g., in a church) but had nonetheless died of neglect and exposure. In the remaining cases, the methods of killing and the ways in which the bodies were dealt with suggest that the killers acted with the intent to kill and with an eye toward hiding the evidence of their crimes. The killers of these newborns and infants, then, do not appear to have acted in ways suggestive of impotent victimhood or psychic disability. The unsystematic and even accidental ways in which these killings came to the attention of authorities also suggest that there were other such killings in these cities that were never discovered. This conclusion is consistent with the claim that homicides of newborns and infants are more likely than any other type of homicide to remain undetected.[38] In some time periods, this "dark figure" of infant homicide is estimated to have made it the most common form of homicide and to have, according to Allen's research in Australia, made "women who killed babies the largest group of people . . . who killed, both in city and country areas."[39]

Two important points can be made about the cases we have documented of neonaticide and infanticide by unknown offenders. First, many if not most of these cases are likely to have been committed by or involved the complicity of the victims' mothers. We base this claim on the following reasons. According to other research, in cases of neonaticide that are initially undetected or unsolved but subsequently solved, as well as in contexts where neonaticide is not a crime, mothers predominate among the killers.[40] In addition, in cases where unidentified older infants' bodies were found, it is difficult to imagine that their mothers would not have informed authorities of their disappearances, unless these women were implicated in some way in the killings.

Second, what we know about the circumstances of these cases suggests that at least some and perhaps most of the killers are likely to depart substantially from the dominant portrayals we have described. If mothers acting on their own killed these newborns and infants, then the women were sufficiently self-possessed to have covered up or explained away either the evidence of their pregnancies and births, in the case of neonaticides, or the disappearance of their infants, in the case of infanticides. They were also resourceful enough to have disposed of their victims' bodies without being discovered and sufficiently composed not to have cracked under the pressure of an investigation or inquiries from friends and family. This is not to overstate the extent to which these women coldly calculated, calmly carried out, and then covered up their killings. However, it does suggest a clear contrast with the portrayal of women who kill their newborns and infants as incapable of acting on their own behalf, as disabled by denial, fear, mental illness, or poverty, and thus powerless in the face of larger structures of oppression to exert some control over their lives. At least as plausible is an account that acknowledges that some women who kill their infants may well be more canny, in control, and attentive to their own needs and interests than has been granted in the dominant narratives.[41]

Deaths of Newborns and Infants in Suspicious or Ambiguous Circumstances

Another sort of evidence speaks to the potential for homicides of newborns and infants to be undercounted and hence for some killers to have remained undetected. That evidence comes from our review of all coroner's death records for Seattle from March 1895 through September 1904. During that ten-and-a-half-year period, twenty-seven deaths of newborns (babies less than a week old) and eighty-one deaths of infants were recorded by the King County coroner. The causes of death in these cases are shown in Table 4.2.

Homicide was listed as the cause of death for only one of the newborns and one of the infants. However, an examination of the other causes of death suggests that some of these deaths are likely to have been neonaticides or infanticides. Consider first the eleven cases in which bodies of unidentified newborns or infants were discovered in public places around Seattle. Five of these were newborns whose bodies were disposed of in waterways and lakes, under sidewalks, or in ash heaps. In four of these five cases, the cause of death was either listed as unknown or left blank, and in the fifth case the death was attributed to "external trauma." Of the six unidentified dead infants, one had been buried in a field, one deposited in a lake, another placed in a tin vessel found floating in a bay, one unearthed from an ash heap, and a fifth stuffed inside a macaroni box and placed in

TABLE 4.2
Deaths of Newborns and Infants in Seattle, March 1895–September 1904

Cause of Death	Number of Newborns	Number of Infants
Gastrointestinal diseases[a]	1	17
Respiratory diseases[b]	0	12
Convulsions	1	4
Selected childhood diseases[c]	0	8
Stillborn (with physician attending)	3	0
Inanition, malnutrition, general debility	12	19
Suffocation, strangulation, overlaying	0	12
Poison	0	1
Bled to death before umbilical cord could be severed; no physician present	1	0
No cause recorded	3	1
Unidentified bodies discovered; cause typically unknown or undetermined	5	6
Homicide	1	1
Total deaths	27	81

[a] Includes cholera, gastritis, inflamed bowels, obstructed bowels.
[b] Includes croup, pneumonia, bronchitis.
[c] Includes measles, scarlet fever, whooping cough, infantile paralysis, smallpox, jaundice.

an alleyway. Similar to the records for the unidentified newborns, the reports of these infants' deaths included few details, but the information available suggests similarities to the cases classified as infanticides by unknown offenders that we described earlier. In a few of these cases the coroners' notes indicate that foul play was suspected, but the condition of the body was such that this could not be verified. Although some of these babies may have died from natural or accidental causes and their parents sought to avoid the costs of a burial or the involvement of authorities, others were almost certainly victims of homicide at the hands or with the complicity of their mothers, for reasons discussed earlier.

A second type of infant death seems a probable source for the dark figure of homicide. During this period, twelve infants died from "overlaying," or being strangled or smothered by bedclothes, in almost all cases while sleeping with their mothers. These cases include an illegitimate child who, according to her sixteen-year-old unmarried mother, suffocated in her bed during the night; a baby who died of asphyxiation from a pillow "accidentally [getting] over the child's head"; and an infant found dead in bed with its mother for whom the coroner listed both suffocation and hereditary syphilis as the causes of death. It is possible that all twelve of these infants died from accidental smothering or from natural causes, such as sudden infant death syndrome (SIDS) or some congenital abnormality. But, as others who have studied infanticide suggest, another possibility is that some parents chose this relatively indirect and difficult-to-detect way to kill infants in order to end the life of children they did not want or for whom they could not provide care.[42] If this is the case, the women who killed by smothering or strangling their babies were able to present themselves to medical officials so that they did not arouse suspicion—unless the medical officials themselves colluded by turning a blind eye and not pressing the mothers by investigating the deaths more thoroughly.[43]

In sum, of the 103 newborn and infant deaths recorded by the King County coroner over a ten-and-a-half-year period, only 2 percent were attributed to homicide. But another 22 percent (or twenty-three cases) were sufficiently suspicious or ambiguous to lend support to the claim that the incidence of newborn and infant homicides was substantially higher.[44] The circumstances of these twenty-three cases, combined with evidence from other research, also suggest that if any were homicides, the mothers of the victims are likely to have been responsible for or implicated in the killings. What emerges is the distinct possibility of mothers killing their infants in ways that required some calculation and preparation of the scene so as not to draw suspicion on themselves—in the case of overlaying—or mothers participating or acquiescing in the killing and disposing of newborns and infants in ways that allowed them to avoid detection. These are the sorts of women envisioned by those who argue that a fuller understanding of infanticidal mothers requires recognizing that some of them are rational, responsible, agentic actors who act within a context that, to borrow Morrissey's words, "enables and produces" these crimes.[45]

Conclusion

We are left, then, with the question with which we opened this chapter: to what extent have accepted knowledge and currently popular characterizations in some of the feminist-oriented research on women who kill their children been systematically biased by studying only cases determined to be homicides and in which offenders have been identified? We have suggested that information on cases of neonaticide and infanticide in which the killers remain unknown, as well as information on cases of newborn and infant deaths not classified as homicides, can help us to think about women who kill their children in more complex ways than implied by dominant narratives of these women as mad, bad, or victims. Explanations and typologies of these homicides must take into account the processes by which (1) a child death is discovered rather than remaining hidden, (2) the death is defined as a homicide rather than as an accident or some other cause, and (3) the homicide is attributed to a particular person.

Some women who kill their children are able, because of their resourcefulness and sense of self-preservation, to shape these processes either to prevent the discovery of the crime or to avoid detection as the killer. This does not deny that these and other women who kill their children may experience psychological distress, gendered forms of inequality, poverty, social isolation, and other personal and contextual factors that constrain the choices they can make about their lives. What it does deny is that these constraints leave women without agency or the ability to choose a course of action that they decide is a legitimate or necessary response to these constraints, even as (or perhaps because) this choice challenges the normative feminine role of mother.

Although we lack information on mothers who were successful at concealing the lethal violence they inflicted on their children, we can speculate about the factors that aided their success. Financial resources presumably mattered. The means to disguise a pregnancy, give birth in private secluded spaces, delay medical attention, or transport a dead body likely decreased the chances that a death would be discovered or that it would be designated a homicide. A second type of resource, social support, is also important. Women who had willing accomplices, whether they were romantic partners, family members, or friends may have been better able to dispose of bodies without being detected. Accomplices' effectiveness was likely influenced by their status in the community and their ability to convince others that a baby was stillborn or died of natural causes. In many instances, investigations of women originated from complaints by neighbors and other community members. Well-connected women and accomplices may have preempted official investigations by convincing others of the mothers' innocence. The converse of these attributes should, then, increase the chances that a woman would be identified as a child killer. Thus, socially isolated women—those who were unmarried, separated from supportive family members, or had affairs with married men—were likely more at risk of detection and less able to dismiss suspicions about the deaths of their newborns or infants. These are the characteristics of the women around whom the dominant narratives of maternal child killing have been constructed.

But beyond the social resources available to a woman, her personal resourcefulness could also increase her ability to successfully hide or disguise the killing of her newborn or infant, as other research has found. Women who had the wherewithal to use common folk knowledge about pregnancy, birth, and infant death could more effectively construct their experiences in ways that convinced others that they were not guilty of the crimes of which they were suspected. These explanations included denying birth by claiming that everyone knew that the pain and complications of childbirth precluded giving birth alone or by continuing on with their daily routines and noting that giving birth would have prohibited them from completing their work duties.[46] Other resourceful women made sure that they left no trace of identification with the abandoned body or that the state of their dead infant indicated that it was stillborn or died of natural causes (e.g., the position of the infant's hands, its entrapment in bed linen, or explaining bruising as evidence of hard labor and not of harm).[47] Conversely, women who could not effectively accomplish such presentations of self—for example, because of physical or mental exhaustion— were more likely to be identified as killers, providing support for constructions of mothers who kill as passive, imbalanced, and disabled.

Of course, more than a woman's attributes and resources matter if her killing is to remain part of the dark figure of child homicide. Historical conditions also play a role. With regard to the period covered by our study, concerns about out-of-wedlock births and the sexual threat of single women, or medical practitioners' "discovery" of child abuse, probably affected the likelihood that a neonaticide or infanticide was appropriately classified and the killer identified. Changes in the knowledge, resources, and disposition of officials also contributed to the likelihood that a birth was reported and that a child's death was defined as a homicide. Midwives, physicians, and coroners wielded considerable power in defining the nature of death and convincing others of the legitimacy of their pronouncements. Variation in these actors' beliefs about pregnancy, birth, women's and men's lives, and other factors contributed to differences in their decisions about the cause of death.[48] Determining how these factors may have influenced the nature and extent of the dark figure of maternal child-killing over this ninety-year period is, however, beyond the scope of our study.

Although it may be tempting to think that the factors contributing to this dark figure are largely confined to the early twentieth century, there is evidence to suggest otherwise. In her work on contemporary women who commit a series of homicides, Schurman-Kauflin describes cases in which one woman killed five children whom she was babysitting and two mothers killed five and eight of their own children.[49] In these cases, only the final deaths led authorities to review the earlier deaths, all of which had initially been classified as resulting from natural causes. Ewigman, Kivlahan, and Land find that less than half of the 384 cases of fatal abuse or neglect substantiated by the Missouri Division of Family Services between 1983 and 1986 are included in the Federal Bureau of Investigation Uniform Crime Reports database;[50] and Johnson demonstrates that states that do not have a special unit to investigate child deaths are significantly less likely to report child homicides.[51] Among the reasons for the continued misclassification of infant homicides, as Wilczynski and Morris argue in their study of filicide in England and Wales in the 1980s, are difficulties in proving that a child was born alive and in distinguishing homicides from accidents, diseases, or SIDS.[52]

Neonaticides and infanticides, like other homicides, involve a much greater variety of motives, purposes, circumstances, and meanings than are reflected in the typologies that have been used to interpret these tragic acts. Yet it is the norm that explanations and typologies—whether in the social sciences or in popular and legal discourses—will be incomplete. Their inability to account for all cases does not make them worthless; instead, they are useful to the extent that they help us understand the most common manifestations of the phenomena under scrutiny. The image constructed in some feminist scholarship of women who kill their children as victims is a useful account. However, we believe that it represents a far smaller proportion of maternal child killings than previous research suggests. Conversely, we believe that a greater proportion of these women more closely resemble the image of the killer as rational actor. We are not suggesting that these women take after the instrumental, hyper-self-interested actor of neoclassical economics. Rather, we argue, as many social historians have, that their actions were chosen from the small set of alternatives created by the untenable situations in which they found themselves.[53] Morrissey urges a similar reading of female killers more generally, pointing out the legal and political implications of existing and partial narratives of the subjectivity of violent women:

Denials of female agency . . . are crucial to decreasing the threat women killers pose to the dominant, male-dominated institutions of heteropatriarchy. If a woman can be found to have been so victimized that she did not know what she was doing when she killed, or if she is portrayed as a mythic, inhuman personification of wickedness, then the radical implications of her acts are muffled, her challenge to oppression nullified, at least as far as the dominant purveyors of cultural meaning are concerned. She is returned to her place of passivity and silence.[54]

Although a wider recognition of women as agents is likely to improve our understanding of maternal child killing, we must resist the tendency to assume that adding another category will exhaust the backgrounds and experiences of women who use violence. As noted by Hoffer and Hull, other mothers (and fathers) will fall between the cracks that separate our categories: "Between the disoriented and the 'rational' infanticidal parents and caretakers, lay men and women, parents of newborns or slightly older children, frustrated at their own lives—who struck out at the immediate cause of their misery. The newborn after a difficult birth, the crying infant, and the disobedient toddler became their victims."[55] Thus, we must ensure that we address the admonitions of many feminists not to essentialize or naturalize women (and men) who take the lives of others. Nor should we force them into categories that obscure rather than illuminate their diversity.

NOTES

1. Deborah Kirkwood, "Female Perpetrated Homicide in Victoria between 1985 and 1995," *Australia and New Zealand Journal of Criminology* 36 (2003): 152–172; Ania Wilczynski, "Mad or Bad? Child-Killers, Gender, and the Courts," *British Journal of Criminology* 37 (1997): 419–437; Allison Morris and Ania Wilczynski, "Rocking the Cradle: Mothers Who Kill Their Children," in *Moving Targets: Women, Murder and Representation,* ed. Helen Birch, pp. 198–217 (Berkeley: University of California Press, 1994).

2. Belinda Morrissey, *When Women Kill: Questions of Agency and Subjectivity* (London: Routledge, 2003), 167.

3. Ibid., 7. Our argument relies heavily on undetected violence by women, and so it is particularly important to avoid the sort of naturalizing tendency evident in early scholarship on women and crime. For example, Otto Pollak, among others, asserted that women committed much more crime than officials were aware of

because of women's natural abilities at deception and concealment—abilities born of their physiological differences from males. See Otto Pollak, *The Criminality of Women* (Westport, CT: Greenwood, 1950). We argue that cultural and structural arrangements surrounding childbirth and childcare provide women who kill newborns and infants distinct opportunities for avoiding detection that are less available to other types of killers.

4. DeAnn K. Gauthier, Nancy K. Chaudoir, and Craig J. Forsytg, "A Sociological Analysis of Maternal Infanticide in the United States, 1984–1996," *Deviant Behavior* 24 (2003): 393–404.

5. These data were collected as part of a larger project we have been conducting on homicide in two American cities (Buffalo and Seattle) and two Canadian cities (Toronto and Vancouver) during the twentieth century. Our access to coroners' records in the American cities for early in the century led us to focus this analysis on Buffalo and Seattle.

6. The sources available to us varied somewhat between the two cities. In Seattle, our primary source of information for the years prior to 1972 was records kept by the King County Medical Examiner's Office, supplemented with newspaper coverage of those deaths deemed homicides from their archives. For Seattle after 1972, we relied primarily on police records, which we supplemented with information from our own search of local newspapers. We also cross-checked the total number of homicides from police records against counts kept by the medical examiner and the FBI. In Buffalo, we relied primarily on police records, including annual reports that provided information on all homicides investigated by the police. We cross-checked and supplemented this information with a systematic search of the archives of the city's main newspaper. To validate further the accuracy of the police data, we also (1) obtained access to death records for a sample of some of the years under study and (2) cross-checked our homicide counts against counts from the FBI's Uniform Crime Reports.

7. The information recorded on these death records is very limited and typically includes the deceased's name, age, sex, address, date of death, cause of death, condition of body, and the name of the physician completing the death record. If a coroner's jury investigated the death, somewhat more information was often recorded. We restricted our search to this ten-year period and to one jurisdiction because of restrictions on time, resources, and access.

8. P. J. Resnick, "Murder of the Newborn: A Psychiatric Review of Neonaticide," *American Journal of Psychiatry* 126 (1970): 73–82; Marie W. Piers, *Infanticide* (New York: Norton, 1978).

9. Ania Wilczynski, "Images of Women Who Kill Their Infants: The Mad and the Bad," *Women and Criminal Justice* 2 (1991): 71–88.

10. Peter C. Hoffer and N. E. H. Hull, *Murdering Mothers: Infanticide in England and New England, 1558–1803* (New York: New York University Press, 1981); Lionel Rose, *The Massacre of the Innocents: Infanticide in Britain, 1800–1939* (Lon-

don: Routledge and Kegan Paul, 1986); G. Hausfater and S. B. Hrdy, eds., *Infanticide: Comparative and Evolutionary Perspectives* (Hawthorne, NY: Aldine de Gruyter, 1984); Martin Daly and Margo Wilson, *Homicide* (Hawthorne, NY: Aldine de Gruyter, 1988).

11. Ann Goetting, *Homicide in Families and Other Special Populations* (New York: Springer, 1995); Charles P. Ewing, *Fatal Families: The Dynamics of Intrafamilial Homicide* (Thousand Oaks, CA: Sage, 1997); Neil Websdale, *Understanding Domestic Homicide* (Boston: Northeastern University Press, 1999).

12. Robert Fiala and Gary LaFree, "Cross-National Determinants of Child Homicide," *American Sociological Review* 53 (1988): 432–445; Rosemary Gartner, "Family Structure, Welfare Spending, and Child Homicides in Developed Democracies," *Journal of Marriage and the Family* 53 (1991): 231–240; Colin Pritchard and Alan Butler, "A Comparative Study of Child and Adult Homicide Rates in the USA and the Major Western Countries, 1974–1999," *Journal of Family Violence* 18 (2003): 341–350.

13. Christine M. Alder and June Baker, "Maternal Filicide: More Than One Story to Be Told," *Women and Criminal Justice* 9 (1997): 15–39; Cheryl L. Meyer and Michelle Oberman, *Mothers Who Kill Their Children: Understanding the Acts of Moms from Susan Smith to the "Prom Mom"* (New York: New York University Press, 2001); Ania Wilczynski, *Child Homicide* (London: Greenwich Medical Media, 1997).

14. Joyce Dougherty, "Women's Violence against Their Children: A Feminist Perspective," *Women and Criminal Justice* 4 (1993): 91–114; Lita Linzer Schwartz and Natalie K. Isser, *Endangered Children* (Boca Raton, FL: CRC Press, 2000).

15. Janna Haapasalo and Sonja Petaja, "Mothers Who Killed or Attempted to Kill Their Child: Life Circumstances, Childhood Abuse, and Types of Killing," *Violence and Victims* 14 (1999): 219–239; Cora Mae Mann, *Women Who Kill* (Albany: State University of New York Press, 1996); Ralph A. Weisheit, "When Mothers Kill Their Children," *Social Science Journal* 23 (1986): 439–448.

16. Vickie Jensen, *Why Women Kill: Homicide and Gender Equality* (Boulder, CO: Lynne Rienner, 2001), 14.

17. Martha Smithey, "Maternal Infanticide and Modern Motherhood," *Women and Criminal Justice* 13 (2001): 66–67.

18. Michelle Oberman, "Understanding Infanticide in Context: Mothers Who Kill, 1870–1930, and Today," *Journal of Criminal Law and Criminology* 92 (2002): 710; also see Michelle Oberman, "Mothers Who Kill: Coming to Terms with Modern American Infanticide," *American Criminal Law Review* 34 (1996): 1–110.

19. Schwartz and Isser, *Endangered Children*, 41.

20. Smithey, "Maternal Infanticide," 81.

21. Jeffrey S. Adler, "'I Loved Joe, but I Had to Shoot Him': Homicide by Women in Turn-of-the-Century Chicago," *Journal of Criminal Law and Criminology* 92 (2002): 875.

22. Hilary Allen noted a similar tendency in her study of legal portrayals of women who kill. See *Justice Unbalanced: Gender, Psychiatry, and Judicial Decisions* (Milton Keynes, UK: Open University Press, 1987).

23. Morrissey, *When Women Kill*, 35–36.

24. Mark Jackson, ed., *Infanticide: Historical Perspectives on Child Murder and Concealment, 1550–2000* (Aldershot, UK: Ashgate, 2002); Randolph Roth, "Child Murder in New England," *Social Science History* 25 (2001): 101–147; Deborah A. Symonds, *Weep Not for Me: Women, Ballads, and Infanticide in Early Modern Scotland* (University Park: Pennsylvania State University Press, 1997); also see Gauthier, Chaudoir, and Forsytg, "Sociological Analysis."

25. Ann-Louise Shapiro, *Breaking the Codes: Female Criminality in Fin-de-Siecle Paris* (Stanford: Stanford University Press, 1996), 130.

26. Kathy Laster, "Infanticide: A Litmus Test for Feminist Criminological Theory," *Australia and New Zealand Journal of Criminology* 22 (1989): 151–166.

27. Johanna Geyer-Kordesch, "Infanticide and the Erotic Plot: A Feminist Reading of Eighteenth-Century Crime," in Jackson, *Infanticide*, 127.

28. Ibid., 126–127.

29. Meyer and Oberman, *Mothers Who Kill.*

30. Laster, "Infanticide," 158.

31. Christine Alder and Kenneth Polk, *Child Victims of Homicide* (Cambridge: Cambridge University Press, 2001), 45. See also Meyer and Oberman, *Mothers Who Kill.*

32. Alder and Polk, *Child Victims of Homicide*, 67.

33. Shapiro, *Breaking the Codes*, 130.

34. Julia Wheelwright, "'Nothing in Between': Modern Cases of Infanticide," in Jackson, *Infanticide*, 285.

35. Nevertheless, two patterns are worth noting: neonaticides in these data were concentrated in the years when abortion and birth control were not widely available (85 percent occurred prior to 1960), whereas infanticides were more evenly distributed over the entire period (about half occurring before 1960 and half afterward). These patterns suggest that neonaticide is more responsive to the expansion of women's reproductive choices than is infanticide; however, this conclusion presumes that these data either reflect the true incidence of these killings or that the "dark figure" of these killings is relatively invariant over time.

36. In the remaining two cases, the victims' mothers were assaulted—in one case by the victim's father, in the other case by an acquaintance of the mother—while they were in the last stages of pregnancy, and the infants were born dead as a consequence.

37. Alder and Polk, *Child Victims of Homicide*, 45.

38. Ania Wilczynski and Allison Morris, "Parents Who Kill Their Children," *Criminal Law Review* 793 (1993): 31–36; Judith A. Allen, *Sex and Secrets: Crimes Involving Australian Women since 1880* (Melbourne, Australia: Oxford University

Press, 1990); Alder and Polk, *Child Victims of Homicide*; Schwartz and Isser, *Endangered Children.*

39. Allen, *Sex and Secrets*, 31.

40. See, for example, Allen, *Sex and Secrets*; Hoffer and Hull, *Murdering Mothers*; Daly and Wilson, *Homicide*; Deborah Schurman-Kauflin, *The New Predator— Women Who Kill: Profiles of Female Serial Killers* (New York: Algora, 2000); Ann Jones, *Women Who Kill* (New York: Fawcett Columbine, 1980).

41. Some of these unidentified killers may have been people who acted with the mothers' acquiescence or at their urging. In more than one case, the coroner argued that the mother would have been too weak to dispose of the body so soon after birth and suggested that someone else must have participated. In at least one case, there is clear evidence that a man was involved, because a newborn's body was discovered in a hotel room immediately after the male customer had checked out. Thus, women who gave birth may have had assistance from—or been managed by—family members, midwives, lovers, or friends who could have carried out the killings and/or disposed of the bodies. If this is the case, then at least some of the mothers who kill their newborns and infants do not fit the image—based on characteristics of known offenders—of women who lack social support and suffer from extreme isolation.

42. Hoffer and Hull suggest a similar interpretation of infant deaths from overlaying, or what they call the "supposedly accidental smothering of infants." Hoffer and Hull, *Murdering Mothers*, 137–138. See also Allen, *Sex and Secrets*.

43. Allen, along with other historians, suggests that this was not an uncommon practice and that particularly in the late nineteenth and early twentieth centuries, there was "a certain fatalism" that "accompanied the death of babies rather than the moralism, shock and suspicion often apparent by the late twentieth century." Allen, *Sex and Secrets*, 33.

44. There is a third group of newborns and infants whose deaths may also have been misclassified but for which the evidence is more ambiguous. These are the thirty-one who died, according to coroners, from inanition, malnutrition, failure to thrive, or general debility—causes often listed when no others were apparent. Twelve of these were newborns who died within hours or a few days of birth and without a physician in attendance, meaning that these babies' mothers would have been the most important source of information on their brief lives. The deaths of nineteen infants, ranging in age from a few weeks to six months, were attributed to the same causes; their death records are strikingly similar and very sparse. In each case, one of the three causes of death was listed, often accompanied by the statement "without attendance of physician" (sometimes adding "to certify death from natural causes") and little else. The one record with more detail describes a baby who died of "inanition and maltreatment" shortly after arriving at the home of a care giver. The coroner's jury concluded that the care giver was not responsible for the death because the jury found the condition existed prior to

the infant going into her care. We cannot state with confidence that any of these deaths were due to homicide, especially given the relatively high infant-mortality rates of the times. Yet if even one or two of these thirty-one cases were homicides, the killers were sufficiently resourceful (or perhaps lucky) to have avoided detection or prosecution and/or to have disguised the cause of death.

45. Morrissey, *When Women Kill*, 35.

46. Constance Backhouse, *Petticoats and Prejudice: Women and Law in Nineteenth-Century Canada* (Toronto: Osgoode Society, 1991).

47. Mark Jackson, *New-Born Child Murder: Women, Illegitimacy, and the Courts in Eighteenth-Century England* (Manchester, UK: Manchester University Press, 1996); Symonds, *Weep Not for Me*.

48. Backhouse, *Petticoats and Prejudice*; Johnson, *New-Born Child Murder*; Symonds, *Weep Not for Me*.

49. Schurman-Kauflin, *New Predator*.

50. B. Ewigman, C. Kivlahan, and G. Land, "The Missouri Child Fatality Study: Underreporting of Maltreatment Fatalities among Children Younger than Five Years," *Pediatrics* 91 (1993): 330–337. Also see P. W. McClain, J. J. Sacks, R. G. Froehlke, and B. G. Ewigman, "Estimates of Fatal Child Abuse and Neglect, United States, 1979 through 1988," *Pediatrics* 91 (1993): 338–343.

51. Keith Johnson, "State Maternal Infanticide Determinations as a Product of Official Concern for Deviant Behavior" (paper presented at the ninety-ninth American Sociological Association Meeting, San Francisco, CA, August 2004).

52. Wilczynski and Morris, "Parents Who Kill Their Children."

53. At least one philosopher, Ian Hacking, also shares this view. After noting that infanticide "is probably far more common among us than is usually acknowledged," he asserts that this "sad reality" is "determined neither by genes nor environment." Instead, it is a consequence of choice, but of choice seen in a particular way: "Of course the mothers have not simply chosen to be cruel. But they have made little choices, day after day, which end in these tragedies. The little choices are often made in unbearable circumstances of poverty, abusive husbands, postbirth depression. But they are choices all the same." Ian Hacking, "Between Michel Foucault and Erving Goffman: Between Discourse in the Abstract and Face-to-Face Interaction," *Economy and Society* 33 (2004): 286–287.

54. Morrissey, *When Women Kill*, 170.

55. Hoffer and Hull, *Murdering Mothers*, 158.

Chapter 5

The Crimes of Poverty
Economic Marginalization and the Gender Gap in Crime

Karen Heimer, Stacy Wittrock, and Halime Ünal

Poverty and economic marginalization have long been identified as key factors in explaining male crime rates and thus, crime rates more generally. Although it is reasonable to assume that poverty also is important for understanding women's crime,[1] quantitative studies of poverty and the gendering of crime are surprisingly rare.

Yet there seems to be a parallel between gender differences in poverty and gender differences in arrest rates over time.[2] The explanation of this association has been referred to as the "economic marginalization thesis."[3] The argument is that the gender gap in crime decreases and females account for a greater proportion of crime when women's economic well-being declines. Although the claim appears in some recent discussions of women's crime rates, there have been very few empirical studies of the economic marginalization thesis with regard to women's crime, and the existing studies have some methodological limitations.

Our study contributes to research on this issue and goes beyond previous research in a couple of ways. First, we treat economic marginalization as a comparative concept that reflects the relative economic circumstances of women and men. Some previous work has examined women's absolute levels of poverty vis-à-vis their offending; other research has examined whether structural variables that capture communities' overall economic health (i.e., not specific to women's economic circumstances) are associated with female crime rates. By contrast, we propose that the *relative* economic well-being of women and men is the key to understanding the gender gap in offending.

Second, we go beyond existing studies of the economic marginalization thesis by simultaneously examining variation over time and across cities in the United States. Specifically, we present an analysis of a novel data set that contains information on the gender gap in arrests and the comparative economic well-being of women and men; our sample includes one hundred large U.S. cities for the period 1970 through 2000.[4]

We set the stage for our research by first discussing research on gender ratios of crime rates and then briefly reviewing research that helps to shed light on the dimensions of women's economic marginalization in recent decades.

Patterns of Gender Ratios of Arrest

Accurately assessing patterns of women's crime requires attention to certain measurement issues, although some research—especially early research—has not taken account of these issues.[5] First, women's crime rates must be population adjusted, such that changes in women's crime can be disentangled from population growth or decline. Second, adjusting female crime rates by male crime rates—either examining *gender rate ratios* or *gender differences in rates*—is essential for assessing relative change.[6] Female rates can increase while the gender rate ratio remains static if, for example, male crime rates are increasing similarly to female rates. This would indicate that the changes in women's offending are not unique and that research need not examine variation in female rates apart from male rates. Third, the magnitudes and variability in gender rate ratios are not the same for all offense types. Aggregating across offense types can obscure important gender differences in magnitudes and trends over time. Consequently, in the patterns reported in this section, we focus on studies of gender rate ratios or gender differences in rates that examine the major types of crime separately.

Early research on gender differences in offending in the United States focused exclusively on changes over time at the national level.[7] The earliest empirical research concluded that during the 1960s and 1970s, there was notable narrowing in the gender gap in arrests for property offenses, such as larceny and fraud.[8] However, more recent studies of national-level data from the 1960s through the 1990s have reported statistically significant long-term convergence in gender rates (i.e., an increase in gender rate ratios) of arrests for other offenses, including violent offenses as well as other property offenses, such as burglary.[9]

Yet there does not appear to be a simple trend that holds across all offenses.[10] Two studies that examine gender rate ratios or gender differences in arrest rates for the United States from 1960 through the middle 1990s show the following general patterns.[11] The gender rate ratio of larceny arrests increased between 1960 and the late 1970s and then leveled off somewhat through the 1980s and the early part of the 1990s. The gender rate ratios in robbery and burglary arrests, by comparison, increased fairly steadily from the early 1960s through the middle 1990s. The gender rate ratios of aggravated assault arrests declined somewhat between 1960 and 1970, were fairly low during the 1970s and 1980s, and then increased in the early 1990s, at a time when violence among males was increasing. The increases in gender rate ratios of arrests for some violent offenses in the early 1990s occurred because female rates were increasing more than male rates.

Although studies show that there has been some convergence over time in gender ratios for some offenses, the specific patterns vary across offense types. Moreover, we note that increases in gender rate ratios have occurred under several scenarios: female arrests increased more than male arrests; female arrests increased while male arrests changed very little or while male crime declined; and female offending decreased at a slower rate than male offending.[12]

Finally, very little research has compared gender ratios of offending across place. Existing research has focused on cross-national differences.[13] Despite the attention to the changing gender gap in crime in the United States, no study published to date has examined variation across U.S. cities. Cities vary greatly in social structural features as well as in crime rates, however, and it seems likely that they would also vary in gender rate ratios of crime. This provides one motivation for our study, which examines variation in the gender gap in crime over time and across cities, simultaneously.

Explaining Changes over Time in the Gender Gap in Crime

The earliest explanation of changes in the gender gap in crime was the liberation thesis, which posited that women's increasing economic and social independence from men had led to increased female crime and, thus, a narrowing in the gender gap of offending. The thesis originated in the work of Rita Simon and Freda Adler, who both noted increases in women's offending that seemed to correspond to the emergence of the women's liberation movement.[14] Whereas Adler focused more on convergence in gender roles and attitudes, Simon focused on the increased labor force participation of women, which was said to create new opportunities for crime among women.

Subsequent research on the liberation thesis, however, produced very little support for it. In a series of studies, Steffensmeier and his colleagues pointed out that the largest increases in female arrests during this era of the women's movement were for larceny-theft, fraud, and forgery, which reflected mostly increases in shoplifting, writing bad checks, welfare fraud, and credit card fraud.[15] These researchers argued that such crimes were more consistent with traditional female roles as consumers and caretakers of families and were not the occupation-related crimes that Simon's version of the liberation thesis emphasized. In addition, other scholars observed that the continued sex-segregation in labor markets has limited women's access to positions of power that would offer the greatest opportunities for the commission of white-collar crimes.[16] In short, the liberation thesis has received little empirical support.

A counterargument to the liberation thesis focuses on the relationship between economic hardship and female offending. For example, Box states, "crimes committed by females have increased considerably in the past decade in both the United Kingdom and the United States. The most plausible reason for this is that more women have become economically marginalised."[17] Indeed, several scholars have argued that increases in women's crime have been associated with the feminization of poverty rather than with economic liberation. This has become a popular explanation of changes over time in the gender gap in offending.

Despite its recent popularity, there has been surprisingly little empirical research assessing the thesis. A few existing studies have offered some support for an economic marginalization argument. Two national-level time-series studies, for example, reported an association between female unemployment rates and female court-conviction rates in England and Wales (1951–1980).[18] Another national-level time-series study, using U.S. data (1965–1986), reported that certain indicators of economic marginalization—the percentage of female-headed households, women's and men's relative unemployment rates, and births out of marriage—were associated with gender rate ratios of arrest for some offenses.[19] Yet, because national-level data were only available for a twenty-year period, the researchers could not include multiple measures of economic marginalization in any one equation, so the reported associations may or may not be reproduced when various dimensions of marginalization are considered simultaneously. Finally, some support for the marginalization thesis comes from a pooled time-series analysis of ten nations over twenty years, which reported that women's conviction rates (aggregated across all offenses) increased along with their economic marginalization, as measured by women's participation in service-sector jobs.[20]

Although these studies offer some support for the economic marginalization thesis, there are methodological limitations that limit the strength of this support. First, some of these studies examined gender differences in aggregated crime rates rather than in offense-specific rates, which can mask important differences in trends across crime types, such as those described previously. Second, only one study examined relative measures of female-to-male economic well-being, which we will later argue is essential for assessing the economic marginalization thesis.[21] Third, all the studies were based on national-level time series and thus may suffer from aggregation bias.[22] Put simply, national-level aggregation can mask important fluctuations in crime rates that are apparent at lower levels of aggregation. Moreover, correlations between variables aggregated to higher-order units are typically stronger than those at the primary measurement unit, making it more difficult to detect effects of covariates above and beyond the effects of other variables in the model, including time. Generally speaking, using data measured at the geographic unit where it is collected is more desirable than aggregating up from these units to higher-order units. The primary unit on which the FBI collects arrest statistics is at the city level, and it is well known that cities vary substantially in crime statistics.[23]

This discussion suggests that a better understanding of changes over time in the gender gap in crime in the United States requires a study that has the following features: a focus on offense-specific gender rate ratios, the inclusion of multiple measures of the relative economic hardships of women and men, and data from a sample of cities over time. We note that examining cities over time also increases the observations available for statistical analysis and thus avoids the statistical power problems that may have plagued previous national-level time-series studies.

Research on Variations across Place in the
Gender Gap in Crime

Research on variation across place in the gender gap in crime also can shed light on the economic marginalization thesis. Unfortunately, we could locate only two studies of variation across place in the gender gap in crime, both of which focused on cross-national differences.

One of these studies was referenced in the previous section—a pooled cross-sectional time-series study of ten nations over twenty years, which reported that women's work in service-sector jobs is associated with increases in women's conviction rates.[24] Another study examined the percentage of arrests accounted for by females across sixty-nine countries.[25] These authors reported that the proportion of arrests accounted for by women was not associated with a measure of occupational segregation among women. However, occupational segregation may not be the best measure of the comparative economic hardship of women and men, given that it only captures differences across occupational categories among working adults and does not tap gender differentials in income, education, or poverty. Indeed, the unemployed are most likely to be poor and thus marginal economically; this group is not included in occupational segregation measures. Also, an index of occupational segregation does not speak to income differentials across jobs.

Although published studies have not examined gender differences in crime rates across U.S. cities, one study has compared the important structural covariates associated with female and male arrests across cities.[26] This study reported that cities with higher levels of economic disadvantage (e.g., poverty, unemployment, female-headship rates) had higher rates of arrests for serious crimes among both females and males. This study shows that absolute levels of economic disadvantage are associated with female and male crime, but it does not claim to speak either to the gender gap in offending or to women's, as compared to men's, economic marginalization.

In short, the existing studies of variation across place in gender differences in offending suggest that economic marginalization may play a role. Although researchers have not examined variation in the gender gap in crime across U.S. cities, the great variation in social structural features and crime rates (not disaggregated by gender) across cities suggests that there may well be important cross-city variation in the gender gap.

Women's Relative Economic Marginalization and the Gender Gap in Crime

We maintain that economic marginalization is best viewed as a comparative construct—as the relative risk of economic disadvantage among women as compared to men. However, most studies of economic marginalization and gender differences in crime focus on women's absolute levels of economic hardship, without comparison to men's levels. Yet, as researchers studying women's poverty point out, absolute levels of poverty in the United States declined since the 1950s; however, during these years, women were more likely to live in poverty than men. The essential fact, therefore, is that poverty is "feminized"—women make up a larger fraction of the poor population than men, regardless of the year. Poverty researchers thus argue that the focus must be on the *relative risk* of women's disadvantage as compared to that of men.[27]

In addition, researchers maintain that the gap between female and male risks of poverty widened between the 1950s and the 1980s.[28] This pattern, referred to as the feminization of poverty, has become widely recognized across the social sciences. What has been rarely recognized, however, is the more recent finding that women's relative risk of poverty declined in the 1980s (because men's rates rose more than women's rates during the recession of the early 1980s) and then stabilized in the late 1980s and 1990s, with women's poverty hovering between 50 percent and 60 percent higher than men's rates.[29] So, although women's risk of poverty still exceeds men's risk, the increases in the gender gap slowed after 1980, likely due to the movement of large numbers of prime-working-age women into good paying jobs during this period. Nevertheless, disaggregation of these figures by age shows that although poverty ratios among thirty- to sixty-four-year-old women declined after the mid-1980s, the relative risk of poverty among very young women continued to increase at least somewhat.[30] The bottom line is not only that women are more likely to live in poverty than men but also that the gender gap in poverty rates for women in the most crime-prone age group continue to increase.[31]

Moreover, the most recent statements on the feminization of poverty have indicated that examining female and male poverty ratios, even when disaggregated by age, may mask important demographic trends.[32] These statements suggest that it is more appropriate to focus attention on the relative poverty of female-headed or mother-only families. For example, the poverty of female-headed families increased in the 1970s (to seven times the poverty rate of two-parent families in 1974) then declined some in the recession of the early 1980s (to five times the poverty rate of two-parent families in 1984) as two-parent families also became poorer.[33] After this time, the proportion of the poor living in mother-only families increased and then leveled off at a rate more than five times the poverty rate of two-parent families. This discussion suggests that operationalizing the relative economic marginalization of women requires a consideration of the proportion of the poor population residing in female-headed families.

But the concept of economic marginalization embodies more than official poverty; it also encompasses financial instability that may not be reflected in poverty statistics. Indeed, economists have emphasized the growing number of the "near poor" in the United States, those who do not fall below the official poverty line but who are also not making ends meet.[34] In addition, many scholars have charged that methods used to determine the poverty line result in an underestimation of the poor population.[35] Some scholars suggest that a focus on income dispersion may be more appropriate. These researchers point out that income dispersion or income inequality—the gap between high- and low-wage workers—increased after the 1970s and that this is accounted for largely by declines in the wages of workers with less than a high school education.[36] Moreover, income inequality is linked to service-sector employment because, on average, service-sector jobs tend to be low-paying, part-time, intermittent, and limited in benefits.[37] These patterns suggest that a consideration of gender differences in education and service-sector employment is important for capturing women's relative economic marginalization. Similarly, the relative unemployment ratios of females as compared to males are pertinent for a comparison of women's and men's economic disadvantage.

The economic marginalization argument suggests that the gap between women's and men's economic hardships over time and across place will correspond to variations in gender rate ratios of crime. Gender rate ratios of crime should increase (i.e., gender differences or gender gaps in crime should decrease) as the gap between women's and men's relative economic marginality increases. The relative economic hardships of women can be captured by examining the proportion of the poor population that is accounted for by mother-only or female-headed families, the relative high school graduation rates of women and men, the proportion of women as compared to men who are working in service-sector jobs, and the relative unemployment rates for women and men. All these indicators emphasize the comparative nature of economic marginalization.

Data

To assess whether the relative economic marginalization of women and men can account for variation in gender ratios of crime over time and across place, we constructed a data set that includes the one hundred largest U.S. cities (in 1970) for each decennial census year, from 1970 through 2000.[38] The sample thus includes four hundred city-year observations. These data are unique for the study of gender and crime because they cover a significant time period and include a large number of urban areas.[39]

The data set contains city-level measures of female and male arrests from the Uniform Crime Reports (UCR) for 1970, 1980, 1990, and 2000. It also contains an array of sociodemographic variables from the censuses of 1970 through 2000.

These data allow us to address some limitations of previous research. First, using the city as our unit of analysis avoids potential aggregation bias, as discussed earlier. In addition, it should be easier to disentangle covariate effects from the effects of time with city-level data than with national-level data. Second, the use of data on cities over time gives us a much larger sample size (four hundred city-years) than is possible in national-level data analyses. We thus have sufficient statistical power to examine the partial effects of covariates that are themselves correlated, such as gender rate ratios of unemployment and education. Previous research has often been able to focus only on one or two economic covariates per model, due to small samples sizes and thus limited statistical power. Third, our strategy allows us to examine variability across cities, as well as over time, in the association between economic marginalization and the gender ratio of offending.

Variable Construction

Our dependent variables are the population-adjusted gender rate ratios of arrests for aggravated assault, robbery, other assault, burglary, and larceny. All of the offenses, except for other assault, are UCR Part I index offenses. We include larceny because this is the offense that received the greatest attention in early studies of the gender gap in arrests. But we also examine more serious and traditionally "male" crimes, such as assaults, robbery, and burglary. As noted earlier, recent research demonstrates some decrease in the gender gap in these offenses.[40] Our argument is that the poverty and economic marginalization of women should be associated with increases across violent as well as property crime, just as economic marginalization and poverty are linked to both types of crime in other areas of criminology, such as in research on race and class differences.

The analyses that we report use the main agency arrest data for females and males over fifteen years of age for each of the one hundred cities in our sample.[41] We select age fifteen as the lower bound because, as the most recent reports on the feminization of poverty note, very young women are among the most strongly affected by economic marginalization. The arrest rates for females and males are population adjusted using gender-disaggregated population figures from the census.[42] We smooth the arrest rate data for each gender by taking multiyear averages for years proximal to 1970, 1980, 1990, and 2000.[43] Then we compute the gender ratios of smoothed population-adjusted arrest rates for each of the crime types in our study. In the analyses that follow, we model the natural logarithms of these gender rate ratios.

Measures of Women's Relative Economic Marginalization

We obtained information on our covariates from U.S. Census reports for each of our one hundred cities for the period 1970 through 2000. Specifically, we collected information on the following six variables, which combine to give a picture of the relative economic hardships of women and men:

1. *concentration of poverty in female-headed families* = proportion of all poor families that are female-headed;
2. *relative rates of high school education* = female-to-male population-adjusted rates of graduation from high school;
3. *relative rates of unemployment* = female-to-male population-adjusted unemployment rates;
4. *relative rates of service work* = female-to-male rates of employment in service-sector industry.[44]

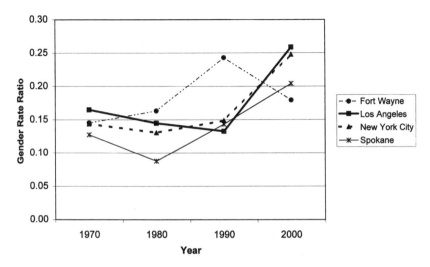

Fig. 5.1. Aggravated Assault Arrest Gender Rate Ratio, 1970–2000.

Higher values on these covariates indicate increased economic marginalization among women and thus should be associated with increases in gender rate ratios of both property and violent offending.

Describing Patterns of Female-to-Male Arrests

Figures 5.1 and 5.2 illustrate typical patterns of gender rate ratios of arrests in our data. We show trends in four cities, including two very large cities (New York and Los Angeles) and two moderately sized cities (Fort Wayne and Spokane); the trends in these cities are representative of patterns in similarly sized cities. The figures show trends for one violent crime (aggravated assault) and one property crime (larceny). The figures depict the gender rate ratios; if this number is multiplied by one hundred, it gives female arrest rates as a percentage of male arrest rates.

Figure 5.1 depicts the gender rate ratios of aggravated assault for the four cities. This graph shows variation across cities. It also shows some declines in gender rate ratios between 1970 and 1980 (Los Angeles, Fort Wayne, and Spokane). It also shows an upward trend in New York and Los Angeles between 1990 and 2000, as well as an increase in Spokane that

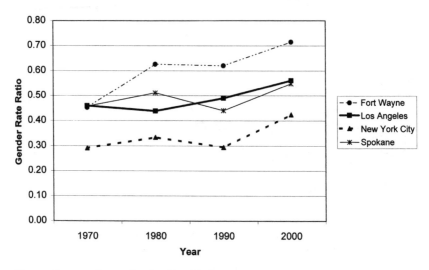

Fig. 5.2. Larceny Arrest Gender Rate Ratio, 1970–2000.

appears to begin in 1980. For example, in 1990, female arrest rates for aggravated assault were about 14 percent of male rates in 1990 and climbed
to almost 26 percent of male rates by 2000. New York shows a somewhat
similar overall pattern. There is a decline in the gender rate ratio between
1990 and 2000 in Fort Wayne, however.

Figure 5.2 shows the gender rate ratios of larceny arrests for the four
cities. The graph illustrates both an upward trend over time in all cities, as
well as variation in the magnitude of the ratios across cities. For example,
in Fort Wayne, female arrests for larceny were about 45 percent of male
arrest rates in 1970 but were over 70 percent of the male rates by 2000. In
New York, by comparison, female arrest rates for larceny were under 30
percent of male rates in 1970 and had increased to about 42 percent of
male rates by 2000. Not only do absolute values of the gender rate ratio
differ across cities, but the size of the increase over time also varies across
cities. This highlights the importance of examining city-level data; such
variation would be masked by using data aggregated to higher-order geographic units.

Overall, these figures show that gender rate ratios of arrest vary across
crime types, over time, and across cities, indicating the need for a structural explanation to account for these patterns. Both figures also show that

there is greater fluctuation in gender rate ratios in the moderately sized cities than in the larger cities. This is expected because the lower population base leads to more chance variability. This variability indicates the need to conduct analyses weighted by city size to account for heterogeneity in the variances across cities.

Statistical Modeling Procedures

Our dependent variables are the logarithms of gender rate ratios of arrest for all offenses listed in Table 5.1. For each offense type, we specify a mixed model (random and fixed effects) that includes all the covariates listed earlier, as well as city population size (in millions). We weight the data by city population size to address the tendency for smaller cities to show greater fluctuations in arrest rates over time, as depicted in the figures. Weighting leads to more efficient estimates because the variance is more likely to be specified correctly.

We include in all equations a fixed linear effect for the four time periods covered by our data—1970, 1980, 1990, and 2000. We treat time as linear because this provided a better fit to the data than did including time as a categorical variable.

We also include a random effect for city in each equation estimated, to account for unobserved heterogeneity across cities not accounted for by the other variables in our model. Because it is likely that the other covariates in the model are correlated with the city random effect, violating a key assumption of mixed models, we center the data within each city (i.e., subtract the mean value for that city from the value of each covariate).

For each dependent variable, we also assess whether the effects of any of our covariates vary across cities (i.e., whether the effects of random coefficients are significant). For burglary, we find that the random coefficient for decade (i.e., the decade variance component) is significant and thus retain this term in this model.

We specify our model as a general linear mixed model and fit it using PROC MIXED in SAS. In addition to the city random effect, we allow for first autocorrelated errors across time within city. (First autocorrelated errors are significant and thus retained in all equations, except for the equation predicting the burglary gender rate ratio.) We based our tests of significance of effects on Wald statistics that use the empirically adjusted

TABLE 5.1
Women's Relative Economic Marginalization and Gender Rate Ratios of Arrest

Covariates	Aggravated Assault	Robbery	Other Assault	Burglary	Larceny
Poverty Concentration in Female-Headed Families	−0.386 (0.329)	1.00** (0.372)	−0.349 (0.318)	0.014 (0.345)	−0.746 (0.433)
Relative Rate of High School Education	−1.625*** (0.423)	−0.446 (0.404)	−0.209 (0.617)	−0.199 (0.474)	0.099 (0.456)
Relative Rate of Unemployment	0.678*** (0.174)	0.141 (0.201)	0.382** (0.147)	0.523*** (0.152)	0.392** (0.135)
Relative Rate of Service Work	−0.050 (0.048)	−0.054 (0.093)	−0.070 (0.065)	−0.048 (0.053)	0.095 (0.062)
Decade	0.062 (0.042)	0.086** (0.032)	0.097 (0.053)	0.262*** (0.043)	0.094* (0.044)
City Population (in millions)	0.068 (0.103)	0.172 (0.162)	0.255*** (0.072)	0.053 (0.127)	−0.102 (0.107)
City Variance Component	0.009 (0.006)	0.005 (0.007)	0.012* (0.006)	0.050*** (0.017)	0.025*** (0.007)
Decade Variance Component	—	—	—	0.003*** (0.001)	—

NOTE: Numbers in parentheses are standard errors.
* $p \leq 0.05$; ** $p \leq 0.01$; *** $p \leq 0.005$
All models include an AR 1 error process, except for the model predicting burglary.

standard errors.[45] This procedure gives a robust and consistent estimate of the standard error, even if we have misspecified it in our model. We estimate our models using REML (Residual Maximum Likelihood) estimation.

We report the best-fitting model for each offense type, as indicated in Table 5.1. The models that we use control for unobserved heterogeneity across cities and accommodate within-city autocorrelation among responses over time. We use a relatively robust estimation method, thus analyses are arguably conservative.

Findings: Economic Marginalization and Gender Rate Ratios of Arrest

We estimate the model described above for each of the gender arrest rate ratios in Table 5.1. Our analyses use the 385 data points that remain after deletion of missing data. The pattern of findings is consistent with an economic marginalization explanation of variation across time and city in the gender rate ratios of arrest, for both violent and property offenses. Although the specific covariates capturing women's economic marginalization vary somewhat across equation, every crime type examined is associated with at least one dimension of women's disadvantage relative to men.

For example, Table 5.1 shows that even after controlling for unobserved heterogeneity across cities, population size, and decade, the gender rate ratio of aggravated assault is largest when women's rates of unemployment are higher relative to men's rates. In addition, as women's relative rates of high school completion increase, the gender rate ratio of arrests for aggravated assaults is reduced. We see some similarity in our analysis of the gender rate ratio of other assault: as women's rates of unemployment climb relative to those of men, the gender rate ratio of other assault increases. Our analysis does not, however, uncover an important association between the gender rate ratios of high school graduation and other assault.

In the case of robbery, we find that the gender rate ratio of arrests is largest when poverty is most concentrated in female-headed families. We do not find that the gender rate ratio of unemployment is associated with the gender gap in robbery. Overall, however, our findings show that indicators of economic marginalization are associated with variation in the gender gap in three violent offenses that have received little attention in the literature on gender and crime. These findings are consistent with other findings in criminology that link economic disadvantage with increases in violence.[46]

With regard to property offenses, Table 5.1 shows that the gender rate ratios of both burglary and larceny increase along with women's relative unemployment rates. When women's unemployment rates climb relative to those of men, the gender gaps in arrests for burglary and larceny are both reduced. We do not find evidence that either high school graduation or the concentration of poverty in female-headed families is important once unobserved differences across cities and the other variables in our model are controlled.

In short, these analyses present evidence consistent with an economic marginalization explanation of changes in gender ratios of crime, for both violent and property offending. Interestingly, a key indicator of women's economic marginalization—the ratio of female-to-male unemployment rates—appears to be consequential for all but one of the offenses examined here.

Finally, we note that the city variance components are significant for other assault, burglary, and larceny (see Table 5.1). In addition, the linear time trend—the decade effect—remains significant for robbery, larceny, and burglary. This indicates that after controlling for the covariates in Table 5.1, variation across cities in the rate ratios of some offenses and variation over time in the rate ratios of other offenses are still substantial. Furthermore, the variance component for decade also is statistically significant in the equations predicting other assaults and burglary, indicating that the decade or time trend in the gender rate ratios of these offenses are not the same across all cities in the sample. Together, this indicates that our substantive variables are not explaining all the variability over time and across cities in the gender rate ratios of crime. Future research on this issue should seek to identify other covariates that might add to our understanding of this unexplained variability. We suggest some potential candidates in the conclusion.

Conclusions

The present study extends the scant previous research on the association between the gender gap in offending and women's economic hardships. Specifically, we present analyses of unique data that allow for the simultaneous examination of variation across a sample of U.S. cities and over three decades. Because we use a robust estimation method, the findings from our analyses are arguably conservative. Our findings offer support for an economic marginalization explanation of variation over time and across cities in gender rate ratios of violent as well as property crime.

Generally, we find that in cities and times when women are socioeconomically disadvantaged relative to men, the gender rate ratio of arrests increases, indicating that women are accounting for a bigger share of arrests. Most important, we find that as women's unemployment rates increase relative to those of men, women account for a larger proportion of arrests for most of the crimes examined here. We also find that when poverty is concentrated in female-headed families, the gender gap in one violent crime, robbery, is decreased. Finally, we find that as the relative rates of female-to-male high school graduation decrease, the gender rate ratio of aggravated assault increases.

Our findings not only indicate support for the economic marginalization thesis, but they also highlight the need to view women's economic circumstances in comparison with men's, consistent with recent statements on women's poverty.[47] Moreover, our findings demonstrate important variation in the gender gap in crime across cities, as well as over time, which has been neglected in the literature on women's crime to date. All this is to say that the gender gap in crime does, in fact, vary across place as well as time and that the economic marginalization of women relative to men helps to explain these patterns.

We note that although we did not set out to test a liberation explanation of variation on gender rate ratios, our findings are inconsistent with this perspective. Indeed, the logic of the liberation argument would predict that as women's employment and education increase relative to men's, the gender gap should narrow. Our findings, of course, are just the opposite. Indeed, our study suggests that economic oppression, rather than economic liberation, may be at the root of the narrowing of the gender gap in crime over the past four decades.

In addition, our findings are not consistent with the argument made by some scholars that increases in women's crime are tied to the proliferation of consumerism combined with women's primary family roles as consumers.[48] Our findings regarding serious street crimes—aggravated assault, robbery, and burglary—do not support this variant of the opportunity explanation. The consumerism explanation may be better suited to our findings regarding larceny and fraud, yet even here, considering the role of economic marginalization seems important for understanding changes over time.

We do not propose that the analyses reported here capture the complete substantive picture of variation across time and place in the gender gap in crime. Indeed, we found a significant degree of remaining variation across cities in gender rate ratios for some crimes, even after we had taken all our measures of economic marginalization into account. One very important dimension of women's economic well-being that is not addressed by the analyses reported here is the role of the welfare safety net. Government entitlement programs have been steadily reduced since the 1970s.[49] Moreover, the Personal Responsibility and Work Opportunity Reconciliation Act of 1996 (PRWORA) has reduced benefits and restricted time limits for assistance, which may have affected the economic well-being of women relative to men in ways that are not captured in the present analysis. Indeed, several scholars have argued that PRWORA will increase poverty and make the lives of low-income families qualitatively worse.[50] What we know to date is that changes in welfare programs have further eroded the safety net and made it more difficult for the poor—most notably female-headed families—to make ends meet. Consequently, future research on women's relative economic marginalization and gender ratios of crime will do well to consider the role of welfare reforms.

We also have not considered how the increased criminalization of drug offenses and corresponding increases in mass imprisonment of women and men may figure into the processes described here.[51] These important social phenomena may well have compounded the marginalization of poor women in the United States in ways that have yet to be explored. This is another issue that will be important for future research on economic marginalization explanations of the gender gap in crime.

In sum, the present study brings new data to bear on an unresolved question regarding women's offending. The empirical findings suggest that gendered patterns of offending across time and cities are linked with women's economic hardships, yet understanding this phenomenon more fully will require further research.

NOTES

1. Steven Box, *Recession, Crime, and Punishment* (London: Macmillan, 1987).

2. Karen Heimer, "Changes in the Gender Gap in Crime and Women's Economic Marginalization," in *Criminal Justice 2000*, vol. 1, *The Nature of Crime and Continuity and Change*, ed. Gary LaFree, pp. 427–483 (Washington, DC: National Institute of Justice, 2000).

3. See Darrell Steffensmeier, Emilie Allan, and Cathy Streifel, "Development and Female Crime: A Cross-National Test of Alternative Explanations," *Social Forces* 68(1989): 262–283; Gwen Hunnicutt and Lisa M. Broidy, "Liberation and Economic Marginalization: A Reformulation and Test of (Formerly?) Competing Models," *Journal of Research in Crime and Delinquency* 41 (2004): 130–155.

4. We selected the one hundred largest U.S. cities in 1970, based on population counts published by the U.S. Census Bureau.

5. For discussion, see Steven Box and Chris Hale, "Liberation and Female Criminality in England and Wales," *British Journal of Criminology* 23 (1983): 35–49.

6. Gender rate ratios are typically computed as female arrest rate (population adjusted) divided by male arrest rate (population adjusted). Gender ratios are number of female arrests divided by number of male arrests and are therefore not population, or rate, adjusted. Gender differences in arrest rates are typically computed as female rate subtracted from male rate.

7. See, for example, Darrell J. Steffensmeier, "Sex Differences in Patterns of Adult Crime, 1965–1977: A Review and Assessment," *Social Forces* 58 (1980): 1080–1108; Darrell J. Steffensmeier and Michael J. Cobb, "Sex Differences in Urban Arrest Patterns, 1934–79," *Social Problems* 29 (1981): 37–50.

8. Steffensmeier, "Sex Differences in Patterns of Adult Crime."

9. Robert M. O'Brien, "Measuring the Convergence/Divergence of 'Serious Crime' Arrest Rates for Males and Females," *Journal of Quantitative Criminology* 15 (1999): 97–114; Heimer, "Changes in the Gender Gap."

10. It is possible that the gender rate ratios in offending also vary across age groups. However, there is no existing study of this, and because some of the key variables that tap economic marginalization are not available for different age groups, we do not address this issue in the present chapter.

11. The two most recent studies of gender differences in arrest rates over time, which include data for the 1990s, are by O'Brien and Heimer. See O'Brien, "Measuring the Convergence/Divergence"; Heimer, "Changes in the Gender Gap."

12. Heimer, "Changes in the Gender Gap."

13. Darrell J. Steffensmeier and Dana Haynie, "Gender, Structural Disadvantage, and Urban Crime: Do Macrosocial Variables Explain Female Offending Rates?" *Criminology* 38 (2000): 403–439; Hunnicutt and Broidy, "Liberation and Economic Marginalization."

14. Freda Adler, *Sisters in Crime* (New York: McGraw-Hill, 1975); Rita James Simon, *Women and Crime* (Lexington, MA: Lexington Books, 1975).

15. For example, see Darrell J. Steffensmeier, "Crime and the Contemporary Woman: An Analysis of Changing Levels of Female Property Crime, 1960–75," *Social Forces* 57 (1978): 566–584; Steffensmeier, "Sex Differences in Patterns of Adult Crime"; Darrell J. Steffensmeier, "National Trends in Female Arrests, 1960–1990: Assessment and Recommendations for Research," *Journal of Quantitative Criminology* 9 (1993): 413–441; Darrell J. Steffensmeier and Emilie Allan, "Gender and Crime: Toward a Gendered Theory of Female Offending," *Annual Review of Sociology* 22 (1996): 459–487; see also Peggy C. Giordano, Sandra Kerbel, and Sandra Dudley, "The Economics of Female Criminality: An Analysis of Police Blotters, 1890–1975," in *Women and Crime in America,* ed. L. H. Bowker, pp. 65–82 (New York: Macmillan, 1981).

16. See, for example, Kathleen Daly, "Gender and Varieties of White-Collar Crime," *Criminology* 27 (1989): 769–794.

17. Box, *Recession, Crime, and Punishment,* 42–43.

18. Steven Box and Chris Hale, "Liberation/Emancipation, Economic Marginalization, or Less Chivalry: Relevance of Three Theoretical Arguments to Female Crime Patterns in England and Wales, 1951–1980," *Criminology* 22 (1984): 473–497; Box and Hale, "Liberation and Female Criminality in England and Wales."

19. Darrell J. Steffensmeier and Cathy Streifel, "Time-Series Analysis of the Female Percentage of Arrests for Property Crimes, 1960–1985: A Test of Alternative Explanations," *Justice Quarterly* 9 (1992): 77–103.

20. Hunnicutt and Broidy, "Liberation and Economic Marginalization."

21. Steffensmeier and Streifel, "Time-Series Analysis."

22. Robert M. O'Brien, "Levels of Analysis," in *Encyclopedia of Sociology,* ed. E.

Borgatta and M. Borgatta, pp. 1107–1112 (New York: Macmillan, 1992); Marc Ridel, "Sources of Homicide Data," in *Homicide: A Sourcebook of Social Research,* ed. M. D. Smith and M. A Zahn, pp. 75–95 (Thousand Oaks, CA: Sage, 1999).

23. U.S. Federal Bureau of Investigation, *Crime in the United States* (Washington, DC: Federal Bureau of Investigation, U.S. Department of Justice, 2000).

24. Hunnicutt and Broidy, "Liberation and Economic Marginalization."

25. Steffensmeier, Allan, and Streifel, "Development and Female Crime."

26. Steffensmeier and Haynie, "Gender, Structural Disadvantage, and Urban Crime."

27. Suzanne M. Bianchi, "Feminization and Juvenilization of Poverty: Trends, Relative Risks, Causes, and Consequences," *Annual Review of Sociology* 25 (1999): 307–333; Sara S. McLanahan and Erin L. Kelly, "The Feminization of Poverty: Past and Future," in *Handbook of the Sociology of Gender,* ed. Janet Saltzman Chafetz, pp. 127–145 (New York: Kluwer, 1999).

28. Diana Pearce, "The Feminization of Poverty: Women, Work, and Welfare," *Urban and Social Change Review* 11 (1978): 128–136; Annemette Sorensen and Sara McLanahan, "Married Women's Economic Dependency, 1940–1980," *American Journal of Sociology* 93(3) (1987): 659–687.

29. Bianchi, "Feminization and Juvenilization of Poverty"; McLanahan and Kelly, "Feminization of Poverty."

30. Bianchi, "Feminization and Juvenilization of Poverty," 311, fig. 1. Note that the relative risk of poverty increased most for elderly women (over sixty-five) during this period.

31. We note that all the studies reported here are based on national-level data and may be prone to some of the issues of aggregation bias that we discussed earlier with regard to arrest data.

32. Bianchi, "Feminization and Juvenilization of Poverty"; McLanahan and Kelly, "Feminization of Poverty."

33. Ibid. See also Mary Jo Bane and Daniel T. Ellwood, "One Fifth of the Nation's Children: Why Are They Poor?" *Science* 245 (1989): 1047–1053.

34. See Kathryn Edin and Laura Lein, *Making Ends Meet: How Single Mothers Survive Welfare and Low-Wage Work* (New York: Russell Sage Foundation, 1997); John Iceland, *Poverty in America* (Berkeley: University of California Press, 2003).

35. Ibid. See also Harrell R. Rodgers Jr., *American Poverty in a New Era of Reform* (Armonk, NY: M. E. Sharpe, 2000).

36. See Peter Gottschalk, "Inequality, Income Growth, and Mobility: The Basic Facts," *Journal of Economic Perspectives* 11 (1997): 21–40; Richard B. Freeman and Lawrence F. Katz, eds., *Differences and Changes in Wage Structures* (Chicago: University of Chicago Press, 1995); Jared Bernstein and Lawrence Mishel, "Has Wage Inequality Stopped Growing?" *Monthly Labor Review* (December 1997): 3–6.

37. See Suzanne M. Bianchi, "Changing Economic Roles of Women and Men,"

in *State of the Union: America in the 1990s,* vol. 1, ed. R. Farley, pp. 107–154 (New York: Russell Sage Foundation, 1995); Edin and Lein, *Making Ends Meet*; Emily Northrup, "The Feminization of Poverty: The Demographic Factor and the Composition of Economic Growth," *Journal of Economic Issues* 24 (1990): 145–161; Joan Smith, "The Paradox of Women's Poverty: Wage-Earning Women and Economic Transformation," *Signs* 10 (1982): 291–310.

38. The 1970 population figures for the cities in our sample ranged from over one hundred thousand (115,420) to over seven million (7,867,760). There were thirty-one cities with populations less than two hundred thousand and six cities with populations greater than one million in 1970.

39. We include data from sixteen northeastern cities, twenty-eight midwestern cities, thirty-five southern cities, and twenty-one western cities.

40. O'Brien, "Measuring the Convergence/Divergence"; Heimer, "Changes in the Gender Gap." Note that we do not examine murder in the present study. Unlike for every other UCR offense category, the gender rate ratio of arrests for murder has shown a steady decline since 1960. Because this offense clearly shows a different pattern than all others, its explanation likely requires a very different theoretical approach, which is beyond the scope of the present chapter.

41. The arrest data for 1970, 1980, and 1990 come from publicly available data archived by the Intercollegiate Consortium on Political and Social Data at the Institute for Social Research, University of Michigan. The data are from Study #2538 archived by the Inter-University Consortium for Political and Social Research, Principal Investigators, Roland Chilton and Dee Weber, "Uniform Crime Reporting Program Data [United States]: Arrests by Age, Sex, and Race for Police Agencies in Metropolitan Statistical Areas, 1960–1997." From this file, we extracted the data associated with the Originating Agency Identifier (ORI) representing the main agency in each city in our sample. For each decade, we extracted data on the three most proximal years for which data were available, to allow us to take a three-year average to "smooth" the data. Data for 1999 and 2000 were obtained from the Federal Bureau of Investigation. The smoothing of the 2000 data is therefore based on two rather than three values.

42. We population adjust the raw arrest figures using census data because the Uniform Crime Report population counts are not disaggregated by gender. We recognize that the census and UCR figures may not correspond perfectly. However, because we measure arrest rate *ratios,* we only need to know the female-to-male population count ratio, *not* the two disaggregated population counts. It is reasonable to assume that the population count ratio reported by the census is similar to the unreported UCR ratio.

43. As noted, our smoothing procedure uses three-year averages for 1970, 1980, and 1990 and a two-year average for 2000.

44. We note that our measure of service-sector work is not optimal because it

includes a range of service-sector employment, from low-paid unstable jobs to better-paid stable work. This measure was the only available industry measure that was comparable across the census years studied, however.

45. P. J. Huber, "The Behavior of Maximum Likelihood Estimates under Non-standard Conditions," *Proceedings of the Fifth Berkeley Symposium on Mathematical and Statistical Probability* 1 (1967): 221–233; Halbert White, "A Heteroskedasticity-Consistent Covariance Matrix Estimator and a Direct Test for Heteroskedasticity," *Econometrica* 48 (1980): 817–838.

46. See, for example, Lauren J. Krivo and Ruth D. Peterson, "Extremely Disadvantaged Neighborhoods and Urban Crime," *Social Forces* 75 (1996): 619–648.

47. Bianchi, "Feminization and Juvenilization of Poverty."

48. See, for example, Steffensmeier, "Crime and the Contemporary Woman"; and Steffensmeier, "National Trends in Female Arrests."

49. Frances Fox Piven, "Welfare Policy and American Politics," in *Work, Welfare, and Politics: Confronting Poverty in the Wake of Welfare Reform*, ed. F. F. Piven, J. Acker, M. Hallock, and S. Morgan, pp. 19–33 (Eugene: University of Oregon Press, 2002).

50. Randy Albelda and Chris Tilly, *Glass Ceilings and Bottomless Pits: Women's Work, Women's Poverty* (Boston: South End Press, 1997).

51. Meda Chesney-Lind, "Imprisoning Women: The Unintended Victims of Mass Imprisonment," in *Invisible Punishment: The Collateral Consequences of Mass Imprisonment*, ed. Marc Mauer and Meda Chesney-Lind, pp. 79–94 (New York: Free Press, 2002).

Part II

Gendered Victimization
Trajectories, Social Contexts, and Justice

Chapter 6

The Violent Victimization of Women
A Life Course Perspective

Candace Kruttschnitt and Ross Macmillan

Over the past two decades our knowledge and understanding of women's experiences with violent victimization has grown tremendously. Such growth is due in no small part to the public's and the federal government's concern with this problem and the acknowledgment that women's experiences of violent victimization have some unique characteristics.[1] Women are subject to violence across a range of social relationships, notably from parents, siblings, acquaintances, dates or boyfriends, and both current and former partners.[2] Further, women's risks of intimate-partner violence, sexual assault, and stalking are comparatively greater than they are for men. Likewise, their chances of recurrent violent victimization and multiple types of victimization within an intimate relationship are also greater.[3] The current challenge for those interested in understanding violence against women is organizing these facts into a comprehensive understanding of women's victimization.

In general, efforts to formulate a broader understanding of women's victimization have been limited by the relatively narrow research focus, which has followed one of two paths. First, much of the research on women's victimization is relationship specific. This approach is exemplified by work that addresses whether women's experiences with spousal violence differ in form, cause, and consequence from violence in other relationships.[4] Other work contrasts violence from "known men" with violence from strangers and asks similar questions.[5] A key limitation of this approach is that it ignores the possibility, if not likelihood, of violence transcending given relationships; giving attention to this possibility may provide a more accurate "biographical" image of victimization, including its unique risk factors and consequences. Second, there is a complementary body of research that considers differences in the types of violence experienced. Most prominent here is research on sexual victimization and the idea that risk (and consequences) of sexual victimization is distinct from risk (and consequences) of other types of violence.[6] Unfortunately, work in this tradition seldom considers the possibility that different types of violence occur at the same time, because of their association with either a particular offender or particular situations or behaviors.[7] In general, the possibility of violence extending across relationships, forms, and time has received little attention.

In this chapter, we develop and assess a life course perspective to account for women's experiences of violent victimization. This perspective draws attention to the ways in which victimization experiences may unfold over time and across relationships. Augmenting this, sociometric considerations emphasize the types of social relationships and ties that exist and how their unfolding produces distinct patterns of risk over the life span. The identification of life course patterns of victimization also allows us to consider the risk factors for violence and the broader links between sociohistorical context and the patterning and risk of violence against women. We conclude by discussing the implications of both our approach and our findings for theory, research, and public policy.

Women's Victimization over the Life Span: A Life Course Approach

A life course approach to women's victimization can be organized around three issues: relationships with others, individual experiences over a life span, and sociohistorical context.

Relationships and Linked Lives

To what degree do relationships shape the types of violence that occur within them? A key principle in life course research is the notion of linked lives.[8] Individuals are tied to others socially and psychologically, and the nature of these ties influences their experiences and interactions. As Blumstein and Kollock note, relationships have their own internal dynamics and properties. These include patterns of interdependence, interpersonal norms, private cultures, mutual regulation and control, interactional habits, and styles of conflict resolution. Consequently, personal relationships affect people at both a personal (psychological) and social level.[9]

In the context of violence against women, two issues are important. First, the type of relationship likely influences motivations for offending. There is a large body of research that examines violence in the context of relationship dynamics, conflict, and stress. Research associated with the New Hampshire School of Family Violence, for example, views spousal violence as intimately connected to conflicts over domestic matters.[10] Here, violence is directed at a particular partner because that partner has not (or is perceived as having not) lived up to expectations of financial support, domestic responsibility, fidelity, or sexual access. The motivation to offend is thus a direct function of the ongoing relationship. From a different perspective, Macmillan and Gartner suggest that the importance of male "breadwinner" status within marital relationships can produce threats to masculinity and violent reactions when husbands are unable to live up to this expectation.[11] Unemployment among men married to employed women may be particularly problematic and may induce men to attempt to reexert their status and authority through the use of serious, systematic violence. By contrast, acquaintance or stranger relationships are unlikely to produce this kind of motivation.

A second important issue is the opportunity structure for victimization. Put simply, relationships structure how much time is spent with particular individuals, where their time is spent, and the types of activities in which people engage. In a seminal series of papers, Cohen, Felson, and colleagues drew attention to the "necessary conditions" for crime,[12] specifically the convergence in time and space of (a) a potential or motivated offender, (b) a suitable target, and (c) an absence of capable guardianship. While the nature of relationships shapes motivation and determines, by extension, who might be suitable targets, it may also influence the degree to which motivated offenders and suitable targets share time and space and whether this occurs in public or private spaces. For example, stranger relationships may be characterized by "diffuse" motivation in which any female may be a suitable target of victimization, but the relationship may still be conditioned by time (i.e., night rather than day) and location (i.e., secluded rather than open). In contrast, acquaintance relationships may involve a more specific "target," as in the case of acquaintance sexual assault, and may present more opportunity for victimization because of greater time spent together, particularly in private places without others present. Spousal and other family relationships present even greater opportunities for victimization because individuals typically share the same residence and activities in private environments that lack guardianship.[13] Clearly, then, relationships help to determine the form and patterning of violent incidents. Yet aside from some research on intimate partners, little work has empirically assessed the role of relationships in structuring violence against women.

Life Course Linkages

A second aspect of life course theory is the longitudinal progression of lives, or the way in which individual experiences and behaviors are linked over the life span.[14] In what is often referred to as "state dependence," particular experiences are thought to influence later ones by changing the ways people think or act or by altering the social environment in which they live their lives. When considered in the context of women's life histories of victimization, violence experienced at one point in time can influence its existence at another and in multiple relationships across the life span. The notion of *sociometry*, which refers to the patterning of social relationships, rather than focusing on a specific relationship, provides a framework for understanding this type of state dependence.[15] Specifically, sociometry leads us to consider how violence can permeate social networks over time and across relationships. By definition, this directs attention toward various relationships at distinct points in the life span, such as parent-child relationships in childhood, dating/peer relationships in adolescence, and spousal and co-worker relationships in adulthood. It also directs attention to the patterning of violence across relationships. With sufficient detail, this approach can provide individual "biographies of violence," setting the stage for analyses that examine for whom and why such patterns exist.

In the study of violence, most "life course" work has focused on the role of violence in childhood, either physical punishment or child abuse, and its relation to offending and victimization in later life.[16] Some scholars argue that exposure to child abuse provides scripts to individuals that may influence who they choose for a partner[17] and, ultimately, their risk of intimate violence.[18] Others suggest that preferences for particular situations and activities produce "routine activities," both normative and deviant, that may increase exposure to potential offenders and decrease guardianship.[19] For example, research on the consequences of victimization suggests that child abuse increases alcohol and substance use in later life,[20] which, in turn, increases the risk of victimization and, especially, sexual assault.[21] Research on homeless adolescents similarly indicates the co-occurrence of family violence, high-risk life circumstances, and repeated violent victimization in young adulthood.[22]

Beyond such work, efforts to consider the broad patterning of victimization, and the risk factors associated with such patterns, have been quite limited. Some work demonstrates associations between violence in one's family of origin and later spousal victimization, but comparatively little work has considered consequences beyond the family.[23] Other research has examined the relationship between child sexual abuse and sexual victimization in later life,[24] as well as links between child physical abuse and dating violence among college students.[25] Although there is some speculation on an association between dating violence and marital (or cohabitation) violence, supporting evidence is largely anecdotal and does not extend to violence from other individuals.[26] In general, generic links between physical and sexual violence at different stages of the life course have not been explored. Consequently, efforts to differentiate those whose risk of victimization is multifaceted from those whose risk is specific to a given offender or a given relationship are nonexistent.

Gender, Victimization, and Sociohistorical Context

In understanding both the patterning of violence within relationships and of violence across relationships, it is also necessary to consider sociohistorical context, a third key aspect of life course theory. In his classic study *Children of the Great Depression,* Elder meticulously documents how the experience of living through the Great Depression profoundly shaped the life course fortunes of individuals.[27] The experience produced a social structure that influenced how people thought about organizing their lives, the degree to which interpersonal roles and relationships were sources of opportunity or constraint, and whether people were able to exercise agency and actively construct their life experiences in accordance with their aspirations and expectations.[28] Although there have been some efforts to situate aggregate levels of violence in a sociohistorical context,[29] implications at an individual level have received little attention, especially with regard to female victimization.[30] Nevertheless, the sociohistorical context of violence against women is important because it influences the meaning of particular relationships, the routine activities embedded in these relationships and social roles, and even the motivations to offend.

Women's social roles and accompanying relationships have undergone significant transformations over the past half century. This has occurred along several dimensions and has specific consequences for women's experiences with violence. Huber and others, for example, argue that the large-scale movement of women into the paid workforce during the twentieth century had significant consequences for women's experiences in the home.[31] Some scholars have suggested that women's increased labor force participation has created a "backlash" against women and increased the likelihood of their being victims of physical and sexual violence.[32] Moreover, changes in cultural norms regarding sexuality and family have altered behavioral expectations among acquaintances, dates, spouses, and parents, leading some scholars to speculate that this has increased women's risks of victimization, particularly sexual victimization.[33] Finally, although changes in the sociolegal context of families, notably the divorce revolution, have increased women's opportunities for escaping violent relationships, these changes may also have increased their risk of becoming a victim of stalking and serious violence.[34] The changing context surrounding interpersonal relationships, both intimate and other, points to the necessity of considering dimensions of risk within specific sociohistorical contexts.

Summary

There is little question that research on specific types of violence, and studies of contemporary social problems such as dating violence and stalking, have contributed to our understanding of violence against women. Still, the general compartmentalization of the field into distinct types of violence and associated risk factors has resulted in a number of limitations. Most important among these is the failure to either conceptualize or model broader biographical patterns, or distinct typologies, of violent victimization among women that span types of violence, relationships, and the life course. Additionally, there has been no attempt to examine risk factors that may be associated with such patterns and that may illuminate unique causes, causal structures, and consequences.

Consistent with these concerns, the remainder of this chapter has three objectives. First, we use data from a large-scale victimization survey of American women to examine patterns of physical and sexual victimization both within and across a range of victim-offender relationships and the life course. Second, we consider individual risk factors for the life course patterns of victimization we identify. Third, we examine similarity and difference in risk factors for victimization across birth cohorts to illuminate the general influence of sociohistorical context on life course patterns of violence among women. Overall, our research seeks to provide a more historically grounded, biographical account of women's experiences with violence and serves as an initial statement of a life course theory of women's victimization.

Data

The data to be used in this research are unique in their documentation of women's experience with violence. The National Violence against Women Survey (hereafter NVAWS) was jointly sponsored by the National Institute of Justice (NIJ) and the Centers for Disease Control and Prevention (CDC).[35] NVAWS gathered data, from November 1995 to May 1996, from a national sample representative of all households with a telephone in fifty states and the District of Columbia. Overall, a total of 8,000 women and 8,005 men were interviewed using a computer-assisted telephone interviewing system. Our analyses focus on female respondents, although future research should examine similarities and differences in the patterns of victimization across genders. The participation rate for the survey was 72 percent, consistent with other high-quality surveys of crime and violence.[36] As violence is a statistically rare phenomenon and multiple victimization both within and across relationships is even rarer, the large sample size of the NVAWS is necessary to provide enough statistical power for our analyses.

A unique feature of the NVAWS is the breadth of its measurement of violence experienced by women. A key criticism of prior research on violence against women, including the National Crime Victimization Survey, is that it does not effectively measure the various forms of violence experienced by women.[37] This includes sexual and physical violence perpetrated by family members, dates, spouses, and other men known to the victim. An explicit objective of the NVAWS was to document the various types of violence that women experience while simultaneously identifying the wide range of social relationships in which women are embedded. Our analyses will examine the multifaceted prevalence of violence in the context of *parents, other relatives, partners, dates, acquaintances,* and *strangers.*[38] This set of relationships provides a reasonable index of Blumstein and Kollock's "property space" of relationships, which differentiates kin versus nonkin, sexual-romantic versus non-sexual-romantic, cohabiting versus noncohabiting, and hierarchical versus egalitarian relationships and includes both cross-sex and same-sex relationships.[39]

The types of violence considered include sexual assault,[40] stalking,[41] and different types of physical violence such as being pushed, grabbed, or shoved; being slapped or hit; having hair pulled; being kicked or bitten; being choked or beaten up; having someone throw something at them or being hit with some object; or being threatened or attacked with a gun or some other form of weapon. For the purposes of our research, we restrict our sample to those who reported at least one current or prior relationship (N = 6,937) in order to incorporate partner victimization into our analyses.

Prevalence of Victimization

Table 6.1 reports the likelihood of victimization by the type of victimization and the victim-offender relationship. Although general risk of victimization is low, relationship type has a strong impact on the nature and extent of the violence women experience. The risk of being stalked is highest among partner relations (3.8%), more than double that found with acquaintances (1.5%) or strangers (1.7%); risk is lowest among relatives (0.2%) and dates (0.8%). Sexual victimization is also high in partner relationships (2.8%) and among relatives (2.9%) and acquaintances (2.2%), but it is somewhat lower among dates (1.5%) and strangers (1.4%).

Physical victimization shows a different pattern of risk. In general, risk is highest in the context of parent-child relationships and partner relationships. One-third of women report being slapped by a parent, and more than 15 percent had an object thrown at them, were hit with an object, or were pushed, grabbed, or shoved. Risk of other forms of violence, ranging from having hair pulled to being threatened or attacked with a weapon, varies from 2 to 10 percent.[42] At the same time, more than 15 percent of women reported being pushed, grabbed, shoved, or slapped by a partner, and between 8 and 10 percent had their hair pulled, had something thrown at them or were hit with something, or were choked or beaten up. Approximately 5 percent of women were kicked or threatened or attacked with a weapon by a partner. Risk of physical violence of any sort is lower among dates, acquaintances, and strangers, typically affecting

TABLE 6.1
Rates of Victimization: Type of Victimization by Relationship, NVAWS, 1995

	Parent	Relative	Partner	Date	Acquaintance	Stranger
Stalking	N/A	.2%	3.8%	.8%	1.5%	1.7%
Sexual assault	N/A	2.9%	2.8%	1.5%	2.2%	1.4%
Choked or beaten	5.1%	.6%	10.1%	.9%	.7%	.7%
Object, thrown at or hit with	17.7%	.6%	8.6%	.8%	.9%	.6%
Weapon, threat or use	1.7%	.2%	5.1%	.5%	.6%	1.3%
Kicked	2.1%	.3%	5.3%	.5%	.6%	.4%
Pulled hair	10.6%	.7%	8.6%	1.0%	1.0%	.7%
Slapped	33.4%	1.2%	15.1%	1.9%	1.5%	1.1%
Pushed	15.0%	1.1%	17.1%	2.3%	2.1%	1.7%

only about 2 percent or less of the women in this sample. The lowest rates of physical violence occur among relatives.

Violence within Relationships

Our examination of the patterns of victimization over time and across relationships uses latent class analysis.[43] Latent class analysis provides a direct means of assessing whether different relationships are characterized by distinct patterns of violence within them. It does so by cross-classifying different types of violent acts and then examining the degree to which particular classes or clusters of violent acts appear within a given relationship. For example, Macmillan and Gartner demonstrate that partner relationships are characterized by several distinct classes of violence that reflect variation in the number and extent of violent acts, but we expect that stranger relationships will involve fewer types of violence, perhaps distinguishing between sexual and physical violence.[44]

Latent class analysis accounts for the association between a set of manifest variables by specifying a latent construct that accounts for their association. However, latent class analysis is distinct from other latent variable approaches, notably covariance structure or "LISREL" models, in that it makes possible the characterization of a multidimensional, discrete latent variable from a cross-classification of two or more observed discrete variables. Most generally, this can be expressed as:

$$\pi_{ij...mt}^{AB...EX} = \pi_{it}^{\bar{A}X} \times \pi_{jt}^{\bar{B}X} \times ... \times \pi_{mt}^{\bar{E}X} \times \pi_{t}^{X},$$

where $\pi_{ij...mt}^{AB...EX}$ is the probability that a randomly selected case will be located in the i, j, m, t cell, $\pi_{it}^{\bar{A}X}$ is the conditional probability that a case in class t of the latent variable X will be located in category i of variable A, $\pi_{jt}^{\bar{B}X}$ is the conditional probability of being in category j of variable B, $\pi_{mt}^{\bar{E}X}$ is the conditional probability of being in category m of variable E, and π_t^X is the probability of a randomly selected case being in class t of the latent variable X.

A latent class approach produces a latent variable that defines the relevant classes of violence and the types of violence that characterize them. This generates an empirical typology of violence that is characterized by the *pattern* of violent victimization that an individual respondent experiences. This approach permits examination of whether all forms of violence cohere in distinct patterns or whether distinct patterns exist for specific types of violence. This provides a lens for assessing the utility of prior practices of examining the causes and consequences of distinct types of female victimization (i.e., sexual versus physical victimization), as well as a framework for examining patterns of violence across relationships.

Three sets of statistics guide our analyses. First, goodness of fit statistics indicate (a) whether a set of variables has any significant association and (b) the number of classes that are necessary to adequately represent the data. Our analyses include the likelihood ratio chi-square statistic (L^2) and its corresponding degrees of freedom and p-value, the index of dissimilarity (Δ), and the BIC statistic. A nonsignificant likelihood ratio chi-square statistic, an index of dissimilarity less than .05, and a large negative BIC statistic indicate a good fit to the data. In general, we look for consistency in fit across indictors. Second, conditional probabilities for specific types of violence indicate risk associated with particular classes. Such probabilities range from 0 to 1, with higher values indicating increased risk. Conditional probabilities apply to each type of violence examined and together indicate cumulative risk. In other words, a particular class that has high probabilities on more than one type of violence indicates multifaceted risk. Finally, latent class probabilities associated with particular classes indicate the expected prevalence of a particular pattern of violence and identify the size of the population that could be expected to experience it. This indicates more or less common patterns of violence.

Results

Goodness of fit statistics in Table 6.2 reveal significant variation in the patterning of victimization across relationships. A one-class model fits

TABLE 6.2
Goodness of Fit Statistics: Type of Violence by Relationship Type, NVAWS, 1995

Relationship	Number of Classes	L2	df	P-value	ID	BIC
Parent	I	6623.68	120	0.000	0.32	5563.75
	II	959.59	112	0.000	0.08	−29.78
	III	172.16	104	0.000	0.02	−746.44
	IV	124.59	97	0.031	0.01	−732.19
Relative	I	153.15	502	1.000	0.01	−4268.35
	II	183.44	493	1.000	0.01	−4158.79
	III	119.34	485	1.000	0.01	−4152.43
	IV	110.43	483	1.000	0.01	−4143.73
Partner	I	6252.65	502	0.000	0.28	1831.15
	II	1370.78	492	0.000	0.07	−2962.65
	III	529.71	482	0.066	0.03	−3715.64
	IV	393.33	473	0.997	0.03	−3772.75
Date	I	548.62	502	0.074	0.03	−3872.81
	II	264.79	492	1.000	0.01	−4068.55
	III	185.79	482	1.000	0.01	−4068.29
	IV	159.04	473	1.000	0.01	−4059.81
Acquaintance	I	437.44	502	0.983	0.02	−3984.29
	II	238.54	492	1.000	0.01	−4095.1
	III	201.71	482	1.000	0.01	−4043.85
	IV	167.57	479	1.000	0.01	−4051.56
Stranger	I	117.68	502	1.000	0.01	−4303.98
	II	195.84	493	1.000	0.01	−4146.54
	III	137.04	485	1.000	0.01	−4134.88
	IV	120.41	479	1.000	0.01	−4098.66

the data by conventional criteria in the cases of relatives, dates,[45] acquaintances, and strangers. This indicates that risk of any specific violent act is essentially independent of the risk of experiencing other violent acts within these relationships. People who experience one type of violence are not significantly more likely to experience another form of violence. Thus, there are no identifiable patterns of violence in each of these relationships.[46] In contrast, both parent-child and partner relationships are characterized by more complex patterns of violence. In parent-child relationships, three distinct patterns of violence are apparent.[47] And in partner relationships, four patterns of violence provide an adequate fit to the data.

For parent-child relationships (see left panel, Table 6.3), the first class involves a relatively low probability of experiencing any form of violence. All probabilities are less than .16, and all except one are below .05. In addition, there is virtually no likelihood of being threatened or attacked

TABLE 6.3
*Latent Class and Conditional Probabilities: Parent and
Partner Victimization, NVAWS, 1995*

| | Relationship Type | | | | | | |
| | Parent | | | Partner | | | |
Violence Type	I	II	III	I	II	III	IV
Throw/hit	0.037	0.562	0.911	0.002	0.216	0.432	1.000
Push	0.012	0.510	0.984	0.009	0.715	0.969	0.993
Pull hair	0.016	0.298	0.892	0.007	0.101	0.598	0.975
Slapped	0.156	0.883	0.978	0.006	0.494	0.981	0.992
Kicked	0.004	0.026	0.482	0.001	0.016	0.318	0.828
Beaten/choked	0.002	0.093	0.817	0.001	0.135	0.792	0.951
Weapon	0.002	0.034	0.349	0.001	0.115	0.250	0.642
Sexual assault	NA	NA	NA	0.006	0.056	0.126	0.244
Stalking	NA	NA	NA	0.005	0.081	0.159	0.478
Latent Class Probability	0.754	0.199	0.047	0.813	0.082	0.071	0.033

with a weapon, being beaten or choked, or being kicked (.002, .002, and .004, respectively). With a latent class probability of .754, this pattern of violence characterizes almost three-quarters of the sample. We define this pattern as essentially *no violence.*

A second class involves a very high likelihood of being slapped (.883), a high likelihood of having something thrown at them or being hit with an object (.562) and of being pushed, grabbed, or shoved (.510), and a moderate risk of having hair pulled (.298). Equally important, the risk of more severe and more systematic[48] violence is relatively low for this group, who comprise almost 20 percent of the sample (.199). We consider this class of violence to be characteristic of *physical aggression.*

A final class involves multifaceted violence and substantial risk of the more severe and systematic types of violence. The risk of having something thrown at them or being hit with an object, being pushed, grabbed, or shoved, having hair pulled, and being slapped are very high, as are their risks of being beaten up or choked (.817 to .984), being kicked or bitten (.482), and being threatened or attacked with a weapon (.349). The combined high probabilities for multiple types of violence indicate a combination of many different violent acts, making this group distinct. When combined with the increased prevalence of the more serious forms of violence, this suggests a pattern of *abuse* that characterizes almost 5 percent of the sample.

Patterned violence is also characteristic of partner relationships with four distinct classes (see right panel, Table 6.3). A first class involves a very low, almost negligible risk of violence. All probabilities are below .01, indicating that less than 1 percent of the women in this class can be expected to experience any type of violence. This pattern can be seen to characterize over 80 percent of the sample (.813) and can be considered as essentially *no violence*. A second class involves a generally high risk of being pushed, grabbed, or shoved (.715), moderate risk of being slapped (.494), and low but non-negligible risk of having something thrown at them or being hit with an object (.216). The risk of encountering other types of violence, including sexual assault and stalking, is also generally low (< .14). The nature of these probabilities suggests that this pattern of violence is not multifaceted, does not involve more serious and injurious types of violence, and does not typically involve sexual assault or stalking. This pattern characterizes just over 8 percent of the sample (.082) and might best be regarded as *interpersonal conflict violence.*[49]

A third class characterizes a similar proportion of the sample (.071), but this pattern of violence is more multifaceted. It involves very high probabilities of being pushed, grabbed, or shoved (.969), being slapped (.981), and being beaten up or choked (.792). Likewise, the risk of having hair pulled (.598), having something thrown at them or being hit with an object (.432), being kicked (.318), and being threatened or attacked with a weapon (.250) are substantial. Still, this pattern of violence is largely confined to physical assaults, as the risk of being sexually assaulted (.126) and being stalked are comparatively low (.159). As the violence in this class is multifaceted but generally confined to physical violence, we define this pattern of violence as *physical abuse.*

A final class of violence is also multifaceted, but it involves a comparatively greater risk of the more injurious types of violence and both sexual assault and stalking. In general, this pattern of violence involves having something thrown at them or being hit with an object (1.000), being pushed, grabbed, or shoved (.993), having hair pulled (.975), being slapped (.992), being beaten up or choked (.951), and being kicked (.828). Likewise, the risk of being threatened or attacked with a weapon is high (.642), as is the risk of being stalked (.478). This pattern of violence involves physical violence combined with a comparatively high risk of sexual assault (.244). Characterizing just over 3 percent of the sample (.033), this pattern typifies the kind of *systematic abuse* that has been the focus of considerable public policy and criminal justice attention.[50]

Violence across Relationships and the Life Course

To examine the issue of whether there are distinct patterns of victimization across relationships and across the life course, we cross-classify victimization risk across the six relationship types described earlier and then perform a second latent class analysis.[51] Goodness of fit statistics are shown in Table 6.4. A one-class model provides a very poor fit to the data according to all criteria and indicates a patterning to violence *across relationships*. A three-class model provides a good fit to the data according to the likelihood ratio chi-square test (183.17, 162 *df*, p > .10) and the index of dissimilarity (.02).[52] Substantively, this indicates that three distinct patterns of violence across relationships and the life course characterize the sample of American women.

Table 6.5 shows conditional and latent class probabilities for the three-class model and reveals the nature and extent of these specific patterns of risk. The first class involves those women whose risk of violence is low across all relationships. There is a small likelihood of physical punishment in childhood (.066) but virtually no risk of abuse (.001). This is combined with very little risk of violence from relatives (.010), dates (.029), acquaintances (.028), and strangers (.031). These women also have only a small probability of experiencing interpersonal conflict violence (.064) or the more serious and multifaceted types of partner violence (.040 and .013 for physical and systematic abuse, respectively). This pattern of violence encompasses almost three-quarters (.746) of the sample. We characterize this pattern of violence as *atypical violence*.

A second pattern of violence involves a high likelihood of physical aggression in childhood (.687) but a relatively low likelihood of abuse (.052). This is also combined with low risks of violence from relatives (.101), dates (.093), acquaintances (.140), and strangers (.109). However, these women do have a moderate risk of experiencing partner violence, particularly

TABLE 6.4
Goodness of Fit Statistics: Sociometry of Victimization, NVAWS, 1995

Number of Classes	L2	df	P-value	ID	BIC
I	1211.65	182.00	0.000	0.14	−388.09
II	245.11	173.00	0.000	0.03	−1275.52
III	183.17	162.00	0.122	0.02	−1240.78
IV	153.53	154.00	0.496	0.02	−1200.10
IV-Fixed	182.71	161.00	0.116	0.03	−1232.44

TABLE 6.5
Latent Class and Conditional Probabilities: Sociometric Analysis, NVAWS, 1995

Relationship			Violence Pattern		
			I	II	III
Parent	I	None	0.934	0.261	0.374
	II	Physical aggression	0.066	0.687	0.119
	III	Abuse	0.001	0.052	0.507
Relative	I	No	0.990	0.899	0.708
	II	Yes	0.010	0.101	0.292
Date	I	No	0.971	0.907	0.900
	II	Yes	0.029	0.093	0.100
Acquaintance	I	No	0.972	0.860	0.804
	II	Yes	0.028	0.140	0.196
Stranger	I	No	0.968	0.891	0.855
	II	Yes	0.031	0.109	0.145
Partner	I	None	0.883	0.567	0.426
	II	IPCV	0.064	0.222	0.140
	III	Physical abuse	0.040	0.142	0.179
	IV	Systematic abuse	0.013	0.069	0.255
Latent Class Probability			0.746	0.193	0.061

interpersonal conflict violence (.222) or physical abuse (.142), but their risk of systematic abuse is low (.069). In general, this pattern does not suggest a multifaceted risk of victimization across relationships or the life span. Instead, it suggests that women's experiences of violence are largely confined to family relationships. This pattern characterizes almost 20 percent of the sample (.193). We define this pattern of victimization as *parent-partner violence*.

The final pattern of violence we uncovered is multifaceted, stretching across relationships and across the life span. It involves a high risk of violence in childhood, particularly abusive violence (.507), and it is coupled with a comparatively high risk of violence from relatives (.292), dates (.100), acquaintances (.196), and strangers (.145). This pattern of violence also involves greater risk of more-serious partner violence, particularly systematic abuse (.255). Given the elevated risk of violence that appears across relationships, we define this pattern as *multifaceted-multirelationship violence*.

Risk Factors

Previous research on specific types of violence (e.g., sexual assault) and on the nature of violence within specific relationships (e.g., partner violence, child abuse) indicates a number of important risk factors. Prior research has not, however, examined such risk factors in the context of patterned violence across relationships and the life span. We do so in the following section with respect to *age, race, employment status, educational attainment, personal income, household income, poverty, marital status,* and *parenthood.* In general, these demographic, economic, and relationship factors are thought to be important for understanding variation in individual risk of victimization.[53] A full description of these variables is provided in Appendix 6.1.

We emphasize that our objective here is simply to document factors that are associated with different patterns of risk. We cannot conclude that such factors are causes of violence because (a) our descriptions of victimization experiences span multiple years and some violent incidents occurred before our risk factors were measured (for example, employment, marriage, parenthood), and (b) it is very likely that several of these factors may be influenced by victimization experiences. Victimization and its consequences likely have notable effects on educational and income attainments and on social relationships over the life span.[54] Nonetheless, it is important to identify factors that are associated with the different patterns of risk we have identified.

Before discussing the results, it is important to note that age has unique significance in these analyses. All our violence measures indicate lifetime prevalence of victimization. Age is thus best viewed as a measure of cohort, and age effects reveal cohort variation in the patterns of violence that women experience. Specifically, they reveal whether women born in the latter decades of the twentieth century have different types of risks than those that were born earlier. As such, it provides some evidence of the importance of sociohistorical context in shaping women's experiences with violence both within and across relationships. Later we use this variable to consider changing dimensions of risk based on age cohort.

To examine risk factors for the different patterns of violence over time and across relationships, we employ multinomial or polychotomous logistic regression.[55] In a multinomial logistic regression equation, the expected probabilities of having a particular pattern of violence depend in nonlinear ways on a set of K risk factors that predict them. The relationship is given by a multivariate logistic distribution function:

$$P_{ij} = \frac{e^{\Sigma \alpha + \beta_{kj} X_{kji}}}{\sum^{J} e^{\Sigma \alpha + \beta_{kj} X_{kji}}}$$

where p_{ij} = the probability that the ith case is in the jth category of the dependent variable. In substantive terms, this models the overall likelihood that a particular individual experiences a particular pattern of violence. Similar to conventional, binomial logistic regression, parameter estimates β can be interpreted in terms of the effect of the particular factor on the log-odds of experiencing a particular pattern of violence or by extension, through e^β, their effect on the odds of victimization. As the risk factors we consider have considerable association with one another, we examine their effects in a multivariate context, explicitly considering the independent effects of each risk factor. In each case, the reference category indexes those respondents reporting *no violence*. These results are shown in Table 6.6.

Results

Beginning with the comparison of risk of *atypical violence,* there is a curvilinear relationship to age. Specifically, risk increases through the midthirties and then declines thereafter. As indicated earlier, we interpret this as showing greater risk of violence among the younger cohorts in the NVAWS sample. Although race differences are few, American Indians are almost twice as likely to experience atypical violence ($e^{.613} = 1.85$). Variation in employment status and education are negligible. Other measures of socioeconomic resources are, however, important. First, those respondents who did not report their personal income are considerably less likely to experience isolated violence ($e^{-.447} = .64$), suggesting that those at the upper end of the income range were least likely to respond to the income question. Equally important, respondents who reported that they had been without phone service, our proxy for poverty, had odds of isolated violence that were 69 percent higher than for other respondents ($e^{.527} = 1.69$). Finally, marital status is a particularly important risk factor. Respondents with disrupted (separated or divorced) relationships are twice as likely to report isolated violence ($e^{.700} = 2.01$), and those who are married have odds of violence that are 39 percent lower ($e^{-.495} = 0.61$).

The risk of *parent-partner violence* shows the same curvilinear pattern as the risk of atypical violence. There are again few race differences in victimization. Only African Americans show any significant difference, with their risk being 87 percent lower than that of non-Hispanic whites ($e^{-2.034} = 0.13$). With the significant association between race and socioeconomic status, this variation is difficult to interpret and may reflect the

TABLE 6.6
Multinomial Logit Coefficients: Risk Factors for Violence Patterns, NVAWS

	Violence Contrasts		
	Atypical Violence vs. No Violence	Parent-Partner Violence vs. No Violence	Multifaceted-Multipartner Violence vs. No Violence
Age	.069**	.116**	.056
	(.013)	(.043)	(.039)
Age squared	−.001**	−.002**	−.001**
	(.000)	(.000)	(.000)
Race			
Black	−.159	-2.034	−.702**
	(.103)	(.600)	(.332)
Asian	−.453	.504	.062
	(.250)	(.538)	(.612)
American Indian	.613**	.543	.761
	(.274)	(.643)	(.574)
Mixed	−.015	.139	.878**
	(.135)	(.338)	(.253)
Employment			
Part-time	−.021	−.048	.256
	(.089)	(.287)	(.246)
Unemployed	.324	.545	1.06**
	(.174)	(.435)	(.347)
Student	.333	.645	.424
	(.192)	(.475)	(.443)
Other	−.007	.223	.341
	(.076)	(.226)	(.218)
Education	.025	−.168**	.118
	(.027)	(.085)	(.076)
Personal income	−.029	.059	.001
	(.019)	(.059)	(.052)
Personal income—missing	−.447**	−.684**	−1.448**
	(.073)	(.237)	(.291)
Household income	.023	−.050	−.062
	(.018)	(.058)	(.051)
No phone	.527**	1.010**	1.324**
	(.162)	(.356)	(.291)
Marital status			
Disrupted	.700**	.050	.992**
	(.112)	(.296)	(.274)
Married	−.495**	−1.060**	−.485**
	(.089)	(.244)	(.248)
Parent	.119	.853**	.248
	(.077)	(.295)	(.217)
Intercept	−.896	−2.171	−3.015
	(.335)	(1.068)	(.941)

** p < 0.05 (two-tailed)
NOTE: Standard errors in parentheses.

ability of middle- and upper-class blacks to insulate themselves from violence. Unlike atypical violence, there are significant effects of education. Specifically, higher levels of education decrease the odds of parent-partner violence by over 15 percent ($e^{-.168} = 0.85$). Effects of other socioeconomic measures are even more pronounced. Women that did not report their personal income, again a group that we expect to have very high income, have odds of parent-partner violence that are 50 percent lower than for other women ($e^{-.684} = 0.51$). Even more dramatic, poor women (as indicated by lack of phone service) had a risk of victimization that was almost three times greater than for other women ($e^{1.010} = 2.75$). Although there were surprisingly no effects for marital disruption, women who were married reported significantly less parent-partner violence ($e^{-1.060} = 0.35$). Parents were also less likely to report this pattern of violence.

We next consider risk of *multifaceted-multirelationship violence*. Age differentiation is also curvilinear but somewhat flatter than that seen for the former patterns of violence. Racial differentiation in risk is somewhat more pronounced. African American women have somewhat lower odds of victimization ($e^{-.702} = .496$), while mixed-race women were almost two and a half times more likely to report experiencing multifaceted-multipartner violence ($e^{.878} = 2.41$). Employment status is also an important consideration. Women who reported being unemployed were almost three times more likely to experience the most extensive and severe pattern of violence ($e^{1.060} = 2.87$). Although education differences were negligible, we find significant effects for income and poverty that are entirely consistent with our previous findings: women living in poverty had odds of victimization that were almost four times greater than those not living in poverty ($e^{1.324} = 3.76$). Marital disruption also increases the odds of victimization ($e^{.992} = 2.70$), and being married decreases this risk ($e^{-.485} = 0.62$).

Cohort Variation in Risk Factors

In our final set of analyses we consider similarity and difference in effects based on birth cohort or, by extension, sociohistorical context. We differentiate cohorts by those younger than thirty-eight years of age (in 1995) and those thirty-eight and older. Based on this division, members of the older cohorts were born prior to 1957 and moved into adulthood (after age eighteen) prior to 1977. This is important for three reasons. First, it represents a period in U.S. history during which the proportion of women in paid labor was peaking. Second, it indexes the onset and diffusion of laws associated with the "divorce revolution." Third, the late 1970s are widely regarded as the period during which mores of sexual liberation, particularly for females, were solidified. This age differentiation also has the advantage of dividing the sample into the youngest third of the sample and the oldest two-thirds, thus providing reasonable statistical power for the analyses undertaken.

Because we found considerable variation in effects of risk factors across models in the full-sample analysis and because there is an imbalance in sample size across cohorts, we focus less on the significance of any given parameter and more on the degree to which there are significant differences in effect size across models. We examine this using a conventional z-test:

$$z = \frac{\beta_1 - \beta_2}{\sqrt{(se_1^2 + se_2^2)}}$$

Specifically, we consider coefficients to be significantly different when (a) either or both of the coefficients are statistically significant and (b) the z-score is sufficiently large to indicate a statistically significant difference. In general, this should be regarded as a rather conservative test.

Results

Table 6.7 shows coefficients for parallel models of risk factors predicting pattern of violence for the two cohorts. Beginning with risk of atypical violence, socioeconomic resources are generally consistent with our previous findings: women living in poverty have a higher risk of victimization, although the effect for the younger cohort just fails to achieve statistical significance.[56] But perhaps what is most notable in this analysis is the clear differences with respect to marital status. Marital disruption is associated with a 28 percent increase in risk of isolated violence ($e^{.246} = 1.28$) in the younger cohort but with a remarkable 143 percent increase in the older cohort ($e^{.889} = 2.43$). Complementing this, married women in the younger cohort have odds of victimization that are 61 percent lower ($e^{-.941} = 0.39$), and married women in the older cohort have odds of victimization that are less than 23 percent lower ($e^{-.256} = 0.77$). Clearly both marriage and

TABLE 6.7
Multinomial Logit Coefficients: Risk Factors for Violence Patterns by Cohort, NVAWS

| | Violence Contrasts | | | | | |
| | Atypical Violence vs. No Violence | | Parent-Partner Violence vs. No Violence | | Multifaceted-Multipartner Violence vs. No Violence | |
	Younger	Older	Younger	Older	Younger	Older
Age	.265**	.093**	.228	.075	.009	.151
	(.121)	(.031)	(.348)	(.108)	(.269)	(.120)
Age squared	−.004**	−.001**	−.004	−.001	−.001	−.002
	(.002)	(.000)	(.006)	(.001)	(.005)	(.001)
Race						
Black	−.293	−.088	−2.421**	−1.825**	−.724	−.647
	(.168)	(.132)	(1.031)	(.735)	(.464)	(.483)
Asian	−.693**	−.164	.553	.222	−.693	.969
	(.347)	(.367)	(.644)	(1.037)	(1.046)	(.760)
American Indian	.547	.659	.552	.186	.549	.965
	(.399)	(.378)	(.810)	(1.092)	(.812)	(.821)
Mixed	−.046	.000	−.451	.597	.696**	1.306**
	(.179)	(.208)	(.551)	(.439)	(.352)	(.367)
Employment						
Part-time	.109	−.096	−.095	−.028	.729**	−.334
	(.143)	(.116)	(.439)	(.383)	(.326)	(.409)
Unemployed	.011	.575**	.532	.696	.521	1.698**
	(.249)	(.251)	(.598)	(.651)	(.544)	(.460)
Student	.240	NA	.735	NA	.519	NA
	(.230)		(.552)		(.485)	
Other	−.095	.031	−.339	.497	.318	.365
	(.127)	(.097)	(.382)	(.294)	(.331)	(.295)
Education	−.005	.039	−.231	−.136	.053	.170
	(.048)	(.033)	(.144)	(.106)	(.121)	(.101)
Personal income	−.017	−.037	.247**	−.060	−.045	.082
	(.030)	(.024)	(.098)	(.075)	(.074)	(.078)
Personal income—missing	−.418**	−.456**	−.630	−.651**	−1.044**	−1.833**
	(.130)	(.089)	(.391)	(.299)	(.420)	(.408)
Household income	.003	.036	−.163	.024	.025	−.176**
	(.030)	(.024)	(.100)	(.071)	(.071)	(.076)
No phone	.393	.639**	1.256**	.806	1.433**	.863
	(.227)	(.236)	(.465)	(.573)	(.365)	(.529)
Marital status						
Disrupted	.246	.889**	.318	−.122	.967**	.871**
	(.211)	(.136)	(.515)	(.367)	(.404)	(.400)
Married	−.941**	−.256**	−.735	−1.339**	−.985**	−.065
	(.151)	(.114)	(.412)	(.314)	(.347)	(.372)
Parent	.097	.155	.935**	.776	.116	.442
	(.114)	(.108)	(.407)	(.434)	(.285)	(.365)
Intercept	−3.160	−1.945	−3.492	−.905	−1.908	−5.376
	(1.759)	(.881)	(5.047)	(2.940)	(3.826)	(3.178)
N	2154	4154	2154	4154	2154	4154

** $p < 0.05$ (two-tailed)

NOTE: Standard errors in parentheses. Bordered coefficients are significantly different from each other (z-test).

marital disruption were more facilitative of violence among the older cohort than among the younger.

There are fewer differences with respect to parent-partner violence. The only clear difference was for personal income. Among the younger cohort, personal income is associated with significantly greater risk of parent-partner violence ($e^{.247} = 1.28$) but with slightly lower risk among the older cohort ($e^{-.060} = 0.94$). This may be indicative of a backlash or the degree to which greater income attainment among women produces conflict in interpersonal relationships.

Variation in effects is most pronounced with respect to multifaceted-multirelationship violence. Of particular note, employment status appears to interact strongly with cohort in shaping risk of violence. Here, younger women who work part-time are *twice* as likely to experience the more extensive and extreme pattern of violence ($e^{.729} = 2.07$), but older women of similar employment appear less likely to experience this form of violence ($e^{-.334} = 0.716$). Equally important, younger women who are unemployed have odds of multifaceted-multirelationship violence that are 68 percent higher ($e^{.521} = 1.68$), and unemployed older women have odds that are almost five and a half times greater ($e^{1.698} = 5.46$). Unemployment among older women bears a strong association with violence that spans relationship and time. Because these older women entered the job market at the time when employment was becoming normative for women, and because employment provides a number of avenues for escaping violent relationships, it may well be that the violent intimate relationships of these women prevented them from obtaining gainful employment.[57] Similar to the effects of unemployment, poverty also increases the risk of this type of violence, but here the effects appear to be larger for the younger cohort. These findings support other research that has demonstrated that social factors are critical determinants of patterns in intimate-partner homicides.[58] Specifically, it has been argued that the recent cuts in welfare benefits limited the opportunities for abused women to leave their partners and increased the likelihood that their violent encounters would escalate. Complementing this interpretation, there is considerable variation in the effect of being married across cohorts. Although marital disruption appears to generically enhance risk (effects on odds are 2.63 and 2.39 for the younger and older cohorts, respectively), younger women ($e^{-.985} = 0.37$) who are married have dramatically lower odds of multifaceted-multirelationship victimization than married women in the older cohort ($e^{-.065} = 0.94$). The increase in the separation and divorce rates over the past twenty-five years means that women are now more likely to exit an abusive relationship and that they may be more selective about the men they marry.[59] More generally, these findings provide reasonable support for our speculation that sociohistorical context shapes risk factors for violence against women.

Discussion

We believe there are two general implications of our findings, as well as a number of important policy imperatives. First, the findings highlight the diversity of violence against women. Although the majority of women are not victimized, those that are have very different experiences. For some, an incidence of victimization is a relatively isolated and atypical experience. For others, violence tends to be multifaceted but largely confined to family relationships. For still others, violence is multifaceted and occurs in a variety of relationships, both within and beyond the family. In recognizing this diversity, our work points to the utility of expanding our conceptualization of women's experiences with violence beyond discrete forms of violence or violence in discrete relationships.

Second, our findings highlight the need to know more about the factors that produce variation in the types of victimization that women experience across the life span. Our work highlights the importance of early victimization in cumulative patterns of victimization through later life, but it cannot explain *how* early violence produces patterned victimization over the life span. Likewise, we have shown that socioeconomic deprivation is a major risk factor, but we do not know why it is important. It may be that poverty embeds individuals in neighborhood and network contexts that are characterized by greater violence.[60] Or it may be that low income coupled with fragile interpersonal relationships creates economic imperatives for women's participation in crime and deviance, ultimately heightening their risk for further victimization.[61] Or, as we have noted in our focus on historical context, it may be that a lack of economic resources prevents women from leaving abusive relationships or limits the choice set in selecting new partners.

While our analysis informs our understanding of women's risk for violence across relationships and the life course, a next stage of research would move beyond our descriptive analyses to identify the mechanisms that produce patterned victimization over the life span. Despite all its advantages, the NVAWS data unfortunately do not contain a rich set of measures that would allow the examination of such issues in detail. As a result, our work highlights the need for further data collection that would allow us to understand personal, social, and ecological factors that both produce and inhibit the different patterns of violence that we identify. Such data should also focus on factors in later life that may produce "turning points" in a violent life course, either increasing women's risks of violence or shielding women from the violence they have previously experienced.

Our findings also have implications for public policy. These variations in victimization experiences suggest the need to tailor interventions so that they can be more readily implemented in the context of ongoing relationships. This would involve victim services being less uniform and more adaptable to patterned victimization. For example, the criminal justice system may be uniquely beneficial in dealing with atypical and isolated incidents of violence. In this case, criminal justice sanctions can target a specific offender or offenders. In other cases, notably parent-partner violence, providing financial assistance may greatly improve the odds that women will leave abusive situations. At the same time, women who experience multifaceted-multirelationship violence may benefit more from counseling and general relocation assistance. Consideration of effective response begins with the recognition of variation in victimization type.[62]

Those who deal directly with victims of violence might consider the use of diagnostic instruments, similar to those used in medical screening, to identify the broader pattern of violence that may not be conveyed through current practices. This would facilitate the collection of information that would allow law enforcement and practitioners to understand both the biography of violence and the likely variation in the consequences of this broader pattern.

The significance of abuse in family of origin in the general patterning of multifaceted-multirelationship violence further suggests the importance of early intervention. Removing abused children from dangerous situations, increasing public awareness of the long-term consequences of such abuse, and providing extensive victim services to abused children may go a long way toward limiting subsequent victimization in later life.

Finally, we return to our starting point by drawing attention to the ways in which violent experiences are linked across relationships and over the life span. Our use of the life course perspective forces us to rethink how we conceptualize and understand women's victimization. It directs attention to the ways in which relationships structure the types of violence women encounter and how the timing of these encounters influences subsequent victimization experiences. Given its focus on historical period, this perspective also directs attention to the ways in which risk markers for victimization are bound by time and place.[63] As such, we see the life course perspective on violent victimization as particularly relevant to furthering our understanding of the form, the risks, and the consequences of women's violent experience.

APPENDIX 6.1
Descriptions and Univariate Statistics

Variable	Description	Mean	SD
Sociodemographics			
Respondent's age	Age in years	46.29	15.47
Race	Respondent's self-reported race		
Black	(1 = Black; 0 = other)	0.08	0.28
Asian	(1 = Asian; 0 = other)	0.01	0.12
American Indian	(1 = American Indian; 0 = other)	0.01	0.10
Mixed	(1 = Mixed; 0 = other)	0.05	0.21
Ethnicity			
Hispanic	Respondent's self-reported ethnicity (1 = Hispanic; 0 = other)	0.07	0.26
Employment			
Full-time	Employed full-time	0.46	0.50
Part-time	Employed part-time	0.13	0.33
Unemployed	Unemployed and looking for work	0.03	0.17
Student	In school	0.02	0.15
Other	Other (1 = Category; 0 = other)	0.36	0.48
Education	Total educational attainment (from 1 = no schooling to 7 = postgraduate)	4.72	1.18
Personal income	Total personal income (from 1 = less than $5,000 to 10 = more than $100,000)	4.27	2.00
Household income	Total household income (from 1 = less than $5,000 to 10 = more than $100,000)	5.44	2.24
Poverty proxy	Lost telephone service in last twelve months	0.03	0.18
Marital status			
Married	Respondent married	0.71	0.45
Disruption	Respondent separated/divorced	0.13	0.33
Parent	Respondent has children	0.83	0.37

NOTES

1. Candace Kruttschnitt, Brenda L. McLaughlin, and Carol V. Petrie, eds., *Advancing the Federal Research Agenda on Violence against Women,* Steering Committee for the Workshop on Issues in Research on Violence against Women, National Research Council (Washington, DC: National Academy Press, 2003).

2. Nancy Crowell and Ann Burgess, *Understanding Violence against Women* (Washington, DC: National Academy Press, 1986); Holly Johnson, *Dangerous Domains: Violence against Women in Canada* (Toronto: Nelson, 1996); Patricia Tjaden and Nancy Thoennes, *Prevalence, Incidence, and Consequences of Violence against Women: Findings from the National Violence against Women Survey*, Research in Brief, NCJ 172837 (Washington, DC: U.S. Department of Justice, National Institute of Justice, November 1998).

3. See Demie Kurz, "Separation, Divorce, and Woman Abuse," *Violence against Women* 5 (1986): 243–256; Patricia Mahoney and Linda M. Williams, "Sexual Assault in Marriage: Prevalence, Consequences, and Treatment of Wife Rape," in *Partner Violence: A Comprehensive Review of Twenty Years of Research*, ed. Jana L. Jasinski and Linda M. Williams (Thousand Oaks, CA: Sage, 1998); Patricia Tjaden and Nancy Thoennes, *Full Report of the Prevalence, Incidence, and Consequences of Violence against Women*, NCJ 183781 (Washington, DC: National Institute of Justice, November 2000).

4. See Jeff Fagan and Sandra Wexler, "Crime at Home and in the Streets: The Relationship between Family and Stranger Violence," *Violence and Victims* 2 (1987): 5–23; Gerald Hotaling, Murray Straus, and Alan J. Lincoln, "Intrafamily Violence and Crime and Violence outside the Family," in *Physical Violence in American Families: Risk Factors and Adaptations to Violence in 8,145 Families*, ed. Murray A. Straus and Richard Gelles, pp. 431–470 (New Brunswick, NJ: Transaction, 1990); Terrie E. Moffitt, Robert F. Krueger, Avshalom Caspi, and Jeff Fagan, "Partner Abuse and General Crime: How Are They the Same? How Are They Different?" *Criminology* 38 (2000): 199–232.

5. For example, Ronet Bachman, *Violence against Women: A National Crime Victimization Survey Report*, NCJ-145325 (Washington, DC: Bureau of Justice Statistics, U.S. Department of Justice, 1994); Ronet Bachman, "The Factors Related to Rape Reporting Behavior and Arrest: New Evidence from the National Crime Victimization Survey," *Criminal Justice Behavior* 25 (1998): 8–29; Ronet Bachman and Linda E. Saltzman, *Violence against Women: Estimates from the Redesigned Survey*, NCJ-154348 (Washington, DC: Bureau of Justice Statistics, U.S. Department of Justice, 1995).

6. For example, Bachman, "Factors Related to Rape Reporting"; Crowell and Burgess, *Understanding Violence against Women*; Maria Testa and Kurt Dermen, "The Differential Correlates of Sexual Coercion and Rape," *Journal of Interpersonal Violence* 14 (1999): 548–561.

7. See, for example, Candace Kruttschnitt, Rosemary Gartner, and Kathleen Ferraro, "Women's Involvement in Serious Interpersonal Violence," *Aggression and Violent Behavior* 7 (2002): 529–565.

8. Glen H. Elder, "Time, Human Agency, and Social Change: Perspectives on the Life Course," *Social Psychology Quarterly* 57 (1994): 4–15.

9. See Phillip Blumstein and Peter Kollock, "Personal Relationships," *Annual Review of Sociology* 14 (1988): 467–490.

10. See Murray A. Straus and Richard Gelles, *Physical Violence in American Families: Risk Factors and Adaptations to Violence in 8,145 Families* (New Brunswick, NJ: Transaction, 1990).

11. Ross Macmillan and Rosemary Gartner, "When She Brings Home the Bacon: Labor Force Participation and Risk of Spousal Violence against Women," *Journal of Marriage and the Family* 61 (1999): 947–958.

12. Lawrence E. Cohen and Marcus Felson, "Social Change and Crime Rate Trends," *American Sociological Review* 44 (1979): 505–524.; Lawrence E. Cohen and David Cantor, "The Determinants of Larceny: An Empirical and Theoretical Study," *Journal of Research in Crime and Delinquency* 17 (1980): 140–159; Lawrence E. Cohen, James R. Kluegel, and Kenneth C. Land, "Social Inequality and Predatory Criminal Victimization: An Exposition and Test of a Formal Theory," *American Sociological Review* 46 (1981): 505–524.

13. In the case of spousal violence, potential guardians, such as spouses or parents, are transformed into potential offenders.

14. See Elder, "Time, Human Agency, and Social Change."

15. See Mark Granovetter, "The Strength of Weak Ties," *American Journal of Sociology* 78 (1973): 1360–1380.

16. For example, Murray A. Straus and Carrie L. Yodanis, "Corporal Punishment in Adolescence and Physical Assaults on Spouses in Later Life: What Accounts for the Link?" *Journal of Marriage and the Family* 58 (1996): 825–841; Cathy Spatz Widom, "Child Abuse, Neglect, and Violent Criminal Behavior," *Criminology* 27 (1989): 251–271; Cathy Spatz Widom, "Childhood Victimization: Risk Factor for Delinquency," in *Adolescent Stress: Causes and Consequences,* ed. Mary Ellen Colton and Susan Gore, pp. 201–221 (New York: Aldine de Gruyter, 1991).

17. See Robin Malinowsky-Rummel and David J. Hansen, "Long-Term Consequences of Child Physical Abuse," *Psychological Bulletin* 114 (1993): 68–79.

18. See review in Crowell and Burgess, *Understanding Violence against Women.*

19. See discussions in Michael Hindelang, Michael Gottfredson, and James Garofalo, *Victims of Personal Crime* (New York: Ballinger, 1978); Janet Lauritsen, Robert Sampson, and John Laub, "The Link between Offending and Victimization among Adolescents," *Criminology* 29 (1991): 265–292.

20. See Malinowsky-Rummell and Hansen, "Long-Term Consequences"; Ronald Kessler and William Magee, "Childhood Adversities and Adult Depression: Basic Patterns of Association in a U.S. National Survey," *Psychological Medicine* 23 (1993): 679–690.

21. Crowell and Burgess, *Understanding Violence against Women,* 72–73.

22. See Arlene McCormick, Ann Burgess, and Peter Gaccione, "Influence of Family Structure and Financial Stability on Physical and Sexual Abuse among a

Runaway Population," *International Journal of Sociology of the Family* 16 (1986): 251–262; Arlene McCormick, Mark-David Janus, and Ann Burgess, "Runaway Youths and Sexual Victimization: Gender Differences in an Adolescent Population," *Child Abuse and Neglect* 10 (1986): 387–395; John Hagan and Bill McCarthy, *Mean Streets: Youth Crime and Homelessness* (New York: Cambridge University Press, 1997); Les B. Whitbeck, Danny R. Hoyt, and Kevin A. Ackley, "Abusive Family Background and Later Victimization among Runaway and Homeless Adolescents," *Journal of Research on Adolescence* 7 (1997): 375–392; Les B. Whitbeck and Ronald L. Simons, "Life on the Streets: The Victimization of Runaway and Homeless Adolescents," *Youth and Society* 22 (1990): 108–125.

23. See Gerald Hotaling and David Sugarman, "An Analysis of Risk Markers in Husband to Wife Violence: The Current State of Knowledge," *Violence and Victims* 1 (1986): 101–124; Jane A. Siegal and Linda M. Williams, *Risk Factors for Violent Victimization of Women: A Prospective Study,* NCJ 189161 (Washington, DC: National Institute of Justice, 2001).

24. See Mary E. Collins, "Factors Influencing Sexual Victimization and Revictimization in a Sample of Adolescent Mothers," *Journal of Interpersonal Violence* 13 (1998): 3–24; Kathleen A. Kendall-Tackett, Linda M. Williams, and David Finkelhor, "Impact of Sexual Abuse on Children: A Review and Synthesis of Recent Empirical Studies," *Psychological Bulletin* 113 (1993): 164–180; Barbara Krahe, Renate Scheinberger-Olwig, Eva Waizenhofer, and Susanne Kolpin, "Childhood Sexual Abuse and Revictimization in Adolescence," *Child Abuse and Neglect* 23 (1999): 383–394; Azmaira H. Maker, Markus Kemmelmeier, and Christopher Peterson, "Child Sexual Abuse, Peer Sexual Abuse, and Sexual Assault in Adulthood: A Multi-risk Model of Revictimization," *Journal of Traumatic Stress* 14 (2001): 351–368; Charlene Muehlenhard, "The Sexual Revictimization of Women and Men Sexually Abused as Children: A Review of the Literature," *Annual Review of Sex Research* 9 (1998): 177–223.

25. See Bonnie S. Fischer, Francis T. Cullen, and Michael G. Turner, *The Sexual Victimization of College Women,* NCJ 182369 (Washington, DC: National Institute of Justice, 2000); Diane R. Follingstad, Rebekah G. Bradley, James Laughlin, and Leslie Burke, "Risk Factors and Correlates of Dating Violence: The Relevance of Examining Frequency and Severity Levels in a College Sample," *Violence and Victims* 14 (1999): 365–380; Helen M. Hendy, Kristin Weiner, and John Bakerofskie, "Comparison of Six Models for Violent Romantic Relationships in College Men and Women," *Journal of Interpersonal Violence* 18 (2003): 645–665.

26. See Crowell and Burgess, *Understanding Violence against Women.*

27. Glen H. Elder, *Children of the Great Depression* (Boulder, CO: Westview, 1999).

28. Michael J. Shanahan, Richard A. Miech, and Glen H. Elder, "Changing Pathways to Attainment in Men's Lives: Historical Patterns of School, Work, and Social Class," *Social Forces* 77 (1998): 231–256; Michael J. Shanahan, Glen H. Elder,

and Richard Miech, "History and Agency in Men's Lives: Pathways to Achievement in Cohort Perspective," *Sociology of Education* 70 (1997): 54–67.

29. See, for example, John E. Conklin, *Why Crime Rates Fell* (New York: Allyn and Bacon, 2003); Michael Eisner, "Long-Term Historical Trends in Violent Crime," *Crime and Justice* 30 (2003): 83–142; Ted Gurr, "Historical Trends in Violent Crime: A Critical Review of the Evidence," *Crime and Justice* 3 (1981): 295–331.

30. An exception is Rosemary Gartner and Bill McCarthy, "The Social Distribution of Femicide in Urban Canada, 1921–1988," *Law and Society Review* 25 (1991): 287–311.

31. See Joan Huber, "Macro-Micro Links in Gender Stratification: 1989 Presidential Address," *American Sociological Review* 55 (1990): 1–10; and Paul England and George Farkas, *Households, Employment, and Gender: A Sociological, Economic, and Demographic View* (New York: Aldine de Gruyter, 1986).

32. See, for example, Rachel Bridges-Whaley and Steven F. Messner, "Gender Equality and Gendered Homicide," *Homicide Studies* 6 (2002): 188–210; Lynne M. Vieraitis and Marion R. Williams, "Assessing the Impact of Gender Inequality on Female Homicide Victimization across U.S. Cities: A Racially Disaggregated Analysis," *Violence against Women* 8 (2002): 35–63.

33. See Menachem Amir, *Patterns in Forcible Rape* (Chicago: University of Chicago Press, 1971); Richard Felson, *Violence and Gender Reexamined* (Washington, DC: American Psychological Association, 2002).

34. See, for example, Laura Dugan, Daniel Nagin, and Richard Rosenfeld, "Explaining the Decline in Intimate Partner Homicide: The Effects of Changing Domesticity, Women's Status, and Domestic Violence Resources," *Homicide Studies* 3 (1999): 187–214; Laura Dugan, Daniel Nagin, and Richard Rosenfeld, "Exposure Reduction or Retaliation? The Effects of Domestic Violence Resources on Intimate Partner Homicide," *Law and Society Review* 37 (2003): 169–198; Patricia Tjaden and Nancy Thoennes, *Stalking in America: Findings from the National Violence against Women Survey,* NCJ 169592 (Washington, DC: National Institute of Justice, 1998).

35. General discussions and main findings for the NVAWS data are found in Tjaden and Thoennes, *Prevalence, Incidence, and Consequences,* and Tjaden and Thoennes, *Full Report of the Prevalence.*

36. Holly Johnson, *Dangerous Domains* (Toronto: Nelson Canada, 1996).

37. See Crowell and Burgess, *Understanding Violence against Women*; Mary Koss, "The Underdetection of Rape: Methodological Choices Influence Incidence Estimates," *Journal of Social Issues* 48 (1992): 61–75; Wes Skogan, "The Polls—a Review: The National Crime Survey Redesign," *Public Opinion Quarterly* 54 (1990): 256–272.

38. The relationship categories are defined as follows:

Parents: parent, stepparent or guardian.

Other relatives: brother, stepbrother, brother-in-law, uncle, grandfather, step-grandfather, male cousin, son/stepson, son-in-law, nephew, nephew-in-law, grandmother, step-grandmother, aunt, sister, stepsister, sister-in-law, other male relative, other female relative.

Partners: current husband, ex-husband, current male partner, current female partner; former male partner; former female partner.

Dates: boyfriend or date.

Acquaintances: boss, supervisor, co-worker, co-volunteer, employee, ex-employee, client, customer, patient, student, doctor, nurse, other health professional, teacher, professor, instructor, coach, landlord, minister, priest, rabbi, clergy, friend, acquaintance, neighbor, roommate, service worker, hired hand, parent of friend, family friend.

Stranger: male stranger, female stranger, both male and female stranger.

39. See Blumstein and Kollock, "Personal Relationships."

40. Sexual assault is generally measured by the question "Has a man or boy ever made or tried to make you have sex by using force or threatening to harm you or someone close to you?" Variants in the survey included specific cues about vaginal sex, oral sex, and anal sex.

41. Stalking victimization was measured by the respondents' being followed or spied on, being sent unsolicited letters or written correspondences, receiving unsolicited calls, having someone stand outside their home or place of work or recreation, having someone show up at places they were even though he or she had no business being there, having someone leave unwanted items for them to find or try to communicate with them against their will, or a variety of volunteered behaviors (e.g., vandalized property). Following prior work, we only included acts in which the respondents felt that they or someone close to them would be seriously harmed or killed when the perpetrator was following or harassing them or when the respondents felt "somewhat frightened" or "very frightened."

42. Respondents were not asked to report either stalking incidents or incidents of sexual assault in childhood that involved parents or guardians.

43. See Clifford Clogg, "Latent Class Analysis," in *Handbook of Statistical Modeling for the Social and Behavioral Sciences,* ed. Gerhart Arminger, Clifford Clogg, and Michael Sobel (New York: Plenum Press, 1995); Allan McCutcheon, *Latent Class Analysis* (Newbury Park, CA: Sage, 1987).

44. We assess the patterning of violence within relationships by examining goodness of fit statistics for models that predict one (functional independence between the different types of violence and no patterning), two, three, and four classes of violence. Models that provide a good fit to the data (discussed in Appendix 6.1) suggest the optimal number of classes or patterns of violence.

45. Dating violence is a borderline case. It provides a good fit to the data using a .01 and .05 criterion but has BIC statistics that support a more complex model. We assess the nature of the more complex models and conducted robustness assessments (see note 46) and concluded that the one-class model was indeed the optimal model.

46. In some cases, the BIC statistic suggested support for a more complex model. In each of these cases, we investigated the latent class and conditional probabilities associated with each class. Consistent with the problem of "over-fitting," each of the cases had latent class probabilities that were too small for reasonable estimation (less than .01) and showed considerable distortion from the observed data. We further assessed whether a correction for empty cells, specifically the addition of small constants to all cells (i.e., 0.1, 0.25, 0.5, 0.75) changed the results. It did not.

47. In this case, a four-class model provides a slightly better fit by two of the three criteria and a poorer fit by the third. We selected the three-class model on the grounds that the additional class was not clearly distinguishable from the third class and that its latent class probability was too small for adequate estimation (< 0.01).

48. Following Macmillan and Gartner, "When She Brings Home the Bacon," we consider violence to be systematic if it requires a sustained use of force (e.g., beating someone up, choking them) or requires some form of planning (e.g., getting a weapon).

49. We use terminology similar to that developed in Macmillan and Gartner, "When She Brings Home the Bacon."

50. See discussions in R. Emerson Dobash and Russell P. Dobash, *Women, Violence, and Social Change* (New York: Routledge, 1992); Michael Johnson, "Patriarchal Terrorism and Common Couple Violence: Two Forms of Violence against Women," *Journal of Marriage and the Family* 57 (1995): 283–294; Macmillan and Gartner, "When She Brings Home the Bacon."

51. Specifically, we cross-classify the three patterns of child victimization with the four patterns of partner victimization and with the two categories of relative, date, acquaintance, and stranger victimization. For the latter relationships, we simply differentiate between victims and nonvictims. This procedure yields a general *victimization matrix* composed of 192 cells.

52. Although a two-class model has the lowest BIC statistic (−1275.52 versus −1240.78), this model has a poor fit to the data based on the likelihood ratio test (p < .001). We opt for a three-class model on the grounds that it provides a good fit based on all criteria. Like the earlier analyses, we assessed robustness by adding small constants to each cell in order to assess the degree to which model selection was being influenced by zero cells. These models confirmed our choice of selecting the three-class model.

53. See discussion in Hotaling and Sugarman, "An Analysis of Risk Markers."

54. See Ross Macmillan, "Violence and the Life Course," *Annual Review of Sociology* 27 (2001): 1–22.

55. George Bohrnstedt and David Knoke, *Statistics for Social Data Analysis*, 3rd ed. (Itasca, IL: F. E. Peacock, 1994).

56. Based on the magnitude of the effects in the full-sample analyses, an effect

of the size seen for the younger cohort would have been statistically significant had the sample been as large.

57. See also Johnson, "Patriarchal Terrorism."

58. Dugan, Nagin, and Rosenfeld, "Exposure Reduction or Retaliation?"

59. Dugan, Nagin, and Rosenfeld, "Explaining the Decline."

60. See Deborah R. Baskin and Ira B. Sommers, *Casualties of Community Disorder: Women's Careers in Violent Crime* (Boulder, CO: Westview, 1998).

61. Beth Richie, *Compelled to Crime: The Gender Entrapment of Battered Black Women* (New York: Routledge, 1996).

62. See also Carolyn Block, "How Can Practitioners Help an Abused Women Lower Her Risk of Death?" *NIJ Journal* 250 (2003): 4–7.

63. See also Gartner and McCarthy, "Social Distribution of Femicide."

Chapter 7

Predictors of Violent Victimization
National Crime Victimization Survey Women and Jailed Women
Laura Dugan and Jennifer L. Castro

The goal of the research presented in this chapter is to learn more about the victimization of *all* women by comparing the predictors and circumstances of violent victimization for two distinct groups of women. The first group is a national U.S.-based sample; the second group is drawn from a setting that is excluded from the sampling frame of the first, a public jail. We inform this research by using the most dominant theory of victimization, lifestyle/routine-activities theory. According to this perspective, women in both samples will have a higher likelihood of victimization if their activities increase their chances of exposure to a motivated offender in the absence of a capable guardian.[1] Can this broadly stated theory explain the violent experiences of *all* women, including those who live marginalized lifestyles?

Much of what we already know about violence against women comes from the National Crime Victimization Survey (NCVS), the largest self-report survey of victimization in the United States. The original goal of the NCVS was to create crime estimates to account for criminal events not reported to police. Although this survey has supplemented our knowledge of crime patterns for nearly three decades, limitations in the NCVS sampling strategy raise concerns that important criminal events still remain unrecorded. For individuals to be included in the NCVS they must live at an address identified by the Census Bureau.[2] The types of living quarters covered include a wide range of low-income or nontypical housing, such as public housing, dormitories, mobile homes, motel housing units, and quarters within a rooming house. However, individuals who are homeless and individuals who live in military barracks and institutions such as nursing homes, jails, and prisons are excluded from NCVS samples.

Although the exclusion of persons in need of assisted living is unlikely to bias resulting crime estimates, missing data from military personnel, homeless persons, or incarcerated persons likely will. In this research we examine the theoretical and practical implications of omitting information from the last group—incarcerated persons—in a general study of violence against women.

Why is missing data from incarcerated women problematic? Women who behave outside the parameters of the law may be more vulnerable to dangerous associates, which, according to routine-activities theory, will increase their odds of criminal victimization. Indeed, extremely high rates of victimization have been found among samples of incarcerated women.[3] Female offenders, even more so than male offenders, have a greater likelihood of violent victimization than nonoffenders.[4] In addition to the risky lifestyles many offenders pursue, these women are usually unprotected by capable guardians. Thus, women involved in illegal activities make desirable targets of violence because perpetrators know they are unlikely to call the police.[5] In fact, the proportion of unreported violence among female offenders is likely much higher than that among nonoffenders, which is substantial when one considers that only half of all nonoffender victimizations are ever reported.[6] Clearly, we want to include frequently victimized women in any study that purports to describe the nature of violence against women.

Furthermore, incarcerated women represent one of the most marginalized and vulnerable populations of potential victims. If such women fail to receive services that enable them to cope with the consequences of their victimizations, they are likely to return to the illegitimate and potentially socially harmful resources with which they are most familiar (e.g., substance use).[7] Without a proper understanding of the victimizations that incarcerated women have experienced, criminal justice practitioners and treatment providers will be at a loss to provide much-needed services.

In the current research, we explore whether NCVS sampling limitations impair our understanding of the nature and extent of routine-activities theory and violence against women. Using predictors that are drawn from routine-activities theory, we compare risk and protective factors for violent victimization among female respondents to the NCVS with those among a sample of women incarcerated in Baltimore, Maryland. We also examine the situational characteristics of violent events experienced by victims within each group. By virtue of their incarceration, women in the Baltimore jail sample were excluded from the NCVS despite the fact that their life circumstances place them at high risk for violent victimization. Our research points to the importance of conducting victimization studies on highly marginalized populations.

Predictors of Violence against Women

Routine-activities theory generally predicts that persons who pursue activities outside the household have a greater likelihood of violent victimization, especially if those activities are carried out at night and involve social contact with persons likely to offend. However, the relationship between women's activities away from home and the likelihood of violent victimization depends on the source of violence. Because women are more likely to be victimized by nonstrangers (such as partners or family members) than by strangers, a woman's home may not be such a safe haven. Routine-activities theory may best apply to violence against males and to only stranger (or nonintimate) violence against women. Studies that have not examined females exclusively or distinguished stranger from intimate violence have found that nighttime activities away from the home significantly predict the risk of violent victimization, even when other individual-level and even community-level risk factors are controlled.[8]

Thus far, research has shown that the demographic characteristics of the most frequent victims of violence match the predictions of routine-activities theory. Those who are most likely to live in areas with a high prevalence of violent offenders are most likely to be violently victimized. From the NCVS and from smaller-scale general-population surveys, we know that age, gender, race, and socioeconomic status are key predictors of violent victimization.[9] Young, black, low-income (and unemployed) males are the most frequent victims of violence. Older, white, upper-class women are least likely to be victimized. However, for certain violent crimes such as rape and simple assault (which includes family violence), women are equally if not more likely to be victimized than men.[10] Black women, especially, have been disproportionately victimized by the violent crimes of homicide, rape, and robbery.[11]

Rates of violent victimization peak when women are in their early twenties.[12] In fact, the risk of violent victimization is highest for women under twenty-five years of age.[13] Also, women who live in urban areas are at a greater risk of being victimized than women who live in nonmetropolitan areas.[14] The city of Baltimore, Maryland, from which most of our incarcerated sample came, has one of the highest rates of violent victimization.[15]

Marital status is also empirically related to women's risk of violent victimization; however, the nature of this relationship is complex. Marriage can be considered one form of guardianship and is therefore typically conceptualized as a protective factor that inhibits the likelihood of victimization. However, because much of the violence that women suffer is perpetrated by intimate partners, marriage can also imply exposure to a motivated offender and thus serve as a risk factor for violent victimization.[16] Without distinguishing intimate from stranger violence, unmarried persons overall are at greater risk of violent victimization.[17]

The demographic characteristics described here are not the only individual-level predictors of violence against women; a host of lifestyle activities are thought to contribute as well. Some researchers who have studied intimate violence against women have found that the likelihood of victimization increases when a woman engages in nontraditional activities, but only if these activities are carried out in an environment where patriarchal expectations dominate.[18] In such environments, women who delay marriage, divorce, rear children alone, or are employed may have a higher likelihood of intimate victimization. However, receiving a higher education appears to buffer this effect, perhaps because women who attend school are better able to establish networks of social support.

Finally, violent victimizations against women can be characterized by a variety of situational circumstances. These circumstances can include the presence and type of weapon, drug or alcohol intoxication, the role of bystanders or third parties, and victim resistance and retaliation.[19] In our research, we explore whether situational characteristics vary across samples of NCVS and incarcerated women.

Research Design

The purpose of our research is to compare experiences of violent victimization among a sample of NCVS women with those among a sample of incarcerated women and to determine the applicability of routine-activities theory to each group. Our analyses involve two separate datasets collected from two different samples of women. This section describes each of these data sets and the methods of statistical comparison we employ.

Data

Sample of NCVS Women

The National Crime Victimization Survey (NCVS) is the largest victimization data source documenting characteristics of victims and nonvictims, age twelve and older, living within sampled housing units. In addition to detailed information on each interviewed household and individual, respondents report their recent experiences as crime victims, including details of each event and its consequences.[20] Since 1972, data collection has used a rotating panel designed to interview about 100,000 residents in select housing units seven times during a three-year period.[21] Our sample includes all females age eighteen or older who were interviewed using the redesigned NCVS between January 1992 and June 2000 inclusive $(N = 646,549)$.[22]

Sample of Incarcerated Women

Data for the incarcerated women comes from in-person interviews conducted between January 2001 and March 2002 with women detained in the Baltimore City Detention Center in Maryland. These interviews were completed as part of a multisite study funded by the National Consortium on Violence Research (NCOVR).[23] Interviewers used a computerized life-event calendar to collect detailed monthly information regarding each woman's life circumstances, including any experiences with violence, in the three years prior to her current incarceration.[24] From all women reporting experiences of violence, detailed information on the situational context of each violent event was collected, including qualitative narratives in the women's own words, for up to eight incidents involving partners and eight involving nonpartners. Very few women had events numbering beyond this sampling threshold during the three-year calendar period.

Female inmates over eighteen years of age were recruited for the study, provided that they had appeared before court and were aware of the possible sentence for their current charge. Of the 361 women originally recruited, only 6 women refused to be interviewed at the time of the actual interview, yielding an overall response rate of 98 percent. Of the 355 women who agreed to be interviewed, 4 were transferred, were released, or stopped the interview before it was complete.[25] The final number of valid interviews completed was 351.[26] The experiences of these women can be generalized to those of other female offenders who live in urban areas (and are predominantly African American), a population that has historically experienced some of the highest rates of violent victimization.[27]

Methods

Our analysis proceeds in two stages. First, we predict the probability of violent victimization separately within each data set and compare predictors of violent victimization among NCVS women with those among incarcerated women. Second, we restrict our attention to victims of violence and describe how situational characteristics of their victimization experiences vary by sample.

Predicting Violent Victimization

The dependent variable for these analyses is a binary-response variable indicating whether the respondent reported being a victim of a violent crime within the previous six months. Women interviewed for the NCVS reported any incidents within six months prior to their interview date, and women from the incarcerated sample reported any incidents within six months prior to their incarceration date. Within both samples, violent crimes include completed or attempted incidents of rape or sexual assault, robbery, and assault.

The statistical models we use predict victimization separately for each sample of women.[28] Our choice of variables is based on two criteria. First, we selected measures that had some predictable impact based on routine-activities theory. Second, we were limited to variables that could be constructed from both data sets. Thus, while each data set had a wealth of information on the routine activities and lifestyle of the women, we were restricted to the variables identified in the equation in note 28. In that equation, PF refers to variables that are expected to protect women from violence. These factors reflect stability and attachment to community. The length that a woman has lived at her residence clearly shows an investment and familiarity with her environment. Also, by living in the same home for an extended period of time, natural guardianships emerge among neighbors, providing an additional level of protection. As discussed earlier and in the research literature, being married can also provide protection to a woman, since our dependent variable does not exclusively measure partner violence.

The second set of variables, RF, represents risk factors. Some of these variables characterize less stable environments and are predicted to increase the risk of violence due to the high potential for offender contact (e.g., high mobility, public housing, one-adult household with at least one child, and going out every night). Other variables suggest a low level of social and economic achievement, which may indicate that these women live in lower socioeconomic neighborhoods that have higher exposure to violent predators. We include here measures of low income and lower levels of education (with having at least four years of post–high school education as the reference category).

We name the final set of predictor variables UnC, for uncertain. The two measures here could relate to violence either positively or negatively. Routine activities would predict that a woman is protected by living in a multiple-unit dwelling, if the others living in the building serve as informal guardians. However, multiple-unit dwellings could also provide more exposure to potential offenders who have access to her building through other tenants. We also include employment in this category because, by having a job, a woman may be able to afford housing in safer neighborhoods. Yet she will need to travel to her job, which increases her exposure to potential violent encounters.

The final categories serve as controls for this model. *Dem* (demographics) includes race and measures of age broken into several categories: 18 to 24, 25 to 34, and 50 or older (35 to 49 is the reference category). *SI* (survey issues) controls for over- or underreporting due to the survey design and missing data. Survey issues include controls for whether another person was present during the interview, for proxy and unbounded interviews, as well as for the interview period.[29] Also, because NCVS respondents sometimes fail to answer questions pertaining to income, employment, education, and length of residence, all variables that relied on these data were coded zero if missing. Four dummy variables were then included in the model to control for potential biases resulting from this coding scheme. Finally, year dummies were included to control for temporal trends in violence. See Appendix 7.1 for a full listing of all variables.

NCVS collections are based on a cluster sampling technique that interviews residents in adjacent housing units.[30] Females living in the same neighborhood may have similar propensities of victimization. The consequence of not having fully independent observations is that the estimated standard errors will be smaller than the true value. To account for this, we adjust the NCVS model's standard errors by an estimated "design effect" as determined by the STATA command survey logit.[31]

Model Limitations

There are at least two sources of violation of independence across observations within the NCVS data set. First, because the sampling strategy of the NCVS is to interview all persons in selected housing units, females living together could be victimized by the same offender. For example, the husband of a victim of spousal violence may also abuse his daughter. Second, because of the panel design of the sampling strategy, residents of housing units are potentially interviewed six times (not including bounding interviews). Therefore, a sample of females compiled by pooling NCVS interviews across multiple years *will* contain repeated interviews of the same woman and thus, by definition, violate the assumption of independence across observations. This problem can be framed as an issue of spatial autocorrelation. Uncorrected autocorrelation for linear models deflates coefficient standard errors and underestimates the model variance, thus exaggerating model fit.[32] However, although there is likely to be bias in the standard errors, the coefficient estimates will remain unbiased.

Situational Context of Female Victimization

The second stage of our analysis is restricted to those females who reported being violently victimized. Our interest is in comparing the characteristics of victimization found among NCVS victims with those among incarcerated victims. Because respondents can report more than one incident during an interview, only the first (or most recent) incident was used.[33] By discarding the remaining incidents we were able to reduce potential problems associated with dependence across observations.

The situational characteristics are sorted into three categories (see Appendix 7.2). *Offender characteristics* include the victim-offender relationship and the offender's race, gender, and age. *Incident characteristics* include the offense type, incident location, presence of a weapon, whether there were multiple offenders, and whether the offender was under the influence of a psychoactive substance. *Consequences* include level of injury, immediate action taken by the victim in response to the incident (e.g., attacking or threatening offender), and whether the police were informed.

For each predictor, we calculate a mean for each sample as defined earlier (since the predictors are binary, the means are interpreted as proportions). We then conduct a *t*-test comparing each pair of means. This method is a useful way to describe overall patterns of victimization between distinct groups.

Results

Predicting Violent Victimization

Results from the logistic models described above are found in Table 7.1. The table lists the odds ratios for each variable for the model using NCVS women and for the model using incarcerated women (note that the demographic, survey issue, and other control variables are omitted to save space).[34] Since we list odds ratios, variables that are positively associated with victimization will have values greater than one, and those that are negatively associated with victimization will have values between zero and one. The first notable finding is that, as expected, the victimization rate is much higher for the marginalized population. Nearly half (47 percent) of all incarcerated females were violently victimized within six months of serving jail time. This compares to only 1.4 percent of women drawn from the general population.

Before reviewing the model results it is important to note that they were generated from data sets with very different sample sizes. Almost 650,000 women were interviewed in the NCVS, and only 350 women were interviewed in the Baltimore City Detention Center. Because the NCVS is so large, most estimates are going to be significantly different from zero. For this reason we will pay greater attention to the magnitudes of the odds ratios. As shown in Table 7.1, most of the significant dummy variables have magnitudes of 1.2 or greater for positively related measures or 0.83 (1/1.2) or less for negatively related variables.[35] In contrast, the sample drawn from incarcerated women is a small data set. With such low statistical power, few of the variables are going to be significantly different from zero. In the instances where a finding is insignificant, we still find value in visually comparing the results generated from the incarcerated women data to that from the NCVS data.

Turning first to the results for NCVS women, it is immediately apparent that most of the selected variables neatly follow the predictions of routine

TABLE 7.1
*Logistic Odds Ratios Predicting Violent Victimization for
NCVS and Incarcerated Women*

Variable[a]	NCVS Women[b] (n = 646,549)	Incarcerated Women (n = 342)
Percent Victimized	1.40%	47.08%
Protective Factors		
Months at residence	0.997***	0.999
Married	0.558***	1.257
Risk Factors		
High mobility	2.123***	0.665
Public housing	1.196**	0.568
One Adult with kid(s)	2.071***	1.087
Out Every night	1.399***	1.691**
Low income	1.196***	0.949
In school	1.080	0.619
Less than high school	1.109**	1.438
High school diploma/GED	1.062	1.838
Some college	1.173***	2.312
Uncertain		
Multiple-unit dwelling	0.964	1.431*
Job	1.465***	0.707
Pseudo R-square	0.0920	0.0526

* = p ≤ 0.10, ** = p ≤ 0.05, *** = p ≤ 0.01, all tests one-tailed.
[a] In the interest of saving space, estimate associated with the demographics and survey issues are omitted from this table. Please contact the authors for copies of the entire table.
[b] All standard errors have been adjusted to account for the clustered survey design except for the 1992 dummy variable. Design effects could only be estimated for the years 1993 to 2000.
NOTE: All odds ratios greater than 1.0 are associated with increases in violent victimization, and all odds ratios less than 1.0 are associated with decreases.

activities. Both Protective Factors have odds ratios less than one, and all but two of the Risk Factors have odds ratios greater than one. Of the Uncertain variables, only having a job is significant; it turns out to be a risk factor for this group of women. When comparing these findings to those generated from the marginalized group of women, we find a number of inconsistencies. Looking first at the Protective Factors, we find that although living at the same residence for an extended period of time could arguably be said to provide some protection to the jailed population (positive but insignificant), marriage fails to provide any protection, as it had to the more general population. The vast difference between the two odds ratios (0.558*** versus 1.257) cannot be attributed to the low power of the

Baltimore sample because the direction of the marriage effect is positive, not negative.

The two samples of women only appear to have one Risk Factor with common significance and magnitude: going out every night appears to be a risk for women regardless of whether they are representative of the general population or more marginalized from the mainstream. Also, low educational attainment appears to similarly affect both groups of women (the nonsignificance of the Baltimore group could simply be due to low statistical power). However, two strong differences are found among the expected Risk Factors of high mobility and public housing. In each case, the finding is positive and significant for the NCVS females and negative and insignificant for the Baltimore females (i.e., odds ratio less than one). The marginalized women seem to be immune to the predictions of lifestyle/routine-activities theory with regard to these two factors. One possible explanation is that these women are less sensitive to the types of adverse conditions that are more common in their lives. They are likely accustomed to moving frequently and may therefore be better able to protect themselves from the types of risks that high mobility could impose. Similarly, the marginalized population may be more accustomed to living in public housing, making them less vulnerable to victimization in that setting.[36] Finally, it appears as if living in a household with only one adult and at least one child and having a low income are only risk factors for the general sample of women. The findings for the Baltimore sample have magnitudes very close to one.

We find different results for the two variables with uncertain predictions according to routine-activities theory. The results show that risk of violent victimization is higher for the jailed women when they lived in multiple-unit buildings. However, this is not the case for the NCVS sample. Their victimization risk is the same regardless of their dwelling type (after controlling for public housing and poverty, of course). This divergence may highlight an important difference in the situational context for these two groups of women living in multiple-unit buildings. For the Baltimore sample, the multiple-unit dwellings are undoubtedly more likely to be located in disadvantaged neighborhoods and occupied by similarly marginalized populations, providing a rich assortment of possibly motivated violent offenders. Multiple-unit dwellings for other women provide no additional protection but do seem also to be unrelated to risk. The other finding also highlights the divergence between these two groups. Although having a job appears to induce risk among the general population of women, it is not risky for the marginalized population. In fact, the small odds ratio of the job variable for the Baltimore women suggests that having a job could protect them from violence.

Situational Context of Female Victimization

To illustrate the similarities and differences in violent victimization experiences between the sample of women from the general population and that from the marginalized group, we present five bar graphs (Figures 7.1–7.5). Each graph compares the percent of victims whose incident matched the characteristics described for that series. The first series, found in Figure 7.1, shows the relationship of the offender to the victim for both samples. Note that significant differences are marked with an asterisk.[37] The offender types are arranged in the order of most intimate to least intimate, moving from spouse to stranger. Significant differences between the NCVS and Baltimore samples are found in the extreme groups (intimates and strangers). Among intimates, the most apparent difference is that women from the general population are more likely than the marginalized to be victimized by their husbands. This is strikingly different from the findings for nonmarital partners. The marginalized women are almost four times more likely to be victimized by their nonmarital intimate partners (boy/girlfriends) than are mainstream women. This may reflect more

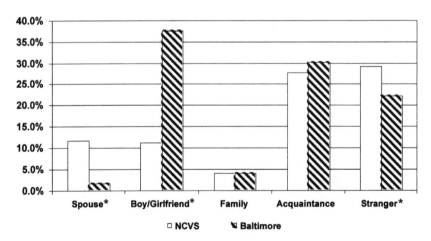

Fig. 7.1. Relationship of Offender to the NCVS and Baltimore Victims. * = p ≤ 0.05, two-tail test.

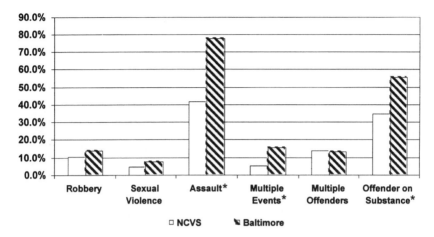

Fig. 7.2. Victimization Circumstances for NCVS and Baltimore Victims. * = p ≤ 0.05, two-tail test.

the patterns of domesticity than violence. Note that the NCVS women are almost equally likely to be victimized by a spouse or by a boy/girlfriend, whereas the Baltimore sample is more than twenty times more likely to be victimized by their boy/girlfriend than their spouse. Only about 15 percent of the Baltimore women are married, compared to 57 percent of the NCVS women. Still, even with these differences, there is undeniably a strong tendency for the marginalized women to be violently victimized by nonmarital partners.[38] The final and rather surprising difference is that the marginalized women are less likely to be violently victimized by strangers than the NCVS women (22.4 percent versus 29.2 percent). Perhaps this group of women is more "street smart," making them better able to negotiate public spaces where strangers abide.

Figure 7.2 presents data on the contextual circumstances surrounding the violence experienced by each group of victims. Three differences are significant. The Baltimore women are more likely to be victims of assault, have multiple victimizations that are indistinguishable, and be attacked by someone who is using drugs or alcohol. The difference in assault between the two groups is particularly striking given that the marginalized group of women is nearly twice as likely to have been assaulted as the general population.

Figure 7.3 compares the different locations of violent victimizations. All locations show a difference between the two groups of women, except for

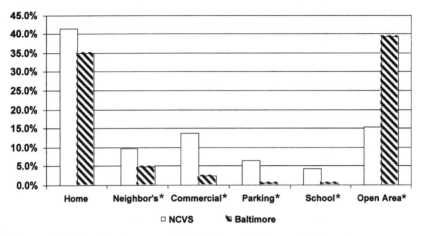

Fig. 7.3. Victimization Locations for NCVS and Baltimore Victims. * = p ≤ 0.05, two-tail test.

home. Interestingly, all women regardless of whether they are from the general population or are marginalized have a high likelihood of being violently attacked at home (between 35 to 42 percent). The differences in the remaining findings support predictions of lifestyle/routine-activities theory. The NCVS women are more likely than the Baltimore women to be victimized in locations that they may also be more likely to visit— namely, a neighbor/friend's home, a commercial establishment, a parking lot or facility, or a school. The Baltimore women, however, are more likely to be victimized in an open area, such as the street. Narratives provided by the Baltimore women reveal that street victimizations are frequently related to some type of drug transaction, as the following examples illustrate:

> I was selling a bag of pills for him, and I kept three of them for myself. And he wanted to fight over them. And he grabbed me and started punching me, and he hit me in my eye. Made it black—gave me a black eye. The police was riding down the street and he ran. I didn't call them; they just rolled past. I didn't give him no money, but I worked it off. [thirty-nine-year-old Respondent #112]

> We were arguing about because he thought I should sell [drugs] up this end and I thought I should stay at another end. He called me by my name

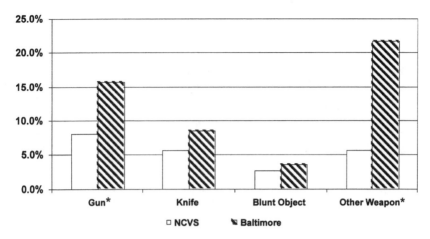

Fig. 7.4. Weapons Used on NCVS and Baltimore Victims. * = p ≤ 0.05, two-tail test.

[cursed at respondent] and I called him by his name, and he jumped on me. I was walking away; he just leaped on me and landed on top of me. I fell to the ground, and people grabbed him off me and took him one way and took me the other. [thirty-year-old Respondent #235]

The types of weapons used in all incidents are shown in Figure 7.4. First, we find that victims from the Baltimore sample were more likely to have a weapon used against them. In fact, nearly half had a weapon used against them (49.7 percent), compared to less than a quarter of the NCVS victims (22.2 percent). Women from the Baltimore sample are most likely to have had a gun used against them, followed by an assortment of other types of weapons (the distribution of weapon type for the NCVS victims was similar). Many of the victimizations of the Baltimore women that involved weapons stem from drug-related disputes or robberies on the street, where the presence and availability of guns is practically commonplace. The following narratives illustrate the context of these street robberies:

Okay, I was on the street. And I copped [purchased drugs]. And a guy come up to me and told me, "I got coke and dope." I said, "I'm fine, thank you." And he followed me around the corner and stuck a gun in my face, and said, "Give me all your shit, bitch, or I'll shoot you." And that was it. I gave it to him. [thirty-two-year-old Respondent #833]

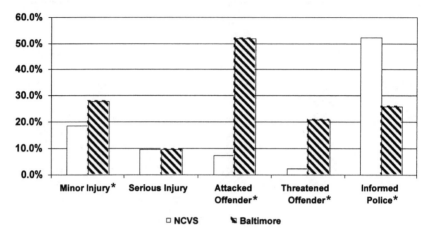

Fig. 7.5. Consequences of Victimizations for NCVS and Baltimore Victims. * = p ≤ 0.05, two-tail test.

> I was up on Monroe and Baltimore Street. I was selling drugs for a guy. Had been selling most of the day. Two guys get out a car, come up to me like they were going to buy drugs. Pull out a gun, say "You know what time it is?" I was so upset and scared I just dropped everything on the ground and started running. The boy, one guy, ran after me to make sure I didn't have any more money or any drugs, 'cause I was at the end of the pack [of heroin]. He didn't believe I had that little bit, 'cause I had just turned the money in. So he just like hit me in the back of the head and ran off. That was the end of that. [forty-two-year-old Respondent #103]

Finally, Figure 7.5 presents the consequences of the violent acts. While nearly all the observed differences are significant, the most striking is the victim's response. More than 70 percent of the Baltimore women retaliated either with an attack (52.1 percent) or a threat (20.9 percent). In contrast, less than 10 percent of the women from the general population retaliated (9.9 percent). Instead, most of these women contacted the police (52.3 percent). Finally, marginalized women were more likely to be injured than other women (37.6 percent versus 28.6 percent). However, this difference was found only among minor injuries. All women were equally likely to have been seriously victimized.

Conclusion

We began this chapter by discussing the importance of considering the experiences of incarcerated women when studying violence against women. Because most information on such violence comes from surveys administered to victims, we compare the victimization data from the general population to that collected from a group of highly marginalized women incarcerated in the Baltimore City Detention Center. We framed this research with the guidance of routine-activities theory, which is a rich theory that provides a clear set of predictions that should be consistent regardless of the group under study. In fact, the first prediction we derived was supported. The incarcerated women had experienced far more violence than women drawn from the general (noninstitutionalized) public. In fact, the jailed women were more than thirty-three times more likely to have been violently attacked during the six months prior to incarceration than were mainstream women during any given six-month period. One concern is that violence against these highly marginalized women rarely appears in official crime and victimization statistics.[39] As suspected, only a small percentage of these women report their victimization to the police. Instead they are more likely to take matters into their own hands by attacking or threatening the perpetrator. Without intervention or prevention, this pattern will serve to perpetuate an ongoing and destructive cycle of violence.

The research conducted in this chapter suggests that routine-activities theory may not be well suited to predict the violence encountered by women living under marginalized circumstances. Although a few factors appeared to similarly affect all women regardless of marginalization—such as dropping out of high school, going out nightly, and being victimized in the home—the most important results are found in the differences between the two groups of women. Two patterns emerge from the findings. First, partnering with a man fails to protect marginalized women from the risk of violent victimization. Unlike mainstream women, marriage does not translate into a safer lifestyle. In fact, the findings suggest that marriage puts these women at a higher risk of violence. Furthermore, the decision not to marry can also increase risk. If violently attacked, the marginalized woman was most likely targeted by her boyfriend.

The second pattern revealed by this research is that the highly marginalized women appear to be better able to negotiate certain types of risk than mainstream women. Lifestyle characteristics that are consistently associated with violent victimization seem to not significantly affect these women. Moving from place to place, living in public housing, having a relatively low income, and being a single parent do not increase their risk of victimization. Further, by comparison to mainstream women, marginalized women derive some protection from crime victimization if they are employed. Perhaps by reducing the suitability of the targeted victim herself certain factors inhibit victimization despite an increased likelihood of interaction with motivated offenders. Many of these findings challenge predictions of routine-activities theory; and by doing so, they offer an opportunity to advance theory.

Clearly, context matters. The situational predictors and circumstances of violence against women can differ by the type of woman being studied. Marginalized women spend much of their time on the street and are frequently involved in the volatile drug market. Thus, they are more often than mainstream women violently victimized on the street by a perpetrator who uses a weapon. If we keep relying exclusively on the experiences of *mainstream* women to learn about the experiences of *all* women, we will continue to perpetuate naive characterizations of women whose victimization patterns fall neatly into those predicted by routine activities. We cannot be content to learn about violence against women with NCVS data or with data from other mainstream populations. Studying populations of incarcerated women helps us understand important components of the nature and extent of violence against *all* women.

APPENDIX 7.1
Variables Used in the Logistic Models Predicting Violence

Variable	Possible Values	Description
Protective Factors		
Months at Residence	$[0, \infty]$	The number of months the respondent has lived at her current residence (NCVS women) or last residence (incarcerated women). All values at thirty-six months or greater are recorded as thirty-six for incarcerated women.
Married	0, 1	The respondent is married.
Risk Factors		
High Mobility	0, 1	The respondent has moved at least five times over the past five (NCVS women) or three (incarcerated women) years.
Public Housing	0, 1	The respondent lived in public housing.
One Adult with Kid(s)	0, 1	The respondent lived in a household that includes only one adult with at least one child.
Out Every Night	0, 1	The respondent reported spending almost every

APPENDIX 7.1 *(continued)*

Variable	Possible Values	Description
		evening away from home for work, school, or entertainment (NCVS women) or the respondent reported going out at least five evenings a week for fun and recreation (incarcerated women).
Low Income	0, 1	Household income was less than $15,000 per year.
In School	0, 1	The respondent was currently attending school.
Less Than High School	0, 1	The respondent did not finish high school and was nineteen years or older.
High School Diploma / GED	0, 1	The respondent reported completing only twelve years of education (NCVS women) or obtained her GED (incarcerated women).
Some College	0, 1	The respondent had less than four years of post–high school education and was twenty-three years or older.
Uncertain		
Other Units	0, 1	The respondent lived in a multiple-unit dwelling (e.g., apartment, hotel).
Job	0, 1	The respondent had a job.
Demographics		
Nonwhite	0, 1	The respondent is not white.
18 to 24	0, 1	The respondent is between eighteen and twenty-four years old.
25 to 34	0, 1	The respondent is between twenty and twenty-nine years old.
35 to 49	0, 1	The respondent is between thirty-five and forty-nine years old.
50 or Older	0, 1	The respondent is age fifty or older.
Survey Controls (Incarcerated Women)		
Past 36 Months	0, 1	The respondent lived at their previous residence for at least thirty-six months.
Missing Public Housing	0, 1	No information on public housing was collected.
Survey Controls (NCVS)		
Others Present	0, 1	Another person was present during the interview.
Proxy Interview	0, 1	Someone else provided information for the respondent.
CATI	0, 1	The interviewer used Computer Assisted Telephone Interviewing.
Unbounded	0, 1	The respondent just moved into the sample during the current interview period.
Interview Period	0, 1	The current interview period.
Missing Job Info	0, 1	The respondent provided no information on employment.
Missing Educ Info	0, 1	The respondent provided no information on education.
Missing Month Info	0, 1	The respondent provided no information on months at residence.
Missing Income Info	0, 1	The respondent provided no information on income.
Year 1992–1999	0, 1	An indicator for each year.

APPENDIX 7.2

Variables Used in Analyses Describing Violent Incidents

Variable	Possible Values	Description
Offender Characteristics		
Spouse	0, 1	At least one offender is currently or formerly married to the victim.
Boy/Girlfriend	0, 1	At least one offender is a current or former boyfriend or girlfriend to the victim.
Family Member	0, 1	At least one offender is a nonintimate immediate family member to the victim.
Acquaintance	0, 1	At least one offender is known to the victim but is not an intimate or family member.
Stranger	0, 1	All offenders are not known to the victim.
Incident Characteristics		
Robbery	0, 1	The incident was a completed or attempted robbery (use or threat of force to take something from the respondent).
Sexual Violence	0, 1	The incident was a completed rape or sexual attack with assault (NCVS women) or the incident involved an opponent's use or threat of force to make the respondent have sexual relations (such as vaginal penetration, anal penetration, or oral penetration with a penis or an object) (incarcerated women).
Assault	0, 1	The incident was a completed aggravated assault or simple assault (NCVS women) or the incident involved a physical attack by an opponent against the respondent, including use of a weapon, throwing something (e.g., rock, bottle), punching, slapping, choking, kicking, or throwing to the ground or against a wall (incarcerated women).
Multiple Events	0, 1	Multiple incidents of violence that women could not clearly distinguish in their minds.
Home	0, 1	The incident occurred in or near respondent's own home (e.g., in yard or on street adjacent to home) or in detached building on property.
Neighbor/Friend's	0, 1	The incident occurred at, in, or near a known third party's home, e.g., friend's, relative's, or neighbor's home.
Commercial Area	0, 1	The incident occurred in a commercial place, e.g., restaurant, office, bar.
Parking Lot	0, 1	The incident occurred in a parking lot or garage.
School	0, 1	The incident occurred inside school or on school property.
Open Area	0, 1	The incident occurred in an open area, on the street, or on public transportation.
Gun	0, 1	The offender had a gun.
Knife	0, 1	The offender had a knife.
Blunt Object	0, 1	The offender had a blunt object.
Other Weapon	0, 1	The offender had some other weapon.
Offender on Substance	0, 1	The offender was on drugs or alcohol.
Multiple Offenders	0, 1	There was more than one offender.

APPENDIX 7.2 *(continued)*

Variable	Possible Values	Description
Consequences		
Minor Injury	0, 1	Respondent was injured, but it was not identified as serious (NCVS women) and the respondent received no medical attention (incarcerated women).
Serious Injury	0, 1	The reported injury included broken bones, loss of teeth, internal injuries, loss of consciousness, or any injury requiring two or more days of hospitalization or was a completed rape where the victim sought professional medical help (NCVS women), or the injury included knife/stab wounds, gunshot/bullet wounds, or injuries to breasts or genitalia (incarcerated women).
Attacked Offender	0, 1	The victim attacked the offender with or without a weapon or chased off the offender ("chased off" was only asked of NCVS women).
Threatened Offender	0, 1	The victim threatened the offender with or without a weapon—or yelled at the offender or turned on the lights (NCVS women)—or demanded compliance (incarcerated women).
Informed Police	0, 1	The police were informed about the incident.

NOTES

1. Lawrence E. Cohen and Marcus Felson, "Social Change and Crime Rate Trends: A Routine Activity Approach," *American Sociological Review* 44 (1979): 588–608; Michael J. Hindelang, Michael R. Gottfredson, and James Garofalo, *Victims of Personal Crime: An Empirical Foundation for a Theory of Personal Victimization* (Cambridge, MA: Ballinger, 1978).

2. Bureau of Justice Statistics, *National Crime Victimization Survey, 1992–1999* (Computer File and Documentation), conducted by the U.S. Department of Commerce, Bureau of Census (9th ICPSR ed.) (Ann Arbor, MI: Inter-university Consortium for Political and Social Research [producer and distributor], 2001).

3. Beth E. Richie, "Exploring the Link between Violence against Women and Women's Involvement in Illegal Activity," in *Research on Women and Girls in the Justice System: Plenary Papers of the 1999 Conference on Criminal Justice Research and Evaluation—Enhancing Policy and Practice through Research,* vol. 3, ed. B. E. Richie, K. Tsenin, and C. S. Widom (Washington, DC: National Institute of Justice, 2000).

4. Robert J. Sampson and Janet L. Lauritsen, "Deviant Lifestyles, Proximity to Crime, and the Offender-Victim Link in Personal Violence," *Journal of Research in Crime and Delinquency* 27 (1990): 110–139; Candace Kruttschnitt, "Gender and Interpersonal Violence," in *Understanding and Preventing Violence,* vol. 3, ed. A. J.

Reiss Jr. and J. A. Roth, pp. 293–376 (Washington, DC: National Academy Press, 1994).

5. Deborah R. Baskin and Ira B. Sommers, *Casualties of Community Disorder: Women's Careers in Violent Crime* (Boulder, CO: Westview, 1998); Richie, "Exploring the Link."

6. Kruttschnitt, "Gender and Interpersonal Violence."

7. Richie, "Exploring the Link."

8. Pamela Wilcox Rountree, Kenneth C. Land, and Terance D. Miethe, "Macro-Micro Integration in the Study of Victimization: A Hierarchical Logistic Model Analysis across Seattle Neighborhoods," *Criminology* 32 (1994): 387–414; Robert J. Sampson and Janet L. Lauritsen, "Violent Victimization and Offending: Individual-, Situational-, and Community-Level Risk Factors," in Reiss and Roth, *Understanding and Preventing Violence*, 1–114.

9. Sampson and Lauritsen, "Violent Victimization and Offending"; Callie Marie Rennison, *Criminal Victimization 1999 Changes 1998–99 with Trends 1993–99* (Washington, DC: Bureau of Justice Statistics, U.S. Department of Justice, 2000); Kruttschnitt, "Gender and Interpersonal Violence"; Diane Craven, *Sex Differences in Violent Victimization, 1994: Bureau of Justice Statistics, Special Report, NCJ-164508* (Washington, DC: U.S. Department of Justice, 1997); Nancy A. Crowell and Ann W. Burgess, *Understanding Violence against Women* (Washington, DC: National Academy Press, 1996).

10. Kruttschnitt, "Gender and Interpersonal Violence."

11. Robert J. Sampson and Janet L. Lauritsen, "Racial and Ethnic Disparities in Crime and Criminal Justice in the United States," in *Crime and Justice*, vol. 21, ed. Michael Tonry, pp. 311–374 (Chicago: University of Chicago Press, 1996); Sampson and Lauritsen, "Violent Victimization and Offending"; Kruttschnitt, "Gender and Interpersonal Violence"; Candace Kruttschnitt, Rosemary Gartner, and Kathleen Ferraro, "Women's Involvement in Serious Interpersonal Violence," *Aggression and Violent Behavior* 7 (2002): 529–565; Ross Macmillan, "Violence and the Life Course: The Consequences of Victimization for Personal and Social Development," *Annual Review of Sociology* 27 (2001): 1–22.

12. Candace Kruttschnitt, "Violence by and against Women: A Comparative and Cross-National Analysis," in *Interpersonal Violent Behaviors: Social and Cultural Aspects*, ed. R. B. Ruback and N. A. Weiner, pp. 89–108 (New York: Springer, 1995).

13. Sampson and Lauritsen, "Violent Victimization and Offending."

14. Kruttschnitt, "Gender and Interpersonal Violence."

15. Keith Harries and Eric Kovandzic, "Persistence, Intensity, and Areal Extent of Violence against Women: Baltimore City, 1992 to 1995," *Violence against Women* 5 (1999): 813–828.

16. Crowell and Burgess, *Understanding Violence against Women*; Patricia Tjaden and Nancy Thoennes, *Full Report of the Prevalence, Incidence, and Conse-*

quences of Violence against Women, report from the National Institute of Justice and the Centers for Disease Control and Prevention (Washington, DC: U.S. Department of Justice, 2000); Bureau of Justice Statistics, *National Crime Victimization Survey, 1992–1999.*

17. Sampson and Lauritsen, "Violent Victimization and Offending."

18. Rosemary Gartner, Kathryn Baker, and Fred C. Pampel, "Gender Stratification and the Gender Gap in Homicide Victimization," *Social Problems* 37 (1990): 593–612.

19. Sampson and Lauritsen, "Violent Victimization and Offending."

20. Bureau of Justice Statistics, *National Crime Victimization Survey, 1992–1999.*

21. The Bureau of Justice Statistics uses the first interview for bounding purposes only. It is not included in these data.

22. Proxy interviews are also included in this data. Proxy interviews are interviews given by a representative of the respondent in place of the respondent.

23. The Women's Experience of Violence (WEV) Project is a multisite study examining women's experiences as offenders and victims of violence. The four principal investigators directing the WEV Project are Julie Horney, State University New York at Albany; Sally Simpson, University of Maryland at College Park; Rosemary Gartner, University of Toronto; and Candace Kruttschnitt, University of Minnesota.

24. The computerized life-event calendar used in our research was a revised version of the instrument originally used with incarcerated male offenders by Julie Horney, D. Wayne Osgood, and Ineke Haen Marshall, "Criminal Careers in the Short-Term: Intra-individual Variability in Crime and Its Relation to Local Life Circumstances," *American Sociological Review* 60 (1995): 655–673.

25. Also, two women completed the study twice. We chose to count only their first interview as valid.

26. Each respondent received fifteen dollars for her participation.

27. Our sample was 92 percent African American.

28. In all models, we estimate the likelihood that a person is victimized by a violent crime using the cumulative logistic function:

$$P(Violent = 1) = \frac{\exp(\beta_0 + \beta_1 PF + \beta_2 RF + \beta_3 UnC + \beta_4 Dem + \beta_5 SI)}{1 + \exp(\beta_0 + \beta_1 PF + \beta_2 RF + \beta_3 UnC + \beta_4 Dem + \beta_5 SI)}$$

29. For discussion of issues related to these measures, see Albert D. Biderman and David Cantor, "A Longitudinal Analysis of Bounding, Respondent Conditioning, and Mobility as Sources of Panel Bias in the National Crime Survey," *Proceedings of the Section for Survey Research Methods, American Statistical Association* (1984): 708–713; Bureau of Justice Statistics, *Technical Background on the Redesigned National Crime Victimization Survey* (Washington, DC: Bureau of Justice Statistics, U.S. Department of Justice, 1994).

30. See Bureau of Justice Statistics, *National Crime Victimization Survey, 1992–1999*.

31. In order to calculate the design effect, NCVS data must provide two values of the secucode (or half sample code) for each pseudostratum (or geographic unit). When we began to examine females of smaller racial and ethnic groups, not all pseudostrata have two secucodes, making it impossible to use that pseudostratum to calculate the design effect. Further, observations from 1992 omit all values for the pseudostratum and secucode. Because we wanted to include all observations in the analysis, we first ran survey logit models on the limited sample to obtain estimates of the true design effect. We then ran the entire data set using regular logistic regression and adjusted the standard errors by the estimated design effect.

32. John Johnston, *Econometric Methods*, 3rd ed. (New York: McGraw-Hill, 1984).

33. Seven incarcerated women reported experiencing both a partner and non-partner victimization in the same most recent month. We flipped a coin to determine which incident to include for each woman.

34. Readers may contact the authors for the complete list of odds ratios and a table of summary statistics.

35. Note that the variable Months at Residence is not a dummy variable. Each additional increment measures one month, thus making the odds ratio of .997 incomparable to the other ratios.

36. Data on public housing in the Baltimore sample was less consistent. Because the question was added after interviews had begun, almost 40 percent of the sample had no data on whether or not they had lived in public housing. These cases were marked as non-public-housing cases and then flagged with a dummy variable. The dummy variable was positive and significant, suggesting that those who never mentioned whether they had lived in public housing have a higher risk of victimization. Thus, the insignificant public-housing coefficient only reflects the sample of women who reported living in public housing.

37. Two-tail significance levels are shown here to emphasize that this is an exploratory comparison. We make no a priori claims regarding the direction of any differences.

38. Although the marginalized women are predominantly African American, this finding is not entirely a function of race. Laura Dugan and Robert Apel, in "An Exploratory Study of the Violent Victimization of Women: Race/Ethnicity and Situational Context," *Criminology* 41 (2003): 959–980, show that only 18 percent of the African American females victimized in the NCVS were harmed by their nonmarital partner. This figure is only half as high as that from the women in the Baltimore sample.

39. Such women can appear in NCVS statistics during periods of nonincarceration, but even that likelihood is low given that they are a highly transient population and spend much of their time out on the street.

Chapter 8

Female and Male Homicide Victimization Trends
A Cross-National Context

Gary LaFree and Gwen Hunnicutt

Gender, along with age, has long been regarded by criminologists as the most conspicuous predictor of criminal behavior.[1] And differences between women and men are widely assumed to be especially great for violent crime. Although there are a handful of studies examining the so-called gender gap in female and male rates of homicide victimization, this research literature is in several respects extremely selective. First, although some prior research examines changes in the gender gap in annual homicide victimization, we could not identify a single study of convergence in gender-specific criminal victimization trends. Second, although generalizations about the gender gap in crime are frequently assumed to apply to women and men everywhere, much of the research on gender and crime trends is based on data from the United States. And finally, while many of the theoretical expectations about the magnitude and direction of female homicide victimization trends are made in comparison to male homicide victimization trends, much of the research has either examined only female trends or has examined male-female victimization ratios that may obscure different trends for men and women.

In this chapter, we respond to these neglected research topics by examining annual homicide victimization rates for women and men in thirty-five nations during the last half of the twentieth century. Our study explores cross-national, longitudinal similarities and differences in male and female homicide victimization rates. We employ a gender equality framework to interpret these similarities and differences and consider the implications of the results for theory and future research.

Homicide data are universally judged to be the most valid crime data,[2] and among cross-national comparative sources, the World Health Organization (WHO) data are widely believed to be the most valid single data source.[3] For much of the analysis, we take advantage of econometric time-series methods that allow us to provide consistent and efficient estimates of female and male trends, to test these trends with significance tests, and to correct for statistical biases. For convenience, we have arranged our analysis into a series of five research questions about trends in female and male homicide victimization rates during the past half century. Before considering these questions, we first describe the homicide victimization data that are the main source of our analysis.

Homicide Victimization Data

We assembled annual time-series data from WHO on homicide victimization rates per 100,000 females and males in thirty-five countries from 1950 to 2001. The length of the series and the countries included were determined by data availability—the sample and time frame maximized the number of countries and years available for analysis. We did not extrapolate values to the beginning or the end of any individual series. Because data were missing for Puerto Rico after 1992, Bulgaria before 1960, and Hungary for 1956, comparisons involving these countries were truncated accordingly. We excluded nations that had missing data for more than three consecutive years.[4] Because Iceland had no homicides for several years, it was impossible to compute a meaningful measure of relative difference between women and men in Iceland, and we excluded it. Rates for Israel are reported only for the Jewish population. We interpolated three years for Israel that included deaths from the Sinai campaign (1956, 1957) and the Six-Day War (1967).

Several political changes affected the geographical boundaries and hence the homicide rates of the nations included. Our analysis of Czechoslovakia is based on data from only the Czech Republic after the political breakup of 1992. Our analysis of the Federal Republic of Germany (West Germany) becomes an analysis of unified Germany after 1991. And finally, because French statistics include Algeria until 1962, we limit our analysis of France to the years since Algerian independence.

As is universally true in this type of research, our analysis is dominated by North American and West European nations, which comprise eighteen countries (51.4 percent) in the sample. In addition, the sample includes six Latin American/Caribbean countries, four East European countries, five countries from the Western Pacific, one from Africa, and one from the Middle East.[5] In 1990 these thirty-five nations accounted for 18 percent of the total world population and an estimated 9 percent of total world homicides.[6] Next we turn to our analysis of the five research questions.

Are Male Homicide Victimization Rates Universally Higher Than Female Rates?

Nearly all studies that examine the gender gap in homicide victimization begin with the assumption that male homicide victimization rates are universally higher than female rates.[7] Hence, of all the questions we might ask about female and male trends in violent victimization over the past fifty years, this one at first seems to be the most obvious. The gender equality model of violence against women is probably the dominant explanation of the gender gap in homicide.[8] This model holds that female homicide victimization is an expression of patriarchal control and that as social, political, and economic disparities between men and women gradually decline, violence against women will also decline. In other words, the assumption is that male homicide victimization rates have long been higher than female rates and that this difference will further widen over time as women's social status improves relative to men.

Another feature of the literature on the gender gap in homicide victimization is that most of it has been done in the United States, which has very distinctive homicide rates compared to other highly industrialized countries.[9] Although the assumption that male homicide victimization rates are considerably higher than female rates may be true for the United States, it may not hold for other nations. Thus, it is unclear whether the gender equality model that has been based mostly on data from the United States also applies to other countries. Instead, it could be that gender-specific behaviors are characteristic of broad cultural patterns that vary across nations and regions. In fact, this seems plausible because we know that gender roles are in large part socially constructed and vary by culture.[10] For example, Smith and Brewer show that the relative risk of homicide victimization for women and men differs substantially across different geographical areas.[11] Further, Daly and Wilson have found major cross-national differences in male and female homicide rates, depending on different combinations of victim and offender age and gender.[12]

Employing the use of cross-national data may help us better understand the extent to which female-male victimization trends in the United States generalize to other nations.

Table 8.1 shows female and male homicide rate victimization means and standard deviations for several groups of nations and for the individual nations included in our analysis. According to Table 8.1, male victimization rates are considerably higher than female rates for all the groups of nations compared. Rates for both women and men are highest for the full sample. Exclusion of the less industrialized nations[13] reduces the male rate by 56.9 percent and the female rate by 33.8 percent. Female and male rates for industrialized nations are further reduced if the United States is excluded from the analysis. Female and male homicide victimization rates for the European Union nations[14] included in the analysis are somewhat lower than the rates for the industrialized nations. For men, average national homicide victimization rates range from a high of 35.13 per 100,000 for Mexico to a low of .85 per 100,000 for Ireland. For women, the highest homicide victimization mean rate is for Puerto Rico (3.53), followed closely by Mexico (3.40) and the United States (3.37). The lowest female rate is for Spain (.31), followed closely by Ireland (.34).

Consistent with the argument that male homicide victimization rates are universally higher than those for women, the male mean rate is greater than the female rate for every group comparison and for all thirty-five nations in the sample. Among the group comparisons, the male-female ratio is greatest for the full sample (4.00) and least for the EU sample (2.05). Although men have higher homicide victimization rates than women in all these nations, the size of the male-female ratio varies considerably, ranging from a low of 1.06 for Denmark to a high of 10.32 for Mexico. Moreover, the ratio of male to female homicide victimization differs greatly by geographic region. Thus, the four nations with the smallest ratio of male to female homicide victimization rates are all West European: Denmark (1.06), Switzerland (1.14), Belgium (1.28), and Austria (1.29). By contrast, the three nations with the highest ratio of male to female homicide victimization are all Latin American: Mexico (10.32), Venezuela (9.84), and Chile (7.10).

Because data from the United States have dominated the research literature on trends in female and male crime, we begin by examining U.S. trends. Figure 8.1 compares female and male homicide victimization rates for the United States from 1950 to 1999. The male trend is relatively flat until the early 1960s, rises rapidly in the 1960s and early 1970s, remains

TABLE 8.1
Descriptive Statistics, Male and Female Homicide Victimization Rates, 1950–2001

Country/Group	Years	Males Mean	Males Standard Deviation	Females Mean	Females Standard Deviation
Groups					
European Union	1956–1998	1.629	0.369	0.795	0.153
Industrial nations	1956–1998	2.245	0.403	0.862	0.144
Industrial—no U.S.	1956–1998	1.703	0.287	0.995	0.166
Full sample	1956–1998	5.215	0.796	1.303	0.195
Countries					
Australia	1950–1999	2.174	0.437	1.286	0.235
Austria	1950–2001	1.386	0.334	1.074	0.218
Belgium	1954–1998	1.379	0.573	1.079	0.423
Bulgaria	1960–2000	4.472	1.723	1.480	0.505
Canada	1950–1998	2.314	0.744	1.265	0.352
Chile	1954–1999	5.886	2.212	0.829	0.311
Costa Rica	1955–2000	7.145	2.137	1.449	0.597
Czechoslovakia/Czech Republic	1953–2000	1.889	0.896	1.174	0.456
Denmark	1950–1998	1.013	0.680	0.951	0.373
England/Wales	1973–1999	1.284	0.244	0.899	0.092
Finland	1950–2000	4.374	1.068	1.728	0.494
France	1963–1999	1.233	0.224	0.722	0.123
West Germany/Germany	1950–1999	1.357	0.182	0.911	0.153
Greece	1956–1999	1.563	0.679	0.592	0.225
Hong Kong	1960–2000	2.007	1.037	0.877	0.380
Hungary	1955–2001	3.573	1.225	1.870	0.653
Ireland	1950–1999	0.850	0.446	0.344	0.268
Israel	1951–1998	1.692	0.922	0.827	0.446
Italy	1950–1999	2.409	0.901	0.623	0.100
Japan	1950–1999	1.626	0.765	0.940	0.358
Mauritius	1955–2000	3.030	1.794	0.911	0.576
Mexico	1956–1999	35.133	9.882	3.403	0.817
Netherlands	1950–1998	0.974	0.472	0.463	0.209
New Zealand	1950–1999	1.657	0.733	0.938	0.395
Norway	1950–1999	1.064	0.564	0.598	0.295
Poland	1955–2000	2.244	1.035	0.983	0.370
Portugal	1955–2000	2.001	0.520	0.633	0.154
Puerto Rico	1955–1999	24.640	12.220	3.529	0.904
Singapore	1954–2000	2.685	0.893	0.768	0.420
Spain	1950–1999	0.941	0.548	0.306	0.156
Sweden	1950–1999	1.224	0.458	0.798	0.223
Switzerland	1950–1999	1.063	0.344	0.928	0.287
Trinidad & Tobago	1951–1998	9.369	3.392	3.144	1.319
United States	1950–1999	11.877	3.551	3.366	0.812
Venezuela	1950–2000	18.151	7.076	1.845	0.390

high until the early 1990s, and then declines substantially. Female trends are clearly correlated with male trends ($r = .87$) but remain at much lower levels throughout the series. Overall, the mean male rate is 3.53 times higher than the mean female rate.

In order to directly address the question posed in this section, we examined each of the thirty-five nations in the data set to determine whether there were any cases in which female homicide victimization rates exceeded those of men. We found that for eleven nations in the sample (31.4 percent), female homicide victimization rates were higher than male rates for at least one year in the series. In fact, female rates exceeded male rates eighty-nine times for these eleven nations in the years spanned by our data. This raises serious conceptual difficulties for the concept of convergence, which is the focus of our second question.

Convergence between male and female victimization trends assumes a situation in which male rates exceed female rates at time one, but this gap significantly diminishes at time two. Such an analysis makes sense for female-male comparisons in the United States in the 1970s because male rates were unambiguously higher than female rates. But the meaning of

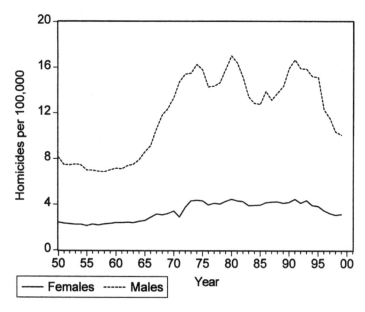

Fig. 8.1. Female and Male Homicide Victimization in the United States, 1950 to 1999.

TABLE 8.2

Nations and Years in Which Women Have Higher Homicide Victimization Rates Than Men, 1950 to 2001

Nation	Years before 1975	1975 and Later	Total
Denmark	21	10	31
Switzerland	10	6	16
Austria	2	6	8
Israel	8	0	8
Sweden	7	0	7
Belgium	6	0	6
New Zealand	4	1	5
Ireland	4	0	4
Mauritius	2	0	2
Hong Kong	1	0	1
Norway	1	0	1
Total	66	23	89

convergence is far less clear in situations in which female rates exceed male rates for part of the series. In fact, the timing of cases in which female rates exceed male rates is important for interpreting the results. Thus, if female rates are far below male rates during the first half of a series but sometimes exceed male rates during the second half of a series, it might be a strong indication of convergence in trends. On the other hand, if female rates are higher than male rates in the first half of a series, then testing for convergence makes little sense, but we could nevertheless still test for divergence in rates during the second half of a series.

To illustrate these differences, Table 8.2 shows for the eleven nations with overlapping female and male rates the total number of years in which female homicide victimization rates exceeded male rates and indicates whether the higher female rate-years occurred in the first or second half of the series. According to Table 8.2, Denmark reported the largest total number of years in which women had higher homicide victimization rates than men—thirty-one out of forty-nine years available for analysis (63.3 percent). After Denmark, the nation with the next highest total (sixteen) is Switzerland. By contrast, both Hong Kong and Norway report only one year in which women's homicide rates exceed those of men.

Table 8.2 shows that women's homicide rates exceeded men's rates almost three times more frequently during the first half of the series than the second half. In fact, we did not observe a single nation in which female rates were higher than male rates for a year after 1975 but not for a year before. For seven of the eleven nations, all the years in which women's rates exceeded men's occurred in the first half of the series. In short, it became *less* common for female homicide victimization rates to exceed male rates in the years after 1975. It is also clear from Table 8.2 that the nations that experienced at least one year in which female homicide victimization rates exceeded those of males are by no means a random sample of the nations in the study. Instead, seven of the eleven nations are West European democracies, and three others (New Zealand, Hong Kong, and Israel) are nations with strong connections to the West.

What all these nations have in common is very low homicide rates for both women and men throughout the period spanned by the data. The tiny island nation of Mauritius—which reported higher female than male victimization rates for just two years—is the single exception to this pattern. Unlike the other nations with overlapping male and female rates, Mauritius's average homicide rate for males during the series (3.03) puts it in the highest one-third of the homicide victimization averages among the nations in the study. According to Table 8.2, only four nations recorded higher female than male homicide victimization rates during at least one year in the first half and one year in the second half of the series (Denmark, Switzerland, Austria, and New Zealand). We compare the female and male homicide trends for these four nations in Figure 8.2.

Figure 8.2 shows how closely intertwined female and male homicide victimization rates are for these four nations. Testing for convergence makes little sense in any of these nations because all four begin the period with overlapping rates. And of the four nations, only New Zealand provides any indication of divergence during the second half of the period spanned by the data. Although New Zealand experienced one year after 1975 in which female homicide victimization rates exceeded those of males (1982), it does appear that female and male rates are diverging somewhat in New Zealand in the more recent half of the series. Accordingly, we later include New Zealand in our formal statistical tests for divergence.

Consistent with previous expectations, average male homicide victimization rates are higher than female rates for all thirty-five nations in the sample. In fact, of the more than 1,700 nation-years included in the analysis, female rates exceeded male rates only 5 percent of the time. Nevertheless, for almost one-third of the nations in our study, female rates did exceed male rates for at least one year in the series. And for Denmark, female victimization rates were actually higher than male rates for more than half of the years in the series. Thus, our results suggest that male homicide victimization rates are not universally higher than female rates. And for a

a. Austria

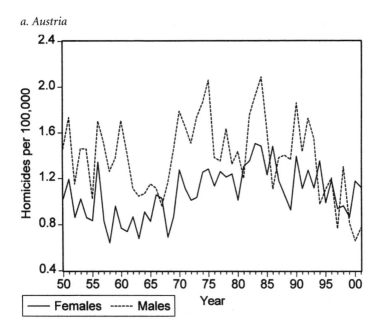

b. Denmark

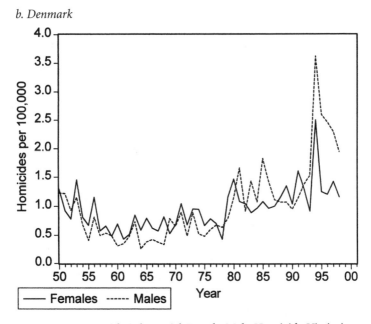

Fig. 8.2. Nations with Substantial Female-Male Homicide Victimization Overlap, 1950–1999

c. New Zealand

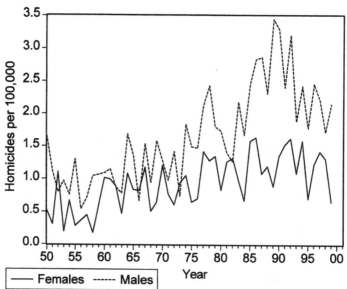

d. Switzerland

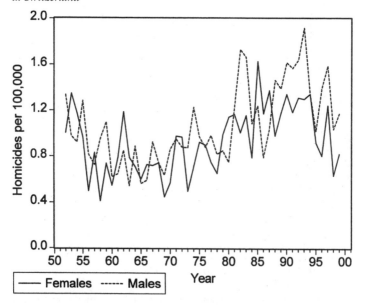

Fig. 8.2 *(continued)*

small number of mostly West European democracies, female and male rates of homicide victimization are virtually identical.

Are Female and Male Homicide Victimization Rates Converging or Diverging over Time?

Although we could identify no prior cross-national research that has examined whether female and male violent victimization rates are converging (or diverging) over time, there is research that examines variation in the gender gap in homicide victimization.[15] Typically, these studies explore whether the narrowing of the gender gap in homicide victimization is related to gender stratification in a given society. Those supporting a gender equality argument claim that gradual improvement in women's economic, social, and political position should reduce their exposure to violent victimization.[16] Given that male victimization rates are generally higher than female rates, this argument suggests a widening in the gap between male and female rates as gender equality brings greater power and protective resources to women.

In support, Gartner, Baker, and Pampel find that nations in which women's autonomy, independence, and social status increase experience a widening of the gender gap in homicide victimization.[17] But in a study of female homicide victimization in the United States, Smith and Brewer do not find a significant connection between increasing gender equality and a widening of the gender gap in homicide victimization.[18] In fact, Smith and Kuchta find that women's risk of homicide relative to men in the United States has been surprisingly stable from 1946 to 1990 and that the relative risk of female homicide victimization is more a function of shifts in male than in female homicide victimization rates.[19]

Although these studies have been useful for drawing our attention to relative changes in female and male homicide victimization rates over time, none of them has specifically tested for convergence or divergence in female and male homicide victimization rates within the nations they have studied. In the next section, we describe our methods for applying such tests to the thirty-five nations included in our study.

TESTING FOR CONVERGENCE AND DIVERGENCE

We use a constant multiplicative relationship between two series of homicide rates over time as a standard for measuring convergence and divergence between women and men in each of the nations in our study.

We compute the multiplicative relationship between female and male rates as the yearly difference of the log of each rate.[20] For example, in testing for convergence between female and male homicide rates for Australia, we compute the yearly logged difference as:

log (total male homicide rate)$_t$ − log (total female homicide rate)

Applying this formula to all comparisons produces a separate series of logged scores for each. We compute these scores by subtracting female rates from male rates at the beginning of the time series.[21] We tested each series of logged scores for evidence of convergence, divergence, or stability. For simplicity, we refer to these logged scores as "convergence scores."

We first classify each series of convergence scores as stationary, trend stationary, or difference stationary.[22] A stationary time series has a mean, variance, and autocovariance that are constant over time.[23] Scores vary by year, but they never move far away from their mean. If a series of convergence scores is stationary, the relative difference between the two component homicide rates does not change significantly over time. A stationary series therefore represents neither convergence nor divergence between female and male homicide rates.

In order to classify each series of convergence scores as stationary, trend stationary, or difference stationary, we used the augmented Dickey-Fuller procedure to test for the presence of a unit root.[24] This test involves estimating the following equation for each series of convergence scores:[25]

$$y_t = \alpha + \beta t + \rho y_{t-1} + \sum_{i=1}^{q} \theta_i \Delta y_{t-i} + \epsilon_t$$

If $\rho = 1$, the null hypothesis, then the series contains a unit root and is difference stationary, although the order of differencing is unknown. If ρ is significantly different from 1, then the series does not contain a unit root, and standard hypothesis tests can be used to determine whether the series contains a significant linear trend (trend-stationary series) or not (stationary series).[26] Note that these tests require adding lagged differences of the series (Δy_{t-i}) to the model until the residuals are uncorrelated.[27] For stationary and trend-stationary series, we report coefficients and significance tests for the slopes of the linear trend terms. A significant negative slope indicates that the component homicide rates are converging, and a significant positive slope indicates that the component homicide rates are diverging.

If a series contains a unit root, it is difference stationary or stochastic and we cannot test for convergence (or divergence) using the coefficient for the trend term. Instead, we apply a procedure developed by O'Brien that tests for convergence/divergence for difference-stationary series based on the regression of first differences of the convergence scores on an intercept and sufficient lags to remove autocorrelation among the residuals:[28]

$$\Delta y_t = \alpha + \sum_{i=1}^{q} \theta_i \Delta y_{t-i} + \epsilon_t$$

If the intercept is significant and negative, we conclude that the relative difference between the two component homicide rates has been declining on average (i.e., converging) during the time period, and if it is significant and positive, we conclude that the relative difference between the two rates has been increasing on average (i.e., diverging). Thus, for difference-stationary series, we report coefficients and significance tests for the intercepts of the regressions using first differences. This amounts to determining whether the mean yearly increase or decrease in a series is statistically significant over a period of years.

CONVERGENCE AND DIVERGENCE RESULTS

In Table 8.3 we present the results of the convergence tests for the four groups summarized earlier and the thirty-five individual nations in the study. For each comparison, we first determine whether the series is stationary, trend stationary, or difference stationary and then report the appropriate coefficient. We report slope coefficients for the stationary and trend-stationary series and intercept coefficients for the difference-stationary series. Negative coefficients in Table 8.3 indicate convergence; positive coefficients indicate divergence. As noted earlier, for three nations in which female rates exceed male rates in both the first and second halves of the series, convergence tests are inappropriate. For eight nations in which female rates exceeded male rates only during the first half of the series, we test only for divergence.[29] We discuss the group results first and then turn to the results for the individual nations.

According to Table 8.3, we find no evidence of convergence among any of the four tests for groups of nations. In fact, only one of these group comparisons (the full sample) is in a negative (i.e., converging) direction. The four parts of Figure 8.3 show annual female and male homicide victimization trends for the four groups of nations identified in Table 8.3. Perhaps the most striking feature of these figures is how little the gap between male and female homicide victimization rates has changed over the forty-three years spanned by the data. For example, in 1957 the ratio of male to female homicide victimization for the full sample of thirty-five

TABLE 8.3
Trend or Intercept [in brackets] Coefficients from the Convergence Tests for Male and Female Homicide Victimization Rates in Thirty-Five Countries, 1950 to 2001

Groups/Countries	Years	Male-Female Convergence
Groups		
European Union	1956–1998	0.003
Industrial	1956–1998	0.001
Industrial—no U.S.	1956–1998	0.000
Full sample	1956–1998	−0.000
Countries		
Australia	1950–1999	0.003
Austria	1950–2001	INAP
Belgium	1954–1998	Diverge only: 0.006
Bulgaria	1960–2000	0.001
Canada	1950–1998	0.003
Chile	1954–1999	0.003
Costa Rica	1955–2000	0.006
Czechoslovakia/Czech Republic	1953–2000	-0.000
Denmark	1950–1998	INAP
England/Wales	1973–1999	0.022*
Finland	1950–2000	0.001
France	1963–1999	0.002
West Germany/Germany	1950–1999	[−0.005]
Greece	1956–1999	−0.003
Hong Kong	1960–2000	Diverge only: [−0.013]
Hungary	1955–2001	−0.003
Ireland	1950–1999	Diverge only: 0.012
Israel	1951–1998	Diverge only: 0.037*
Italy	1950–1999	[0.001]
Japan	1950–1999	−0.009*
Mauritius	1955–2000	Diverge only: 0.001
Mexico	1956–1999	−0.008*
Netherlands	1950–1998	0.001
New Zealand	1950–1999	Diverge only: 0.002
Norway	1950–1999	Diverge only: 0.007
Poland	1955–2000	−0.001
Portugal	1955–2000	−0.002
Puerto Rico	1955–1999	[0.030]
Singapore	1954–2000	−0.022*
Spain	1950–1999	0.010*
Sweden	1950–1999	Diverge only: 0.013*
Switzerland	1950–1999	INAP
Trinidad & Tobago	1951–1998	−0.001
United States	1950–1999	[0.000]
Venezuela	1950–2000	0.015*

* p < .05

a. Full Sample

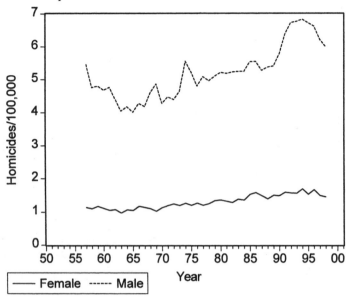

b. Industrialized Nations

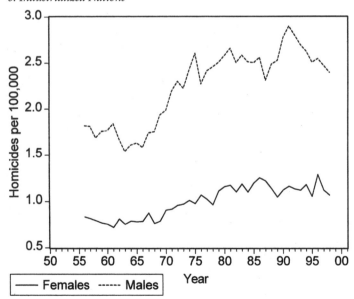

Fig. 8.3. Female and Male Homicide Victimization Rates, 1956 to 1998.

c. Industrial Nations without U.S.

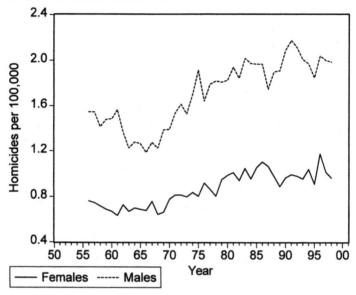

d. European Union

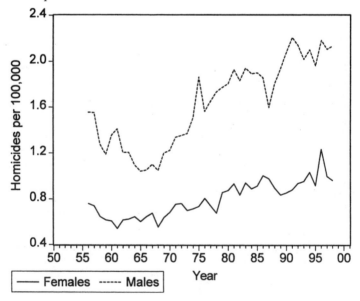

Fig. 8.3 *(continued)*

nations was 4.79 (Figure 8.3a). In 1998 it was down only slightly to 4.14. For the industrialized nations (Figure 8.3b) the male to female ratio increased slightly from 2.17 in 1956 to 2.25 in 1998. Male-female comparisons for Figures 8.3c and 8.3d tell much the same story. These grouped comparisons suggest that if there has been convergence between female and male homicide victimization rates in these nations over time, it must be limited to trends in some subset of individual nations.

Beyond the central observation that there is little evidence of female-male convergence among these groups of nations, it also appears that there has been a general upward trend in homicide victimization rates for both men and women and in all four group comparisons. For the full sample, mean male homicide victimization rates rose from 5.46 in 1957 to 6.00 in 1998, and female victimization rates rose from 1.14 in 1957 to 1.45 in 1998. Similarly, for the industrialized nations, male rates increased from 1.82 in 1956 to 2.40 in 1998, and female rates rose from .84 in 1956 to 1.07 in 1998. Table 8.3 shows that of the twenty-four nations for which we were able to perform meaningful convergence tests, only three nations showed statistically significant signs of convergence (Japan, Mexico, and Singapore). And of the thirty-two nations for which we were able to do divergence tests, only five nations (England/Wales, Israel, Spain, Sweden, and Venezuela) showed statistically significant signs of divergence. These findings suggest that neither convergence nor divergence is very common among this sample of nations and that if anything, there are more national examples of female and male violent victimization rates growing significantly farther apart than significantly closer together during the past fifty years.

For Nations That Are Experiencing Either Female-Male Convergence or Divergence in Homicide Victimization Rates, Are These Changes Being Produced Mostly by Changes in Female Rates, Changes in Male Rates, or Both?

In studies that consider the gender gap in homicide victimization there is often an implicit assumption that the narrowing or widening of the gender gap is driven mostly by changes in female rates.[30] In order to determine whether changes in the relationship between female and male homicide victimization rates over time are being produced mostly by changes in female trends, male trends, or both, we use methods very similar to those described earlier in the convergence tests but instead apply these

TABLE 8.4
*Trend or Intercept [in brackets] Coefficients for Female Homicide
Victimization Rates in Thirty-Five Countries, 1950–2001*

Country	Years	Female Trends	Male Trends	Comparisons
Australia	1950–1999	0.010*	0.021*	+ +
Austria	1950–2001	0.004*	−0.006	+ 0
Belgium	1954–1998	0.028*	0.040*	+ +
Bulgaria	1960–2000	0.029*	[0.117]	+ 0
Canada	1950–1998	[0.004]	[0.009]	0 0
Chile	1954–1999	−.007*	−0.053*	− −
Costa Rica	1955–2000	0.007	0.130*	0 +
Czechoslovakia/Czech Republic	1953–2000	0.026*	[0.027]	+ 0
Denmark	1950–1998	0.013*	0.038*	+ +
England/Wales	1973–1999	−0.003	0.027*	0 +
Finland	1950–2000	0.010*	0.052*	+ +
France	1963–1999	[−0.001]	[−0.006]	0 0
West Germany/Germany	1950–1999	[−0.002]	[−0.007]	0 0
Greece	1956–1999	0.009	0.030	0 0
Hong Kong	1960–2000	0.004	−0.023	0 0
Hungary	1955–2001	0.040*	0.098*	+ +
Ireland	1950–1999	0.006*	0.023*	+ +
Israel	1951–1998	[−0.007]	0.054*	0 +
Italy	1950–1999	[−0.005]	[−0.006]	0 0
Japan	1950–1999	−0.021*	[−0.042]*	− −
Mauritius	1955–2000	[0.035]	0.016	0 0
Mexico	1956–1999	[−0.061]	[−0.859]	0 0
Netherlands	1950–1998	0.014*	0.035*	+ +
New Zealand	1950–1999	0.017*	0.040*	+ +
Norway	1950–1999	0.016*	0.035*	+ +
Poland	1955–2000	[0.015]	[0.041]	0 0
Portugal	1955–2000	0.006*	0.013	+ 0
Puerto Rico	1955–1999	0.033*	[0.492]	+ 0
Singapore	1954–2000	[−0.006]	−0.026*	0 −
Spain	1950–1999	[0.005]	[0.926]*	0 +
Sweden	1950–1999	0.004*	[1.708]*	+ +
Switzerland	1950–1999	0.009*	0.016*	+ +
Trinidad & Tobago	1951–1998	0.070*	[0.175]	+ 0
United States	1950–1999	[0.014]	[0.060]	0 0
Venezuela	1950–2000	[0.030]	[0.972]	0 0

* p < .05

methods to the individual female and male homicide trends in each nation.[31] As in the tests described earlier, these tests allow us to determine
whether the individual series for women and men are stationary, trend
stationary, or unit root and whether there is evidence of significant declines (or increases) in their slopes (for the stationary series) or intercepts
(for the unit root series). Table 8.4 shows the results for the thirty-five
nations in the sample.

We concentrate first on the results for the three converging nations. Figure 8.4 shows female and male trends for Japan, Mexico, and Singapore. For women in Japan, we found that the homicide series was stationary with a significant negative trend (for results, see Table 8.4); for Japanese men, the series was unit root with a significant negative intercept. For women in Mexico, we found that the series was unit root with a nonsignificant negative intercept; for men in Mexico the series was also unit root with a nearly significant negative intercept. And for women in Singapore, the series was stationary with a nonsignificant trend term; and for men in Singapore, the series was stationary with a significant negative trend. Despite substantial individual differences, the dynamics of convergence between female and male rates in each of these comparisons are similar: in all three nations, both female and male rates are gradually declining, but male rates are declining more rapidly than female rates. Thus, in the case of Japan, both women and men experienced significant declining rates, but the size of the decline is greater for men than women. In the case

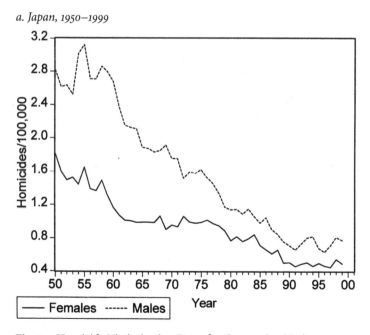

a. Japan, 1950–1999

Fig. 8.4. Homicide Victimization Rates for Converging Nations.

b. Mexico, 1956–1999

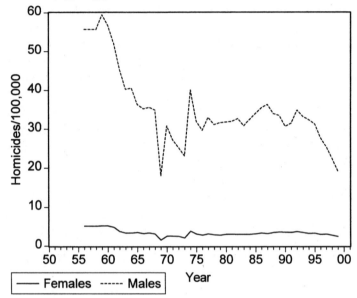

c. Singapore, 1954–2000

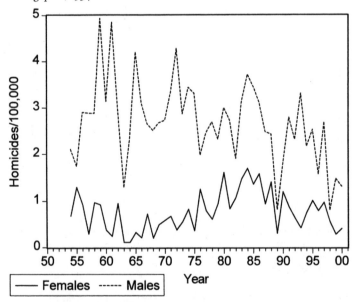

Fig. 8.4 *(continued)*

of Mexico, neither men nor women experienced a significant decline (although the male rate is close, *p* = .09), nevertheless the decline for men is greater than the decline for women. And in the case of Singapore, both female and male rates decline, but only male declines are statistically significant.

Trends for the five nations with significantly diverging female and male homicide victimization rates are shown in the five parts of Figure 8.5. Two of the diverging nations (Israel and Sweden) are among those that actually had higher female than male homicide victimization rates in some of the years during the first half of the series—eight years in the case of Israel and seven years in the case of Sweden. Although England/Wales and Spain show no years in which female homicide victimization rates exceeded those of men, male and female rates were fairly similar for both nations in the earliest years for which we had data. In Venezuela, by contrast, the gap between male and female homicide victimization rates that was already wide in the first half of the series grew even wider during the second half of the series.

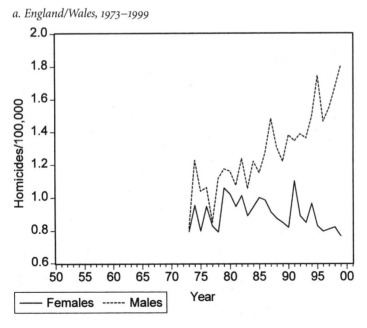

Fig. 8.5. Homicide Victimization Rates for Diverging Nations.

b. Israel, 1951–1998

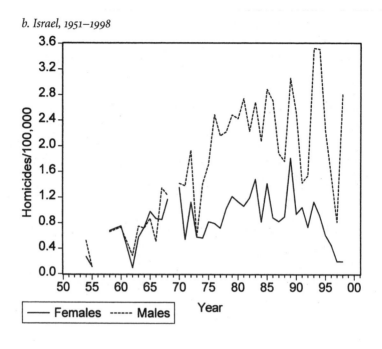

c. Spain, 1950–1999

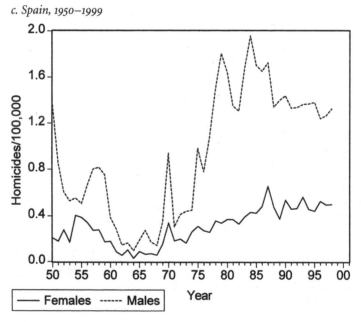

Fig. 8.5 *(continued)*

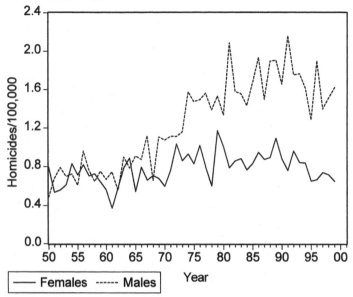

d. Sweden, 1950–1999

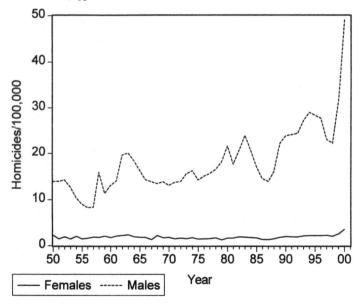

e. Venezuela, 1950–2000

Fig. 8.5 *(continued)*

According to Table 8.4, for England/Wales, the female series is stationary with a nonsignificant negative trend; for men the series is stationary with a significant positive trend. For Israel, the female series is unit root with a nonsignificant negative intercept; for men, the series is stationary with a significant positive trend. For Spain, the female series is unit root with a nonsignificant positive intercept; for men, the series is unit root with a significant positive intercept. For Sweden, the female series is stationary with a significant positive trend; for men, the series is unit root with a significant intercept. And for Venezuela, the female series is unit root with a nonsignificant intercept; for men, the series is unit root with a nonsignificant positive intercept. Again, although there is substantial variation in the relationship between female and male homicide victimization rates in the five diverging nations, the basic process by which divergence occurs in all five nations is similar: female rates remain relatively flat (in the case of England/Wales, Israel, Spain, and Venezuela) or increase gradually (in the case of Sweden), and in each case male rates significantly increase.

To summarize, the previous section shows that examples of convergence and divergence in female and male homicide victimization rates are relatively uncommon from 1950 to 2001 in this set of thirty-five nations. In this section we demonstrate further that when convergence or divergence does occur, it is driven more by changes in male than female rates.

To What Extent Do Homicide Victimization Trends for Women and Men in These Nations Differ over Time?

For the past two decades researchers have explored whether theories of crime are gender neutral,[32] whether trends in offending and victimization are similar,[33] and whether the circumstances and correlates of male and female offending and victimization are similar.[34] Disaggregating crime and victimization rates has become a common practice in the study of homicide victimization, where trends and risk factors associated with distinct subpopulations are frequently examined. With specific regard to gender, some researchers contend that the disaggregation of male and female homicide victimization rates is an appropriate practice because the etiology of homicide victimization of women may be different from that of men.[35] Others suggest that by disaggregating male and female homicide victimization rates, researchers ignore their similarities.[36]

One way that we can address these issues in greater detail with our data is by comparing the overall direction of female and male homicide victimization trends over the past fifty years for the thirty-five nations in our sample. We have summarized these comparisons in Table 8.4 (last column) by indicating for each nation whether female and male trends have significantly increased (+), significantly decreased (−), or shown no significant change over time (o).

As already suggested by the group trends shown in Figure 8.3, the number of nations experiencing significant increases in their rates of female and male homicide victimization during the past fifty years far exceeds the number experiencing significant declines. According to Table 8.4, homicide rates increased significantly for women in seventeen nations (48.6 percent) and for men in fifteen nations (42.8 percent). By contrast, homicide rates declined significantly for women in only two nations (5.7 percent) and for men in only three nations (8.6 percent).

In Table 8.5 we show results for the nine possible outcomes derived from comparing the direction of trends (increasing, decreasing, or no change) for women and men. We further divide these nine combinations into three categories. First, we classify as "no difference" those cases in which female and male trends are in the same direction. Second, we classify as "weak difference" those cases in which either female or male rates are statistically significant but the corresponding rate from the other gender is insignificant. Finally, we classify as "strong difference" the cases in which female trends are significantly increasing while male trends are

TABLE 8.5
Comparing the Direction of Female and Male Homicide Victimization Trends, 1950–2001[a]

Categories	Women	Men	N	%
No Difference	+	+	11	31.4
	−	−	2	5.8
	0	0	11	31.4
Subtotal			24	68.6
"Weak" Difference	+	0	6	17.1
	0	+	4	11.4
	−	0	0	0
	0	−	1	2.9
Subtotal			11	31.4
"Strong" Difference	+	−		
	−	+		
Grand Total			35	100.0

[a] Based on analysis in Table 8.4.

significantly declining or in which male trends are significantly increasing while female trends are significantly declining.

Table 8.5 shows that in twenty-four nations (68.6 percent) included in our sample trends for women and men are in the same direction. In eleven of these cases, female and male trends are significantly positive, in eleven more they both show no change, and in another two cases both female and male trends are significantly negative. We classify the final eleven cases in the "weak difference" category. This includes six nations that had significant positive increases for women but no significant change for men, four cases with significant increases for men but no change for women, and one case with significant declines for men but no change for women. Not a single nation in the sample fit into the "strong difference" category; that is, there were no cases in which female and male rates were both statistically significant and trending in opposite directions. In short, although levels of homicide victimization between women and men differ a great deal in these nations, the overall direction of trends within individual nations shows considerable similarity. Especially telling is the fact that more than two-thirds of the female and male trends for the nations in our sample are either not significantly changing or are significantly changing in the same direction and not a single nation in the sample shows men and women with significant trends in opposite directions.

Is There Support in the Data for a "Backlash" of Violence against Women?

Supporters of a gender equality argument assume that improvements in women's economic, social, and political position should reduce their exposure to violent victimization,[37] but supporters of the backlash hypothesis argue that increased power for women might actually increase their exposure to violence.[38] Those supporting the backlash argument point out that the friction caused by changes in social roles for men, particularly in the second half of the twentieth century, could result in an increase in violence by men directed against women. To the extent that male rates of violent victimization are higher than female rates, the backlash hypothesis predicts that the gender gap in violent victimization might actually *narrow* as women achieve a more equal footing with men.

Whaley and Messner test a backlash hypothesis with gender-specific homicide rates in 191 U.S. cities and find that support is limited mostly to the South.[39] They argue that the construction of masculinity in the South may be such that gender equality there is particularly threatening to men. Similarly, in a study of female homicide victimization rates in 158 U.S. cities, Vieraitis and Williams find that in cities with a high percentage of women employed in executive, managerial, and administrative positions, female homicide victimization rates are higher.[40] Although these studies lend partial support to the backlash thesis, they are limited to U.S. cities and, in the case of Vieraitis and Williams, examine only female homicide victimization rates.[41]

The drawback of examining only female rates is clear in the results shown in Table 8.4. Based on our analysis of these thirty-five nations, we find that in seventeen nations female homicide victimization rates increased significantly during the second half of the twentieth century. However, the likelihood that these increases can unambiguously be attributed to a male backlash is greatly compromised by the fact that in fifteen nations men also experienced significant increases in homicide victimization during the same period. In other words, the backlash position, like the gender equality thesis, implies that female rates behave independently of male rates, but our results suggest considerable similarity between female and male trends over time.

To the extent that the backlash argument predicts an increase in violent victimization that is unique to women, strong evidence of backlash might be found in nations in which female homicide victimization rates significantly increase while male rates decline or stay the same. By examining Table 8.4 we can see that this outcome actually occurred in six nations (Austria, Bulgaria, the Czech Republic, Portugal, Puerto Rico, and Trinidad/Tobago). However, Table 8.4 also shows that the opposite situation— significantly increasing male rates coupled with no change in female rates —happened in four nations (Costa Rica, England/Wales, Israel, and Spain). In short, if the backlash argument is best indicated by a situation in which female homicide victimization rates significantly increase while male rates decline or remain the same, we can identify little support in this international sample. And the fact that this outcome happens in our analysis almost as often for men as women further weakens the case.

Discussion and Conclusions

In this chapter, we assembled cross-national homicide victimization data for thirty-five nations to answer a series of research questions about female and male homicide victimization trends during the second half of the twentieth century. Cross-national studies in general and our study in particular suffer from at least two major methodological challenges. First, cross-national crime samples are intrinsically biased in that not all nations of the world are equally likely to be studied. Thus, our sample was limited to a small proportion of the nations of the world and greatly overrepresented high-income, Western-style democracies. Interestingly, our results did not suggest that convergence in homicide trends was more or less common in the highly industrialized nations in our sample, nor did we find any consistent patterns in the direction of female and male trends for either highly industrialized or lesser industrialized nations. However, we did find that female and male homicide victimization rates were more similar in highly industrialized than lesser industrialized nations. Moreover, other important differences may well have gone undetected or may not be apparent based on the convenience sample that was available for analysis.

Second, because of cross-national variation in legal definitions and uncertain reporting and recording rates, this study, like most other recent studies of cross-national crime, is limited to homicide victimizations and excludes all other types of crime. It is quite possible that our conclusions about female-male convergence might not apply to these other crime types.

With these two caveats in mind, we offer six conclusions.

1. Although National Homicide Victimization Rates for Men Are More Often Higher Than Rates for Women, There Are Frequent Exceptions

The assertion that homicide victimization rates both in the aggregate and for individual nations will be higher for men than women is one of the most common assumptions in criminology. Nevertheless, we found that female rates exceeded male rates for at least part of the series in eleven nations (about one-third of the sample). These results cast doubt on the assumed inevitability of long-standing differences in the violent victimization rates for women and men.

The nations and times in which female rates were higher than male rates were also clearly patterned. Nearly all the examples of years in which female homicide victimization rates were greater than male rates occurred in West European democracies (Denmark, Switzerland, Austria, Sweden,

Belgium, Ireland, Norway) or nations with strong links to Western democracies (Israel, Hong Kong, New Zealand). In support of earlier research by Gartner and her colleagues[42] these patterns suggest that the gap in homicide victimization for women and men is smaller in nations with less gender stratification. Interestingly, examples of women having higher homicide victimization rates than men were about three times more common before 1975 than after. This pattern is explained mostly by the post-1975 increases in homicide victimization rates for men in the predominantly West European nations that have had the smallest gender gap in homicide victimization rates for men and women.

2. There Is Little Systematic Evidence That National Homicide Victimization Rates of Men and Women Have Converged during the Second Half of the Twentieth Century

Given the incredible scope of change experienced by women and men during the second half of the twentieth century, it seems remarkable that there is so little evidence of converging victimization rates between women and men during this period for the nations in our sample. In fact, compared to convergence, we found slightly more evidence of female-male divergence in homicide victimization rates. Of course, part of the reason for the low rates of convergence is that a fundamental assumption of the gender equality hypothesis—that male rates have in the past been consistently higher than female rates—did not apply to almost one-third of the nations in our study. For these nations, female and male homicide victimization rates have been similar for years, so there was little room for convergence. But for the majority of nations in our sample, the gender gap in homicide victimization either stayed the same or widened in the years spanned by our data.

In a recent analysis of how the women's movement affected national policies on abortion during the second half of the twentieth century, Ferree and Gamson conclude that although there has been a growing presence of women's movements throughout the world and although these movements have some common features with respect to goals and strategies, the impact of the women's movement on the abortion debate within individual nations has operated very differently.[43] Similarly, our results suggest that female and male homicide victimization rates in the nations in our sample do not appear to be increasingly the result of supranational global forces but instead appear to depend to a large extent on specific differences between nations.

3. Examples of Convergence or Divergence in Female-Male National Homicide Victimization Rates That Do Occur Are More Likely to Be Explained by Changes in Male Than Female Rates

Supporters of the gender equality and backlash hypotheses have often assumed that changes in the relationship between female and male violent victimization will be produced mostly by changes in *female* victimization rates. But the cases of convergence and divergence we identified in our data were instead due more to changes in male than female rates. This finding suggests that even when the main question being addressed in a research project concerns changes in female victimization rates, it may nevertheless be misleading to exclude men from the analysis.

4. National Rates of Female and Male Homicide Victimization Are Highly Correlated; We Did Not Observe a Single Nation in Which Trends for Women and Men Were Both Statistically Significant and in Opposite Directions

There has been much debate in recent years about the utility of disaggregating crime trends by gender. In general, our analysis shows that there are large cross-national differences in the levels of homicide victimization for women and men but a fair degree of similarity in the trends for women and men within nations. In fact, in nearly 70 percent of the nations in the sample, female and male trends for the past half century were in the same general direction. Moreover, in the eleven nations in which the direction of trends for women and men was not the same, trends for either men or women were significantly increasing or decreasing while trends for the opposite gender group were insignificant.

Although there was relatively little difference in trends among male and female homicide victimization rates within nations, there was substantial difference in both level and trend between nations. These results coincide with some prior research that supports the similarity position (at least for the United States), finding that male and female homicide victimization rates trend similarly and that change in these rates is relatively stable over time.[44]

5. We Found Little Evidence in Support of a "Backlash" Interpretation of National Female and Male Homicide Rates

Researchers supporting a backlash argument have advanced the proposition that increased friction between men and women caused by profound changes in gender roles during the second half of the twentieth century has resulted in growing rates of female violent victimization. Although homicide rates for many of the nations included in our sample increased during the past fifty years, there is little evidence that these increases affected only women. In fact, we found only six nations in which female homicide victimization rates significantly increased while male rates remained the same. And we found four nations in which male homicide victimization rates significantly increased while female rates remained the same. But although our research did not support the backlash hypothesis, we believe that it is premature to abandon it. It could well be that backlash effects might play out in complex ways that are not evident in an aggregate analysis of national homicide trends. For example, Bailey and Peterson recently found support for the backlash argument in a study of female victims of acquaintance killings.[45] Results such as these remind us that different aspects of gender inequality might contribute to different types of violent victimization and that there may well be important subnational differences in these relationships.

6. There Are Substantial and Enduring Differences between Female and Male Homicide Victimization Rates within Nations

Although there was relatively little difference in trends among male and female homicide victimization rates within nations, there was substantial difference in both level and trend between nations. Because female and male homicide victimization rates vary so much by nation, it is critical that future research focus on the social, historical, demographic, economic, and political variables that explain this variation. In fact, considerations such as these suggest that it might be helpful to rethink our use of concepts such as "crime convergence" and "backlash" when it comes to their rival predictions about female and male crime trends. In addition to looking for concepts that describe all cross-national patterns, it is also important to remain alert to individual cases that fit a particular model. For example, although we found little evidence of convergence in female and male homicide victimization rates in general, the convergence we did find in Japan, Mexico, and Singapore might provide very useful case studies. Projecting from this finding, we might suggest that to the degree that women's vulnerability to homicide remains more confined to the domestic arena, it will also remain less accessible to the social conditions which mitigate men's victimization rates.

NOTES

1. An earlier version of this chapter was presented at the annual meeting of the American Society of Criminology, November 2003. We would like to thank the World Health Organization for supplying the homicide victimization data and Robert O'Brien for helpful comments on an earlier draft. The original project on which this chapter is based included our friend and colleague, Kriss Drass.

2. Dane Archer and Rosemary Gartner, *Violence and Crime in Cross-National Perspective* (New Haven: Yale University Press, 1984); W. S. Wilson Huang and Charles F. Wellford, "Assessing Indicators of Crime among International Crime Data Series," *Criminal Justice Policy Review* 3 (1989): 28–47; James P. Lynch, "Crime in International Perspective," in *Crime,* ed. J. Q. Wilson and J. Petersilia (San Francisco: ICS Press, 1995).

3. Rosemary Gartner, "The Victims of Homicide: A Temporal and Cross-National Comparison," *American Sociological Review* 55 (1990): 92–106; Steven F. Messner and Richard Rosenfeld, "Economic Discrimination and Societal Homicide Rates: Further Evidence on the Cost of Inequality," *American Sociological Review* 54 (1997): 597–611.

4. We interpolated missing values for Mexico (1956–1957, 1984), New Zealand (1959), Poland (1980–1982), Puerto Rico (1967–1968, 1978), Trinidad/Tobago (1965–1966, 1969), and Venezuela (1984, 1991). Also, for England and Wales we use homicide victimization rates supplied directly by the British Home Office.

5. In this analysis we treat Hong Kong and Puerto Rico as countries.

6. Avid Reza, James A. Mercy, and Etienne G. Krug, *A Global Concern: The Impact of Violence-Related Deaths throughout the World* (Atlanta: Division of Violence Prevention, National Center for Injury Prevention and Control, 2001).

7. See, for example, Rosemary Gartner and Bill McCarthy, "The Social Distribution of Femicide in Urban Canada, 1921–1988," *Law and Society Review* 25 (1991): 287–308; and M. Dwayne Smith and Victoria E. Brewer, "Female Status and the 'Gender Gap' in U.S. Homicide Victimization," *Violence against Women* 1 (1995): 339–350.

8. Diana E. H. Russell, *The Politics of Rape: The Victim's Perspective* (New York: Stein and Day, 1975); William C. Bailey and Ruth D. Peterson, "Gender Inequality and Violence against Women: The Case of Murder," in *Crime and Inequality,* ed. J.

Hagan and R. D. Peterson (Stanford: Stanford University Press, 1995); Lynne M. Vieraitis and Marian R. Williams, "Assessing the Impact of Gender Inequality on Female Homicide Victimization across U.S. Cities," *Violence against Women* 8 (2002): 35–63.

9. Gary LaFree and Kriss A. Drass, "Counting Crime Booms among Nations: Evidence for Homicide Victimization Rates, 1956 to 1998," *Criminology* 40 (2002): 769–800; Gartner, "Victims of Homicide."

10. Edwin M. Schur, *Labeling Women Deviant: Gender, Stigma, and Social Control* (Philadelphia: Temple University Press, 1984); James W. Messerschmidt, *Masculinities and Crime: Critique and Reconceptualization of Theory* (Lanham, MD: Rowman and Littlefield, 1993).

11. Smith and Brewer, "Female Status and the 'Gender Gap.'"

12. Martin Daly and Margo Wilson, "Who Kills Whom in Spouse Killings? On the Exceptional Sex Ratio of Spousal Homicides in the United States," *Criminology* 30 (1992): 189–215.

13. Based on the World Bank (2000) classification.

14. Based on the fifteen European Union nations before the expansion of the EU in 2004.

15. See, for example, Rosemary Gartner, Kathryn Baker, and Fred C. Pampel, "Gender Stratification and the Gender Gap in Homicide Victimization," *Social Problems* 37 (1990): 593–609; and Smith and Brewer, "Female Status and the 'Gender Gap.'"

16. Janet Saltzman Chafetz, *Sex and Advantage: A Comparative Macro-Structural Theory of Sex Stratification* (Totowa, NJ: Rowman and Allanheld, 1984); Bailey and Peterson, "Gender Inequality and Violence against Women."

17. Gartner, Baker, and Pampel, "Gender Stratification and the Gender Gap."

18. Smith and Brewer, "Female Status and the 'Gender Gap.'"

19. M. Dwayne Smith and Ellen S. Kuchta, "Female Homicide Victimization in the United States: Trends in Relative Risk, 1946–1990," *Social Science Quarterly* 76 (1995): 665–672.

20. For a more complete description, see Robert M. O'Brien, "Measuring the Convergence/Divergence of Serious Crime Arrest Rates for Males and Females: 1960–1995," *Journal of Quantitative Criminology* 15 (1999): 97–114; and LaFree and Drass, "Counting Crime Booms among Nations."

21. This is equivalent to placing the smaller rate in the denominator of the fraction and computing the relative difference between rates.

22. Charles R. Nelson and Charles I. Plosser, "Trends and Random Walks in Macroeconomic Time Series," *Journal of Monetary Economics* 10 (1982): 139–162; James D. Hamilton, *Time Series Analysis* (Princeton, NJ: Princeton University Press, 1994).

23. Walter Enders, *Applied Econometric Time Series* (New York: John Wiley, 1995).

24. Ibid.; O'Brien, "Measuring the Convergence/Divergence."

25. It is also possible to estimate this equation without the intercept and trend, or with the intercept but without the trend. We estimate the equation with an intercept and a trend because the coefficient for the trend term provides us with a direct way of testing for convergence and divergence.

26. Hypothesis testing for the augmented Dickey-Fuller test requires nonstandard critical values for the t distribution. We performed these tests using values supplied by eViews, *User's Guide* (Irvine, CA: Quantitative Micro Software, 2000).

27. To determine the appropriate number of lags in these models, we added lag terms one at a time until no additional terms were statistically significant ($p < .05$).

28. O'Brien, "Measuring the Convergence/Divergence."

29. Because New Zealand experienced only one year with higher female than male victimization rates during the second half of the series, we tested it only for divergence.

30. See Smith and Brewer, "Female Status and the 'Gender Gap'"; and Gartner, Baker, and Pampel, "Gender Stratification and the Gender Gap."

31. For a complete description of the methods used, see LaFree and Drass, "Counting Crime Booms among Nations."

32. Gwen Hunnicutt and Lisa M. Broidy, "Liberation and Economic Marginalization: A Reformulation and Test of (Formerly?) Competing Models," *Journal of Research in Crime and Delinquency* 41 (2004): 130–155; Douglas A. Smith and Raymond Paternoster, "The Gender Gap in Theories of Deviance: Issues and Evidence," *Journal of Research in Crime and Delinquency* 24 (1987): 140–173.

33. M. Dwayne Smith and Ellen S. Kuchta, "Trends in Violent Crime against Women, 1973–89," *Social Science Quarterly* 74 (1993): 28–45; Smith and Kuchta, "Female Homicide Victimization in the United States."

34. Thomas B. Marvel and Carlisle E. Moody, "Female and Male HVR: Comparing Trends and Regressors," *Criminology* 37 (1999): 879–902.

35. See, for example, Gartner and McCarthy, "Social Distribution of Femicide."

36. See, for example, Marvel and Moody, "Female and Male HVR."

37. Chafetz, *Sex and Advantage*; and Gartner, Baker, and Pampel, "Gender Stratification and the Gender Gap."

38. Edem F. Avakame, "Females' Labor Force Participation and Intimate Femicide: An Empirical Assessment of the Backlash Hypothesis," *Violence and Victims* 14 (1999): 277–291; and Russell, *Politics of Rape*.

39. Rachel Bridges Whaley and Steven F. Messner, "Gender Equality and Gendered Homicides," *Homicide Studies* 6 (2002): 188–210.

40. Vieraitis and Williams, "Assessing the Impact of Gender Inequality."

41. Ibid.

42. Gartner, Baker, and Pampel, "Gender Stratification and the Gender Gap."

43. Myra Marx Ferree and William A. Gamson, "The Gendering of Abortion

Discourse: Assessing Global Feminist Influence in the United States and Germany," in *Social Movements in a Globalizing World,* ed. D. Della Porta, H. Kriesi, and D. Rucht (New York: St. Martin's, 1999).

44. See, for example, Smith and Kuchta, "Female Homicide Victimization in the United States."

45. Bailey and Peterson, "Gender Inequality and Violence against Women."

Chapter 9

Restorative Justice for Victims of Sexual Assault

Kathleen Daly and Sarah Curtis-Fawley

Studies of the experiences of sexual assault victims in the criminal justice process come to similar conclusions: despite decades of legal reform, the police and courts continue to fail victims.[1] To be sure, some cases proceed to court, pleas are entered, and defendants are convicted at trial; but scholars and advocates agree that existing law and procedure, coupled with social attitudes about gender and sexual violence, thwart just outcomes for victims. As we have known for years, the majority of sexual assault victims do not report the offense to the police;[2] and for the victims who do report, the likelihood of their case reaching the prosecutor's desk is low. What can and should be done?

On this question, there is considerable debate. Some scholars propose more inclusive definitions of sexual violence, which shift citizens' and criminal justice officials' understandings away from the "real rape template" to "the realities of rape." Added to a more inclusive definition are calls for further legal reform to make court processes more responsive to victims.[3] Other scholars are skeptical that further legal reform can assist victims. Smart argues that because law disqualifies women's accounts and experiences of sexual violence, thereby further damaging abused women and children, nonlegal sites of activism should be pursued.[4] Likewise, Carrington proposes a shift in emphasis from law, police, and courts to "alternative technologies" for "the policing of sexual violence." This entails a reconstruction of ethical sexual behavior for masculine citizenship in extralegal sites such as schools, families, and sports activities.[5]

Some propose a blend of state (or legal) and extralegal intervention.[6] Assuming that an offender has admitted responsibility for an offense to the police, an alternative to court prosecution is a conference, one type of restorative justice practice.[7] Still other proposals include specialized courts for sexual violence, the use of civil law, and diversion and treatment programs for specific categories of offenders (e.g., adolescents or intrafamilial violence).[8]

Our focus is on the role that restorative justice (RJ) can play in sexual assault cases. RJ can be used when diverting cases from court or as presentencing advice to judicial officers. At present there are only two jurisdictions in the world, South Australia and New Zealand, that routinely use RJ in youth sexual assault cases. In New Zealand, conferences are used in court diversion and for presentencing advice. In South Australia, conferences are currently used largely in court diversion. No jurisdiction currently uses RJ routinely for cases of adult sexual assault.[9]

In this chapter, we describe in detail two sexual assault cases that were diverted to conference. Both cases had youthful male offenders (seventeen at the time of the offense) and female victims (twelve and thirteen), and both were finalized by a family conference in South Australia. In a conference, an admitted offender, victim (or victim representative), their supporters, and other relevant parties, along with a police officer and a facilitator, meet to discuss the offense, why it came about, how it affected the victim and others, and to decide on a penalty.[10] We shall document the victims' experiences with the police and the conference process, what they hoped would happen at the conference, and what did occur in their face-to-face encounter with the offender. Along with the girls' views are the facilitators' thoughts on the case, their concerns in planning and running the conference, and their opinions of the conference dynamics and its benefits (or not) for the victim.

The two cases were drawn from an in-depth study of fourteen sexual and family violence cases finalized by a conference in the second half of 2001. Joined with the in-depth study is our archival analysis of 387 sexual offenses involving youthful offenders and finalized over a period of six and a half years (1995 to mid-2001) by formal caution, conference, or in the Youth Court in South Australia. From the archival study, we can compare the legal journey and outcomes of court and conference cases; and with the in-depth study, we can explore the aftermath of crime and conference dynamics largely, although not exclusively, from the viewpoint of victims. Ours is the first study to shed light on the potential and limits of court versus conference processes for victims of sexual violence. Before presenting the cases, we review what happens in the criminal justice system in response to sexual assault and what is known about victims' experiences with the legal process.

Attrition: Lost and Dropped Cases

Any study of sexual assault and the criminal justice process confronts the problem of attrition, which occurs at multiple sites. First, most victims do not report the offense to the police; estimates of rates of report range from 5 to 30 percent.[11] Of cases reported to the police, 22 to 40 percent reach the prosecutor's desk, because victims withdraw the complaint, there is insufficient evidence for conviction, no suspect is apprehended, or cases are determined by the police to be "unfounded" or are "no crimed."[12] Third is the prosecutor's decision to go forward with the case; an estimated 16 to 33 percent of cases reported to the police are prosecuted. Fourth is whether the defendant is convicted (including guilty pleas and lesser included offenses); this figure ranges from 10 to 26 percent of cases reported to the police and is typically 10 to 15 percent of cases. With substantial attrition at earlier phases of the criminal process, the likelihood of conviction (including guilty pleas and lesser included offenses), once a case is prosecuted, is considerably higher, ranging from 40 to 80 percent, and is typically 65 to 70 percent of cases.

High rates of attrition are well documented in cases involving adult offenders and victims, but less is known about attrition when children or young people are victims or offenders.[13] Piecing together several sources,[14] we find that added to the "downstream" convictability assessments prosecutors make in adult offender–adult victim sexual assault cases,[15] there are heightened levels of attrition when cases involve young people or children as offenders and victims. For example, in a re-analysis of Wundersitz's data on sexual offenses with child victims in South Australia in 2000–2001,[16] we find that of the cases that were prosecuted, the conviction rate was higher in the Adult Court (66 percent) than the Youth Court (50 percent).[17]

Victims' Experiences in Court

If a case has survived the many hurdles to reach the stage of prosecution, victims "may be dismayed that their identity is a matter of public record, that they are expected to testify about graphic details of sexual assault in open court, and that rape shield laws fail to protect them from questions about their social and sexual history."[18] The impersonal and intimidating courtroom environment, defense "attorney questioning that exacerbates self-blame, and [a] perpetrator's unmoving stance that he is not guilty of a crime" are further sources of legal victimization.[19] A major Australian study of 150 sexual assault trials and hearings found that despite legal reform, victims faced the same problems they had decades earlier: inappropriate questions at cross-examination about provocation and the introduction of sexual history evidence.[20]

What, then, of child or youth victims? Eastwood finds that in two of three Australian states, a minority of young victims whose cases went to court said that they would again make the choice to report the sexual abuse because "the process was not worth the trauma."[21] Three problems were repeatedly identified by young victims: long periods of waiting for their cases to proceed, seeing the defendant in the courtroom, and being cross-examined. Eastwood calls for a "paradigm shift," arguing that "we have lost sight of the fact that what the child wants most of all is to be listened to, and be believed."[22] Likewise, Morgan and Zedner's research on child victims in England revealed that "above all child victims want their accusations to be believed."[23] Kelly suggests that the central problem is the adversarial process, in which the "defense's strongest tactic will be to attempt to undermine children's credibility."[24]

Potential Problems and Benefits of RJ

In part arising from the failures of the police and courts to respond adequately to sexual violence, RJ has been proposed as an alternative. Much controversy surrounds this idea, although most debate has centered on using RJ for partner violence.[25] Critics assume RJ is another form of diversion, which treats offenders too leniently, or that it is another form of mediation.[26] Although there is overlap in the dynamics of partner and sexual violence, there are also important points of difference. For example, partner violence is typically an ongoing pattern, but sexual violence may or may not be; and evidentiary problems tend to loom larger in sexual violence cases.

The potential problems of RJ for victims are the following:[27]

Victim safety. As an informal process, RJ may put victims at risk of continued violence; it may permit power imbalances to go unchecked and reinforce abusive behavior.

Manipulation of the process by offenders. Offenders may use an informal process to diminish guilt, trivialize the violence, or shift the blame to the victim.

Pressure on victims. Some victims may not be able to effectively advocate on their own behalf. A process based on group consensus building may minimize or overshadow a victim's interests. Victims may be pressured to accept certain outcomes, such as an apology, even if they feel it is inappropriate or insincere. Some victims may want the state to intervene on their behalf and may not want the burdens of RJ.

Mixed loyalties. Friends and family may support victims but may also have divided loyalties and collude with the violence, especially in intrafamilial cases of abuse.

Cheap justice. Offenders may view RJ processes as a "soft" option, reinforcing their belief that their behavior is not wrong or can be justified. Penalties may be too lenient to respond to serious crimes like sexual assault.

In reviewing this list, some of these same elements may also feature in sexual assault cases dealt with in court. Victims can be intimidated by offenders in the court room; there are just as likely to be mixed loyalties; if an offender is not convicted, he may believe he did nothing wrong; and often the penalties handed down in court could be deemed "too lenient," as the results of our archival analysis (discussed later) suggest.

The potential benefits of RJ for victims are the following:[28]

Victim voice and participation. Victims have the opportunity to voice their story and to be heard. They can be empowered by confronting the offender and by participating in making a decision on the appropriate penalty.

Victim validation and offender responsibility. A victim's account of what happened can be validated, acknowledging that she is not to blame. Offenders are required to take responsibility for their behavior.

Communicative and flexible environment. The process can be tailored to child and adolescent victims' needs and capacities. Because it is flexible and less formal, it may be less threatening and better able to respond to the individual needs of victims.

Relationship repair (if this is a goal). The process can address violence between those who want to continue the relationship. It can create opportunities for relationships to be repaired, if that is what is desired by the victim.

When reviewing this list, some factors may also feature in court, albeit in an attenuated form. If a case goes to trial, a victim may be able to tell her story of what happened, but this will be constrained by what is deemed to be legally relevant and will be subject to cross-examination. If an offender pleads guilty or is convicted, the victim may submit a victim impact statement, describing how the offense affected her, portions of which may be read in court before sentencing. Erez suggests that although victims derive satisfaction from participating in the sentencing process, victim impact statements have "little effect on the criminal justice system and on victims' satisfaction with it."[29] When it is successful, court prosecution can validate a victim's experience.[30] However, as the attrition data show, the frequency of a successful prosecution, once a case is reported to the police, is low.

On balance, RJ may have much to offer victims. Its main problems are ensuring safety for victims, overcoming the potential for power imbalances in a face-to-face encounter, and the appearance of too lenient processes and penalties. We must emphasize one crucial advantage for all victims participating in an RJ process: because the offender has admitted to the police that he committed an offense, victims do not experience the negative and disabling consequences of an adversarial process.

Court or Conference: Which Is Better for Victims? Results from the Archival Study

One of the major questions posed in our archival study of sexual offenses was, from a victim's point of view, is it better for one's case to be dealt with by way of a restorative justice process (a conference) or to go to court?[31] We gathered police documents, family conference files, court records, and criminal histories for all youth sexual offenses that were finalized from 1 January 1995 to 1 July 2001 in South Australia and that began with one or more sexual offenses charged by the police. There were a total of 227 court cases, 119 conferences, and 41 formal cautions. A detailed coding scheme containing over two hundred variables was created, which described the offender's biography and orientation to the offense, the number of victims (with detailed information on the primary victim), the context and elements of the offense, how the offense was reported to the police and the time from offense to disposition, the legal history of court cases from initial charges to finalization (including whether an offense was proved or not), the features of conference cases, and penalties imposed. In addition, the offenders' criminal histories (for all types of offending behavior) were coded.

Overall, we found that victims were better off if their case went to conference rather than court. The principal reason was that in conference cases, *something happened,* that is, there was an admission by the offender and a penalty (also termed an "undertaking" or "agreement") was decided. If the case went to court, the chances of any sexual offense being proved was 51 percent,[32] with the remaining cases being withdrawn or dismissed. We concluded that the potential problems of RJ in sexual assault cases (that is, the potential revictimizing dynamics or power imbalances of a face-to-face encounter) may be less victimizing than what occurs in a court process. So long as those accused have the right to deny offending, a right enshrined in the adversarial process, a court process can do little for victims of sexual assault. The potential of RJ is that it opens up a window of opportunity for those who have offended to admit to what they have done.

Using several measures of seriousness (legal and offense elements), we found that the cases referred to court started out as more serious than those referred to conference. However, by the time the cases were finalized as proved (convicted), the court and conference cases were of similar seriousness.[33] Cases that began with the most serious charge (rape) were the least likely to be proved of *any* sexual offense in court. Although the more serious cases and those with extrafamilial victim-offender relations and nonadmitting offenders were more likely referred to court, the cases *proved* in court were *less* serious and involved *intra*familial victim-offender relations. Court cases took over twice as long to finalize compared to conference cases: using the mean, the time from a report to the police to case finalization was 6.6 months for court cases and 3.2 months for conference cases. Victims would have had to attend court, on average, six times to follow their case to finalization, and nearly 20 percent would have had to attend ten or more hearings. If victims came to court on the day of finalization, half would learn that their case had been dismissed or the charges withdrawn. On all our measures of the legal process from a victim's point of view, the court appeared to be less validating and more difficult for a victim to negotiate.

Contrary to Coker's notion that RJ may be "cheap justice,"[34] we found that conference penalties did more for victims than those imposed in court. A higher share of conference than court offenders apologized to victims, carried out community service, were ordered to stay away from the victim, and undertook an intensive counseling program for adolescent sex offenders, the Mary Street Programme.[35] The court's greater power is its ability to impose a detention sentence. However, of the 116 proved court cases, 20 percent of offenders received a detention sentence; in all but three, the sentence was suspended. A small number of court cases was set for trial ($N = 18$). Of these, six offenders eventually pled guilty and twelve entered no plea or a not guilty plea. Of the twelve, eight were dismissed and three were found not guilty. One case was proved at trial.

From the archival study, we learned about the character of youth sexual offending, the kinds of cases that move through the system or are dropped, the circumstances in which offender admissions of guilt are more likely, among many other elements. We came away from the study with a degree of confidence that conferences have the potential to offer victims a greater degree of justice than court. However, the study design did not permit us to interview victims retrospectively, and we felt it was inappropriate to do so as a matter of ethical research practice.

In-Depth Study of Conference Cases

In order to document the experiences of victims, we decided to track a set of conference cases as they moved contemporaneously through the system during a six-month period, 1 July to 31 December 2001.[36] Our in-depth study had eight cases of sexual assault and six of family violence. Of these, we have selected two sexual assault cases for analysis in this chapter; both involved older child victims (twelve years or older), whom we interviewed directly.[37] Interviews were carried out with the victims two to six weeks after the conference, and with each Youth Justice Coordinator (YJC) both before and after the conference.

Because so little is known about RJ in cases of sexual assault, this chapter chronicles the cases in considerable detail as they moved through the conference process. In doing so, the emotions and effects of the crime and the legal process can be brought to light more fully. The two cases show complexity and ambiguity; they challenge proponents and skeptics alike to reconsider their claims of the benefits and problems of RJ in cases of sexual assault.

Rosie's Case: Sexual Assault at a Military Camp

Rosie was a strong and confident young teenager who knew what she wanted from the conference process. Her experiences with it were generally positive, although she was critical of several aspects.

The Offense, Report to the Police, and Immediate Aftermath

Rosie, who was twelve at the time of the offense, and Rick, who was seventeen, were attending an army cadet training camp. One evening, the cadets were participating in an exercise in which they were to go to a site by using cover and concealment techniques. Rosie had injured her ankle earlier in the day and had difficulty walking; Rick ordered the other cadets to go ahead, leaving Rosie alone with him. As Rosie and Rick walked up a hill, Rick pushed her to the ground and lay down next to her. He began to rub Rosie's breasts and her bottom through her clothing. He then pushed his hand between her legs and grabbed her in the vaginal region. According to Rosie, this continued for about four minutes. Rick attempted to undo her pants, but she resisted. Rosie then elbowed Rick in his stomach, stood up, and tried to run away. Rick reached up and grabbed her belt to prevent her from running, but Rosie was able to get away. She immediately reported the assault to another cadet.

About three hours later, a police officer came to the camp to interview Rosie. Rosie was highly positive toward the officer, remembering, "I had a female police officer and she was really good about it. She spoke to me because I was still shaking, and she could get it out of me. She was really nice." Rick was taken to a local police station to be interviewed with his parents present. He admitted that he had rubbed Rosie's breasts and back but denied touching her in the vaginal area. He was charged with indecent assault.

In her statement to the police, Rosie's grandmother said that when she saw Rosie the next day, she had two small bruises on her inner left thigh.[38] A strong and disturbing memory for Rosie was that the army would not let her leave to go home right away; rather, she had to sit alone in a room at the camp for most of the next day while various army officials spoke to her about what had happened. This made her feel that she had done something wrong.

Rosie reported a variety of effects from the offense, including a fear of being alone, an increased distrust of others, a loss of self-confidence, problems concentrating, and a fear of men, including her grandfather. She began to have panic attacks and was referred to a psychiatrist, who prescribed antianxiety medication. She was very angry and frightened of Rick before the conference. He was known for wearing a red baseball cap, and Rosie recalled that every time she saw a male wearing a red cap she would become scared and anxious.

Leading Up to the Conference

The period of time between Rosie's report to the police and the date of the conference was very long, nearly fifteen months.[39] The case was delayed partly because the police were slow to refer the matter to court (it took four months); and once it was in court, Rick's case was listed four times. The case was then referred from court to conference. The YJC was concerned with the lengthy delay, thinking the conference "would have been more useful twelve months ago." She said that both Rick and Rosie had "suffered a lot because of the delay" and that Rick's father was particularly angry about it.

Before the conference, Rick met several times with Gwen, a counselor at the Mary Street Programme. Gwen told the YJC that Rick was taking responsibility for the assault, and because of this, she did not believe he required long-term therapy: "he's taken responsibility, he knows he did the wrong thing, and he just wants to get on with his life."

The YJC spoke by phone with Rick three times before the conference. She said he was placing high priority on the conference and was taking full responsibility for his behavior. Rick's mother told the YJC that the incident had "rocked the whole family, giving up Rick's hopes for going into the army." According to the YJC, Rick's mother was "very supportive" of the conference process. "She is very grateful it's out of court, and so is Rick." At the same time, the YJC believed that Rick's mother was minimizing the assault, saying things like "there are much worse types of assaults." The YJC recalled that she "did a lot of work" to counter these views from Rick's mother.

In her preconference phone conversations with Rosie, the YJC could sense that Rosie was nervous about attending the conference because she had expressed concerns that she'd have to stand up and give evidence. This misconception about the conference process gives us insight into those aspects of a court process that can trouble victims: the courtroom is an intimidating environment, and yet it is only this setting that victims can imagine, if they should decide to engage the criminal process. The YJC explained the conference process again, reminding Rosie that she was the victim and had not done anything wrong. The YJC was concerned that she was not able to meet Rosie before the conference (the distance was too great because Rosie lived in a country town over five hours' drive from the city), and she had deliberately not met with Rick for this reason. Typically, a YJC will meet with both the victim and the offender at least once when preparing for a conference for a serious offense.

Rosie said she was "all for" the conference, and when the YJC proposed that she could participate by video link-up (rather than a face-to-face meeting), Rosie was adamant that she wanted to come to Adelaide "to face up to it." She had some idea of what would happen at the conference and what her role was, but she did not know what the possible outcomes could be. She hoped that by attending the conference she would be able to "get my side across" and that everyone would listen to her story. Her comments show the importance to victims of recounting what happened, of being heard and believed.[40] She hoped that the details of the offense would not be discussed because she would feel "weird" about this: "you just feel really weird when they talk about it; it's a mixture between embarrassment and shame." She also worried that Rick's parents would "glare" at her.

The Conference

On the day of the conference, Rosie and her grandmother took an early morning bus to Adelaide from their home, a trip that took over five hours. After the conference was over, they returned by plane that evening. They bore all the costs of the trip; the YJC could only offer to pay for a taxi fare to the airport. The conference participants were Rick, his mother and father, his Mary Street counselor (Gwen), Rosie, and her grandmother. Some imbalance in conference participation was evident in that Rosie's counselor could not attend (due to the travel distance); thus, Rosie had only one supporter, her grandmother, while Rick was supported by both of his parents and a counselor. The YJC ran the meeting, and a male police officer, who had considerable experience working on the police force's sexual assault team, was present.

By this time, Rick was eighteen years old and Rosie was thirteen. Going into the conference, Rosie said the most important thing was to tell Rick how the offense affected her. She also wanted answers from him about the offense, to hear his account of what happened, to have him apologize, and to be reassured that he would not do it again.

Rosie said that when she walked into the conference room, Rick and his parents were already there, and this was "intimidating" for her. During the conference, she felt "scared and angry" when Rick talked about what had happened. He disagreed with part of the police statement, maintaining that there had been no vaginal contact. When this was being discussed, Rosie recalled that Rick "crossed his arms like he was blocking it out." She believed that Rick minimized the offense through his denials of vaginal contact, and she was upset that his parents and Gwen concentrated on how the experience had affected Rick, "like he was the victim."

At the same time, Rosie was surprised to learn that the incident affected Rick "in all sorts of ways" and felt that he "showed heaps of remorse" through his body language and the way he talked. She "definitely" was able to say everything that she wanted and said she never felt controlled or frightened by Rick during the conference, saying that he was "very placid." She expected Rick to act "cocky, big, and tough," but instead he was like a "gentle giant."

Rosie said that it occasionally felt like Rick's parents were "ganging up" on her. She also found Gwen to be intimidating and was angry that she repeatedly defended Rick. Unfortunately, in the middle of Rosie's account of the offense, the YJC had to stop her because Gwen had to leave to attend another appointment and wanted the chance to talk about Rick's participation in the Mary Street Programme. Gwen shared how hard Rick was working in counseling; she suggested that he did not need a whole year of sessions but that a few would suffice. Gwen's ability to interrupt Rosie's story suggests that professionals may be granted concessions and priority over victims during a conference.

In the early phase of the conference, Rick's father acted withdrawn and angry. The YJC recalled that his "body language through all of this was significant. He had his arms folded and had his back pushed so far back against the chair that the chair was leaning backward, and he was really pushing away from everything. It was remarkable. He did talk later, but he had a hard time coming into the conference, and he was really angry."

When the YJC asked Rick about the assault, he did not use specific language, saying things like "when it happened." The YJC did not permit this evasiveness and corrected him by saying "when you indecently assaulted Rosie." These comments reveal that the YJC can and does intervene in conferences when the offender or his supporters are attempting to minimize the offense. The police officer was also highly supportive of Rosie: he was firm in explaining to Rick that he had broken the law and was lucky his case was referred to a conference.

When Rosie began to tell her story, the YJC observed that "Rick didn't see Rosie as a human being at all. He was there for himself, and there were some things he said that indicated that if she hadn't have struggled [during the assault], he would have gone further. . . . Although he wasn't uninvolved, you could tell he was quite anxious about the whole thing. It [the conference] was meaningful to him, but he didn't show empathy to Rosie."

The YJC was concerned that Rosie would have difficulty talking about the offense, but her stance was confident and forthright. "She talked about how frightened she was, and she talked directly to Rick, and that was the significant thing. I would ask her a question and she would turn directly to Rick and say 'you did this.'" The YJC remarked that Rosie is "so much the winner in all of this." She continued:

> The most significant moment for me . . . was when Rosie turned to Rick and said, "you're so much bigger than me, I was frightened of you and I couldn't get away from you. I had to fight you, and I'm a really little person." You know, she said those things, and it was absolutely amazing, really amazing. And I guess for me the conference gave her a chance to express that, and I think that must have been a really satisfying moment for her.

Ultimately, Rick did not admit to Rosie's version of events (touching her in the vaginal area, trying to undo her pants). Although this could be interpreted as revictimization, the YJC felt it was not revictimization because everyone believed Rosie: "It was giving him an opportunity, and Rosie knows he didn't take it, but it gave her the opportunity to say, 'well, I know from my point of view this is what happened, and I put it to this group of people.'" In her strength and presence, "Rosie was far more powerful in the conference than Rick," according to the YJC.

Apology and the Agreement

Rick did not apologize directly to Rosie. Rather, according to the YJC, "he apologized, and he did that spontaneously. . . . He regretted having done it, and he sort of again apologized into the ether, but saying he wished that he hadn't done it." At this point in the conference Rick's mother said, "'Rick, turn and talk to Rosie.' She was absolutely aware that Rosie had been contained enough to turn and speak to Rick, but that Rick had never spoken to Rosie." The YJC continued:

> He regretted it off into some distant corner. . . . And he talked about it ruining his life too, you know, it was all me, me, me. And Rosie knew that, she was amazing. She just floated above it. She said "look Rick, I'm not afraid of you anymore. I accept your apology, and I know you'll never do this to anyone again." Those were the three things she said to him, straight to his face. What a powerful thing to give her, what a powerful thing for her to be able to have achieved. Amazing!
>
> At the moment of the apology, the YJC remembered that Rosie just soaked it in. She leaned toward him and just took it in; it was just what she wanted to hear. You could see she had been waiting for this moment when he responded to her. It was really incredible; she just changed completely. She put her glass of water down on the table, and she actually leaned forward and she accepted his apology. She told him she believed he was never going to do it again and told him she wasn't afraid of him anymore. It was really significant. It absolutely burned in my memory, that kid moving towards him.

The main criticism Rosie had of the conference was that the undertaking was unfair in two respects. First, she felt that it was procedurally unfair. She thought "we would all have a say," but in fact she had no say during the discussion of what should be included in the agreement. Rather, Rick's parents and Gwen were the main people who decided the content of the agreement. Rosie recalled that she was thinking, "What's the point of being here if they already know what should happen to him?" Rosie wanted Rick to do community service, perhaps in a nursing home, but she felt that the YJC was not supportive of her suggestion. Moreover, Rick's mother said he occasionally visited his grandmother after work, so he should not have to do any more community service. Second, Rosie believed the agreement was too lenient. Another young person she knew had been in court for a similar offense, and "he got one hundred hours of community work." However, she was not given an opportunity to object to what was finalized in the agreement, in which Rick was to (1) continue counseling at Mary Street for a period of time to be determined by Gwen, Rick, and his parents and (2) send a written apology to Rosie.

Respect and Safety

Rosie said the YJC and police officer treated her in a respectful manner, she felt safe at the conference, and it helped her to resolve important issues.

Postconference

Rosie left the conference feeling better, saying it was a "fresh start. Now I can put it behind me. . . . I felt like the world had been lifted off my shoulders." Talking about what happened, hearing what Rick had to say, and seeing his remorse were very helpful. She left the conference feeling that "it just helped me get over it. It was like, hearing everything, it just helped me close the book. That was like the last chapter."

After the conference, Rosie was not at all angry or frightened of Rick, and she had a more positive attitude toward him because he seemed remorseful. The conference had helped her to deal with the negative effects of the assault: she could concentrate better, felt more self-confident, and was more trusting of others. She was "a lot happier," although she was still taking antianxiety medication.

Despite her criticism of the agreement, Rosie was satisfied with how her case was handled. She was glad she did not have to go to court because she would "have [had] to stand up and talk in front of everyone," and the court requires that "you prove your side." She recommended conferencing to other victims of sexual assault because the conference process is "so laid back" and the court is "scary."

Reprising Problems and Benefits through Rosie's Case

Let us now consider the list of problems and benefits of RJ in light of Rosie's experience.

Problems. Contrary to the concerns of RJ critics, Rosie felt safe at the conference. However, power imbalances were evident in the larger number of people supporting the offender, including his counselor. Rosie was initially intimidated by their presence, body language, and the things they said; but over time, Rick was increasingly isolated in his efforts to minimize the assault. Although he attempted to downplay the effects and extent of his offending, the YJC, the police officer, Rick's mother, and Rosie effectively checked this. Rosie felt pressure to accept the agreement, but contrary to the concerns of critics, the apology process was a significant triumph for her. She took charge of the conference in ways that Rick could not. In so doing, she redefined herself away from the status of "victim." Thus, the conference process helped her "to close the book." She willingly accepted the burdens that the conference process required, traveling a great distance and at significant expense to attend it. She faced no divided familial loyalties since the offense was extrafamilial, and her grandparents (her primary caretakers) supported her fully. We do not know if Rick thought the outcome was a "soft" option, but we do know that the official response to his sexual assault had already hurt him considerably. Rosie wanted a stiffer penalty to be imposed and saw the conference outcome as too lenient.

Benefits. Rosie was definitely able to tell her story effectively and to be heard by Rick and the other conference participants. Although she felt empowered by participating in the conference, she was disappointed that her views on the agreement were not considered. Rosie validated her own account of what happened, with the encouragement of the YJC and her grandmother. However, Rick only took partial responsibility for what he did, denying any vaginal contact. Rosie said the conference process was more comfortable ("laid back") than what she imagined court would be ("scary"). There was no aim of relationship repair in this case.

Tanya's Case: Intrafamilial Sexual Intercourse

Compared to Rosie, Tanya's experience was less positive. There was victim blaming by her mother, her stepfather, and her stepfather's parents; a pathologizing and medicalizing of the offender's behavior; and conflict between the offender and his father before and during the conference.

The Offense, Report to Police, and Immediate Aftermath

When Tanya was twelve years old, her mother, Nancy, married Nick; and he and his two sons, Andy (eleven years) and Zac (sixteen years), moved into the house. A year later, Tanya (now thirteen) said that her stepbrother Zac (now seventeen) began to touch her sexually, initially over her clothing. Over the next five to six months, this sexual contact occurred from time to time but then increased in frequency. It escalated one day when Zac asked Tanya to come to his trailer, where he lived in the family's backyard. Zac began to touch and kiss her, and because Tanya did not want anything else to happen, she went back into the house. Zac persuaded her to come back out to his trailer and had sexual intercourse with her. This occurred several more times over the next three months. In her interview, Tanya recounted that Zac was "a very violent person" and would "throw you against the wall and knock you out. . . . A few times I had all these bruises and cuts on my back." Thus, although she appeared to "go along" with the sexual activity, it occurred in a context of fear and intimidation.

About four months later, Zac was interviewed by the police. He admitted to having sexual intercourse with Tanya six times but claimed that she consented. He also said that he was using marijuana or alcohol each time. He was charged with unlawful sexual intercourse.

After the offenses were reported, Tanya moved to her grandparents' home. Zac was kicked out of the parental home because he was constantly fighting with his father and stepmother (but notably not because of Tanya's disclosure of the sexual contact between herself and Zac). He moved to his mother's house, but after he held a knife to her throat, she asked him to leave. He had no fixed address at this point. He was hospitalized in a mental facility for a short period of time after he was charged, and his father was sure that this was caused by the stress of police involvement. Zac did not attend Mary Street before the conference but was seeing a psychiatrist for treatment of bipolar disorder.

Initially Tanya did not tell anyone about the sexual relations because she was scared of Zac. The disclosure came about when Tanya's teacher called her mother because Tanya had been acting up in school. Her grandmother picked her up at school and wanted to know why she was not behaving, and Tanya told her about Zac. She was unsure who made the police report but thinks it was her grandmother. She was glad it was reported because "I don't really like Zac, and he shouldn't just get away with it." She was satisfied with the way the police handled the case but then was frustrated because it seemed to take a long time for anything to happen.[41] The conference was held four months after Zac was charged by the police.

After the police report, Tanya broke out in scabs and sores over her body and face, which her doctor said was caused by stress. She took over three weeks off from school for police interviews, counseling sessions, and for general stress-related reasons. She was fearful of being alone and had headaches and difficulty sleeping, increased suspicion of others, problems concentrating at school, and a loss of self-confidence: "I sort of think I'm dirty." Zac had been spreading rumors about her in their school, and she was embarrassed.

Leading Up to the Conference

In the preconference period, there was much conflict between Tanya, her mother, and her stepfather, as well as between her stepfather and Zac. Her parents did not fully believe she was a victim in that they assumed she and Zac had both played a role in initiating sexual relations.

The YJC asked a female police officer to be part of the conference process to balance his male presence. "I knew that if Tanya decided to come to the conference, that a female perspective was needed and a connection could be made." The YJC and police officer made a home visit to meet Tanya, and they also visited her mother and stepfather. The YJC "wanted to give Tanya the chance to make an informed decision about whether or not to come to conference, given her age and given that this is a case of family sexual abuse; and in the long term, this family is still together, mum and dad, it may be that here was an opportunity for her to confront Zac and say what she wanted to say." The YJC had initially spoken by phone with Tanya's grandfather, who was adamant that Tanya did not want to attend the conference.

Tanya recalled the YJC's home visit. She was upset to learn the case was going to a conference because she had believed that Zac would be imprisoned as a result of the police report. She felt that by going to conference, Zac was "just getting away with it because it's the easiest thing to do, and like yeah, I was really mad." It was clear to her that Zac had committed a crime, and she did not understand why he was not going to get "a life sentence." She did not want to attend the conference because "I didn't want to see him. I didn't want to speak to him." The YJC recalled that Tanya "had said something like 'Zac should be punished, and he should be jailed, and I shouldn't have to bother with this.'"

Tanya was content living with her grandparents and did not want to go back to her mother and stepfather's house because, in the YJC's words, her grandparents "strongly validated her as a victim in all this." Her mother, Nancy, and stepfather were not as supportive. Her mother viewed the sexual activity as caused by "rampant hormones" of both Zac and Tanya and recalled a time when she walked into a room and found Tanya sitting on Zac's lap. She described Tanya as "having been quite prudish until all this, and now all of a sudden she is running around in a negligee." When the

YJC told Nancy that Tanya might not attend the conference, her response was "that's wrong. They should both have to be there, and they should both have to apologize." In her mind, there was mutual culpability for the sexual activity and the fallout it caused in the family.

Tanya recalled that before the conference she was not getting along with her mother, mainly because her mother believed Tanya had seduced Zac. Tanya felt that Nick had convinced Nancy that Tanya had been lying about Zac's taking advantage of her. In fact, Tanya said that Nick came to her grandparents' home one day, telling them, "she's a stupid liar."

Tanya had not planned to attend the conference, but the police officer spoke with her again. At first, her aim was to help Tanya prepare a victim impact statement to be read at the conference. During their conversation, she encouraged Tanya to attend, reminding her of what could happen. Tanya changed her mind, thinking that "maybe I should go 'cause if I'm not there, then they could decide stuff, which I didn't want to happen." She said she had sufficient information about how the conference would work, her role, and possible outcomes. She hoped that Zac would have to do community service and that the offense would be "on his record."

Before the conference, Tanya felt angry toward Zac and frightened of him, and she worried that at the conference "he would start yelling and stuff. He is a scary person." Thus, there were good reasons for Tanya's anxiety about attending the conference: she was fearful of Zac, she had little support from her mother and stepfather, and her grandparents would not be there. She asked to have her social worker attend as her supporter.

The YJC had one phone conversation with Zac before the conference. He believed that Zac was giving "good to high" priority to the case because "he was stressed about what was going to happen to him." However, he was not taking responsibility for his offending because he viewed Tanya as a willing participant. His grandmother defended him and called Tanya "a slut." Thus, Zac's denials were reinforced by several family members. His father, Nick, was concerned about the nature of the potential conference outcomes. He believed that if Zac had to participate in Mary Street counseling or carry out community service, this would further stress Zac and exacerbate his mental illness. At the same time, there was a good deal of conflict between Nick and Zac. Several days before the conference, Zac unexpectedly dropped by his parents' house, and Nick became very angry with him, and they fought physically.

Before the conference, Zac apologized to Nancy for his role in everything that had happened in the family. Despite Nancy's view that Tanya was partly to blame, the YJC anticipated that during the conference she would "go to bat for her daughter." Nancy "saw the conference as a family conference, in the sense that the family would talk about it, as a clearing of the air, more than a legal process."

The Conference

About sixteen months after the initial sexual contact, the conference was held. In addition to the YJC and the female police officer, those attending were Zac, his father, Tanya, her mother, and Tanya's social worker. In light of the conflicts, fights, and angry words during the preconference period, we might anticipate their emergence at the conference. And indeed, they appeared early on.

The YJC said it was a "very dramatic" conference. Zac arrived about thirty minutes early, and the YJC reported that "my very strong first impression was that this kid was quite unwell." Zac started to write things on the white board in a "manic" manner, and initially, the YJC wondered if Zac was competent to participate. In hindsight, the YJC believed it was the right decision to go forward with the conference.

The YJC had to re-arrange the seating in the conference room and then decided to move to another room. "We wanted a bigger table so we could separate people more. We went to a bigger room, and we worked out that it was better for Tanya to be on the end of the table. She needed to be away from the intensity of Zac and his rantings." Later, the seating arrangements were again changed when Nick got very upset with Zac and threatened to hit him.

Going into the conference, it was important for Tanya to be able to tell Zac how the incidents affected her. It was also important to hear his side of the story because she thought it would reveal "how messed up" it was. "I knew he was going to lie, but I wanted to hear what he was saying and see if he was going to lie, which I knew he was, but I wanted to hear his side of the story, how messed up his side of the story is." It was also important to be reassured that it would not happen again and for him to apologize, although she expected that his apology would be insincere. Tanya was hoping that Zac would be punished for his actions, recalling, "I wanted the punishment . . . but that didn't work out."

Right from the start of the conference, Tanya reported feeling intimidated by Zac. "When I walked in the door, he gave me the biggest scariest look. After that, I was scared. I didn't want to go in . . . and I'm like, I'm not going in, I'm not going in, but I did. I was really scared." She had thought a lot about what she wanted to say at the conference, but "when I got there, I forgot everything I was going to do."

In the first phase of the conference, a discussion of the offense normally occurs. The YJC decided not to dwell on the offense facts because before the conference, Zac "said to me that 'I'm the victim here.' You know, he actually used that phrase, and we had to pull him up and say, 'no, you're not the victim, you're the offender. Tanya is the victim.'" The YJC was worried that "it would just blow the whole thing up straight away," so after the police report was read briefly, he steered the conversation in a different direction.

In the YJC's mind, the most important aims for the conference were "to make Zac understand how he's affected Tanya" and "to put into place the things the family wants for him." Tanya felt embarrassed discussing what happened in front of everyone because "everyone was an adult except for me." The YJC felt that Zac was affected by what Tanya said, and having to sit across from her was powerful because they had not seen each other for about six months. "I think being there, he could see the effects of what he's done."

Tanya felt that Zac did not fully acknowledge his offending. In her interview, Tanya repeatedly said that he "lied" and "is a liar." She wanted to object when he downplayed the seriousness of the offense but worried that "we would get into a fight" if she said anything. The police officer warned Zac several times about his behavior and threatened to end the conference if he did not behave appropriately.

The YJC said that Zac acted and spoke in ways that could be interpreted as intimidating and victim blaming, but Tanya did not react strongly: "I think she let it wash over her, and the fact that no one let him get away with it made her feel supported." The YJC surmised that Tanya was not bothered by Zac's actions because "she knew to some degree we were dealing with a person who was unwell and that these were rantings." According to the YJC, Zac did not acknowledge responsibility for the offense and did not even agree that he had broken the law. "His concept of Tanya was that she wasn't a sister, that there was no sister type relationship, so she was fair game." However, the YJC believed that "as the conference moved on, he expressed more and more remorse."

When other people asked Zac questions, he would respond using strange voices (like "a robot," according to Tanya) or by making "weird" faces. When asked why he had initiated sex with Tanya, Zac said "because I thought about that" (pointing to crotch) "instead of like that" (pointing to head). The YJC said it was difficult to manage the conference because "at times Zac seemed to be quite lucid, and then at times he would slip out and say something out of left field or quite over the top. So he'd flip-flop between making headway in the conference to strong victim blaming." Tanya thought that the YJC could have done a better job to "control" Zac and to allow her to speak more.

In light of Tanya's parents' judgments of her before the conference, their behavior at the conference was more supportive. The YJC said that "Nancy was highly effective as a victim supporter. She was very balanced, and I thought she was quite caring to Zac." Nick also showed support for Tanya and was quick to reproach Zac when he said inappropriate things. "He was showing her support, that what his son had done was wrong, and there was no victim blaming at all."

The YJC found that Tanya "was actually very reasonable at the conference and, in fact, quite helpful." She was "highly effective" in discussing the impact of the offense. "She was balanced. I don't think she overstated things, and I think she [focused] on understandable impacts. She was talking about the effects on the family." According to Tanya, however, she was fairly passive. "Everybody was talking to everybody else, and I'm just sitting there and I'm like listening."

Apology and the Agreement

Zac tried to apologize to Tanya and reached out to shake her hand, but she said the apology was insincere:

> He was just saying all that stuff . . . to make, to make the people think that he's trying to make it better, but he was just lying like he does. And [the police officer] said, "Zac, if you're going to say something, please try and say it truthfully." She knew that he was lying.

Zac's agreement contained these elements: (1) apologize to Tanya at the conference, (2) attend drug and alcohol counseling for twelve months, (3) attend a psychiatric consultation, to be arranged by his father, (4) purchase a card and gift for Tanya, including a handwritten apology, (5) obey house rules when visiting his parents' home, (6) not be with Tanya unless under the supervision of a parent, and (7) attend one session of Just Consequences (a program about why young people should avoid offending).

Tanya felt that the conference agreement was unfair because Zac did not have to do very much. She wanted him to do community service but felt that no one paid attention to this suggestion. She also felt that the part of the agreement that required Zac to buy her a gift was "stupid." (For this element, Zac was to draw up a list of ten gift suggestions, and his step-mother was to select and approve a gift for Tanya.)

When discussing the agreement, Nick did not want Zac to do community service because of his poor mental health. The YJC suggested that Zac purchase a gift for Tanya because he knew that she felt Zac "should do something apart from counseling stuff." Zac suggested gifts like roses or a teddy bear, but the police officer pointed out that he was not purchasing a gift for a girlfriend and needed to choose something appropriate. During this discussion, it came out that Tanya's grandparents would be angry if they found out she had accepted a gift from Zac. Tanya did not want to tell her grandparents anything about the conference. They were upset with Zac and did not want her engaged in a process that could be seen as letting him off too easily.

Tanya was not satisfied with how her case was handled, and her dissatisfaction was directly related to her perception that the conference agreement was too lenient. "The whole thing [the agreement] he had to do was really crap." Had the case gone to court, she assumed "it would have been a lot messier, but the agreement would have been a lot better." She understood that she would be required to testify in court, but she preferred this path because she assumed it would result in a harsher penalty. "I wanted him to do community service so, like, he could pick up rubbish on the roofs."

Respect and Safety

Tanya said the YJC and police officer treated her in a respectful manner. She felt safe at the conference because her social worker and mother were there. One problem Tanya raised was the length of the conference. It lasted over three hours, and she was very hungry, but there was no food available during the conference.

Postconference

Tanya was glad she decided to attend the conference because if she had not, everyone would have talked about her without knowing what she thought. After the conference, Tanya felt "pretty mad" toward Zac, compared to being "very angry" before it. Overall, her feelings toward him did not change because "he's an idiot and a liar." She still had a variety of negative psychological and emotional effects (e.g., fear of being alone, lack of self-confidence, among others) and said the conference was not at all helpful in dealing with them. However, she felt "a bit better" after she had seen him at the conference.

The YJC and Tanya had different views of the benefits of the conference: he saw more positives than she did. When asked if he thought the conference validated Tanya and her account of the victimization, he said it did. "That's why it was helpful for her to be there. I think she made a good decision in coming because she did get all that validation. She got it strongly from Nick, she got it strongly from her mum. . . . At various times and increasingly toward the end of the conference, from Zac himself." In contrast, Tanya was "sort of disappointed, but it was OK. It wasn't really a waste of time." She left the conference feeling better because "I finally saw him, not that I was looking forward to it. . . . We spoke about what happened and stuff." Whereas the YJC thought that Tanya could see that Zac's behavior at the conference was largely "rantings," a sign of mental imbalance, Tanya's view was less sanguine and more punitive. To her, although she saw Zac as "messed up," this did not mitigate his responsibility for what he had done; consequently, Tanya believed he deserved to be punished.

The YJC believed that more was achieved in the conference than could have been achieved in court. "I think the victim was able to overcome more this way." In contrast, Tanya wanted the case to go to court. She assumed, perhaps wrongly in light of our archival study, that Zac's case would be proved in court. She also assumed, again perhaps wrongly, that had the case been proved, Zac would have received a more serious penalty.

Reprising Problems and Benefits through Tanya's Case

Let us now consider the potential problems and benefits of RJ in light of Tanya's experience.

Problems. Zac posed a danger to Tanya's safety and to that of others in the room. Zac's father was threatening to hit him, as well. The power imbalance Tanya felt was not only between her and Zac but also between her and the other adults in the room. Zac's "power" was mixed: he attempted to intimidate Tanya, but he was perceived by her and others as mentally unstable. Nick's father and the police officer checked him when he acted or spoke inappropriately. Zac minimized his offending, and he engaged in victim blaming, although his attitude and words were checked by his father, his stepmother, the YJC, and the police officer. Tanya assumed that Zac would lie about his behavior but hoped that this would demonstrate to others "how messed up" his story was. She viewed his apology as insincere but assumed that it would be. Her interests were not minimized by the other conference participants except in the agreement discussion. She initially did not want to participate in the conference because she did not want to see Zac, but afterward, she was glad she was there to confront him.

Mixed loyalties were evident leading up to the conference, with Tanya's mother and stepfather thinking the sexual activity was consensual. Tanya's grandparents, on the other hand, were always behind her, even though they were not invited to the conference.[42] Tanya wanted Zac to be punished; indeed, she assumed he would be jailed. The conference outcomes were therefore too lenient in her opinion. We do not know if Zac viewed the conference as a "soft" option. His father appeared to be protecting him from Mary Street counseling or community service by suggesting that this would cause his son further stress.

Benefits. Although Tanya was effective in describing the impact of the offense, she wanted to say more. From her perspective, she was marginally empowered by attending the conference. She was glad she was there to present her side of the story and believed the conference was not a waste of time, but it did not bring her the things she wanted. From the YJC's perspective, Tanya's account was validated by conference participants (except Zac); but for Tanya, it was simply "OK." Zac did not take responsibility for what he did, but his stance was countered by others in the room.

It is difficult to know if Zac's erratic behavior would have been more restrained in court; it is likely his father would not have threatened violence. Tanya acknowledged that had the case gone to court, "it would have been messier." She would have preferred this because she assumed that a court outcome would have been more punitive on Zac. Relationship repair between Zac and Tanya was not a goal, although Tanya was glad for the opportunity to confront Zac in a controlled environment. Relationship repair between Zac, his father, and his stepmother and between Tanya, her mother, and her stepfather were goals, but it is unclear the degree to which they were realized. We do know that after the conference, Tanya's mother took her out to lunch, and Tanya identified this as a positive step in rebuilding their relationship.

Discussion and Implications

In the debates about the appropriateness of RJ for cases of sexual and family violence, a lack of evidence has fed speculation and polarized positions. The archival and in-depth studies presented here are the first to explore the relative merits of court and conference in sexual assault cases and to document victims' experience with the conference process. The archival study suggests conferences may outperform courts on things that matter to victims: an admission to offending and penalties that may do more to change an offender's behavior. Our examination of Rosie's and Tanya's experiences with and judgments of the conference process adds another layer of understanding. Their cases challenge some of our own presuppositions about the problems and benefits of conferences.

Taking Responsibility

Foremost are contested meanings of an offender's "taking responsibility for an offense" and "an admission." Eligibility for a conference requires that an offender has "admitted" some elements of the offense to the police, but he may deny other elements (as in Rosie's case) or not view what he did as wrong (as in Tanya's case). Although Rick and Zac did not take full responsibility for their behavior, Rosie, Tanya, other conference participants, the YJC, and the police officer challenged and checked their denials. One can interpret this in two ways: as a source of revictimization of victims or as a validation of their accounts by everyone except the offender. These findings also raise questions about the character of an "admission" when offenders plead guilty in court. We suspect (but do not know) that the same level of denial may be present for these offenders. The difference is that denials and minimizations can be aired and then appropriately checked in a well-run conference, but there is no opportunity for this in a courtroom.

A Victim's "Interest in Punishment"

A major theme for Rosie and Tanya was their desire to see stronger penalties imposed. Rosie wanted a considerable number of community service hours, and Tanya wanted to see Zac jailed but would have accepted a punitive form of community service ("picking up rubbish") as acceptable. Both assumed that had the cases gone to court, Rick and Zac would have received tougher penalties; and both believed their views on penalty were not discussed adequately. Setting aside their erroneous assumption that their cases would definitely have been proved in court, several observations can be drawn about their views. First, contrary to the claims of RJ advocates, Cretney and Davis are correct in saying that a "victim has an interest in punishment," not just restitution and reparation, because punishment "can reassure the victim that he or she has public recognition and support."[43] RJ proponents are on weak ground when they take a principled stand against punishment, although this debate has been stymied by differing definitions of punishment.[44] Second, like some critics of RJ, Rosie and Tanya assumed that court penalties would be tougher than those decided in a conference.[45] Our archival study suggests that such views are inaccurate, especially in South Australia, where the maximum length of time that a conference agreement can operate is longer than other Australian or New Zealand jurisdictions.[46] To be sure, the court has the *potential* to impose a severe sanction of detention time to be served, but the reality is that the Youth Court we studied rarely exercised this option. Third, although RJ proponents emphasize that victims "have a say" in penalty setting, when a victim wants harsher penalties than a facilitator or police officer think appropriate, the victim's views will be "listened to" but rechanneled. This is an appropriate role for a facilitator and police officer; in this jurisdiction, they are bound by law to ensure that a conference penalty is no higher than one imposed in court for a similar offense. Another dynamic arose in the conference process for these adolescent victims: compared to the adults present, Rosie and Tanya felt that they lacked authority and power. They "couldn't object" to what the adults were saying (Rosie) and "everyone was talking, and I was listening" (Tanya). The same experience holds for child and youth victims in court.[47]

Individual Differences and Offense Contexts

Rosie had a far more positive experience with the conference process than Tanya. She left the conference feeling "the world had been lifted off my shoulders," she was able to tell her story and be believed, she thought that Rick was remorseful for his actions, and she neither feared him nor was angry toward him after it was over. In contrast, Tanya remained angry toward and frightened of Zac. Although she was glad she attended the conference, it seemed to do little to assist her psychologically or emotionally. Rosie's circumstances and positive attitude suggest that she was able to use the conference process more effectively than Tanya.

Although we would expect to see individual differences in the ways in which victims cope with and recover from crime, Rosie's and Tanya's cases also exemplify the differing impacts of sexual assault, which are dependent on the context and duration of the sexual violence. Rosie's sexual assault was a discrete incident, whereas Tanya was drawn into, manipulated, and groomed by her stepbrother for sexual relations over a considerable period of time. There were elements of partner violence between Zac and Tanya as well: she feared Zac's potential for physical violence and said he had thrown her against a wall on at least one occasion. Her account of going to his trailer, then wanting to return to the house, and then being convinced to go back to the trailer suggest she was conflicted about what they were doing. She knew it was wrong and was afraid of him; she seemed to be both fearful of him and yet flattered by his attention. As a consequence, Tanya felt an even greater degree of shame and embarrassment than Rosie.

Another difficulty that Tanya faced, which Rosie did not, was her mother's and stepfather's views that she had seduced Zac rather than being assaulted by him. Tanya left her parents' home to live with her grandparents; she did not have the consistent familial support that Rosie had leading up to the conference, and it took some courage for her to attend the conference, knowing that her main source of support, her grandparents, would not be present. In other research we have conducted on victim advocates' views of conferencing for gendered violence, the advocates believed that strong support networks were required for conference cases to be successful.[48] Tanya's experience underscores this point. It would have been preferable to have had another victim supporter at her conference (perhaps a sexual assault counselor) and to have had firmer messages reinforcing the inappropriateness of Zac's behavior (and even that of his father). These practice areas can and should be improved.[49]

Conclusion

As advocates and critics debate the merits of RJ for sexual violence, we would do well to heed the complexity and variety of victims' experiences in the aftermath of crime, not just with the legal process but also with everything surrounding it. When reading these cases, we come away less sure of the meaning of "revictimization," "power imbalances," "victim empowerment," or "victim recovery." These are analytical shortcuts, and they are necessary for understanding and making sense of victims' experiences, especially when drawing from detailed materials. However, as Rosie's and Tanya's cases show, these concepts are not static or settled experiences for victims, nor are they produced solely by the legal process. It is possible that had Rosie's and Tanya's cases gone to court and been proved, Rosie would have also judged the court process more positively than Tanya. In other words, what victims bring to a legal process (whether court or conference)—memories of the assault and its context, their resilience and outlook, and other people who surround the case—all may be just as consequential as the legal process itself.

We can be more sure that a victim's account of the offense and its impact can be brought forward in a conference in a way not currently possible in court. We also know that a key source of victim validation and vindication is an offender's admission of wrongdoing. When a case is prosecuted in court, victims cannot be sure that an offender will be convicted of (or plead guilty to) an offense; the probabilities of conviction (and associated victim validation) range from 40 to 80 percent of adult cases and just over 50 percent in the South Australian Youth Court. A case can only go to conference if an offender has admitted that he has committed an offense and is willing to accept responsibility for his behavior. Although such admissions may later be contested by an offender, they are checked and challenged by conference participants and professionals. This is the power of the conference process in cases of sexual assault, although it is dependent on the participants' and the professionals' modes of intervention. Yet this fragile power may be one way of redefining the realities of rape and sexual assault.

NOTES

1. We thank the members of the South Australian Family Conference Team, the South Australian Police, and the South Australian Courts Administration Authority for their assistance and support in conducting this research and Brigitte Bouhours for research assistance. An Australian Research Council grant and Australian-American Fulbright Fellowship provided funding for the research.

Please note that the Sexual Assault Archival Study statistics given in this chapter were correct as of November 2004, when this paper went to press. Subsequent analyses and data cleaning show that there were 385, not 387, cases in the total sample (one less court and conference case each). Three cases, not one, were proved at trial. Two, not three, court youth were sentenced to serve time in detention. These small *N* changes have a negligible effect on the results. Subsequent papers will present the data with these changes in *N* size.

Throughout this article we use the term *sexual assault* to be inclusive of rape and other forms of sexual violence; we use the term *victims* rather than *survivors*; and we use the male pronoun for offenders and the female pronoun for victims of sexual assault.

2. Liz Kelly, *Routes to (In)justice: A Research Review on the Reporting, Investigation, and Prosecution of Rape Cases* (London: Her Majesty Crown Prosecution Services Inspectorates [HMCPSI], 2001), 9–10, lists and discusses the reasons for reporting and not reporting sexual assault, concluding that the "closer the circumstances are to the real rape template, the greater the likelihood that it will be reported."

3. Ibid., 43. The real rape template has these elements: committed by a stranger, outdoors, with a weapon, and with victim injury. By contrast, these "conditions are rare" for the reality of most rape victims (ibid., 5). See also Liz Kelly and Jill Radford, "'Nothing Really Happened': The Invalidation of Women's Experiences of Sexual Violence," in *Women, Violence, and Male Power,* ed. M. Hester, L. Kelly, and J. Radford, pp. 19–33 (Philadelphia: Open University Press, 1996), 32; Sue Lees, "Unreasonable Doubts: The Outcomes of Rape Trials," in *Women, Violence, and Male Power,* ed. M. Hester, L. Kelly, and J. Radford, pp. 99–115 (Philadelphia: Open University Press, 1996), 112.

4. Carol Smart, *Feminism and the Power of Law* (London: Routledge, 1989), 161 (disqualification) and 26 (pursue nonlegal sites). On this point, see also Mary Heath and Ngaire Naffine, "Men's Needs and Women's Desires: Feminist Dilemmas about Rape Law 'Reform,'" *Australian Feminist Law Journal* 3 (1994): 30–52.

5. Kerry Carrington, "Governing Sexual Violence: Criminalization and Citizenship," in *Women's Encounters with Violence: Australian Experiences,* ed. S. Cook and J. Bessant, pp. 219–231 (London: Sage, 1997), 228–231. See also Kerry Carrington and Paul Watson, "Policing Sexual Violence: Feminism, Criminal Justice, and Governmentality," *International Journal of the Sociology of Law* 24 (1996): 253–272. Such positive images and practices for male sexuality can be joined with those for female sexuality. See Nicola Lacey, "Unspeakable Subjects, Impossible Rights: Sexuality, Integrity, and Criminal Law," *Canadian Journal of Law and Jurisprudence* 11(1) (1998): 47–68.

6. John Braithwaite and Kathleen Daly, "Masculinities, Violence, and Communitarian Control," in *Just Boys Doing Business? Men, Masculinities, and Crime,* ed. T. Newburn and E. A. Stanko, pp. 189–213 (London: Routledge, 1994); Kathleen Daly, "Sexual Assault and Restorative Justice," in *Restorative Justice and Family Violence,* ed. H. Strang and J. Braithwaite, pp. 62–88 (Cambridge: Cambridge

University Press, 2002); Barbara Hudson, "Restorative Justice: The Challenge of Sexual and Racial Violence," *Law and Society* 25 (1998): 237–256; Barbara Hudson, "Restorative Justice and Gendered Violence: Diversion or Effective Justice?" *British Journal of Criminology* 42 (2002): 616–634; Mary Koss, "Blame, Shame, and Community: Justice Responses to Violence against Women," *American Psychologist* 55 (2000): 1332–1343; Dianne L. Martin, "Retribution Revisited: A Reconsideration of Feminist Criminal Law Reform Strategies," *Osgoode Hall Law Journal* 36 (1998): 151–188; Linda G. Mills, *Insult to Injury: Rethinking Our Responses to Intimate Abuse* (Princeton, NJ: Princeton University Press, 2003); Allison Morris and Loraine Gelsthorpe, "Re-visioning Men's Violence against Female Partners," *Howard Journal of Criminal Justice* 39 (2000): 412–428; Lois Presser and Emily Gaarder, "Can Restorative Justice Reduce Battering? Some Preliminary Considerations," *Social Justice* 27(1) (2000): 175–195.

7. A key element in any restorative justice practice is that an offender has admitted to an offense; thus, the focus is on the penalty rather than the fact-finding phase of the criminal process.

8. Crime and Misconduct Commission (CMC), *Seeking Justice: An Inquiry into the Handling of Sexual Offences by the Criminal Justice System* (Brisbane, Australia: Crime and Misconduct Commission, Queensland, 2003), 149–156. See also Kelly, *Routes to (In)justice*, 37, on sexual violence courts.

9. For exceptions, see Quince C. Hopkins and Mary Koss, "Incorporating Feminist Theory and Insights into a Restorative Justice Response to Sex Offenses," *Violence against Women* 11(5) (2005): 693–723, for Tucson RJ pilot in adult sexual assault cases; and Therese Lajeunesse, *Community Holistic Circle Healing, in Hollow Water Manitoba: An Evaluation* (Ottawa, Canada: Solicitor General Canada, Ministry Secretariat, 1996), for a Canadian First Nations response to sexual abuse of women and children (on file with the senior author).

10. For an introduction to the RJ literature, see Gerry Johnstone, *Restorative Justice: Ideas, Values, Debates* (Cullompton, UK: Willan, 2002); Gerry Johnstone, ed., *A Restorative Justice Reader: Texts, Sources, Context* (Cullompton, UK: Willan, 2003); and Allison Morris and Gabrielle Maxwell, eds., *Restorative Justice for Juveniles: Conferencing, Mediation, and Circles* (Oxford, UK: Hart, 2001). One major benefit of court diversion to conference for an offender is that no conviction is noted.

11. Kelly, *Routes to (In)justice*, 16; Mary Koss, "Hidden Rape: Sexual Aggression and Victimization in a National Sample of Students in Higher Education," in *Rape and Society: Readings on the Problem of Sexual Assault*, ed. P. Searles and R. J. Berger, pp. 35–50 (Boulder, CO: Westview, 1995), 36; Lees, "Unreasonable Doubts," 101–102.

12. Statistical data for outcome, prosecution, and conviction come from sources in England and Wales, the United States, and Australia. For England and Wales, they are Kelly, *Routes to (In)justice*, 15; Jeanne Gregory and Sue Lees, "Attrition in

Rape and Sexual Assault Cases," *British Journal of Criminology* 36 (1996): 1–17, 14; and Susan Lea, Ursula Lanvers, and Steve Shaw, "Attrition in Rape Cases," *British Journal of Criminology* 43 (2003): 583–599, 595. For the United States, Patricia A. Frazier and Beth Haney, "Sexual Assault Cases in the Legal System: Police, Prosecutor, and Victim Perspectives," *Law and Human Behavior* 20 (1996): 607–628, 608–609. And for Australia, CMC, *Seeking Justice*, 58; and Joy Wundersitz, "Child Victims of Sexual Offences: Tracking from Police Incident Report to Finalisation in Court—Briefing Paper" (Adelaide: Office of Crime Statistics and Research, 2003), 9. "Unfounded" and "no crimed" are U.S. and UK police terms, respectively, for dropping cases.

13. Children and young people are those under the age of seventeen or eighteen, depending on the jurisdiction. It is of some interest to observe that in analyzing victimization, most researchers use "child," whereas in analyzing offending, most use "young people" (to refer to those ten years of age or older).

14. Julie Brownlie, "'An Unsolvable Justice Problem'? Punishing Young People's Sexual Violence," *Journal of Law and Society* 30 (2003): 506–531, 511–514; CMC, *Seeking Justice*, 59, on child prosecution in South Australia; Hudson, *RJ and Gendered Violence*, 622. For a contrary view, see Kelly, *Routes to (In)justice*, 16, "cases involving children [as victims] are more likely to be prosecuted and to result in conviction."

15. Lisa Frohmann, "Discrediting Victims' Allegations of Sexual Assault: Prosecutorial Accounts of Case Rejections," *Social Problems* 38 (1991): 213–226; Cassia Spohn and David Holleran, "Prosecuting Sexual Assault: A Comparison of Charging Decisions in Sexual Assault Cases Involving Strangers, Acquaintances, and Intimate Partners," *Justice Quarterly* 18 (2001): 651–688.

16. Wundersitz, "Child Victims of Sexual Offences," 9.

17. Our calculations assume that the 22–23 percent of unfinalized cases in each court will result in convictions (or case proved). Overall, convictions (or case proved) were 15 percent of incidents reported to police.

18. Koss, "Blame, Shame, and Community," 1335.

19. Ibid. See also Kelly, *Routes to (In)justice*, 30–38.

20. New South Wales Department for Women, *Heroines of Fortitude: The Experiences of Women in Court as Victims of Sexual Assault* (Woolloomooloo, Australia: Department for Women, New South Wales Government, 1996).

21. Christine Eastwood, "The Experiences of Child Complainants of Sexual Abuse in the Criminal Justice System," *Trends and Issues in Crime and Criminal Justice* 250 (Canberra, Australia: Australian Institute of Criminology, 2003), 2. See also the larger report by Christine Eastwood and Wendy Patton, *The Experiences of Child Complainants of Sexual Abuse in the Criminal Justice System* (Canberra, Australia: Criminology Research Council, 2002).

22. Eastwood and Patton, *Experiences of Child Complainants*, 34.

23. Jane Morgan and Lucia Zedner, *Child Victims: Crime, Impact, and Criminal*

Justice (Oxford, UK: Clarendon, 1992), 101. See also 116–117 for the problems that child victims of sex abuse face in the prosecution and sentencing phases of the court process.

24. Liz Kelly, "Remembering the Point: A Feminist Perspective on Children's Evidence," in *Children's Testimony: A Handbook of Psychological Research and Forensic Practice,* ed. H. Westcott, G. Davies, and R. Bull, pp. 361–376 (Chichester, UK: John Wiley & Sons, 2002), 375.

25. For example, all but one contribution to volume edited by Heather Strang and John Braithwaite, *Restorative Justice and Family Violence* (Cambridge: Cambridge University Press), analyzed RJ and partner, domestic, or family violence.

26. Ruth Lewis, R. Emerson Dobash, Russell P. Dobash, and Kate Cavanagh, "Law's Progressive Potential: The Value of Engagement for the Law for Domestic Violence," *Social and Legal Studies* 10 (2001): 105–130; Kelly and Radford, "Nothing Really Happened," 31 (critiques of diversion); Presser and Gaarder, "Can Restorative Justice Reduce Battering?" (comparing mediation and RJ).

27. Note that in the string of citations in this and the next note, problems and benefits can feature in any one article, and advocates and critics of RJ may identify both benefits and problems; it is a matter of emphasis. Ruth Busch, "Domestic Violence and Restorative Justice Initiatives: Who Pays If We Get It Wrong?" in *Restorative Justice and Family Violence,* ed. H. Strang and J. Braithwaite, pp. 223–248 (Cambridge: Cambridge University Press, 2002); Donna Coker, "Enhancing Autonomy for Battered Women: Lessons from Navajo Peacemaking," *UCLA Law Review* 47 (1999): 1–111; Donna Coker, "Transformative Justice: Anti-Subordination Processes in Cases of Domestic Violence," in *Restorative Justice and Family Violence,* ed. H. Strang and J. Braithwaite, pp. 128–152 (Cambridge: Cambridge University Press, 2002); Lewis et al., "Law's Progressive Potential"; Joanna Shapland, "Victims and Criminal Justice: Creating Responsible Criminal Justice Agencies," in *Integrating a Victim Perspective within Criminal Justice: International Debates,* ed. A. Crawford and J. Goodey, pp. 147–164 (Aldershot, UK: Ashgate, 2000); Julie Stubbs, "Shame, Defiance, and Violence against Women: A Critical Analysis of 'Communitarian' Conferencing," in *Women's Encounters with Violence: Australian Experiences,* ed. S. Cook and J. Bessant, pp. 109–126 (London: Sage, 1997); Julie Stubbs, "Domestic Violence and Women's Safety: Feminist Challenges to Restorative Justice," in *Restorative Justice and Family Violence,* ed. H. Strang and J. Braithwaite, pp. 42–61 (Cambridge: Cambridge University Press, 2002); and Julie Stubbs, *Restorative Justice, Domestic Violence, and Family Violence,* Issues Paper 9 (Sydney, Australia: Australian Domestic and Family Violence Clearinghouse, 2004), http://www.austdvclearinghouse.unsw.edu.au/publications.htm.

28. Braithwaite and Daly, "Masculinities, Violence, and Communitarian Control"; Daly, "Sexual Assault and Restorative Justice"; Hudson, "Restorative Justice"; Koss, "Blame, Shame, and Community"; Martin, "Retribution Revisited"; Mills,

Insult to Injury; Morris and Gelsthorpe, "Re-visioning Men's Violence"; Presser and Gaarder, "Can Restorative Justice Reduce Battering?"

29. Edna Erez, "Integrating a Victim Perspective in Criminal Justice through Victim Impact Statements," in *Integrating a Victim Perspective within Criminal Justice: International Debates*, ed. A. Crawford and J. Goodey, pp. 165–184 (Aldershot, UK: Ashgate, 2000), 178.

30. Morgan and Zedner, *Child Victims*, 115, citing arguments for prosecution, when it is successful, but noting it "is always fraught with difficulties."

31. For major findings and study methods, see Kathleen Daly, Sarah Curtis-Fawley, and Brigitte Bouhours, *Sexual Offence Cases Finalised in Court, by Conference, and by Formal Caution in South Australia for Young Offenders, 1995–2001: Final Report* (Brisbane, Australia: School of Criminology and Criminal Justice, Griffith University, 2003); and idem, *SAJJ-CJ Technical Report No. 3: Archival Study of Sexual Offence Cases Disposed of in Youth Court and by Conference and Formal Caution* (Brisbane, Australia: School of Criminology and Criminal Justice, Griffith University, 2003), http://www.griffith.edu.au/school/ccj/kdaly.html.

32. An additional 4 percent were proved of a nonsexual offense.

33. This was caused by guilty pleas to less serious offenses and by the more serious cases being dismissed or withdrawn.

34. Coker, "Enhancing Autonomy," 85.

35. The Mary Street Adolescent Sexual Abuse Prevention Programme "promotes safety in families and communities by helping young people to stop sexual abuse and sexual harassment of others." Young people charged with sexual offenses can receive counseling before or after a conference or sentencing. Without a treatment program like Mary Street in place, we would hesitate to support conferencing for sex offending. Further information can be found at http://www.wch.sa.gov.au/dmh/asapp.html; and see also summary in Daly et al., *SAJJ-CJ Technical Report No. 3*, 45.

36. During September to December 2001, the research group was based in Adelaide, and we were able to conduct this study as cases were referred to the Family Conference Team.

37. For the remaining cases, the average victim age was six years; for these cases, we interviewed a victim representative, typically a parent or close family member.

38. Rosie had lived with her grandparents since she was an infant.

39. From the archival study, the span of time from report to the police to holding a conference ranged from .5 to 11.2 months; thus, this case is well outside the range for conference cases.

40. Amanda Konradi and Tina Burger, "Having the Last Word," *Violence against Women* 6 (2000): 351–395, 365, find that there are three sets of reasons victims give for participating in the sentencing process: to influence the outcome, to

tell their story and monitor the process, and to overcome negative psychological effects of the assault. See also Erez, "Integrating a Victim Perspective," 175–178.

41. File information is not precise on dates. It appears that the first sexual contact began in July, escalated to the trailer sex in December, and ended in March or April. The disclosure and police apprehension occurred in July, and the conference was held in November.

42. The YJC was concerned that their presence would create even greater conflict and animosity in the conference.

43. Antonia Cretney and Gwynn Davis, *Punishing Violence* (London: Routledge, 1995), 178. This "interest in punishment" is also evident in Konradi and Burger's "Having the Last Word," a study of rape victims' reasons for participating in sentencing. Ten of the twenty-five victims said "they wanted substantial prison time for their assailants" (366).

44. For overviews and debate, see Kathleen Daly, "Revisiting the Relationship between Retributive and Restorative Justice," in *Restorative Justice: Philosophy to Practice,* ed. H. Strang and J. Braithwaite, pp. 33–54 (Dartmouth, UK: Ashgate, 2000); Anthony R. Duff, "Restorative Punishment and Punitive Restoration," in *Restorative Justice and the Law,* ed. L. Walgrave, pp. 82–100 (Cullompton, UK: Willan, 2002); Lode Walgrave, "Restorative Justice and the Law: Socio-Ethical and Juridical Foundations for a Systemic Approach," in *Restorative Justice and the Law,* ed. L. Walgrave, pp. 191–218 (Cullompton, UK: Willan, 2002), 197–202. The importance of punishment for sexual assault victims is discussed in Daly, "Sexual Assault and Restorative Justice."

45. For example, Kelly and Radford, "Nothing Really Happened," 31, discuss the problems of "diversion" in cases of domestic violence and incest. They say that "diversion suggests that 'nothing really happened' or that 'something which happened' is less deserving of legal sanction than other offences." This article, first published in 1990, was written before the advent of RJ, but other critics such as Lewis et al., "Law's Progressive Potential," continue to assume diversion from court will mean less-harsh penalties. See Hudson, "Restorative Justice and Gendered Violence," for a thoughtful review.

46. The maximum length of an agreement in South Australia is twelve months; in other jurisdictions, it is normally no more than six months. The maximum length is important when considering the viability and effectiveness of treatment programs. See Kathleen Daly, Michele Venables, Liz Mumford, Mary McKenna, and Jane Christie-Johnston, *SAJJ Technical Report No. 1: Project Overview and Research Instruments in Year 1* (Brisbane, Australia: School of Criminology and Criminal Justice, Griffith University, 1998), 7, comparing maximum penalties that can be imposed in conference and court in South Australia (http://www.griffith .edu.au/school/ccj/kdaly.html).

47. Eastwood, "Experiences of Child Complainants"; Morgan and Zedner, *Child Victims.*

48. Sarah Curtis-Fawley and Kathleen Daly, "Gendered Violence and Restorative Justice: The Views of Victim Advocates," *Violence against Women* 11(5) (2005): 603–638.

49. In fairness to the South Australian facilitators, we note that they have no power to challenge a police referral to conference if they believe the case does not have the necessary elements to make a conference successful. In other Australian jurisdictions, such as New South Wales and Queensland, facilitators can decide that a case is not appropriate for a conference.

Part III

Intersectionalities
Gender, Race, Poverty, and Crime

Chapter 10

Making Sense of Intersections

Sally S. Simpson and Carole Gibbs

It has been almost forty years since Frances Heidensohn launched the first missile in what has become an ongoing clash between feminist and mainstream criminology.[1] Part of the feminist critique of criminology concentrated on the neglect of women and girls as research subjects and their subsequent absence from theory.[2] A second set of concerns emerged somewhat later, coalescing around issues of essentialism and epistemology. Daly and Maher suggest that these latter issues "raised fundamental questions about how feminist knowledge is (and should be) produced and evaluated."[3] From this development emerged a recognition that a woman's identity was multifaceted, linked to her race, ethnicity, class, and sexuality.[4]

Intersections. Although difficult to characterize sparingly, intersectional feminist approaches emerged from a recognition that fundamental differences exist in the life experiences of women. Consequently, the feminist research subject required "decentering."[5] In criminology, theorists and researchers began to think about and empirically investigate how race and/or class structurally and culturally tailored the crime and justice experiences of girls and women,[6] as well as of boys and men.[7]

Conceptually, scholars began to stretch beyond the simple comparisons of male and female to incorporate multiple social identities. Maher, for instance, observed a clear division of labor in the street-level economy.[8] Race, class, and gender intersections affected participation in illegal activities (e.g., who gets involved in drugs and sex work); the kind of activity that occurs (e.g., who does what and with whom); economics (earnings for services); where the activity takes place; relations with the surrounding community; and who gets hassled by the police. In her study of incarcerated women, Richie suggests compelling ways in which social class and race create distinct cultural frames of reference and socioeconomic

experiences that shape how women perceive family relations when growing up. These early experiences ultimately affect how they comprehend
and respond to battering in their adult relationships, including involvement in criminal activity.[9]

Richie's conceptualization of these developmental processes might be
best described as a *pathways approach* to offending, that is, an analysis of
how gender, race, and social class affect female (and male) initiation into
criminal behavior, continued involvement in offending, and contact with
the juvenile and criminal justice system. Others who share this conceptualization have found important similarities, and key differences, in these
processes for males and females, by socioeconomic class, and by race/
ethnicity.[10] Daly, for instance, found that male pathways into crime were
often linked to excesses of masculinity, bad luck, and masculine gaming.
Uniquely female paths to crime included the defensive use of violence
against abusive partners. Simpson and her coauthors found corresponding
pathways to jail for women, but in contrast to Daly's battered women,
abused women in their sample were primarily whites who did not "fight
back" but who became involved in criminal activities with their abusive
partners. The African Americans had more diverse pathways to jail than
did the whites. The authors also note that one group of women did not fit
with Daly's classifications. These offenders had a much later onset of illegal activity, with few of the salient risk factors for crime (e.g., they were
raised by both parents and had late sexual experience).

In keeping with the pathways approach, Heimer offers an interactionist
understanding of how gender and race inequality (social structure) affect
motivational pathways to delinquency (e.g., grades, self-esteem, and definitions favorable to risk-taking).[11] Although she suggests that risk-taking
is positively linked to delinquency for both sexes, her results show that
risk-taking has different implications for males and females. Girls have
favorable risk definitions when their self-esteem is poor. The converse is
true for males. She also shows that African Americans value risk-taking
less than whites and that their self-esteem is higher, yet African American
male levels of violence are higher than all other groups, perhaps reflecting
the attempts of black males to negotiate masculine identities in the context of structural constraints.

Intersectional analysis has also been used to assess the scope claims of
criminological theory. Cernkovich and Giordano, in several papers, found
similarities and differences by gender and race in the role played by family
dynamics (but not structure) and friendship in delinquent outcomes.[12] In-

deed, their research challenges the rather simplistic conceptions of delinquents as products of broken or dysfunctional homes or as involved in delinquency because they either lack friends (cold and brittle) or they are too easily influenced by friends (intimate fraternity). Cernkovich and Giordano show that with more-refined measures of family dynamics and friendship, intersectional differences become apparent. For instance, family variables are better predictors of delinquency for whites than for nonwhites. But within the different dimensions of family dynamics, instrumental communication matters more for whites, and control and supervision is a better predictor for nonwhites. Similarly, females are less apt than males to characterize their friendships as conflictual or to think friends exerted pressure on them—factors that appear to protect females from delinquent involvement. Along these same lines, Simpson and Elis report that parental and peer influences along with an adverse educational environment influence delinquency differently for males and females, blacks and whites.[13] They also find that lower-class status (compared to other classes) increased violent offending only among disenfranchised white females and black males.

Although criminological studies of intersections represent both qualitative and quantitative approaches, Daly suggests that ethnographic accounts and descriptive analyses of historical and official records are preferable because the phenomenon cannot be easily reduced to quantifiably distinct categories that are separate from one another (and thus treated as additive or interactive in their effects).[14] But qualitative approaches may also dominate because they are more consistent with shifts in feminist epistemology.

Feminist Epistemologies. Drawing from postmodern critiques of scientific positivism, in the 1990s new methodologies were advocated to explore the "matrix-like interaction" of the intersectional systems of domination.[15] Feminists were particularly critical of scientific methodologies that privileged quantitative research, but other issues were equally troubling. As Collins enumerates, concerns also were raised about the kinds of research questions asked (sexist and elitist); analyses that included only male subjects but generalized to broader populations; the hierarchal nature of the relationship between researcher and subject; the illusion of objectivity that accompanied quantitative approaches; and overly simplistic and superficial data collection, analysis, and interpretation.[16]

These kinds of problems led to a variety of epistemological stances in the feminist community. Some feminists completely reject scientific approaches to knowledge, preferring deconstruction and textual analyses of how women are constructed in and by particular discourses (e.g., law, psychiatry, media, medicine, literature, and so forth). This approach ("women of discourse") assumes that constructions are historically specific, socially created, varied, and unstable—a position contrary to scientific assumptions of reason, objectivity, universality, and realism.[17] Others advocate that one of the best ways to change traditional positivism is to "do it better than those you wish to criticize."[18] This approach assumes that women actively construct and engage in life, that is, that women (and men) are concrete actors.[19] Although critics of "feminist empiricism" suggest that this approach fails to challenge the gendered nature of the discipline in which knowledge is produced (in our case, criminology),[20] we believe that quantitative approaches that focus on "real women" can bring useful observations to bear on important criminological questions—especially when their use is circumspect. Our position is consistent with that of Ruddick who suggests that "there is no one starting place for feminist epistemology but rather a range of strategies for making epistemologies serve feminist aims."[21] Additionally informative is Lawson's view that "there is nothing essential to scientific or ontological realism that supposes or requires that objects of knowledge are naturalistic or other than transient, that knowledge obtained is other than fallible, partial, and itself transient, or that scientists or researchers are other than positioned, biased, interested, and practically, culturally and socially conditioned."[22]

Although there are clear differences of opinion among feminist scholars regarding how to study and produce knowledge about gender, these diverse views share core feminist values. Specifically, research should acknowledge any underlying assumptions and values/beliefs that guide the investigation. It should also pay attention to the political and social context regarding the selection of research problems and the interpretation of results.[23] Finally, feminist research should be concerned with who benefits from the undertaking and who does not.[24]

Current Research. Given our interest in intersectionality, crime, and feminist epistemology, we follow Collins's suggestion that intersectional investigators should choose "a concrete topic that is already the subject of investigation and . . . find the combined effects of race, class, gender, sexuality, and nation, where before only one or two interpretive categories were used."[25] We select delinquency participation as our main research subject, and we choose quantitative techniques to investigate how the intersections of gender, class, and race may affect delinquency. Our goal is also to determine whether quantitative methods can reveal unique etiological configurations. Our research strategy is to take four mainstream criminological explanations for delinquent offending purported to be "general theories" (i.e., strain, low self-control, social learning, and control theories) to see whether pooled models provide a better fit to the data (using chi-square tests for nested models) than intersectional models.[26] In conducting this research, we recognize that intersectional categories are fluid, historically specific to a particular time and place (the mid-1990s in the United States), and subject to classification error—especially with regard to race and ethnicity.

Data and Methods

Data for this analysis are taken from the National Longitudinal Survey of Youth (NLSY), collected by the U.S. Bureau of Labor Statistics (BLS), U.S. Department of Labor (DOL).[27] For this chapter, the sample is restricted to males and females age fifteen or sixteen as of December 31, 1996 ($n = 3533$) who responded to wave one and wave two interviews (wave two $n = 3243$). From this group, 527 cases (16 percent) have been lost due to missing data (final $n = 2716$). Group-specific sample sizes are available in Appendix 10.1, Table 1; a detailed description of the variables of interest is available in Appendix 10.1, Table 2; variable means are available in Appendix 10.1, Table 3.

Intersections. The NLSY data are useful for examining intersectional groups for several reasons. First, minority youths are oversampled, which allows meaningful comparisons between race/ethic groups (i.e., race/ethnic intersections). The oversampling also allows race and ethnic breakdowns beyond the typical white-black comparisons that dominate the race and crime literature. The data include a sufficient number of Latino/a youth that this generally neglected group can be included in these analyses. Second, the NLSY data contain several measures related to class status. Although each measure is plagued by missing data, the variety of measures available allows us to construct a measure separating disenfranchised youth from all others. This measure was created by drawing on at least one of the three class measures available for each respondent. Respondents are coded as "disenfranchised" if responses met any one of three conditions: both parents are unemployed (or a single parent is unemployed), the respondent's family receives government aid, or the family income falls below the poverty line.[28]

Dependent Variable. Because the NLSY is a sample of the general population, the proportion of the sample engaging in various criminal and delinquent behaviors is small. To obtain sufficient variation to divide the sample into and conduct analyses on intersectional groups, we use a general dependent variable rather than crime-specific measures. A single "delinquency" participation measure was created to reflect whether the youth committed any of the following acts during the year between the first and second interview: (1) attacked someone; (2) stole something worth less than fifty dollars; (3) stole something worth fifty dollars or more, including stealing a car; (4) damaged or destroyed property; (5) used marijuana; (6) took some other drug or substance; and (7) sold or helped sell drugs. If the youth engaged in any of these behaviors, she or he was classified as delinquent. We recognize that this coding strategy limits the scope of our investigation and that important differences between groups (by crime type or frequency) may not be uncovered.

Independent Variables. To maintain proper temporal order, independent variables consistent with the different theoretical perspectives were selected from wave one of the NLSY. All items were entered into a single and "theory-specific" factor analysis to determine whether face validity held under statistical scrutiny. In some instances additive scales have been created from the measures, but single items are included in some of the theoretical models. For the scales that were retained after factor analysis, the reliability coefficients generally were similar across groups (see Appendix 10.1, Table 4).

Social Learning Theory. Constructs representing social learning theory[29] and differential association theory[30] capture both potentially negative and positive learning influences. One potential negative influence is antisocial peers: an additive scale has been created to capture the presence of individuals in the respondent's grade who drink, smoke, cut class, and/or use drugs. Although this scale does not directly measure delinquent definitions or the transmission of definitions as discussed in differential association/social learning theory, others have suggested that it does provide indirect evidence for the theory.[31]

Other potentially negative associational/learning influences include two indicators of gang prevalence: (1) the presence of gangs in the respondent's neighborhood or school and (2) the respondent's peers' or family members' gang membership. The first set of measures is more general than proxies of differential association used in other studies (i.e., they focus on peer behavior in the school or neighborhood rather than the influence exerted by the respondent's friends). However, the second gang-prevalence measure specifically refers to the respondent's family and peers.

Differential association/social learning theories also acknowledge that individuals will experience a mix of definitions, some favorable to delinquency and some unfavorable to delinquency.[32] To capture prosocial peer presence a second scale was created that measured the percentage of peers in the respondent's grade who are active in the school, plan to attend college, volunteer, and/or regularly attend church services. Again, though not directly testing the transmission of prosocial definitions, our measure can provide indirect support for learning theories.

Self-Control Theory. Our measures of low self-control are consistent with the measurement preferences of Gottfredson and Hirschi.[33] Measures cross multiple domains of problem behavior, including substance use, problems in school, and risky sexual behavior.[34] We created an additive scale to capture early problem behaviors, including whether the respondent smoked, drank, and/or used marijuana at or before the age of twelve. School problems include whether the respondent has ever been suspended from school. Risky sexual practices include reporting more than one sexual partner in the previous year and failing to use birth control during sexual intercourse.[35] We do not have an indicator of opportunity, but the authors of the general theory argue that opportunity is ubiquitous. Given our specific measures of low self-control, we concur with this assessment.[36]

Social Control Theory. Indicators of social control also cover several domains: family, work, and school.[37] Although measures of affective attachment would be ideal, they are not available in our data for the age group of interest. However, we believe that our measures of family bonds/closeness provide a reasonable approximation. These two measures include the respondent's perceptions of the degree of support they receive from a mother and father figure.[38] There are additional work and school measures that are included to capture commitment: (1) an additive scale measuring prosocial expectations for future work and schooling (continuing in school for the following year, receiving a high school diploma, receiving a college degree, and working for pay in the future) and (2) a single measure of the respondent's expectations of being in school and working in the following year.

General Strain Theory. The NLSY data contain several potential sources of strain for respondents which are consistent with those employed in previous studies.[39] For example, Agnew measured school strain in terms of negative relationships with teachers (specifically, being treated unfairly by teachers).[40] Other researchers have also included school and peer hassles as measures of strain, including dissatisfaction in daily dealings with peers, teachers, and other students.[41] Our general scale of strain in school includes the following items: teachers are not good; teachers are not interested in the students; students are not graded fairly; discipline is not fair; and the respondent does not feel safe at school. Two individual indicators of school strain did not "load" with the others in our factor analysis: (1) whether students disrupt learning in school and (2) whether students cheat on tests. We think that these conditions indicate something noxious about the school itself rather than the individual's experience with the school.[42] For these reasons, we have chosen to include the strain scale and the two separate school strain items in our analysis.

Additional strain measures include measures of personal mobility, teen pregnancy, and a negative world view regarding one's future. Personal mobility is measured as the number of schools the respondent ever attended and the number of residences since the respondent was twelve years old. Our argument is that high mobility may increase strain by either removing positively valued stimuli or presenting negative stimuli. It is consistent with a measure of stressful life events used by Paternoster and Mazerolle.[43] Our other measure of stressful life events is whether the respondent reported having been pregnant or having gotten someone pregnant. Here, we assume that teenage pregnancy (by age fifteen or sixteen)—regardless of how welcome the event may be—requires life-altering adjustments and potentially stressful decisions, especially for girls (e.g., termination of pregnancy, marriage, adoption, single parenthood).

Finally, an additive scale of negative expectations for the future (arrest, victimization, serving time, early parenthood) is included in the strain model. Although not often used in major studies of general strain theory, Agnew suggests that anticipating new strains (or that old strains will continue) may also lead to delinquent coping. Agnew finds that anticipated victimization does lead to delinquency and suggests that virtually every type of strain could be examined in terms of anticipation.[44]

Control Variables. Finally, several control measures are included in each theoretical model. Two measures are included for theoretical reasons. Sampson and Laub have suggested that although theories may be general, the specific measures of relevant constructs may vary by age.[45] Older respondents, for instance, may be less affected by perceptions of parental support than those who are younger, and an unplanned pregnancy may be more strain inducing for younger respondents than for older. Thus, we include a continuous measure of age ranging from fifteen to eighteen to control for age-graded differences in predictor variables. However, we note that most of our sample respondents are similar in age. Although the age range is from fifteen to eighteen, most of our respondents are fifteen or sixteen. Because respondents in center-city areas may experience unique life circumstances, a single binary variable is included to represent those respondents living in a metropolitan statistical area (MSA) in the central city.

Additional measures are included to ensure the accuracy of the estimates. The length of time between the wave one and wave two interviews varies by respondent. In order to account for variation in time at risk, the number of months between interview dates is included as a control variable. In addition, a single measure of prior delinquency involvement (yes/no) is included as a control, as the relationship between time-one indicators and time-two delinquency would be insufficient to establish causality without accounting for time-one delinquency.

As is always the case with the use of secondary data, variable construction and measures are limited by the existing data. The theoretical measures selected for analysis are limited and lack some of the detailed nuances that other measures can provide. This can raise model specification problems accompanied by faulty interpretations and conclusions. Thus, appropriate care will be taken when we discuss our results and conclusions.

Analytic Strategy. Our first step in all models is to estimate the likelihood that a person has engaged in delinquency, using the standard normal cumulative distribution function (CDF):

$$p(y = 1) = \phi\ (B_0 + B_1X_1 + B_2X_2 + B_3X_3)$$

where ϕ is the standard normal CDF. We calculate these regression models when all groups are pooled together in a single probit equation and when the sample is broken into various subgroups with separate regressions. Because maximum likelihood estimation has no widely accepted equivalent to the R-squared coefficient in Ordinary Least Squares regression (OLS), we use the likelihood ratio statistic (chi-square test) to assess overall model fit. These comparisons tell us whether as a group the coefficients in the pooled model are significantly different from the coefficients in the group-specific models (sex, race, class, sex/class, race/class, and gender/race/class). After determining which sample breakdowns are significant improvements over the pooled model, we examine the individual coefficients to pinpoint how the theories operate differently across the various intersectional groups.[46] We utilize the formula suggested by Paternoster et al.:[47]

$$Z = \frac{\beta1 - \beta2}{\sqrt{SE_{\beta1}{}^2 + SE_{\beta2}{}^2}}$$

Because probit coefficients have little intuitive meaning, we convert the results for significant pairwise tests into predicted probabilities for ease of interpretation. When necessary, we confirm our results using interaction terms. Results are presented by theory, beginning with the global tests and then moving into specific pairwise differences.

Analysis and Results

Self-Control Theory. In each chi-square table, column one contains all first-round model tests (each grouping against the pooled model) for which we reject the null hypothesis that the group and pooled model coefficients are equivalent. Thus, in the self-control model (Appendix 10.2, Table 1), column one shows that the coefficients in the race, class, and race/class models are significantly different from the coefficients in the pooled model ($p < 0.05$). The next columns show chi-square tests in which more complex interactions are tested against simpler interactions containing the same grouping. For example, in the self-control model, the next step is to determine whether the race/class interaction is a significant improvement over race alone or class alone (column two). The tests show that the coefficients for the race/class interaction model are not significantly different from either the coefficients for the race or the class model ($p > 0.05$). Therefore, two first-order interactions, rather than the second-order interaction, best characterize the data for self-control theory.

To determine how self-control theory operates differently by race and by class, we turn to our pairwise t-tests. Table 2 in Appendix 10.2 provides the pairwise tests for the race-specific models. We conducted thirty pairwise tests (ten coefficients, three groups) and would expect three to be significantly different by chance (10 percent). Because only three tests indicate a significant difference across race groups, we cannot necessarily assume that the observed differences are substantive ones.

In fact, when examining the specific tests, all of the significant differences are for control variables (prior behavior [two tests], class). Generally, the theoretical variables operate in the same direction and at similar significance levels across race. Thus, it appears that self-control theory performs in a consistent manner for each racial and ethnic group; the global chi-square tests are merely picking up differences in the effects of control variables which may actually be due to chance.

Table 3 in Appendix 10.2 provides pairwise t-tests for the class-specific models. Out of twenty-two pairwise tests (eleven coefficients, two groups) we expect two to be significant by chance. In fact, we find two significant comparisons; one is for a control variable (Latino ethnicity), and the other is for having multiple sex partners (more than one in the previous year). For nondisenfranchised kids, moving from zero/one to two or more sex partners in the previous year increases the probability of delinquency by 39 percent. Having multiple partners barely influences disenfranchised kids, decreasing the probability of delinquency by 7 percent. Thus, having multiple sex partners seems to matter for one group but not for the other. To better assess whether this sole difference is a meaningful or a chance finding, we conduct a pooled regression analysis including an interaction between class and multiple sex partners. The interaction term is significant, thus providing evidence that although overall the theory operates in a similar manner across class, this difference is a substantive one. As we know, sexual activity is not unusual among teens regardless of social-class background. However, this result may suggest that multiple sex partners among youth with a higher social-class background may be a better behavioral measure of low self-control than it is among lower-class youth.

Social Control Theory. Our likelihood ratio (chi-square) test indicates that group-specific analysis also provides a better fit in the social control model. Column one of Table 4, Appendix 10.2, shows that the coefficients in the race/ethnicity, gender/race, race/class, and gender/race/class models are significantly different from the coefficients in the pooled model ($p < 0.05$). However, comparisons of the race model against each of the second-order and the third-order interactions indicate that the more complex intersections are not significantly different from the race/ethnicity model (columns two, three, and four). Therefore, race/ethnicity-specific analysis provides the best characterization of the data for social control theory.

Table 5 in Appendix 10.2 provides coefficient tests for the race-specific models. Five tests indicate a significant difference across groups, two more tests than the three we would expect to be significantly different by chance (thirty-three pairwise tests [eleven coefficients, three groups]). Four of the five significant t-tests are for control variables (male [two tests], class, prior behavior) rather than theoretical variables. The only significant difference among the theoretical variables is found in "support from the respondent's mother figure." Although the effect of mother's support is significant and negative for all three groups, it varies in magnitude by race. In terms of predicted probabilities, moving from "not very supportive" to "very supportive" decreases the probability of engaging in delinquency for black youth by 47 percent, for Latino/a youth by 29 percent, and for white youth by 20 percent. Despite these differences, only the coefficients for black and white youth are significantly different from each other. The black-white difference is consistent with findings from other social control studies.[48]

In order to further explore this potential difference, we run a pooled regression model including only interaction terms for "mom's support" and find that the differences in the coefficients are not significant. Thus, the original findings may have been due to chance. There appear to be few substantive differences in the operation of social control theory by race.

Strain Theory. The strain theory model tests indicate that two separate intersectional breakdowns are necessary to best capture processes within the data. In Table 6, Appendix 10.2, the first column indicates that splitting the data into almost every subgroup possible provides a better fit over the pooled data, with the exception of race-specific and class-specific analysis. When the gender coefficients are tested against the more complex interactions including gender (gender/race in column two, gender/class in column two, and the gender/race/class in column three), we fail to reject the null; thus, the second- and third-order interactions are not significantly different from gender alone. Similarly, column three shows that the gender/race/class model is not significantly different from the race/class breakdown; we fail to reject the null hypothesis of equivalence. Gender-specific and race/class-interaction models provide the best fit for our strain theory model.

Moving to our coefficient tests (Table 7, Appendix 10.2), we would expect three tests to be significant by chance (fifteen coefficients, two groups); we find that two tests are significant. One difference is for a control variable (time between interviews), and the other is for pregnancy. The effect of pregnancy on crime/delinquency is significantly different for males and females. For males, getting someone pregnant increases the probability of engaging in delinquency by 54 percent; pregnancy increases the probability for females by only 1 percent. Because this finding could be due to chance, we conduct a pooled regression analysis including an interaction term for pregnancy by gender. The interaction term is significant, leading us to accept that the observed gender difference is authentic.

Now we turn to the results for strain theory by race and class interaction groups (Table 8, Appendix 10.2). In these models, we conducted 195 pairwise comparisons (thirteen coefficients, six groups) and we expect nineteen to be significant by chance (10 percent); we find twenty-nine significant comparisons. Thirteen of the significant tests are for variables of no theoretical interest (control variables and the intercept), and sixteen are theory related.

When examining the specific theory-related differences, we find that some constructs consistently predict delinquency across groups, some constructs fail to predict delinquency for any group, and some constructs show interesting differences across group. For example, the effect of pregnancy on delinquency is positive and significant for most groups (nonsignificant for disenfranchised whites). Similarly, having negative expectations for the future significantly increases the probability of delinquency for most groups (nonsignificant for disenfranchised Latino/a youth). The school-strain measures also perform in a similar manner across groups; however, the effects are generally insignificant. School strain and disruptive students are unrelated to delinquency for all six groups, and the effect of students cheating in class is only significant for two groups. For each of these measures, only the groups with the largest and smallest effects are significantly different from one another, but the effects for these (high and low) groups are not different from any of the groups that fall in the middle. Thus, any conclusions of substantive differences are precarious ones.

Finally, we turn to our mobility measures. Although the effects of changing schools on delinquency are statistically different for some groups, the effect for each group is insignificant. Therefore, it would be difficult to argue that the differences are substantively meaningful. However, the results for changing homes point to an interesting difference. Moving significantly decreases the probability of delinquency by 14 percent among disenfranchised Latino/a youth, and that effect is significantly different from four of the five remaining groups (for whom the effects are positive but rarely significant). Thus, it seems that the effect for disenfranchised Latino/a youth is unique: moving significantly decreases delinquency for this group but has no effect for any other group.[49]

Social Learning Theory. Chi-square tests for the social learning model point to yet another conclusion regarding the best fit of the data (Table 9, Appendix 10.2). Although several first- and second-order interaction models contain coefficients that are significantly different from the pooled model, none of these interactions are alone sufficient; the gender/race/class coefficients are still significantly different from the second-order interaction between race and class. Thus, a fully intersectional model best characterizes the social learning data.

Table 10 (Appendix 10.2) provides the pairwise coefficient tests. Because we ran 528 tests (eight coefficients, twelve groups), we expect fifty-two comparisons to be significant by chance; we find thirty-seven significant tests, with ten being for control variables. Although we have fewer significant tests than what we would expect by chance, when we run a pooled model with interaction terms for each theoretical variable we find that as a group the interaction terms are significant (chi-square = 123.27; 44 degrees of freedom).

When we attempt to determine how and where specific differences lie, it is much more difficult to make sense of the findings for twelve groups (a three-way interaction). We find effects that are significantly different from others, even though they are not significant themselves. Coefficients are significantly different from some groups but not all groups. We have statistically significant results that are not significantly different from some null results, even though they are statistically different from other null results. The results for antisocial peers provide an example of our frustration. The positive and significant effect of antisocial peers on delinquency among disenfranchised white males is significantly different from seven of the remaining eleven groups. However, the effect for disenfranchised white males is not significantly different from other positive effects, some of which are not significant. In addition, the negative null effect for higher-class black males is significantly different from seven of the eleven remaining groups. Thus, there are four groups for which the effects are not significantly different from higher-class black males. Yet some of these groups are not significantly different from groups with effects equivalent to that of disenfranchised white males. We find this same confusion with each social-learning measure. Simply writing the pattern of results for the reader is a difficult task; determining whether the differences are substantive patterns or meaningless statistical fluctuations is even more daunting. In our opinion, it is at this point that quantitative analysis ceases to be useful.

Summary and Conclusions

Review of Findings. Our goal in conducting this research was to examine whether quantitative techniques could identify and explore gender/class/race intersections *in a meaningful way* as they relate to crime. Overall, the application of quantitative techniques produces mixed results and an interpretive challenge for feminist scholars. The chi-square analysis of each criminological theory demonstrated statistically significant intersectional differences (which varied, depending on the theory); however, additional statistical assessment of these differences challenged the substance and salience of many of these outcomes. Numerous model differences appear to be driven by randomly produced significant differences or by variation across groups in how the control variables affected delinquency (e.g., prior criminality). Though the latter are not uninteresting—the effects of prior criminality, for instance, may capture important missing variables in the models that feminists might prioritize (e.g., prior victimization)—they are not core variables for the criminological theories under investigation. Although our measures of different theoretical constructs are more limited than we would like, it would be hard to attribute the bulk of our findings to model misspecification, especially given that we have comprehensive measures and control variables for several of our theories (e.g., strain, low self-control).

On the other hand, our quantitative analysis did reveal some factors that differed across intersectional groups that point to limitations within the purportedly "gender/race/class-neutral" theories. Low self-control theory, for example, should predict offending across gender, social class, and race groups, accounting for most of the empirically observed differences in crime and delinquency participation across groups.[50] Thus, low self-control (measured through analogous behaviors) should affect crime in a similar manner across groups. However, we find that multiple sex partners are a better predictor of criminal involvement among the higher social classes (working/middle/upper) than among the disenfranchised. Although our quantitative analysis cannot answer the "why" part of the difference since it only provides us with evidence that such a difference exists, the theory itself cannot account for the effect either (differences in opportunity appear irrelevant). Our thinking is that social class may contextualize the negative political message about teen sexuality (abstinence). In the face of constant cultural bombardment about sex, disenfranchised teens discredit the political message. Sexual activity may not carry the same negative interpretation for them nor carry the same stigmatic consequences. Sexual experimentation may, in fact, be viewed as a natural part of growing up. Among higher-class youth, the abstinence message may have found a more receptive audience (both among the teens and their parents). Thus, when teens in this class are more sexually active—with multiple partners—it may be seen as rebelliousness. Participation in delinquency is consistent with youthful rebellion, especially among adolescents.[51]

Similarly, we find a stronger crime inhibition effect for blacks than for whites in the role of mother's social control. Though additional statistical tests challenge the reliability of this difference, intersectional scholars would not find it surprising. Structurally, black families depend disproportionately on mothers (in kinship networks, for steadier employment in the legitimate job market, and because of a greater number of female-headed households in this group relative to Anglos and Latinos).[52] If a mother is viewed by her child as a strong and supportive role model, then the prosocial bond predicted by Hirschi will be enhanced.[53] A strong and positive bond between mother and child also can be seen as an important source of social capital in African American communities, one that may inhibit delinquency.[54] As Hagan and McCarthy define it, social capital emerges in relationships between individuals (e.g., in families) and in aggregations of individuals (e.g., in communities, churches, and so forth).[55] Social capital may inhibit delinquency by generating a sense of obligation and responsibility, norms and sanctions. Social capital is understood to be shaped by structure and culture. Thus, we would expect intersectional differences in its manifestations and consequences.

In our strain model, gender modified the effect of pregnancy on crime. Within the framework of general strain theory, gender differences may emerge in several ways. Gender may affect strain exposure (amount and type), interpretations of whether an event is stressful or not, and the level or type of negative affect, which, in turn, influences the behavioral response to it.[56] For instance, females may react to strain with depression or anxiety rather than with anger. In the theory, anger is seen as a "triggering mechanism" that lessens inhibitions and increases the need for retaliation.[57] Males might respond to an unwanted pregnancy with anger, increasing the likelihood of participation in criminal activity. Further, strain theory discusses how a variety of coping mechanisms (emotional, cognitive, and behavioral) can serve to mediate the strain-crime relationship. Pregnancy, whether wanted or unplanned, forces girls to confront substantial life changes (marriage, single parenthood, adoption, or termination). Girls may be able to draw on support from mothers and extended family, counselors, and medical personnel and, as a result, may better cope with the strain.[58] We should also note that feminist scholars would not find it surprising that pregnancy increases crime for males but has little effect on females. Consistent with a doing-gender perspective, getting a girl pregnant is one way in which masculinity is accomplished for heterosexual males.[59] Crime is another. Although pregnancy (motherhood) is in harmony with hegemonic femininity, women tend not to accomplish their femininity through criminal means.

Finally, we found that household mobility negatively affected offending for our group of disenfranchised Latino/as. Although this finding is counter to what one might expect based on strain theory (in which more frequent moves are expected to create strain for the juvenile and increase delinquent behavior), if we pay attention to the intersection between class and race/ethnicity, mobility may represent something different for this group.

To contextualize this effect we need to ask the question, "Who are the disenfranchised Latino/a youth?" It is likely that many in our sample are the children of migrant laborers who, because work for their parents generally is seasonal, may be constantly mobile as families relocate to seek seasonal or temporary employment.[60] Others are likely the children of immigrants who moved into center-city barrios during the recent waves of Latin immigration, shifting households as they settle in with family or friends.[61] Under both of these conditions, we might expect a negative relationship between mobility and crime.

Because of their lifestyle, migrant youth are more isolated from delinquent opportunities and negative peer influences (e.g., gangs). Many of the youths also work (alongside or without their parents), or they are assigned to watch younger siblings.[62] Finally, they often find themselves serving as translators for their Spanish-speaking parents, who need assistance negotiating social service bureaucracies. Such responsibilities are likely to lessen delinquent involvement. In this case, mobility is merely a proxy for minimizing other delinquency risk factors.

Ironically, for more-recent urban immigrants, frequent changes in households may not indicate transience but rather stability. As Martinez describes it, "families, friends, schools, work, and church . . . provide entrée" for the new immigrant who often "had to *enter* the United States without the benefits of legality."[63] The binding of old with new immigrants in the same community gives the new arrival information and support that leads to employment and affordable apartments or homes (instead of living with family, friends, or previous compatriots)—in short, greater economic and social stability. New arrivals are also apt to understand that their current situation—shifting households, unstable employment, and a language barrier—is still an improvement on how they were living previously. "Immigrants in their daily negotiations with work, settlement, and everyday life in general perceive their new status as infinitely better than where they came from before."[64] Lacking legal status, the new immigrants may be particularly careful to avoid legal authorities, with parents stressing the importance of prosocial behavior.

Implications for Feminist Epistemology. Although we lack the breadth of measures that would constitute a complete test of these general theories, our results suggest that quantitative analysis is a useful tool to detect intersectional differences. All of our tests reveal that intersectional break-downs provide a better fit to the data than the pooled sample across theories. We find these results even though we are not using measures that revealed intersectional differences in other studies (e.g., instrumental communication versus supervision in family dynamics or self-esteem as a motivator for delinquency). Thus, quantitative methods support feminist assertions that so-called general theories are less universal than adherents claim. On the other hand, quantitative techniques break down when observed patterns are nonsensical and numerically overwhelming. Absent information about life context, the interpretation of results often is difficult and downright daunting. To understand what the statistical differences mean and why differences appear across groups—to contextualize the results—re-quires more than quantitative analysis can offer.

Purportedly better suited for theory testing, quantitative research clearly needs assistance from qualitative research. Grounded theory building, which begins with the assumption that intersectionality does matter, can be used to build better models of how social control, differential associations and learning, and strain texture the life experiences of real actors. Specifically, more-nuanced and interpretive studies can give us an idea of where differences lie, so that quantitative research does not result in a blind search for difference. Additionally, participant observation, interviews, and analysis of historical documents may reveal new factors and processes—both structural and cultural—that affect delinquency participation across groups. Such approaches give voice to intersectional members, so that interpretations emerge from the subjects themselves rather than being imposed on them by the researchers. Thus, we believe that a mix of quantitative and qualitative methods will be a more successful research strategy.

We end, however, with a cautionary tale. Intersectional analysis is an important feminist construct that can be explored (in a limited way) using quantitative techniques. However, both the concept and our approach in this chapter emphasize a search for difference. We advocate for a broader conceptualization than this, one that also acknowledges similarities across groups and the general relevance of some theoretical constructs. In the search for difference, some feminists tend to ignore similarities or challenge those who find them. Taking note of similarities allows one to explore how criminogenic processes affect all intersectional members as well as the ways in which ostensibly similar processes may be gendered (or work in *qualitatively* different ways by race or class).[65] Traditional theories are useful in that they identify key constructs that may not vary across groups. But traditional theories are also limited in the way these constructs are understood and measured. Clearly, there is room for modification and extension of existing theories, and quantitative analysis can play a role here. Discovering conceptual nuances or developing new theoretical approaches is likely to be best accomplished with qualitative work.

APPENDIX 10.1

Table 1: Group-Specific Sample Size

Group	N	Percent
Gender		
Males	1,366	50.3
Females	1,350	49.7
Race		
Whites	1,445	53.2
Blacks	710	26.1
Latinos	561	20.7
Class		
Higher Class (HC)	1,878	69.1
Disenfranchised (Dis.)	838	30.9
Sex/Class		
HC Males	957	35.2
HC Females	921	33.9
Dis. Males	409	15.1
Dis. Females	429	15.8
Race/Class		
HC Whites	1,207	44.4
HC Blacks	372	13.7
HC Latin	299	11.0
Dis. Whites	238	8.8
Dis. Blacks	338	12.4
Dis. Latin	262	9.7
Gender/Race/Class		
HC White Males	606	22.3
HC Black Males	183	6.7
HC Latinos	168	6.2
HC White Females	601	22.1
HC Black Females	189	7.0
HC Latinas	131	4.8
Dis. White Males	119	4.4
Dis. Black Males	160	5.9
Dis. Latinos	130	4.8
Dis. White Females	119	4.4
Dis. Black Females	178	6.6
Dis. Latinas	132	4.9

Table 2: Variable Description

Variable	Values	Description
Dependent Variable		
Crime	0,1	Dichotomous Indicator: (1) attacked someone; (2) stole something worth less than fifty dollars; (3) stole something worth fifty dollars or more, including stealing a car; (4) damaged or destroyed property; (5) used marijuana; (6) took some other drug or substance; and (7) sold or helped sell drugs.
Social Learning		
Antisocial peers	1–20	Additive Scale: Percentage of peers in respondent's grade who (1) smoke cigarettes; (2) get drunk one or more times a month; (3) use marijuana, inhalants, or other drugs; and/or (4) cut classes/skip school.
Prosocial peers	1–20	Additive Scale: Percentage of peers in respondent's grade who (1) participate in organized sports, clubs, or school activities; (2) plan to go to college; (3) do volunteer work; and/or (4) go to church or religious services on a regular basis.
Gangs in school/neigh.	0,1	Are there any gangs in your neighborhood or where you go to school? (By gangs, we mean a group that hangs out together, wears gang colors or clothes, has set clear boundaries of its territory or turf, protects its members and turf against other rival gangs through fighting or threats.)
Peers/siblings in gang	0,1	Do any of your brothers, sisters, cousins, or friends belong to a gang?
Self-Control		
Early substance use	0–3	Additive Scale: Respondent began (1) smoking; (2) drinking; and/or (3) using marijuana at or before the age of twelve.
Ever suspended	0,1	Have you ever been suspended from school?
Multiple partners	0,1	Respondent reports more than one sex partner in the previous year.
No birth control	0,1	Did you or your sexual partner use any birth control method or do anything to avoid pregnancy, such as natural family planning, the first time you had intercourse?
Social Control		
Dad's support	1–3	When you think about how he acts toward you, would you say he is not very supportive, somewhat supportive, or very supportive?
Mom's support	1–3	When you think about how she acts toward you, would you say she is not very supportive, somewhat supportive, or very supportive?
Expect prosocial	0–100	Additive Scale: (1) What is the percent chance that you will be a student in a regular school one year from now; (2) What is the percent chance that you will have received a high school diploma by the time you turn twenty; (3) What is the percent chance that you will have a four-year college degree by the time you turn thirty; (4) What is the percent chance that you will be working for pay more than twenty hours per week when you turn thirty?

Table 2 (continued)

Variable	Values	Description
Expect work/school	0–100	If you are in school a year from now, what is the percent chance that you will also be working for pay more than twenty hours per week?
Strain		
School strain	1–20	Additive Scale: Thinking about your (last) school in general, how much do you agree with each of the following statements about your school and teachers (strongly agree, agree, disagree, or strongly disagree): (1) The teachers are good; (2) The teachers are interested in the students; (3) Students are graded fairly; (4) Discipline is fair; (5) I feel safe at this school.
Students disrupt	1–4	Disruptions by other students get in the way of my learning (strongly disagree, disagree, agree, or strongly agree).
Students cheat	1–4	There is a lot of cheating on tests and assignments (strongly disagree, disagree, agree, or strongly agree).
Pregnancy	0,1	Males: Have you ever gotten someone pregnant? Females: Have you ever been pregnant? (Consider all pregnancies even if no child was born).
Number of schools	0–∞	Number of regular schools ever attended as of survey date.
Number of residences	0–∞	Number of different residences (since age twelve).
Negative expectations	0–100	Additive Scale: (1) What is the percent chance that you will be arrested, whether rightly or wrongly, at least once in the next year; (2) What is the percent chance that you will be the victim of a violent crime at least once in the next year; (3) What is the percent chance that you will drink enough to get seriously drunk at least once in the next year; (4) What is the percent chance that you will become the [mom/dad] of a baby sometime between now and when you turn twenty; (5) What is the percent chance you will serve time in jail or prison between now and when you turn twenty; (6) What is the chance you will become pregnant or get someone pregnant within one year?
Control Measures		
Class	0,1	Either both parents are unemployed (or a single parent is unemployed), the respondent's family receives government aid, or the family income falls below the poverty line.
Race/ethnicity	0,1	Two dummy variables: Latino/a and black (white = reference category).
Gender	0,1	Dummy control for male.
Age	15–18	Age at time of interview.
Central city	0,1	Control for respondents residing in central cities.
Time	6–∞	Number of intervals (in months) between interview dates.
Prior crime	0,1	Control for wave one crime and delinquency including: (1) attacked someone; (2) stole something worth fifty dollars or more, including stealing a car; (3) damaged or destroyed property; (4) used marijuana; and (5) sold or helped sell drugs.

Table 3: Means

	Males N = 1,366		Females N = 1,350		Whites N = 1,445		Blacks N = 710		Latino/as N = 561		Higher Class N = 1,878		Disenfranchised N = 838	
	Mean	Std Dev	Mean	Std Dev	Mean	Std Dev	Mean	Std Dev	Mean	Std Dev	Mean	Std Dev	Mean	Std Dev
Dependent Variable														
Crime	0.48	0.50	0.34	0.47	0.44	0.50	0.35	0.48	0.40	0.49	0.41	0.49	0.41	0.49
Social Learning Theory														
Antisocial peers	11.16	3.88	12.15	3.82	11.55	3.79	12.22	3.92	11.19	3.99	11.54	3.78	11.89	4.08
Prosocial peers	11.45	2.78	11.77	2.78	11.91	2.63	11.33	2.97	11.19	2.85	11.89	2.65	10.98	2.97
Gangs in school/neigh.	0.50	0.50	0.47	0.50	0.40	0.49	0.51	0.50	0.70	0.46	0.46	0.50	0.56	0.50
Peers/siblings in gang	0.24	0.43	0.23	0.42	0.15	0.36	0.33	0.47	0.33	0.47	0.20	0.40	0.30	0.46
Self-Control Theory														
Early substance use	0.39	0.72	0.26	0.59	0.40	0.72	0.23	0.54	0.28	0.63	0.33	0.66	0.32	0.67
Ever suspended	0.42	0.49	0.25	0.43	0.25	0.43	0.50	0.50	0.35	0.48	0.28	0.45	0.45	0.50
Multiple partners	0.19	0.39	0.11	0.31	0.11	0.31	0.23	0.42	0.14	0.34	0.13	0.33	0.20	0.40
No birth control	0.09	0.28	0.08	0.27	0.06	0.24	0.10	0.30	0.12	0.32	0.06	0.25	0.12	0.33
Social Control Theory														
Expect prosocial	86.94	15.55	89.74	15.07	90.16	13.16	87.81	16.48	84.30	18.17	90.29	13.55	83.95	18.08
Mom's support	2.71	0.71	2.65	0.70	2.69	0.69	2.67	0.72	2.67	0.73	2.69	0.69	2.66	0.75
Dad's support	1.94	1.28	1.80	1.29	2.16	1.15	1.29	1.35	1.86	1.29	2.16	1.14	1.22	1.36
Single parent	0.32	0.47	0.33	0.47	0.22	0.42	0.53	0.50	0.32	0.47	0.22	0.41	0.56	0.50
Expect work/school	61.34	31.57	59.27	33.62	58.35	33.75	63.44	31.69	61.40	30.42	58.91	33.35	63.45	30.70
Strain Theory														
School strain	10.23	2.26	10.44	2.48	10.07	2.29	10.99	2.44	10.17	2.34	10.16	2.28	10.72	2.52
Students disrupt	2.77	0.84	2.81	0.85	2.75	0.85	2.84	0.88	2.83	0.78	2.79	0.84	2.79	0.87
Students cheat	2.86	0.85	2.99	0.83	2.96	0.84	2.93	0.87	2.82	0.80	2.95	0.84	2.87	0.86
Pregnancy	0.09	0.29	0.08	0.28	0.06	0.23	0.14	0.35	0.10	0.30	0.06	0.25	0.14	0.35
Number of schools	1.88	0.81	1.93	0.84	1.96	0.83	1.85	0.87	1.84	0.77	1.87	0.76	1.97	0.96
Number of residences	1.65	1.28	1.70	1.22	1.62	1.25	1.74	1.21	1.72	1.30	1.51	1.03	2.03	1.58
Negative expectations	14.34	14.54	10.60	12.38	11.78	12.86	12.67	14.16	14.05	14.75	11.49	12.63	14.70	15.43
Control Variables														
Prior crime	0.40	0.49	0.23	0.42	0.34	0.47	0.29	0.46	0.29	0.46	0.31	0.46	0.34	0.48
Age	15.81	0.70	15.80	0.71	15.80	0.71	15.81	0.70	15.82	0.71	15.81	0.72	15.79	0.68
Central city	0.29	0.46	0.33	0.47	0.19	0.39	0.49	0.50	0.41	0.49	0.27	0.44	0.41	0.49
Time	19.83	2.99	19.78	2.76	19.85	2.87	19.88	2.88	19.58	2.87	19.66	2.98	20.13	2.60

Table 4: Cronbach's Alpha

	Antisoc. Peers	Prosoc. Peers	Early Substance Use	Prosocial Expect.	School Strain	Negative Expect.
Pooled	0.81	0.60	0.53	0.64	0.71	0.71
HC WM	0.80	0.54	0.54	0.49	0.64	0.69
HC BM	0.83	0.65	0.38	0.77	0.67	0.77
HC Latino	0.79	0.61	0.59	0.68	0.70	0.74
HC WF	0.82	0.59	0.45	0.37	0.75	0.65
HC BF	0.78	0.60	0.33	0.34	0.69	0.57
HC Latina	0.80	0.54	0.69	0.70	0.73	0.61
Dis. WM	0.83	0.59	0.67	0.68	0.70	0.74
Dis. BM	0.76	0.65	0.58	0.60	0.62	0.74
Dis. Latino	0.83	0.59	0.39	0.62	0.76	0.76
Dis. WF	0.82	0.57	0.64	0.62	0.76	0.67
Dis. BF	0.76	0.62	0.27	0.61	0.70	0.70
Dis. Latina	0.81	0.67	0.37	0.80	0.69	0.76

APPENDIX 10.2

Table 1: Likelihood Ratio (Chi-Square) Tests for Self-Control Theory

	Pooled	Race/class
Race	$P = 0.03^a$	$P = 0.18$
Class	$P = 0.03^a$	$P = 0.14$
Race/class	$P = 0.03^a$	

[a] Significant at $p < 0.05$

Table 2: Pairwise Coefficient Tests for Self-Control Theory by Race

	Whites		Blacks		Latino/as		Significant
	Beta	Std E	Beta	Std E	Beta	Std E	Z Tests
Age	0.02	0.05	−0.10	0.07	−0.07	0.10	
Male	0.07	0.08	0.26^a	0.10	0.23	0.13	
Disenfranchised	−0.02	0.11	0.14	0.12	-0.27^b	0.12	(B,L)
Early substance use	0.13^a	0.05	0.34^a	0.09	0.28^b	0.12	
Ever suspended	0.31^a	0.10	0.35^a	0.10	0.21	0.13	
Multiple partners	0.34^a	0.13	0.21	0.14	−0.20	0.20	
No birth control	0.19	0.17	0.26	0.18	0.39^b	0.20	
Central city	0.08	0.09	0.05	0.11	−0.02	0.11	
Time	0.01	0.01	0.01	0.02	0.01	0.02	
Prior crime	0.96^a	0.08	0.49^a	0.11	0.96^a	0.15	(W,B) (B,L)

[a] Significant at $p < 0.01$; [b] Significant at $p < 0.05$

Table 3: Pairwise Coefficient Tests for Self-Control Theory by Class

	Higher Class (HC)		Disenfranchised (Dis.)		Significant Z Tests
	Beta	Std E	Beta	Std E	
Age	−0.01	0.04	−0.09	0.07	
Male	0.13	0.06	0.22[b]	0.10	
Black	−0.38[a]	0.09	−0.29[b]	0.12	
Latino/a	0.01	0.09	−0.33[a]	0.13	(HC, Dis.)
Early substance use	0.22[a]	0.05	0.13	0.08	
Ever suspended	0.26[a]	0.08	0.35[a]	0.12	
Multiple partners	0.38[a]	0.12	−0.08	0.12	(HC, Dis.)
No birth control	0.21	0.15	0.38[a]	0.14	
Central city	−0.02	0.08	0.16	0.11	
Time	0.01	0.01	0.02	0.02	
Prior crime	0.82[a]	0.08	0.87[a]	0.09	

[a] Significant at $p < 0.01$; [b] Significant at $p < 0.05$

Table 4: Likelihood Ratio (Chi-Square) Tests for Social Control Theory

	Pooled	Gender/race	Race/class	Gender/race/class
Race	$P = 0.02^{b}$	$P = 0.07$	$P = 0.14$	$P = 0.22$
Gender/race	$P = 0.01^{a}$			
Race/class	$P = 0.01^{a}$			
Gender/race/class	$P = 0.04^{b}$			

[a] Significant at $p < 0.01$; [b] Significant at $p < 0.05$

Table 5: Pairwise Coefficient Tests for Social Control Theory by Race

	Whites		Blacks		Latino/as		Significant Z Tests
	Beta	Std E	Beta	Std E	Beta	Std E	
Age	0.02	0.05	−0.11	0.06	−0.07	0.09	
Male	0.14	0.08	0.41[a]	0.10	0.31[a]	0.12	(W,B)
Disenfranchised	−0.03	0.11	0.15	0.12	−0.29[b]	0.12	(B,L)
Expect prosocial	0.00	0.00	0.00	0.00	0.00	0.00	
Mom's support	−0.13[a]	0.07	−0.35[a]	0.08	−0.19[b]	0.08	(W,B)
Dad's support	−0.21[b]	0.07	−0.08	0.09	−0.06	0.08	
Single parent	−0.24	0.17	−0.15	0.26	−0.12	0.23	
Expect work/school	0.00	0.00	0.00	0.00	0.00	0.00	
Central city	0.06	0.09	0.09	0.11	−0.03	0.12	
Time	0.00	0.01	0.02	0.02	0.02	0.02	
Prior crime	1.06[a]	0.08	0.68[a]	0.11	1.06[a]	0.12	(W,B) (B,L)

[a] Significant at $p < 0.01$; [b] Significant at $p < 0.05$

Table 6: Likelihood Ratio (Chi-Square) Tests for Strain Theory

	Pooled	Gender/race	Gender/class	Gender/race/class
Gender	p = 0.02[b]	p = 0.23	p = 0.06	p = 0.06
Gender/race	p = 0.05[b]			
Gender/class	p = 0.01[a]			
Race/class	p = 0.00[a]			p = 0.56
Gender/race/class	p = 0.02[b]			

[a] Significant at p < 0.01; [b] Significant at p < 0.05

Table 7: Pairwise Coefficient Tests for Strain Theory by Gender

	Males		Females		Significant
	Beta	Std E	Beta	Std E	Z Tests
Age	−0.05	0.05	−0.02	0.05	
Black	−0.20[b]	0.10	−0.30[a]	0.10	
Latino/a	−0.09	0.10	−0.15	0.11	
Disenfranchised	−0.06	0.10	−0.08	0.10	
School strain	0.02	0.02	0.02	0.02	
Students disrupt	0.02	0.05	−0.06	0.04	
Students cheat	0.05	0.04	0.11[b]	0.05	
Pregnancy	0.64[a]	0.13	0.01	0.15	(M,F)
Number of schools	0.04	0.06	0.05	0.05	
Number of residences	0.00	0.03	0.07[b]	0.03	
Missing dummy	0.07	0.13	−0.01	0.14	
Negative expectations	0.01[a]	0.00	0.02[a]	0.00	
Central city	0.07	0.09	−0.04	0.09	
Time	0.03[b]	0.01	−0.01	0.01	(M,F)
Prior crime	0.76[a]	0.08	0.95[a]	0.10	

[a] Significant at p < 0.01; [b] Significant at p < 0.05

Table 8: Pairwise Coefficient Tests for Strain Theory by Race/Class

	Higher-Class Whites (HCW)		Disenfranchised Whites (DisW)		Higher-Class Blacks (HCB)		Disenfranchised Blacks (DisB)		Higher-Class Latino/as (HCL)		Disenfranchised Latino/as (DisL)		Significant Z Tests
	Beta	Std E	Beta	Std E	Beta	Std E	Beta	Std E	Beta	Std E	Beta	Std E	
Age	0.04	0.05	−0.19	0.15	−0.07	0.10	−0.22	0.11	−0.32[b]	0.13	0.18	0.12	(HCW,HCL); (DisB,DisL); (HCL,DisL)
Male	0.09	0.08	0.30	0.20	0.39[a]	0.14	0.37[b]	0.16	0.35	0.19	0.06	0.21	
School strain	0.03	0.02	0.07	0.03	0.00	0.03	0.01	0.03	−0.02	0.04	0.03	0.03	
Students disrupt	0.01	0.05	−0.11	0.10	−0.09	0.09	0.01	0.08	0.22	0.12	−0.20	0.12	(DisW,HCL); (HCB,HCL); (HCL,DisL)
Students cheat	0.11[b]	0.05	−0.11	0.11	0.19[b]	0.09	−0.10	0.08	0.07	0.10	0.02	0.10	(DisW,HCB)
Pregnancy	0.63[a]	0.22	−0.38	0.34	0.32	0.19	0.31	0.19	0.77[b]	0.36	0.49[b]	0.24	(HCW,DisW); (DisW,HCL); (DisW,DisL); (HCB,HCL)
Number of schools	0.02	0.06	−0.07	0.08	0.21	0.11	0.05	0.09	−0.13	0.13	0.24	0.14	(DisW,HCB); (DisW,DisL)
Number of residences	−0.03	0.04	0.09	0.07	0.15	0.08	0.14[b]	0.06	0.11	0.07	−0.14[b]	0.06	(DisW,DisL); (HCB,DisL); (DisB,DisL); (HCL,DisL)
Missing dummy	0.08	0.15	0.06	0.54	0.17	0.24	0.44	0.33	−0.38	0.25	−0.23	0.37	(DisB,HCL)
Negative expectations	0.01[a]	0.00	0.03[a]	0.01	0.01[b]	0.01	0.01[b]	0.00	0.02[a]	0.01	0.01	0.01	(DisW,DisB); (DisW,DisL)
Central city	0.00	0.11	0.39	0.19	0.09	0.17	0.01	0.16	−0.17	0.17	0.15	0.18	(DisW,HCL); (HCB,HCL); (HCL,DisL)
Time	0.01	0.01	−0.03	0.03	0.00	0.02	0.04	0.03	−0.03	0.02	0.06	0.04	
Prior crime	0.98[a]	0.09	0.76[a]	0.18	0.36[b]	0.17	0.78[a]	0.15	0.71[a]	0.18	1.09[a]	0.19	(HCW,HCB); (HCB,DisL)

[a] Significant at p < 0.01; [b] Significant at p < 0.05

Table 9: Likelihood Ratio (Chi-Square) Tests for Social Learning Theory

	Pooled	Race/gender	Race/class	Gender/class	Gender/race/class
Race	$p = 0.01^a$	$p = 0.36$	$p = 0.05^b$		
Class	$p = 0.05^b$		$p = 0.01^a$	$p = 0.10$	
Race/gender	$p = 0.02^b$				
Gender/class	$p = 0.02^b$				
Race/class	$p = 0.00^a$				$p = 0.01^a$
Gender/race/class	$p = 0.01^a$				

[a] Significant at $p < 0.01$; [b] Significant at $p < 0.05$

Table 10: Pairwise Coefficient Tests for Social Learning Theory by Race/Gender/Class

	HC WM (1)		HC BM (2)		HC Latinos (3)		HC WF (4)		HC BF (5)		HC Latinas (6)		Dis. WM (7)	
	Beta	Std E	Beta	Std E	Beta	Std E	Beta	Std E	Beta	Std E	Beta	Std E	Beta	Std E
Age	0.09	0.09	-0.07	0.12	-0.28	0.17	0.05	0.08	-0.04	0.15	-0.28	0.19	-0.45[b]	0.19
Antisocial peers	0.05[a]	0.02	-0.03	0.02	0.00	0.03	0.04[b]	0.02	0.06[b]	0.03	0.11[a]	0.04	0.14[a]	0.04
Prosocial peers	0.00	0.02	-0.06	0.03	-0.01	0.04	-0.02	0.02	0.01	0.04	0.01	0.05	-0.06	0.05
Gangs school/neigh.	-0.03	0.12	-0.19	0.20	0.16	0.20	-0.08	0.14	-0.30	0.27	-0.30	0.25	-0.55	0.30
Peers/sib. gang	0.33	0.20	0.26	0.23	0.04	0.23	0.66[a]	0.18	0.37	0.27	-0.37	0.31	0.83	0.44
Central city	0.01	0.14	0.01	0.22	-0.12	0.24	-0.06	0.14	-0.01	0.24	-0.12	0.24	0.63	0.37
Time	0.04[b]	0.02	0.01	0.03	-0.01	0.03	-0.02	0.02	-0.02	0.04	0.01	0.05	-0.04	0.06
Prior crime	1.06[a]	0.12	0.51[b]	0.21	0.74[a]	0.22	1.00[a]	0.14	0.64[b]	0.27	1.17[a]	0.35	0.72[a]	0.25

	Dis. BM (8)		Dis. Latinos (9)		Dis. WF (10)		Dis. BF (11)		Dis. Latinas (12)		Significant Z tests
	Beta	Std E	Beta	Std E	Beta	Std E	Beta	Std E	Beta	Std E	
Age	-0.17	0.16	0.14	0.16	-0.08	0.19	-0.25	0.15	0.23	0.19	(1,3); (1,7); (1,11); (3,12); (4,7); (7,9); (7,12); (11,12)
Antisocial peers	0.04	0.03	0.08[b]	0.04	0.02	0.03	-0.02	0.03	0.05	0.03	(1,2); (1,7); (2,4); (2,5); (2,6); (2,7); (2,9); (2,12); (3,6); (3,7); (4,7); (6,11); (7,8); (7,10); (7,11); (9,11)
Prosocial peers	-0.04	0.03	-0.06	0.05	-0.04	0.05	-0.01	0.04	-0.05	0.06	
Gangs school/neigh.	-0.24	0.24	0.33	0.34	-0.19	0.26	0.69[a]	0.25	0.35	0.29	(1,11); (2,11); (4,11); (5,11); (6,11); (7,11); (8,11); (10,11); (3,7); (7,12)
Peers/sib. gang	0.29	0.22	0.40	0.29	0.37	0.30	0.26	0.22	0.47[b]	0.23	(4,6); (6,7); (6,12); (3,4)
Central city	0.07	0.21	0.18	0.22	0.17	0.26	-0.02	0.24	-0.05	0.31	
Time	0.04	0.04	0.05	0.05	-0.05	0.04	0.02	0.05	0.03	0.07	(1,10); (1,4)
Prior crime	0.64[a]	0.20	0.57[b]	0.24	1.11[a]	0.27	1.12[a]	0.29	1.26[b]	0.37	(1,2)

[a] Significant at $p < 0.01$; [b] Significant at $p < 0.05$

NOTES

1. Frances Heidensohn, "The Deviance of Women," *British Journal of Sociology* 19 (1968): 160–175.

2. Carol Smart, *Women, Crime, and Criminality* (London: Routledge and Kegan Paul, 1976); Eileen B. Leonard, *Women, Crime, and Society* (New York: Longman, 1982); Ngaire Naffine, *Female Crime* (Sydney: Allen & Unwin, 1988).

3. Kathleen Daly and Lisa Maher, *Criminology at the Crossroads* (New York: Oxford University Press, 1998), 3.

4. Angela Y. Davis, *Women, Race, and Class* (New York: Random House, 1981); bell hooks, *From Margin to Center* (Boston: South End, 1984); Kimberlé Crenshaw, "Mapping the Margins: Intersectionality, Identity Politics, and Violence against Women of Color," *Stanford Law Review* 43 (1991): 1241–1309.

5. Elizabeth V. Spelman, *Inessential Woman* (Boston: Beacon, 1988); Patricia Hill Collins, *Black Feminist Thought* (Boston: Unwin Hyman, 1990); Kimberly Christensen, "'With Whom Do You Believe Your Lot Is Cast?' White Feminists and Racism," *Signs* 22 (1997): 617–648.

6. Nicole Hahn Rafter, *Partial Justice* (Boston: Northeastern University Press, 1985); Eleanor M. Miller, *Street Women* (Philadelphia: Temple University Press, 1986); Sally S. Simpson, "Caste, Class, and Violent Crime," *Criminology* 29 (1991): 115–135; Kerry Carrington, *Offending Girls* (St. Leonards, NSW: Allen & Unwin, 1993); Mary E. Odem, *Delinquent Daughters* (Chapel Hill: University of North Carolina Press, 1995); Beth Richie, *Compelled to Crime* (New York: Routledge, 1996); Lisa Maher, *Sexed Work* (Oxford: Oxford University Press, 1997); Deborah R. Baskin and Ira B. Sommers, *Casualties of Community Disorder* (Boulder, CO: Westview, 1998); Marjorie S. Zatz and Coramae Richey Mann, "The Power of Images," in *Images of Color, Images of Crime*, ed. C. R. Mann and M. S. Zatz, pp. 1–12 (Los Angeles: Roxbury, 1998).

7. James W. Messerschmidt, *Masculinities and Crime* (Lanham, MD: Rowman and Littlefield, 1993); Karen A. Joe and Meda Chesney-Lind, "Just Every Mother's Angel," *Gender and Society* 9 (1995): 408–431; Sally S. Simpson and Lori Elis, "Doing Gender: Sorting Out the Class and Crime Conundrum," *Criminology* 33 (1995): 47–81; Karen Heimer and Stacy De Coster, "The Gendering of Violent Delinquency," *Criminology* 37 (1999): 277–318.

8. Maher, *Sexed Work*.

9. Richie, *Compelled to Crime*.

10. Kathleen Daly, *Gender, Crime, and Punishment* (New Haven: Yale University Press, 1994); Sally S. Simpson, Jennifer Castro, and Laura Dugan, "Understanding Women's Pathways to Jail: Analyzing the Lives of Incarcerated Women" (unpublished manuscript, Department of Criminology and Criminal Justice, University of Maryland, 2004).

11. Karen Heimer, "Gender, Race, and the Pathways to Delinquency," in *Crime*

and Inequality, ed. J. Hagan and R. D. Peterson, pp. 140–173 (Stanford, CA: Stanford University Press, 1995).

12. Peggy C. Giordano, Stephen A. Cernkovich, and M. D. Pugh, "Friendships and Delinquency," *American Journal of Sociology* 91 (1986): 1170–1202; Stephen A. Cernkovich and Peggy C. Giordano, "Family Relationships and Delinquency," *Criminology* 25 (1987): 295–321.

13. Simpson and Elis, "Doing Gender."

14. Kathleen Daly, "Different Ways of Conceptualizing Sex/Gender in Feminist Theory and Their Implications for Criminology," *Theoretical Criminology* 1 (1997): 25–51.

15. Johnella Butler, "Difficult Dialogues," *The Women's Review of Books* 6(5) (1989): 16.

16. Patricia Hill Collins, "Moving Beyond Gender: Intersectionality and Scientific Knowledge," in *Revisioning Gender,* ed. M. M. Ferree, J. Lorber, and B. B. Hess, pp. 261–284 (Thousand Oaks, CA: Sage, 1999), 263; see also Sandra Harding, *Whose Science? Whose Knowledge? Thinking from Women's Lives* (Ithaca, NY: Cornell University Press, 1991); and Tony Lawson, "Feminism, Realism, and Universalism," *Feminist Economics* 5 (1999): 25–59.

17. Carol Smart, "The Women of Legal Discourse," *Social and Legal Studies* (March 1992): 29–44; Ngaire Naffine, *Feminism and Criminology* (Philadelphia: Temple University Press, 1996); Daly and Maher, *Criminology at the Crossroads.*

18. Londa Schiebinger, "Introduction: Feminism Inside the Sciences," *Signs* 28(3) (2003): 861.

19. Daly and Maher, *Criminology at the Crossroads.*

20. In particular, critics suggest that empirical work on women without consideration of men (and maleness) simply reproduces the discipline unanalyzed. Feminist empiricism "tends not to comment on the project and methods of the mainstream, that is, the way in which men's lives are documented and interpreted." Naffine, *Female Crime,* 36.

21. Sara Ruddick, "New Feminist Work on Knowledge, Reason, and Objectivity," *Hypatia* 8 (1993): 148.

22. Lawson, "Feminism, Realism, and Universalism," 28.

23. Alessandra Tanesini, *An Introduction to Feminist Epistemologies* (Oxford, UK: Blackwell, 1999).

24. See Harding, *Whose Science?*; and Schiebinger, "Introduction."

25. Collins, "Moving Beyond Gender," 278.

26. These theories are selected based on the availability of measures in the NLSY data set. Other mainstream theories that incorporate gender and class differences (e.g., power-control) cannot adequately be tested using the NLSY data.

27. The data are corrected for the clustering of cases within primary sampling units. Because clustering of this nature biases the standard errors, we used the survey probit command in STATA to correct the standard errors.

28. Our constructed class measure varies in expected ways with other variables in our analysis. For example, 41 percent of the disenfranchised youths reside in the center city, compared to only 27 percent of the nondisenfranchised respondents. In addition, 50 percent of the disenfranchised group report living with a single mother, and only 18 percent of the nondisenfranchised kids report such living arrangements. Finally, our class measure varies by race as one would expect based on the high (but not perfect) correlation between race and class often found in the research literature. Sixteen percent of white youths fall into the disenfranchised category, compared to 48 percent of black kids and 47 percent of Latino/a respondents.

29. Ronald L. Akers, *Deviant Behavior: A Social Learning Approach,* 3rd ed. (1973; Belmont, CA: Wadsworth, 1985).

30. Edwin H. Sutherland, *Principles of Criminology,* 4th ed. (Chicago: J. B. Lippincott, 1947).

31. Mark Warr and Mark Stafford, "The Influence of Delinquent Peers: What They Think or What They Do?" *Criminology* 29 (1991): 851–866.

32. Sutherland, *Principles of Criminology.*

33. Travis Hirschi and Michael R. Gottfredson, "Commentary: Testing the General Theory of Crime," *Journal of Research in Crime and Delinquency* 30 (1993): 47–54.

34. Michael R. Gottfredson and Travis Hirschi, *A General Theory of Crime* (Stanford, CA: Stanford University Press, 1990).

35. Although some may argue that the measure of early substance use is tautological with the dependent variable (Travis C. Pratt and Frances T. Cullen, "The Empirical Status of Gottfredson and Hirschi's General Theory of Crime: A Meta-Analysis," *Criminology* 38 [2000]: 933), the measure is consistent with the measurement recommendations of Gottfredson and Hirschi (*A General Theory of Crime,* 92): "The evidence that offenders are likely to engage in noncriminal acts psychologically or theoretically equivalent to crime is, because of the relatively high rates of these 'noncriminal' acts, even easier to document. Thieves are likely to smoke, drink, and skip school at considerably higher rates than nonthieves. Offenders are considerably more likely than nonoffenders to be involved in most types of accidents, including household fires, auto crashes, and unwanted pregnancies."

36. Gottfredson and Hirschi, *A General Theory of Crime,* 92.

37. Travis Hirschi, *Causes of Delinquency* (New Brunswick, NJ: Transaction, 2002); Robert J. Sampson and John H. Laub, *Crime in the Making: Pathways and Turning Points through Life* (Cambridge, MA: Harvard University Press, 1993).

38. Missing data is a consistent problem with the "dad" measure; many of the youths in the sample do not live with a father figure. Rather than drop these cases, we recoded data for respondents who do not live with a father figure to the lowest response category and included a control measure for the recoded cases.

39. Robert Agnew, "Foundation for a General Strain Theory of Crime and Delinquency," *Criminology* 30 (1992): 47–77.

40. Robert Agnew, "Strain Theory and School Crime," in *Of Crime and Criminality*, ed. S. S. Simpson, pp. 105–120 (Boston: Pine Forge Press, 2000).

41. Raymond Paternoster and Paul Mazerolle, "General Strain Theory and Delinquency: A Replication and Extension," *Journal of Research in Crime and Delinquency* 31 (1994): 235–263.

42. Agnew, for instance, discusses how schools that lack good discipline and have low expectations of students may have higher levels of strain ("Foundation for a General Strain Theory," 13).

43. Paternoster and Mazerolle, "General Strain Theory," 241.

44. Robert Agnew, "Experienced, Vicarious, and Anticipated Strain: An Exploratory Study of Physical Victimization and Delinquency," *Justice Quarterly* 19 (2002): 603–632.

45. Sampson and Laub, *Crime in the Making*, 17.

46. When conducting numerous pairwise tests without corrections for dependence, it is possible to find significant differences merely by chance. Statistical adjustments, such as the Bonferroni correction, are based on the idea that when multiple comparisons are done the chance of at least one test being significant is greater than 0.05. However, because the data do not change based on the number of tests, Perneger argues that Bonferroni corrections are logically flawed and may create more problems (Thomas V. Perneger, "What's Wrong with Bonferroni Adjustments," *British Medical Journal* 316[7139] [1998]: 1236–1238). Instead of using Bonferroni corrections, Perneger suggests that "describing what was done and why, and discussing the possible interpretations of each result, should enable the reader to reach a reasonable conclusion without the help of Bonferroni adjustments" (ibid., 1237). We follow this approach by first calculating (and sharing with the reader) how many of our multiple comparisons one would expect to be significant by chance, using a 10 percent cutoff. We also examine pooled models with interaction terms as a second method to confirm our initial conclusion regarding the pairwise t-test.

47. Although the practice is common in the field of criminology, it is technically incorrect to use the Paternoster et al. formula or interaction terms (Raymond Paternoster, Robert Brame, Paul Mazerolle, and Alex Piquero, "Using the Correct Statistical Test for the Equality of Regression Coefficients," *Criminology* 36 [November 1998]: 859–866) to test for differences in coefficients across groups when using maximum likelihood estimation (Paul Allison, "Comparing Logit and Probit Coefficients across Groups," *Sociological Methods and Research* 28 [November 1999]: 186–206). Thus, we acknowledge that this method only provides an estimation of the differences across groups and should be viewed as exploratory. When differences are found using both of these methods, we examine the difference in

the predicted probabilities as a final "test." The probabilities consistently mirror the estimated statistical differences.

48. Cernkovich and Giordano, "Family Relationships and Delinquency," 315; Simpson and Elis, "Doing Gender," 64.

49. There were some outliers among the disenfranchised Latino/a youth that appeared to pull the regression line down. We recoded the residential-mobility measure and censored it at the ninety-fifth percentile. Although the coefficient was still negative for disenfranchised Latino/a kids, it was no longer significant. However, the effect was still significantly different from three of the five remaining groups. Although this places some doubt on the distinctiveness of the effect for this group, we believe that it is still a substantively interesting finding. Given the population of interest (possibly new immigrants or migrant workers), it is not completely surprising that the most highly mobile youths are also nondelinquent (see discussion section for further explication). If we were to drop these outlier cases, as most would do when utilizing quantitative methods, we may lose a unique aspect of this group.

50. Gottfredson and Hirschi, *A General Theory of Crime*, 11.

51. Terrie E. Moffitt, "Adolescence-Limited and Life-Course-Persistent Antisocial Behavior: A Developmental Taxonomy," *Psychological Review* 100 (1993): 674–701.

52. Miller, *Street Women*; John Hagan and Bill McCarthy, *Mean Streets: Youth Crime and Homelessness* (Cambridge: Cambridge University Press, 1998); Ramiro Martinez Jr., *Latino Homicide: Immigration, Violence, and Community* (New York: Routledge, 2002).

53. Hirschi, *Causes of Delinquency*, 12.

54. Simpson and Elis, "Doing Gender," 21.

55. Hagan and McCarthy, *Mean Streets*, 28.

56. Lisa M. Broidy and Robert Agnew, "Gender and Crime: A General Strain Theory Perspective," *Journal of Research in Crime and Delinquency* 34 (1997): 275–306.

57. Agnew, "Foundation for a General Strain Theory," 12.

58. See, e.g., Lisa M. Broidy, "A Test of General Strain Theory," *Criminology* 39 (2001): 9–36.

59. Simpson and Elis, "Doing Gender," 21; Messerschmidt, *Masculinities and Crime*.

60. In 1992, the U.S. Commission on Agricultural Workers estimated that there were approximately 2.5 million agricultural workers in the United States. Of these, a large majority are foreign born (especially from Mexico and Central America). During the 1990s, the percentage of foreign-born workers increased (to approximately 81 percent of total workers). In 1998, Mexican-born workers constituted 77 percent of all foreign-born workers and Central Americans about 2 percent. Of

the 18 percent U.S.-born migrants, 8 percent are Hispanic or Puerto Rican. David Runsten, Raul Hinojosa, Kathleen Lee, and Richard Mines, "The Extent, Pattern, and Contributions of Migrant Labor in the NAFTA Countries: An Overview" (paper presented at a conference on Agricultural Migrant Labor in North America NAID, 2000).

61. Martinez, *Latino Homicide*, 28.

62. Philip Martin, "Migrant Farmworkers and Their Children," *Eric Digests*, available at www.ericdigests.org/1995-2/migrant.htm; Mary Daniels Brown, "Curriculum: Meeting the Educational Needs of Migrant Students," *Education World*, 1–8, available at www.education-world.com/a_curr/curr347.shtml.

63. Martinez, *Latino Homicide*, 134.

64. Ibid., 138.

65. Daly, *Gender, Crime, and Punishment*; Jody Miller, *One of the Guys: Girls, Gangs, and Gender* (New York: Oxford University Press, 2001).

Chapter 11

The Role of Race and Ethnicity in Violence against Women

Janet L. Lauritsen and Callie Marie Rennison

Over the past twenty-five years, many researchers have noted a correlation between an American woman's risk for violence and her race or ethnicity.[1] Rates of homicide victimization among American Indian and black women have been found to be higher than rates among white women.[2] Rates for nonlethal violence also tend to be higher among black and American Indian women; however, for crimes other than homicide, differences between the groups are much smaller.[3]

Many explanations are offered to account for correlations between race, ethnicity, and violence including an array of cultural and structural hypotheses.[4] Cultural explanations assert that certain race and ethnic groups, for a variety of reasons, are more likely to have norms and attitudes that promote or at least tolerate violence to settle conflicts. These proposed normative differences are thought to make unique causal contributions to the risk for violence. Structural explanations, on the other hand, assert that normative differences are relatively unimportant or even spurious because, if they do exist, they result from the same structural conditions that generate violence. These explanations focus on important social conditions such as economic disadvantage and inequality, institutional imbalances, or social isolation. If violence is correlated with race and ethnicity, it is believed to be the result of a shared association with some form of structural disadvantage.

Recently, research has examined the potential sources of race and ethnic differences in women's victimization using nationally representative data. Bivariate analyses have found that age and marital status are better predictors than income and that income is a stronger correlate than either race or ethnicity.[5] Multivariate analyses have found few significant differences between black, white, and Latina women once differences in family structure or community economic disadvantage are taken into account.[6] These kinds of findings suggest that race and ethnicity should not be the primary focus in studies of violence against women in the United States. They also suggest that cultural differences between the largest racial and ethnic groups, if they exist, may not play as important a role as variations in the structural conditions of everyday life.

Nonetheless, many researchers and advocates are concerned that existing findings may mask important causal differences for women of different racial and ethnic groups. Simply put, this is because the literature has not assessed whether the trends and correlates of victimization are the same for women of different groups. Nationally representative data are inevitably dominated by the experiences of the majority group in a population, and when national findings are reported, it is reasonable to ask whether the same patterns apply for minority women. It is important to know whether recent trends in women's violence vary according to race and ethnicity and whether decreases in risk over time were shared equally across groups for different types of violence. It also is not known whether different factors have the same kinds of influences on violence for black, white, and Latina women. One could argue that if there are group differences in norms about the use of violence, we should find the effects of structural factors to vary across the groups. In groups where cultural values encourage the use of violence, we should expect to see a significantly weaker relationship between victimization and structural factors. Also, there should be less within-group variation in violence (and more between-group variation), and structural factors should be of little use in predicting an individual's involvement in violence.

In this chapter we use data from the past decade of the National Crime Victimization Survey (NCVS) to describe similarities and differences in the levels, trends, and correlates of nonlethal violence against women of different racial and ethnic groups in the United States. The purpose of our analyses is to assess whether the sources of risk are similar for women of different racial and ethnic groups. These comparisons will help determine whether group-based explanations appear to be necessary and will provide indirect evidence about the role of group differences in norms about violence against women. Our findings also will have important implications for policies about violence against women because they will indicate whether there is a need to tailor programs according to a woman's race or ethnicity. Our description of recent trends in violence by race and ethnicity and by victim-offender relationship will help assess whether some groups of women have been neglected by broader social and legislative changes regarding violence against women.

Data

Studies of violence against women often rely on self-report data available in large, nationally representative surveys. Self-report data are preferred for estimating levels and trends in nonlethal violence because they come directly from women rather than from agency records. Women interviewed in the NCVS and in the National Violence Against Women Survey (NVAWS), for instance, report that most nonlethal victimizations do not come to the attention of police departments, emergency rooms, or shelters. In this chapter we use data from the past decade of the NCVS to describe the levels, trends, and correlates of nonlethal violence against American women because it is the only data that can provide reliable information about each of these concerns.

There has been long-standing concern about the quality of data about violence against women. Rand and Rennison, however, have shown that NCVS data are externally valid when compared to data obtained from the NVAWS.[7] The size and representativeness of the NCVS sample is an important strength of these data when the goal is to estimate rates of violence among minority subgroups. Few surveys contain sufficient numbers of interviews with minority-group members to permit reliable estimates of risk. Fortunately, the NCVS data contain a large number of interviews with women each year. Over the past ten years, roughly 900,000 NCVS interviews were conducted with American women in numbers proportionate to their levels in the population. Consequently, we are able to describe recent levels and trends in violent victimization for five groups of women: white, black, Asian, American Indian, and Latina women. For the three largest subgroups in the population (i.e., white, black, and Latina women) we also are able to assess how individual, family, and community factors are related to the risk for violence.

NCVS data are obtained through personal and telephone interviews conducted by the Census Bureau under sponsorship of the Bureau of

Justice Statistics. The information in the survey is derived from a nationally representative sample of housing units and group quarters in the United States, including the District of Columbia. In each selected sample housing unit, all persons age twelve or older are interviewed. The vast majority of interviews are conducted by female interviewers. The survey has been ongoing since 1973. Beginning in 1979, the NCVS underwent a thorough, decade-long redesign to improve the survey's ability to measure victimization in general and certain difficult-to-measure crimes, such as rape, sexual assault, and domestic violence, in particular. This redesign was implemented in 1992 using a split-sample design that allowed for an assessment of the change in reporting. In general, the redesign had the anticipated result of increasing the number of crimes counted by the survey. Rates of violence against women increased more than 110 percent for simple assault, greater than 170 percent for aggravated assault, and 257 percent for rape and sexual assault.[8] Rates of reporting increased more for crimes that had not been reported to the police and for crimes committed by nonstrangers. We limit our analyses of the level and trends of women's violence to the redesign data (1992–2001) because earlier data are less valid for describing women's victimizations. Our multivariate assessment of the individual, family, and community correlates of victimization among black, white, and Latina women relies on a special version of these files known as the "area-identified" NCVS.[9]

To describe recent trends in violent victimization among women, we disaggregated violence according to victim-offender relationship. "Total violence" includes all incidents of attempted or completed assault, robbery, and rape and sexual assault regardless of the relationship between the victim and the offender. "Stranger violence" includes incidents in which the woman reported no prior relationship with the offender. "Nonstranger violence" includes incidents in which the offender was a friend, acquaintance, or family member of the victim. "Intimate-partner violence" is a subcategory of nonstranger violence and includes incidents in which the offender was a spouse, ex-spouse, boyfriend, or ex-boyfriend of the victim.

Race and ethnicity is measured by the Census Bureau using two separate items. We cross-classify these two measures to construct five race-ethnic groupings: black (non-Latina), white (non-Latina), American Indian (non-Latina), Asian (non-Latina), and Latina women. We define race and ethnicity groups in this way because such categories represent popular conceptions of the major racial and ethnic groups in the United States. It is also the case that without this conceptualization, most "Hispanics" would be included with whites, and "Hispanic" versus "non-Hispanic" comparisons would underestimate and confound group differences.

Nonlethal Violence by Race and Ethnicity

Using NCVS data we find that women of different race and Hispanic origins are victimized at different rates: American Indian women experience violent victimization at the highest rate, and Asian women experience similar violence at the lowest rate. In 2001 there were 63 violent victimizations per 1,000 against American Indian women compared to 10 per 1,000 against Asian females. Unfortunately, the relatively small sample sizes for American Indian and Asian women—even over a ten-year period—limit our ability to describe their victimization experiences further. Focusing on the remaining three groups—black, white, and Latina women—demonstrates small but significant differences in victimization among these groups in many years. For example, in 2001, black women experienced nonlethal violence at rates somewhat higher (28.4 per 1,000) than white (22.4 per 1,000) and Latina women (26.9 per 1,000).

Trends in Nonlethal Violence

Figure 11.1 shows that nonlethal violence against all women age twelve or older declined 43 percent—from 41 to 23 violent victimizations per 1,000 women—between 1992 and 2001. This drop resulted in the lowest rate of violence against women ever measured using the NCVS. In addition to an overall decrease in the rate of violence against women, the rate of violence by strangers, nonstrangers, and intimate partners also declined over the 1992 and 2001 period. Stranger violence rates decreased 53 percent, and nonstranger violence rates fell 37 percent. Intimate-partner violence rates —a subcategory of nonstranger violence—declined 43 percent over the same period. Following these substantial declines, women remain at lower risk for stranger violence than for nonstranger violence in 2001 (6.9 versus 16.5 victimizations per 1,000, respectively). And intimate-partner violence against women in 2001 is somewhat less common than stranger violence (5.0 versus 6.9 victimizations per 1,000, respectively).

The declines in violence rates described above are most representative of the majority group in this population, non-Hispanic white females. It is sound to question whether these changes in victimization accurately reflect the experiences of females in other racial and ethnic categories. Figure 11.2 shows that like the overall rates of violence, victimization against black, white, and Latina women decreased between 1992 and 2001. Black women were victims of violence at rates 48 percent lower in 2001 than in 1992 (28 versus 55 victimizations per 1,000). And rates of violence against white females decreased from 39 to 22 victimizations (a 42 percent drop). The smallest drop—26 percent—was measured for Latina females, as victimization rates fell from 36 to 27 victimizations per 1,000.[10]

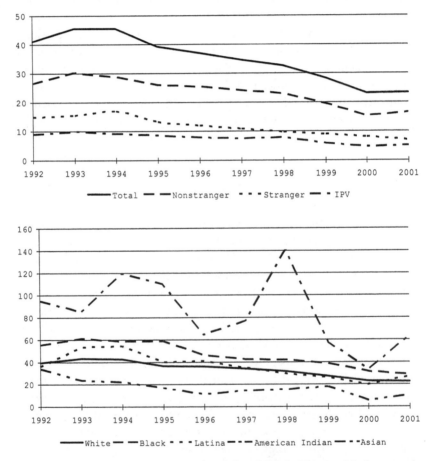

Fig. 11.1. *Top,* Violence against Women by Victim-Offender Relationship (per 1,000).
Fig. 11.2. *Bottom,* Violence against Women by Race and Ethnicity (per 1,000).

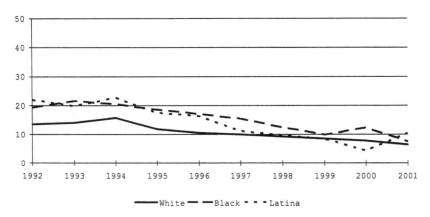

Fig. 11.3. Stranger Violence against Women by Race and Ethnicity (per 1,000).

Drops in rates of overall violence are similar among whites, blacks, and Latinas. But have white, black, and Latina women experienced similar drops in violence when the offender is a stranger? What if the offender is a nonstranger or an intimate partner? Figure 11.3 shows similar declines in stranger violence against white, black, and Latina females between 1992 and 2001 (53 percent, 61 percent, and 52 percent, respectively). In 2001, white, black, and Latina women were victims of nonstranger violence at similar rates in 2001 (6, 7, and 10 victimizations per 1,000, respectively).

A slightly different pattern emerges when considering violence perpetrated by nonstrangers (see Figure 11.4). Black and white females were violently victimized at lower rates in 2001 compared to 1992 (28 percent and 42 percent decreases, respectively). In contrast, violence against Latinas by nonstrangers increased 15 percent, from 14 to 21 victimizations per 1,000. Following these changes, white, black, and Latina women were victims of nonstranger violence at similar rates in 2001 (16, 21, and 21 victimizations per 1,000, respectively).

Some of the changes measured in nonstranger violence reflect changes in rates of intimate-partner victimization between 1992 and 2001. Figure 11.5 shows that intimate-partner violence against whites fell from 9 to 5 victimizations per 1,000 and violence against blacks fell from 11 to 5 victimizations per 1,000 during this period. Intimate-partner victimizations against Latinas increased nominally though not significantly from 2 to 5 victimizations per 1,000 between 1992 and 2001. Though some changes in intimate violence have been measured over the past decade, it is important

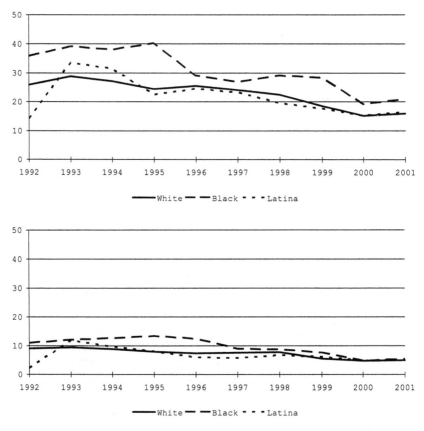

Fig. 11.4. *Top,* Nonstranger Violence against Women by Race and Ethnicity (per 1,000).
Fig. 11.5. *Bottom,* Intimate-Partner Violence against Women by Race and Ethnicity (per 1,000).

to note that it is very difficult to distinguish any statistically significant differences in the levels of intimate-partner violence across these three groups, particularly over the past five years.

Predictors of Nonlethal Violence by Race and Ethnicity

The national trends described in the previous section suggest that recent changes in violence are roughly comparable for women in these race and ethnic groups. To examine whether the predictors of victimization vary depending on a woman's race or ethnicity, we conduct a series of multivariate analyses that allow us to compare the influences of different factors on the various types of violence. In the multivariate models, we are no longer predicting annual victimization rates but rather the likelihood that an individual woman was victimized by violence overall and by stranger, nonstranger, and intimate-partner violence within a six-month period. To do so, we use data from NCVS interviews conducted in 1995. Women who were victims of at least one incident of attempted or completed assault, robbery, or rape or sexual assault were coded as victims. To take into account the possibility that a woman was victimized more than once by more than one type of offender during the six-month period, we estimate the prevalence of victimization separately for each of the different types of violence.

The factors we assess include an array of individual, family, and community characteristics. Existing research has shown that violence in general and violence against women is related to factors at each of these levels.[11] Variables found to be significant in past research form the basis of our comparisons across groups. Individual-level variables include age and "evenings at home," a crude indicator of lifestyle that asks respondents how many evening they spend at home in a typical week. Marital status is examined by comparing currently married women to others (never married, divorced, separated, and widowed).

Family and household measures include self-reported household income and the number of persons living in the household. Length of residence measures the number of years that the family has lived at the current address. Family composition or structure is assessed by comparing women in three different groups: (1) married women living with their spouses, with or without children, (2) women living alone, and (3) women living alone with children. This conceptualization of family structure has been shown to capture important differences in women's risk for violence.[12]

To determine whether the influence of community conditions varies across race and ethnic groups requires use of data from the "area-identified" NCVS, a special release of NCVS data that includes identifiers for the state, county, and census tract in which each woman resides. These identifiers allowed us to link the 1995 NCVS data with tract data available in the census STF3A files.[13] We compare the effects of community conditions in two ways. First, we compare coefficients for three commonly used indices measuring socioeconomic disadvantage, residential instability, and immigrant concentration. Second, we compare four theoretically important components of these indices: the percentage of neighborhood residents living in poverty, the percentage of households with children that are headed by females, the percentage of persons who are under eighteen years of age, and the percentage of persons who are black. In addition, we examine whether the influence of central-city residence (versus suburban and rural) varies across groups.

We provide separate assessments of victimization incidents that occur within one mile of the woman's home because it is reasonable to assume that community factors are more strongly related to violence that occurs near the home than victimization that occurs elsewhere. The neighborhood violence category is used for each type of victimization risk except intimate-partner violence. Intimate-partner violence is not further disaggregated because there are insufficient numbers of incidents that occur more than one mile from home to support reliable analyses.

To determine if the predictors of violence depend on race and ethnicity, we examine six different sets of multivariate models. Each model is analyzed separately for non-Latino white, non-Latino black, and Latina women, and significance tests are performed to assess whether the predictors of violent victimization differ significantly across the groups. Significant differences are determined by conducting a series of z-tests to compare regression coefficients relative to their standard error. American Indian and Asian women could not be included in these group comparisons because their sample sizes in a single year are too small to permit reliable multivariate analyses.

We begin with a description of the prevalence of violence against white, black, and Latina women in 1995. Table 11.1 shows that the bivariate relationship between race, ethnicity, and violent victimization is complex and contingent on the type of violence and the location of the incident. In general, black women were victimized by all types of victimization in significantly greater proportions than were white women. They also reported significantly higher levels nonstranger and intimate-partner violence than Latina women. Latina women had significantly higher rates of stranger violence than white women, especially within their neighborhood. However, levels of nonstranger and intimate-partner violence among Latina women did not differ significantly from those of white women. Thus, Latina women were more similar to black women with regard to stranger violence and more similar to white women in terms of nonstranger and intimate-partner violence risk. The relationship between race, ethnicity,

TABLE 11.1
Violent Victimizations among Females by Race and Ethnic Group[a]

	Total		Stranger	
	All Violence	Neighborhood Violence	All Violence	Neighborhood Violence
Non-Latina Black	26.3 */**	18.6 */**	12.7 *	8.5 *
Latina	18.9	12.5 *	13.0 *	8.4 *
Non-Latina White	15.5	8.0	8.4	3.8

	Nonstranger		Intimate Partner
	All Violence	Neighborhood Violence	All Violence
Non-Latina Black	15.9 */**	12.1 */**	6.8 */**
Latina	8.5	6.1	4.0
Non-Latina White	8.7	5.3	3.9

[a] Prevalence rates (per 1,000 females) represent the proportion of females who reported any violent victimization during a six-month period in 1995.
* Significantly higher than non-Latina white females; ** significantly higher than Latina females.

and victimization in 2001 (described in the previous section) is very similar to that found in the 1995 NCVS data used in the multivariate analyses that follow.

To provide an overview of the possible sources of these differences, Table 11.2 shows how the conditions of life vary for white, black, and Latina women. Among individual factors, average age and marital status tend to differ across the three groups. In the United States, white women are older on average than black and Latina women, and black women are significantly less likely to be married than white or Latina women. These differences are important because both age and marital status are significant correlates of victimization risk.

Differences in family characteristics are more pronounced, especially for household composition and income. Younger black females (i.e., twelve to seventeen years of age) are significantly less likely to be living in two-parent families than white or Latina adolescents. Among women eighteen years and older, Latinas are much less likely to be living alone than black or white women and much more likely to be married with children in the household. Black women are least likely to be married and most likely to be living as single mothers with children. Household income and length of residence in one's current home is highest among whites.

TABLE 11.2
Individual, Family, and Community Characteristics by Race and Ethnicity:
Area-Identified NCVS (1995)

	Non-Latina White	Non-Latina Black	Latina
Individual Characteristics			
Age	43.8	38.4	35.3
Marital Status (1 = Married)	0.54	0.28	0.46
Evenings at Home in a Typical Week	2.4	2.5	2.7
Family Characteristics			
Composition, 12–17 years			
Two Parents (%)	77.2	41.2	64.1
Composition, 18 years and above			
Married, with children	28.2	20.0	40.9
Married, no children	27.0	10.7	11.1
Single, with children	7.8	29.3	18.9
Single, alone	16.8	17.8	8.0
Other (%)	7.9	22.2	21.1
Estimated Household Income	29.2	18.8	20.2
Household Size	2.7	3.0	3.8
Length of Residence (years)	12.1	10.3	7.6
Community Characteristics			
Standardized Index Scores			
Socioeconomic Disadvantage	−0.36	0.93	0.23
Residential Instability	−0.13	0.00	0.14
Immigrant Concentration	−0.21	−0.06	1.79
Other Measures			
Central City (1 = yes)	0.23	0.54	0.49
Percent Non-Latino Black	5.3	54.3	10.1
Percent Latino	4.8	7.7	41.8
Percent Non-Latino White	88.3	39.5	44.9
Percent Below Poverty	10.3	22.4	19.8
Percent Female-Headed Households with Children	16.4	36.9	23.1
Number of Interviews	79,390	10,692	8,019
	(79%)	(12%)	(9%)

The level of economic, race, and ethnic segregation in the United States can be clearly seen in the census tract data describing women's communities. White women tend to live in areas that are overwhelmingly white and with half the levels of poverty and female-headed households compared to black women. In addition, these women are half as likely to be living in central cities as either black or Latina women. Compared to white women, Latina women live in areas that are disproportionately Latino, with nearly twice as many persons living below the poverty line and 50 percent more female-headed households with children. Black women tend to live in areas that are disproportionately black, with the highest levels of female-headed households. The levels of poverty in areas where black women reside are roughly equal to the levels in areas where Latina women live, but the households differ in their family composition.

As seen in Table 11.2, there are significant relationships between race and ethnicity and the contexts of women's lives. Lauritsen and Schaum found that the differences in risk between black, white, and Latina women (in 1995 and other years) can be accounted for by any one of a variety of measures associated with group status.[14] For instance, when household income, community disadvantage, or family composition is taken into account, the differences in nonlethal violence between groups were eliminated. In other words, initial differences in victimization are no longer significant once structural factors associated with race are considered.

To determine whether the predictors of victimization are the same, we examined a series of logistic regression models and compared coefficients across the three groups of women. These comparisons involved six different sets of models containing various combinations of individual, family, and community factors. For the first three sets of models, there were seven dependent variables (total risk, stranger violence risk, nonstranger violence risk, intimate-partner violence risk, and total, stranger, and nonstranger violence risk within the women's neighborhood). For the latter three sets of models, there were four dependent variables (the various forms of neighborhood violence, plus intimate-partner violence). These various combinations of factors resulted in a series of z-tests for 423 group-specific coefficients. A summary of the results is presented in Table 11.3.

TABLE 11.3
Summary of Race and Ethnic Differences in Predictors of
Women's Risk for Nonlethal Violence

Model	Number of Dependent Variables	Number of Independent Variables	Number of Coefficients	Number of Significant Differences
1. Individual	7	3	63	9
2. Family Structure	7	2	42	0
3. Individual and Family	7	6	126	19
4. Community Indices	4	3	36	8
5. Community Items	4	4	48	0
6. Individual, Family, and Community Indices	4	9	108	7
Total Coefficients Compared			423	
Total Significant Differences				40

In the first set of comparisons, we examined whether age, lifestyle, and marital-status effects varied across groups. These three individual characteristics were examined for each of the seven measures of violent victimization, resulting in a comparison of sixty-three ($3 \times 7 \times 3 = 63$) group-specific coefficients. Of these sixty-three coefficients, we found a total of nine to be significantly different. The tests indicated that the relationship between "time spent at home" and victimization risk was significantly different for Latina women than for black and white women. More specifically, Latina women who spent more time at home were less likely to be victimized by intimate-partner violence and nonstranger violence in their neighborhoods, and white women who spent more time at home were more likely to be victims of these crimes. In addition, although time spent at home appears to reduce all women's risk for stranger violence, the effect of this variable was significantly greater for Latina women than for white or black women. There were no differences in the effects of age or marital status across the three groups.

In the second set of models, we examined whether the relationship between family structure and victimization varied—that is, whether the difference between being married and single with children or living alone was similar for black, white, and Latina women. These comparisons revealed no significant differences in the effect of family structure. Regardless of race or ethnicity, the gap between married women and those living alone was similar. Of the forty-two coefficients in these models, none of the differences was statistically significant.

The third set of comparisons examined whether the results from these comparisons persisted in models containing both individual and family factors. Because the measure of marital status is highly correlated with our measure of family structure, we used a simpler marital-status variable (married versus not married) in these models. We included three other household variables in these models: the length of time the family has lived at the current address, whether the household is located in a central-city (versus suburban or rural) place, and household income. Using six predictors and seven outcome variables, we compared a total of 126 coefficients. Significant differences in the effects of "time spent at home" persisted once these variables were included in the models. Several other significant differences emerged among the predictors of nonstranger violence. Most notably, length of residence and central-city residence was a stronger predictor of nonstranger violence for black women than for

Latina and white women. However, the direction of the coefficients was similar. Of these 126 coefficients, 19 were significantly different.

The fourth set of comparisons assessed whether the effects of neighborhood disadvantage, immigrant concentration, and residential instability differed across the three groups. No other covariates were included in this community-factors model. The analyses were restricted to the risk for victimization that occurred within the neighborhood, hence thirty-six coefficients ($3 \times 4 \times 3 = 36$) were compared. We found that white women who lived in areas with greater immigrant concentration and residential instability were at greater risk for stranger, nonstranger, and intimate-partner victimization in their neighborhood. These indices were not, however, significantly associated with victimization risk among black and Latina women. Eight of the thirty-six coefficients exhibited significant differences.

The fifth set of comparisons examined whether selected community characteristics had different relationships with risk for neighborhood stranger, nonstranger, and intimate-partner violence. These four characteristics included central-city residence, percentage of persons living in poverty, percentage of households with children that are headed by females, and percentage black. Of these sixteen coefficients, none was significantly different in strength or magnitude. In other words, these three characteristics had similar effects on white, black, and Latina women's risk for victimization.

In the final set of models, we assessed the differences in individual, family, and community predictors of neighborhood stranger, nonstranger, and intimate-partner violence simultaneously. These models allowed us to assess whether the earlier patterns are contingent on other correlates of victimization. The models included age, time spent at home, marital status, household income, length of residence in the current home, central-city residence, community disadvantage, immigrant concentration, and residential stability. This produced a total of 108 coefficients for comparison ($9 \times 4 \times 3 = 108$). Of these 108 coefficients, only 7 were found to be significantly different across the three groups.

In the full covariate model, we found that among Latina women, more time spent at home was associated with significantly lower rates of nonstranger violence and intimate-partner violence. This same factor was unrelated to black women's risk but positively associated with risk for white women. Length of residence in the current home was significant and negatively associated with black and white women's risk but was not related to Latina women's risk for nonstranger and intimate-partner violence.

The only factor that exhibited a significant difference across groups for stranger violence was length of residence in the current home. For white women, this variable predicted lower levels of stranger victimization, but it was uncorrelated with risk among black and Latina women. The differences noted here persisted across model specifications that controlled for the individual, family, and community correlates noted earlier.

Equally important, no other factors exhibited robust differences across black, white, and Latina women. Less than 10 percent of the comparisons overall resulted in a statistically significant difference in the group-specific coefficients, indicating that the vast majority of these individual, family, and community characteristics had similar influences on violence risk for black, white, and Latina women. Moreover, the number of significant differences that we found is about what one would expect to find on the basis of chance (e.g., 7 out of 108 coefficients in the final model).

Discussion

Although these analyses suggest that nearly all the factors that influence risk do so in similar ways for black, white, and Latina women, the robustness of the difference for the variable measuring time spent at home warrants some comment. Traditional theories of victimization risk do not anticipate this difference. In past research, "time spent at home in the evenings" has been used as a crude measure of one's lifestyle or exposure to offenders. Routine-activities and lifestyle theories propose that, all else equal, greater exposure to offenders occurs outside the home and increases the likelihood of becoming a victim of crime. Feminist research has challenged the key assumption underlying this proposition—that is, that strangers pose greater risks to women than family or friends. This challenge is supported by our finding that black and white women who spend more time at home are *more* likely than those who spend less time at home to become victims of nonstranger and intimate-partner violence.

But Latina women who spend more time at home are *less* likely than other Latina women to be victimized by nonstranger and intimate-partner violence. This may indicate that Latino men inside the home pose less threat to Latina women because they are less likely to be offenders or to be offenders who act violently toward women. To determine if this is so, it would be necessary to collect data that directly studies the nature of male offending across race and ethnic groups, as well as norms and beliefs about violence in general and violence against women in particular.

Alternatively, it may be that Latina women experience less nonstranger and intimate-partner violence if they spend more time at home because there are more capable guardians in their homes (e.g., other adults). Even if Latino men were equally motivated to commit violence against women, they would be less likely to do so if there were more guardians available to deter such situations through intervention or retaliation. Or Latino men could be equally motivated toward violence, but if they are less likely to be home than black or white men, they would have less opportunity to engage in intimate-partner or familial violence. To sort out the veracity of these very different interpretations, it would be necessary to gather new types of data, especially qualitative and contextual information that captures the situational dynamics surrounding everyday activities, especially conflict and its resolution in the home.

The effect of time spent in the home may also reflect an unmeasured variable that varies across groups. For example, compared to black and white women, persons of Latina origin tend to be recent immigrants. Research using data from Chicago has shown that levels of young male offending varied among subgroups of Latinos.[15] First- and second-generation Latinos had significantly lower levels of violent offending than third and subsequent generations. These differences in offending among young Latino males might produce parallel patterns of victimization risk among Latina women. Unfortunately, the NCVS does not contain the data necessary for assessing this issue. But the fact that violent offending is higher among later generations of immigrants points out the importance of acculturation and accommodation to American structural conditions. These processes and adaptations should be explicitly incorporated into studies of violence that seek to understand differences across racial, ethnic, or immigrant groups.

Conclusions

Our assessments of the trends, levels, and correlates of violence point toward the conclusion that race and ethnicity *per se* play a limited role in American women's current risk for nonlethal victimization, at least among the three largest subgroups in the population. Recent trends for black, white, and Latina women are similar and suggest that the broader factors associated with current declines affect women in similar ways. Trends in the victimization of American Indian women and, to a lesser extent, Asian American women show greater fluctuations in part because they are based on relatively small sample sizes. This means that we cannot be certain whether year-to-year changes for the two groups of women reflect actual deviations from general trends or sampling error.

Future research on levels and trends of victimization for American Indian and Asian American women would require substantially larger samples than are currently available on an annual basis in the NCVS. With larger samples, researchers could assess whether higher risks among American Indians and lower risks among Asian Americans also reflect differences in structural conditions. Differences in community socioeconomic status and isolation, as well as individual and family differences, should be assessed before assuming that cultural values account for observed differences.

The similarities in the patterns of risk among black, white, and Latina women suggest that these groups are unlikely to have their own distinct set of norms and attitudes about violence. The same structural conditions that are associated with white women's victimization are correlated with violence against black and Latina women. Hence, there does not appear to be a need to search for race-specific explanations of violence. In fact, there are many reasons not to.

In a powerful critique of race-specific theories of violence, Jeannette Covington argues that the search for collective beliefs among race groups (especially blacks compared to whites) assumes that there are important differences between groups that require illumination and documentation.[16] The resulting comparisons require "that conditions be identified that *liken all blacks to each other while distinguishing them from whites. . . .* Yet, in identifying race-specific risk factors . . . that distinguish blacks from white, theorists construct crude categories that *liken a handful of black killers to millions of black nonkillers.* The necessary diffusion of violent predispositions to many nonviolent blacks seems to be an unfortunate consequence of such racial comparisons."[17] Covington argues that the ongoing search for racial differences lends itself all too easily to stereotypes about blacks and to policies that permit greater surveillance and criminal justice authority over minority males.

Much past knowledge about race, ethnicity, and violence is derived from aggregate studies of homicide, yet this is the most rare form of violence and may have its own unique predictors (e.g., availability of lethal weapons). Also, it is clear that race and ethnic differentials in rates of violent victimization vary depending on the seriousness and rarity of the crime. For instance, over the past decade female homicide rates have been roughly four times higher for black women than for white women. Rape victimization among blacks has been roughly three times greater, and robbery and aggravated assault rates have been roughly twice as high. For simple assault, victimization rates have been approximately equal for black and white women. These differences serve as a reminder that the relationships between race, ethnicity, and violent victimization and offending are complex and contingent on crime type.

Thus, theories of violence against American women should remain race neutral, and future research should focus on more-enduring correlates such as socioeconomic disadvantage, inequality, social isolation, and family functioning. Our understanding of violence against women will improve to the extent that we can specify the conditions under which the level of women's victimization is likely to be high or low and the conditions under which group differences are large or small.

NOTES

1. Support for this research was provided by the American Statistical Association Committee on Law and Justice Statistics. Data for these analyses were made available through the National Consortium on Violence Research under the supervision of the Census Bureau and in cooperation with the Bureau of Justice Statistics. None of the above organizations bears any responsibility for the findings presented here.

2. L. J. David Wallace, Alice C. Calhoun, Kenneth E. Powell, Joann O'Neil, and Stephen P. James, *Homicide and Suicide among Native Americans, 1979–1992, Violence Surveillance Summary Series, No. 2* (Atlanta: U.S. Department of Health and Human Services, National Center for Injury Prevention and Control, 1996).

3. Callie M. Rennison, *Hispanic Victims of Violent Crime, 1993–2002* (Washington, DC: Bureau of Justice Statistics, 2002); Callie M. Rennison, *Violent Victimization and Race, 1993–98* (Washington, DC: Bureau of Justice Statistics, 2001).

4. For a recent overview of these hypotheses, see Darnell F. Hawkins, ed., *Violent Crime: Assessing Race and Ethnic Differences* (Cambridge: Cambridge University Press, 2003).

5. Robert J. Sampson and Janet L. Lauritsen, "Violent Victimization and Offending: Individual-, Situational-, and Community-Level Risk Factors," in *Under-*

standing and Preventing Violence, vol. 3, *Social Influences,* ed. A. J. Reiss Jr. and J. A. Roth, pp. 1–114 (Washington, DC: National Academy Press, 1994); Michael J. Hindelang, Michael R. Gottfredson, and James Garofalo, *Victims of Personal Crime: An Empirical Foundation for a Theory of Personal Victimization* (Cambridge, MA: Ballinger, 1978).

6. Janet L. Lauritsen and Robin J. Schaum, "The Social Ecology of Violence against Women," *Criminology* 42(2) (2004): 323–357.

7. Michael Rand and Callie M. Rennison, "Bigger Is Not Necessarily Better: An Analysis of Violence against Women Estimates from the National Crime Victimization Survey and the National Violence Against Women Survey," *Journal of Quantitative Criminology* (2005, in press).

8. Charles Kindermann, James P. Lynch, and David Cantor, *Effects of the Redesign on Victimization Estimates* (Washington, DC: Bureau of Justice Statistics, 1997).

9. For additional information on the Area-Identified National Crime Victimization Survey, see Brian Wiersema, "Area-Identified National Crime Victimization Survey Data: A Resource Available through the National Consortium on Violence Research," NCOVR, 1997, available at http://www.ncovr.heinz.cmu.edu/docs/Research_Reports/Papers/techpaper.pdf (accessed July 18, 2004).

10. It is beyond the scope of this paper to compare the trends and correlates of male and female victimization. However, it should be noted that the long-standing gap between male and female victimization rates has been closing recently due to faster declines in male victimization risk. Rates of violent victimization against males fell 57 percent between 1992 and 2001. A somewhat larger decline was measured for stranger violence (61 percent) than for nonstranger violence (50 percent), and declines in rates of violent victimization were similar for white males (57 percent drop), black males (52 percent), and Latino males (56 percent).

11. Lauritsen and Schaum, "Social Ecology of Violence against Women"; Janet L. Lauritsen and Norman A. White, "Putting Violence in Its Place: The Effects of Race, Ethnicity, Gender, and Place on the Risk for Violence," *Criminology and Public Policy* 1 (2001): 37–60.

12. Lauritsen and Schaum, "Social Ecology of Violence against Women."

13. Ibid.

14. Ibid.

15. Robert J. Sampson, Jeffrey D. Morenoff, and Stephen W. Raudenbush, "Social Anatomy of Race and Ethnic Disparities in Violence," *American Journal of Public Health* 95 (2005): 224–232.

16. Jeanette Covington, "The Violent Black Male: Conceptions of Race in Criminological Theories," in *Violent Crime: Assessing Race and Ethnic Differences,* ed. Darnell F. Hawkins, pp. 254–280 (Cambridge: Cambridge University Press, 2003).

17. Ibid., 276; emphasis in original.

Contributors

Jennifer L. Castro is a research associate at the Urban Institute's Justice Policy Center in Washington, D.C. She has experience in issues related to prisoner reentry, female offending, neighborhood violence, and youth-program evaluation. She is currently investigating the impact of several multistate, multiyear crime-reduction initiatives, and she conducts research on the causes of crime, including a study of neighborhood and individual-level violence, forthcoming in *Race, Gender, and Class,* and a study of recidivism among released prisoners published in *Justice Research and Policy.*

Stephen A. Cernkovich is Professor of Sociology at Bowling Green State University. His research interests include juvenile delinquency, the long-term behavioral and mental health consequences of early involvement in antisocial behavior, and race and gender variation in deviant behavior. Current projects include an examination of qualitatively distinct female offender types, adolescent nonoffenders, the connection between teenage victimization and delinquent behavior, and a comparative study of positive and negative transitions to adulthood among previously institutionalized Canadian and American adolescent females.

Sarah Curtis-Fawley graduated from the University of Virginia with degrees in psychology and women's studies. After working with both victims and offenders in the United States, Curtis-Fawley came to Australia in 2001–2002 on a Fulbright Fellowship (sponsored by Kathleen Daly) to study restorative justice responses to gendered violence. Today Curtis-Fawley lives in Adelaide, South Australia, and works with the homeless, while continuing to write about restorative justice.

Kathleen Daly is Professor of Criminology and Criminal Justice, Griffith University (Brisbane). She writes on gender, race, crime, and justice and on restorative justice and Indigenous justice. Her book *Gender, Crime, and Punishment* (1994) received the Michael Hindelang award from the American Society of Criminology. From 1998 to 2004, she received three major Australian Research Council grants to direct a program of research on restorative justice and the race and gender polices of new justice practices in Australia, New Zealand, and Canada. She is Vice-President of the Australian and New Zealand Society of Criminology.

Jill A. Deines earned a Master of Arts degree in Sociology with an emphasis in Criminology/Deviance from Bowling Green State University in 2003. Her master's thesis explored the validity of traditional and feminist criminological explanations of juvenile delinquency. Currently, she is a doctoral student in sociology at Bowling Green State University; she is a criminologist and family sociologist. Her primary research interests include juvenile delinquency, gender and crime, religion and marriage, covenant marriage, and qualitative methodology. For the past three years she has served as Field Director for the Marriage Matters project, a five-year study funded by the National Science Foundation that focuses on marriage and divorce in modern America.

Laura Dugan is an assistant professor in the Department of Criminology and Criminal Justice at the University of Maryland. She is a member of the National Consortium on Violence Research and the Maryland Population Research Center. Dr. Dugan is co-investigator on a large-scale project investigating global terrorism. Her published work addresses the causes and consequences of criminal victimization and the efficacy of victimization prevention policy and practice. She also designs methodological strategies to overcome data limitations inherent in the social sciences.

Rosemary Gartner is a professor of criminology and sociology at the University of Toronto. She is coauthor (with Candace Kruttschnitt) of *Marking Time in the Golden State: Women's Imprisonment in California* (Cambridge University Press, 2004) and (with Jim Phillips) of *Murdering Holiness: The Trials of Franz Creffield and George Mitchell* (University of British Columbia Press, 2003). Her research interests include historical and comparative patterns in interpersonal violence and women's experiences of violent victimization and offending.

Carole Gibbs received her master's degree and is currently a Ph.D. candidate in the Department of Criminology and Criminal Justice at the University of Maryland–College Park. Her most recent research involves studying the relationship between corporate social performance, sanctions, and environmental compliance. Her other research interests include criminological theory, gender/race/class and crime, and environmental justice.

Peggy C. Giordano is Distinguished Research Professor of Sociology at Bowling Green State University. Her research has centered on the adolescent period and, more recently, on patterns of continuity and change in offending over the life course. Most of this work focuses on adolescent girls and women and explores the role of basic social network processes in the etiology of criminal onset and desistance.

Karen Heimer is an associate professor of sociology at the University of Iowa. Her research has focused primarily on juvenile delinquency, with a special emphasis on race and gender differences. In other work, she is studying race, gender, politics, and imprisonment patterns in the United States, as well as the link between women's poverty and their criminal offending.

Gwen Hunnicutt is an assistant professor of sociology at the University of North Carolina at Greensboro. Her research interests include gender and crime, stratification and crime, homicide studies, and cross-national crime studies. She is currently working on a project involving the analysis of infant and child homicide victimization data in the United States.

Candace Kruttschnitt received her Ph.D. from Yale University in 1979. Since then, her research has focused primarily on the social control of women offenders and women's involvement in acts of interpersonal violence. She recently completed a monograph, *Marking Time in the Golden State: Women's Imprisonment in California* (Cambridge University Press, 2005), with Rosemary Gartner that focuses on women's experiences of imprisonment in California during the rehabilitative and neoliberal prison eras. Currently, she is involved in a multisite project (with Rosemary Gartner, Sally Simpson, and Julie Horney) that seeks to understand the factors that affect violent victimization and offending, as well as help-seeking behaviors, in a sample of women who have a high propensity toward these three outcomes.

Gary LaFree is a professor of criminology and criminal justice and founding member of the Democracy Collaborative at the University of Maryland and is president elect of the American Society of Criminology. In addition to cross-national comparative research on violent crime, he is analyzing determinants of U.S. crime trends, longitudinal predictors of incarceration risk by race, and the determinants of global terrorism.

Janet L. Lauritsen is Professor and Chairperson of the Department of Criminology and Criminal Justice at the University of Missouri– St. Louis. Her most recent research examines how individual, family, and community factors are related to the risk of violent victimization among women, men, and adolescents. She is currently serving as Visiting Research Fellow at the Bureau of Justice Statistics, Chair of the Committee on Law and Justice Statistics of the American Statistical Association, and Executive Counselor for the American Society of Criminology.

Ross Macmillan is Associate Professor of Sociology and Director of Population Studies at the University of Minnesota. He is also an affiliate of the Life Course Center and the Minnesota Population Center. His current research involves the study of biographies of violence, specifically with respect to gender differences in the extent and etiology of victimization (with Candace Kruttschnitt). He is also involved in a long-term project on the structure of the life course, its etiology, and its consequences in modern society.

Bill McCarthy is a professor in the Department of Sociology at the University of California–Davis. His recent publications focus on danger and other aspects of the decision to offend. His current research interests include a historical study of homicide, the role of mentors, and illegal success.

Jody Miller is Associate Professor of Criminology and Criminal Justice at the University of Missouri–St. Louis. She specializes in feminist theory and qualitative research methods. Her research focuses on situational aspects of gender, crime, and victimization, particularly among urban adolescents, youth gangs, and the commercial sex industry. She is author of *One of the Guys: Girls, Gangs, and Gender* (Oxford University Press, 2001), as well as numerous articles and chapters.

Christopher W. Mullins is Assistant Professor of Criminology at the University of Northern Iowa. He earned his Ph.D. at the University of Missouri–St. Louis from the Department of Criminology and Criminal

Justice. His research interests focus on gender, streetlife, violence, and organizational crime.

Callie Marie Rennison is an assistant professor in the department of Criminology and Criminal Justice at the University of Missouri–St. Louis. Her research focuses on violent victimization, with an emphasis on victimization trends, violence against women, and victimization experienced by minority group members. She is currently a Post-Doctorate Fellow with the National Consortium of Violence Researchers (NCOVR).

Nancy Rodriguez is an associate professor in the Criminal Justice and Criminology Department at Arizona State University in the West campus. Her research interests include sentencing policies, juvenile court processes, and substance abuse. Her work has recently appeared in *Justice Quarterly, Crime and Delinquency,* and *Criminology and Public Policy.*

Sally S. Simpson is Professor and Chair of the Department of Criminology and Criminal Justice at the University of Maryland–College Park. Her research interests mainly focus on criminological theory, female offenders, and corporate crime etiology, prevention, and control. Her work has appeared in a variety of criminology and sociology journals including *Law and Society Review, Criminology, Journal of Quantitative Criminology, American Sociological Review,* and *Social Forces.* She has also published a recent book entitled *Corporate Crime, Law, and Social Control* (Cambridge University Press, 2002). Current research projects involve the WEV study (a multicity study of incarcerated women's experience of violence, with Julie Horney, Candace Kruttschnitt, and Rosemary Gartner), a project on environmental compliance, and an evidence-based assessment of corporate crime intervention and control strategies for the Campbell Consortium Crime and Justice Group (CCJG). She is the incoming president of the White-Collar Crime Research Consortium (2004–2006).

Hilary Smith is a doctoral student in the interdisciplinary Justice Studies Program at Arizona State University. Her research interests include girls and the juvenile justice system, youth and violence, and youth homelessness. She holds a B.S. in criminal justice and sociology from Texas Christian University and an M.S. in justice studies from Arizona State University.

Halime Ünal is Assistant Professor of Sociology at Muğla University, Turkey. She received her Ph.D. in sociology from the University of Iowa. Her research interests focus on gender and crime, violence against women, adolescent violence, and punishment.

Stacy Wittrock received her master's degree and is currently a Ph.D. candidate in the Department of Sociology at the University of Iowa. Her most recent research involves studying the relationships among race/ethnicity, structural disadvantage, and violent delinquency. Her other research interests include the gender differences in crime and delinquency; the intersections between gender, race, and class; criminological theory; and the sociology of punishment.

Marjorie S. Zatz is Professor of Justice and Social Inquiry and Associate Dean of the Division of Graduate Studies at Arizona State University. Her research interests include racial, ethnic, and gender-based discrimination in juvenile and criminal court processing and sanctioning; Chicano and Chicana gangs and the larger communities of which they form a part; gender and the legal profession; and social and legal change in Cuba and Nicaragua. She is the author of numerous journal articles and of *Producing Legality: Law and Socialism in Cuba* (Routledge, 1994), *Images of Color, Images of Crime,* coedited with Coramae Richey Mann (Roxbury, 2002 [first edition 1998]), and *Making Law: The State, the Law, and Structural Contradictions,* coedited with William Chambliss (Indiana University Press, 1993).

Index

NOTE: Boldface type indicates authors and starting pages of articles. The designation "n" refers to footnotes and "t" to tables.